KARL JASPERS

Karl Jaspers

A Biography

NAVIGATIONS IN TRUTH

Suzanne Kirkbright

YALE UNIVERSITY PRESS
NEW HAVEN AND LONDON

For information about this and other Yale University Press publications, please contact:
U.S. Office: sales.press@yale.edu   yalebooks.com
Europe Office: sales@yaleup.co.uk   www.yalebooks.co.uk

Set in Minion by MATS, Southend-on-Sea, Essex
Printed in the United States of America

ISBN 0-300-10242-9

Library of Congress Control Number: 2004110264

A catalogue record for this book is available from the British Library.

The paper in this book meets the guidelines for permanence and durability of the Committee on Production Guidelines for Book Longevity of the Council on Library Resources

10 9 8 7 6 5 4 3 2 1

Excerpt from 'East Coker' in *Four Quartets*, copyright 1940 by T.S. Eliot and renewed 1968 by Esme Valerie Eliot, reprinted by permission of Harcourt, Inc.

Contents

List of Illustrations vii

Acknowledgements ix

Translation and Editorial Note xiii

Chronology xiv

Introduction xvii

PART I   Decisions and Realities

    1   A Classical Education 3

    2   Young Scientist 13

    3   'German Student' 28

    4   Italian Postscript 41

PART II   Devotion, Duty and Family Ties

    5   Gertrud Mayer 49

    6   'In the Clinic' 62

7   *Max Weber 76*

8   *Enno Jaspers 92*

PART III   Artistic Associations

9   *'Ordinarius' in Heidelberg 111*

10   *Paris, Sicily and Vincent van Gogh 120*

11   *Martin Heidegger in the 1920s 129*

PART IV   Absences and Presences

12   *Inside Nazi Germany 141*

13   *Nietzsche Lectures 155*

14   *Keeping Faith 165*

15   *Oxford Connections, Visitors and Loyal Friends 175*

PART V   Pictures of Humanity

16   *'Liberated by Allied Forces' 187*

17   *Citizens of Basel 199*

18   *'Rencontres' in Geneva 208*

19   *Talking Peace 216*

PART VI   'In my end is my beginning'

20   *Butterflies in Sils Maria 225*

21   *'Child Hannah' 230*

Appendix: Karl Jaspers' Family Correspondence 239

Source Material and Abbreviations 269

Notes 280

Selected Bibliography 344

Index 357

Illustrations

Karl Jaspers aged eight, sketch by Karl Jaspers, senior. (Courtesy of Hans Saner) *xxiv*

Karl Jaspers, spring 1919, drawing by Else Engler. (Courtesy of Hans Saner; thanks to Karl–Jaspers–Stiftung.) *46*

Vincent van Gogh, *Fishing Boats on the Beach at Saintes-Maries-de-la-Mer* (1888). *108*

Karl Jaspers, Seminar Strasse, Heidelberg, 1937. (Courtesy of Hans Saner; thanks to Karl–Jaspers–Stiftung.) *138*

Karl Jaspers giving his lecture on the 'Guilt Question' in Alta Aula, University of Heidelberg, 1945/6. (Courtesy of Hans Saner; thanks to Karl–Jaspers–Stiftung.) *184*

Karl Jaspers, Henriette Jaspers and Karl Jaspers, senior, Wangerooge, 1927. (German Literature Archive, Marbach am Neckar.) *222*

between pages 168 and 169

1. Souvenir of Norderney (*Erinnerung an Norderney*), 1898. (Courtesy of Hans Saner; thanks to Karl–Jaspers–Stiftung.)

2. Henriette Jaspers, 1879. (German Literature Archive, Marbach am Neckar.)

3. 'In no "house" group' (*In keiner Vereinigung*). (Courtesy of Hans Saner; thanks to Karl–Jaspers–Stiftung.)

4. The Jaspers family villa, Jever. Painting by Caspar Sonnekes. (Courtesy of Hans Saner; thanks to Karl–Jaspers–Stiftung.)

5. *Rothsandleuchtturm* (Red Sand Light House), watercolour by Karl Jaspers, senior. (Courtesy of Hans Saner.)

6. 'Oath to the Spirit of Science' (*Schwur auf den Geist der Wissenschaft*). Professor Fano, Karl Jaspers and Professor Cornelius, Sils Maria, 1902. (Courtesy of Hans Saner; thanks to Karl–Jaspers–Stiftung.)

7. Gertrud Mayer and Karl Jaspers, Markplaz, Heidelberg, 1907. Photograph by Marie Munk. (German Literature Archive, Marbach am Neckar.)

8. Walter Calé. (Courtesy of Hans Saner; thanks to Karl–Jaspers–Stiftung.)

9. Gertrud and David Mayer, *c.* 1904/5. (Courtesy of Hans Saner; thanks to Karl–Jaspers–Stiftung.)

10. 'Ascher Mayer', Steinstraße, 12, Prenzlau. (Courtesy of Hans Saner; thanks to Karl–Jaspers–Stiftung.)

11. Fritz, Gertrud and Otto Mayer. (German Literature Archive, Marbach am Neckar.)

12. Max Weber. (Courtesy of Hans Saner; thanks to Karl–Jaspers–Stiftung.)

13. Gertrud Jaspers, 29 September 1910. (Courtesy of Hans Saner; thanks to Karl–Jaspers–Stiftung.)

14. Enno Jaspers, 1916/17. (Courtesy of Hans Saner; thanks to Karl–Jaspers–Stiftung.)

15. Karl and Enno Jaspers, Heidelberg, 1930/31. (German Literature Archive, Marbach am Neckar.)

16. Jaspers family portrait photography, *c.* 1917. (German Literature Archive, Marbach am Neckar.)

17. Vincent van Gogh, *Small Pear Tree in Blossom* (1890). (Courtesy of the Van Gogh Museum Foundation, Amsterdam/Vincent van Gogh Foundation.)

18. Vincent van Gogh, *The Bedroom* (1888). (Courtesy of the Van Gogh Museum Foundation, Amsterdam/Vincent van Gogh Foundation.)

19. Vincent van Gogh, *Vase with Sunflowers* (1889). (Courtesy of the Van Gogh Museum Foundation, Amsterdam/Vincent van Gogh Foundation.)

20. Martin Heidegger. (Courtesy of Hans Saner; thanks to Karl–Jaspers–Stiftung.)

21. Plöck 66, Heidelberg. (German Literature Archive, Marbach am Neckar.)

22. Gertrud Jaspers. (German Literature Archive, Marbach am Neckar.)

23. Gertrud Jaspers, Certificate of the Jewish Community of Heidelberg. (Karl Jaspers: Literary Estate, Marbach am Neckar.)

24. Gertrud Jaspers and Erna Dugend, Norderney, 1930. (German Literature Archive, Marbach am Neckar.)

25. Karl Jaspers, senior, Henriette Jaspers, Karl and Gertrud Jaspers, Wangerooge, 1927. (German Literature Archive, Marbach am Neckar.)

26. Paul Gottschalk. (Courtesy of Hans Saner; thanks to Karl–Jaspers–Stiftung.)

27. Gertrud Jaspers and Julia Gottshalk. (Courtesy of Hans Saner; thanks to Karl–Jaspers–Stiftung.)

28. Henriette and Gertrud Jaspers. (German Literature Archive, Marbach am Neckar.)

29. Karl and Gertrud Jaspers, Basel. (Courtesy of Hans Saner; thanks to Karl–Jaspers–Stiftung.)

30. Gertrud Jaspers with Ernst and Ella Mayer, Ausstraße 126, Basel. (German Literature Archive, Marbach am Neckar.)

31. Hannah Arendt, summer 1952. (Courtesy of Hans Saner; thanks to Karl–Jaspers–Stiftung.)

32. Karl Jaspers, St Moritz, 1949. (German Literature Archive, Marbach am Neckar.)

Acknowledgements

THE RESEARCH FOR THIS BIOGRAPHY began in earnest several years ago when I met Hans Saner, Karl Jaspers' assistant at Basel University and author of the first biography of the philosopher in German. Since Jaspers' death in 1969, Saner has fulfilled the role of editor of the Karl Jaspers' literary estate. I am particularly grateful to him for his generous advice about the archive of Jaspers' private family correspondence, an integral part of Jaspers' literary estate which is administered by the Deutsches Literaturarchiv in Marbach am Neckar. Thanks to Saner's generosity, I was able freely to inspect the abundant amount of material in the archive, and I sincerely thank Hans Saner for kind permission to select for publication in this biography those relevant letters from the archive that provide intimate insight into Jaspers' world.

Briefly, to comment upon the lengthy process of deciphering Jaspers' personal correspondence, which is preserved as handwritten letters in their thousands – dating from the late 1880s until the mid-1960s – it is surprising to find that, in private, Jaspers discussed his experiences in a candid and lively manner that may be unfamiliar to those acquainted with his published works of philosophy. A priority of my research was therefore to focus on the reading and transcription of his family letters, whose selection is necessarily guided by the purpose of this biography. To a certain extent, Jaspers' letters to his parents and siblings revealed many facets of his personality that are pertinent for any biography. What became evident was the quality of the letters, which frequently illuminated the context of his published works. It is important to underline, however, that my endeavour was always based on a deep respect for the highly personal nature of this private correspondence. This record of his intellectual life can claim to be a thoroughly researched biography that necessarily includes a philosophical component, but one that is, nonetheless, constantly subjected to the specific constraint of providing a faithful account of his life experience. In other words, this introduction to Jaspers' biography cannot seek to supply a purely philosophical investigation of his major works. Moreover, such a claim would not only be misleading, it would misrepresent the stated desire to respect the private documents and other biographical sources that I was privileged to inspect. It is appropriate to point out here that the letters used in this biography have been translated into English by the author. The discerning reader is alerted to the Appendix of this work, where the original German text has been reproduced. I have largely excluded the original German text of the letters in the notes to individual chapters in the interests of overall clarity. I hope that the scholarly reader will easily find the original words of Jaspers' letters and inspect at leisure the suggested English translations by turning to the Appendix.

This book began when a research project during a sabbatical semester from my lecturing duties in England was transformed into a vocation. The human interest of my work was located on the Continent, and the obvious solution to the issue of research was to relocate to the vicinity of archives in Germany. This change of location gave rise to some unexpected good fortune, not the least of which was two years of generous sponsorship as a Research Fellow by the Alexander von Humboldt Foundation. I am especially grateful for the invitation of my host, Professor Dr Reiner Wiehl, President of the Karl Jaspers-Foundation. The conversations with Professor Dr Wiehl that were made possible under the auspices of the Alexander von Humboldt Foundation highlighted the particular challenges of reading Karl Jaspers' family letters. These conversations opened up a new avenue towards what I hope may be seen as a fresh approach to Jaspers' biography. I also thank the dedicated staff of the Alexander von Humboldt Foundation for their professional support.

The work for a biography of such a prominent personality as Jaspers arouses considerable curiosity and carries a responsibility to consult, wherever possible, with former students, colleagues, friends and even critics of the main protagonist. I am grateful to many such interested parties who have offered me support during the process of research, but I owe a debt of thanks to a special few. In particular, I thank Professor Dr Richard Wisser and his wife for their kind interest in my project. I also thank Professor Dr Renato de Rosa and his wife, whose conversations helped me to develop a picture of Karl Jaspers' *esprit*. Professor Dr Leonard H. Ehrlich and Edith Ehrlich kindly provided advice and several invaluable sources from America. I am especially grateful for their translations of Jaspers' works into English. I also wish to thank Professor Dr Ehrlich for his specific comments on a draft manuscript, many of which were adopted in this work. Equally, Godfrey R. Carr's expert knowledge of Jaspers' philosophy was a constant source of encouragement.

A research visit to Amsterdam would not have come about without the acquaintance of Professor Dr Gottfried Niedhart. I benefited a great deal from his studies on the life and works of the social historian Gustav Mayer. Professor Dr Niedhart's interest in Mayer's biography guided my research to the papers of the Council for Assisting Refugee Academics (CARA), formerly known as the Society for the Protection of Science and Learning (or SPLS). I am grateful to John Akker, Executive Secretary of CARA, for his permission to refer to the relevant papers of the SPLS. My thanks are due, too, to the International Institute of Social History, Amsterdam, for permission to refer to Karl and Gertrud Jaspers' unpublished correspondence with Mayer. I also greatly appreciate the advice of Marije Wissink, Vincent van Gogh Museum, Amsterdam. I thank her for her patience in identifying paintings by Vincent van Gogh that are reproduced in this biography by permission of the Vincent van Gogh Foundation, Amsterdam.

Thanks are also owed to the helpful staff at the Bodleian Library, Oxford, and at the University Archive, Heidelberg. Karl Jaspers' family photographs are reproduced by kind permission of the German Literature Archive. I again thank Hans Saner for his assistance in selecting the photographs and for their reproduction as sponsored by the Karl Jaspers-Foundation.

The German Academic Exchange Service and the British Academy provided small research grants at key stages of research on location at Jaspers' literary estate, Marbach am Neckar. My thanks are due to Dr Jochen Meyer, director of manuscripts at the Deutsches Literaturarchiv. I also thank Dr Ulrich von Bülow for his assistance with Jaspers' family archive and for his advice about Jaspers' life and works. Thomas Kemme and Hildegard Dieke provided constant assistance, in both winter and summer, with Jaspers' family letters and other biographical documents. I also express sincere gratitude to Jutta and Norbert Geißler-Howe.

Among many gifted scholars whom I was privileged to meet in Heidelberg, I am grateful to fellow Humboldtians Denis Thouard, Fosca Mariani Zini and Luca Bagetto, whose lively conversations broadened my horizons and lightened my load. I thank Matthias Bormuth and Gregor Fitzi for their great friendship and scholarship. I am especially grateful to my counterpart Jean-Claude Gens, whose work on a French biography of Karl Jaspers coincided with my research. His gracious interest in my project developed into a friendly flow of information that cannot be overvalued in today's academic climate. Likewise, I acknowledge a debt of thanks to Giandomenico Bonanni for his diligent and knowledgeable research assistance in the task of reading Jaspers' family letters.

I owe sincere thanks to Professor Dr Rüdiger Görner for finding the time to inspect an early draft manuscript. I thank Mechthild Wand for her patient scrutiny of the German sections of the manuscript, and assume responsibility for any lapses due to possible transcription errors. Thanks are expressed to my colleagues at Aston University, Birmingham, England. My sincere gratitude is expressed to Candida Brazil and, last not least, I thank Robert Baldock for believing in this book and for his constant good humour and professional guidance.

For permission to reprint lines from *The Four Quartets* by T.S. Eliot, grateful acknowledgement is made to Faber and Faber Ltd and Harcourt, Inc.

Suzanne Kirkbright
Heidelberg
October 2003

Translation and Editorial Note

Karl Jaspers' unpublished family correspondence, an invaluable source for this biography, is quoted for the first time here by kind permission of Hans Saner and the Deutsches Literaturarchiv, Marbach am Neckar, Germany. The transcription of Jaspers' handwritten German letters is the author's responsibility, but given the number of letters preserved in the Jaspers' family archive, it became necessary to provide the reader, wherever possible, with the original German texts alongside English translations. Much of the original German of the letters is included in the references to the individual chapters, but this proved impractical for Jaspers' letters that are either quoted in full, or else given with minor omissions. Therefore the original German text of these letters is reproduced in an appendix below (pp. 239–68) and the interested reader may wish to clarify my suggested English translations by looking at the original texts.

Needless to say, the task of translation highlighted certain frustrations of working with those available English translations of Jaspers' collected works of philosophy. Wherever possible, I have sought such authorized translations as a preferred and basic source of reference for this biography. However, many English translations of Jaspers' works are no longer in print and the obscurity of some of the existing English ones made it wise to include minor modifications in some cases. Wherever such amendments have been made to the authorized translations, acknowledgements are made, as appropriate, in the references to the individual chapters.

S.K.

Chronology

1883	23 February, Karl Jaspers born in Oldenburg.
1892–1901	Secondary Grammar Education, Großherzogliches Gymnasium, Oldenburg.
1901	April 1901, law studies at the University of Freiburg interrupted by diagnosis of 'bronchiectasis' by Dr Albert Fraenkel in Badenweiler.
	October, enrolment as a law student at the University of Heidelberg.
1902	March–April, journey to Rome. Summer semester, Munich University. August, Sils Maria. Winter semester, Berlin University, student of medicine.
1903–6	Göttingen University. Summer semester 1906–8, University of Heidelberg.
1907	14 July, first meeting with Gertrud Mayer.
1908	December, medical 'state examination' with *summa cum laude*.
1909	Doctoral dissertation on 'Homesickness and Crime' (*Heimweh und Verbrechen*) published in Gross's archive for forensic science.
1909–15	Unpaid medical placement and voluntary assistantship at the Heidelberg Clinic of Psychiatry.
1910	29 September, marriage to Gertrud Mayer, Berlin/Zehlendorf.

1913	Professorial thesis, *General Psychopathology*, accepted as *Habilitation* by Wilhelm Windelband. Unpaid lecturer (*Privatdozent*) for psychology in the faculty of philosophy.
1916	21 November, assistant professorship in psychology (*Extraordinarius*).
1919	'Psychology of World Visions' (*Psychologie der Weltanschauungen*).
1920	14 June, death of Max Weber. 17 July, memorial speech for Max Weber. Associate professorship in philosophy as successor to Hans Driesch.
1921	*Ruf* to Kiel University and Greifswald University declined. October, *Ordinarius* in philosophy at Heidelberg University as successor to Heinrich Maier.
1922	*Strindberg and van Gogh.*
1923	'The Idea of the University' (*Die Idee der Universität*).
1924	21 May, speech for the bicentenary birthday celebration of Immanuel Kant.
1928	*Ruf* to Bonn University declined.
1931	7 March, suicide of Enno Jaspers. October, *Man in the Modern Age* (*Die geistige Situation der Zeit*).
1932	*Philosophy* (3 Vols). 'Max Weber. German Essence in Political Thought, Science and Philosophizing' (*Max Weber. Deutsches Wesen im politischen Denken, im Forschen und Philosophieren*).
1935	*Reason and Existenz*, 25–29 March, guest lectures in Groningen.
1936	*Nietzsche. An Introduction to his Philosophical Activity.*
1937	'Descartes and Philosophy' (*Descartes und die Philosophie*), published in *Revue Philosophique*. Guest lectures, *Philosophy of Existence*, at the Freie Deutsche Hochstift (home of the Goethe Foundation), Frankfurt am Main. September, dismissal by Nazi régime.
1938	Planned emigration to Oxford fails.
1940	Invitation to Paris fails after death of Lucien Lévy-Bruhl. 24 February, death of father.
1941–2	Guest professorship at Basel University fails after refusal of Gertrud Jaspers' exit visa. 31 January, death of mother.
1942	A revised, fourth edition of *General Psychopathology* refused publication.

1943   Official publication ban by *Reichschrifttumskammer*.

1945   1 April, liberation of Heidelberg by American forces. Jaspers
        reinstated as professor of philosophy. 15 August, speech
        'Rejuvenation of the University' (*Erneuerung der Universität*)
        for reopening of medical faculty.
        Winter semester 1945/6, lecture series, *The Question of German
        Guilt*.

1947   Guest lectures at Basel University, *The Perennial Scope of
        Philosophy* (*Der philosophische Glaube*).
        Award of Goethe Prize. Honorary doctorate, University of
        Lausanne. 'On Truth' (*Von der Wahrheit*).

1948   Relocation to Basel, accepts professorship as successor to Paul
        Häberlin. Inaugural lecture at Basel University, *Philosophy and
        Science*.

1950   Guest lectures in Heidelberg, on *Reason and Anti-Reason in Our
        Time*. Radio broadcast, *Way to Wisdom* (*Einführung in die
        Philosophie*).

1953   Honorary doctorate, University of Heidelberg.

1955   'Schelling' (*Schelling. Größe und Verhängnis*).

1957   *The Great Philosophers*.

1958   Peace Prize of the German Book Trade. *The Atom Bomb and the
        Future of Man*.

1959   Erasmus Prize. Honorary doctorates from Sorbonne, Paris and
        University of Geneva.

1960   Professor Emeritus at Basel University and retirement lectures,
        'Ciphers of Transcendence' (*Chiffren der Transzendenz*).
        'Freedom and Unity' (*Freiheit und Wiedervereinigung*).

1964   Ordre pour le Mérite (highest award of Federal Republic of
        Germany).

1967   Citizenship of Basel. Hans Saner authorized to publish Jaspers'
        autobiographical memoirs, 'Destiny and Will' (*Schicksal und
        Wille*).

1969   26 February, Karl Jaspers dies in Basel on Gertrud Jaspers'
        ninetieth birthday.

Introduction

A YEAR AFTER ALBERT EINSTEIN'S DEATH on 18 April 1955, Karl Jaspers delivered a short radio talk, on the atom bomb and the future of mankind.[1] One of the aspects that Jaspers spoke about in his lecture was the dynamic advance of man's scientific knowledge and the technological achievements that contributed to the overwhelming success story of modern man. The success derived in part from the prospects for greater self-fulfilment, inner peace and prosperity. Jaspers characterized the sources of that success as rare gifts of the individual's intellectual and creative capacities that foster a deeper understanding of the environment through scientific knowledge.[2]

Jaspers' lecture was an impressive example of his ability to inspire a mood of change, to strengthen the resolve of his listener to adopt a fresh approach to the challenges ahead. He talked about achieving an inner renewal, something that was within the grasp of the creative individual who was able to reverse attitudes about life – insofar as they required change. His message of vitality and hope was all the more remarkable considering the demands bearing down upon him during his lifetime. In some respects, Jaspers' experiences were similar to those that influenced the lives of a wave of German Jewish émigré scientists, Einstein among them, who fled to America. This generation of scientists became indirectly involved in the feverish attempt to stop Hitler. In 1939, Einstein dictated his letter to President Roosevelt in which he explained the necessity and danger of exploring what might be entailed by the discovery of the splitting of the atom by Otto Hahn and Fritz Strassmann.[3] Their scientific endeavours had been carried out in an attempt to find a deterrent to an aggressively nationalistic agenda and to the ideology of achieving mastery of the globe. When Jaspers later focused his attention on this scientific breakthrough as a disturbing fact of modern life, he addressed the implications of the potential of atomic technology to overturn man's ability to investigate the physical conditions in which he sought to thrive. Jaspers saw that, when placed in the hands of modern dictators, the technology to produce weapons of mass destruction could devastate the planet. Unless a different perception of the technology itself were encouraged, scientific know-how could be misused, or even demonized as a threat to world peace.

The impact of Jaspers' thinking on this question was as powerful in the immediate post-war period as his message remains today. What he inspired in his lectures was a belief in the integrity of the individual to respond to seemingly oppressive circumstances. During his lifetime, his contribution significantly raised the tone and quality of objective debate. His high-pitched, rather thin and watery voice had a curiously moving effect that enhanced his reputation as one of Germany's leading intellectuals.

Jaspers' university career began at the turn of the twentieth century, when the conditions for training such gifted scholars were naturally different from today's. Jaspers was an undergraduate student at Germany's oldest seat of learning, Heidelberg University, where he was to spend most of his professional life. Early on in his lecturing career, he recognized that his special gift as a speaker was to engage directly with his audience, and he gradually obtained a position of influence within the academic community in Heidelberg, earning respect for his contribution to the discipline of psychiatry. The reception of his philosophical works, however, was rather impeded by the idea that he was schoolmasterly or aloof. Perhaps these perceptions of his contribution resulted in his work being treated as a monument to the German system of education. Jaspers was not one of those who subscribed to the notion of the ineffability of German science. After the outbreak of the First World War, he was increasingly critical of what he identified as a failure of the system to cultivate an atmosphere in which truly independent research could flourish. Perhaps that assessment explained why he developed his distinctive lecture style as an appeal to his listener's sense of reason. If he later turned his experiences of war, destruction and his miraculous survival of Hitler's régime into a convincing case for individual engagement, whether by the scientist, thinker, politician or private citizen, he also recognized the need to accept responsibility for living with others in a free world. Jaspers saw the world as potentially a better place than it was. In his view, the individual participates in a free world, insofar as his aim is to realize his sense of freedom out of the constraints of his circumstances.

Jaspers' début work of philosophy, entitled simply *Philosophy* (1932), was written during the 1920s after he had obtained a full philosophy professorship at Heidelberg University. In that challenging work, Jaspers read the individual's situation as an open question, whose status hinges upon maintaining a keen awareness of the political climate in which he lives and works. His philosophy was closely associated with the magnum opus of his friend and contemporary Martin Heidegger, which suggests how uniquely perceptive these thinkers were about the human predicament, in which man is deprived of the thinking space to reflect upon his actions. It cannot be the task of this Introduction to illustrate the complexities of Jaspers' and Heidegger's theories about mankind's existence. But it is worth recalling a profound thought of Jaspers' former student Hannah Arendt. As a German Jewish émigrée and American citizen, Arendt gave a speech in honour of Jaspers' acceptance of the Peace Prize of the German Book Trade that he received for his book, *The Atom Bomb and the Future of Man* (1958). In this speech, she went so far as to identify the essence of Jaspers' work as relevant to modern life, even hinting that his fame as a public figure was more important than that of her great friend and mentor Martin Heidegger. Arendt did not expressly refer to Heidegger in her speech, nor did she develop her praise of Jaspers' humanity other than to state that it was reflected in his personality.[4] She implied that she was aware of the fact that, at heart, Jaspers was a scrupulous and gifted scientist as well as an eminent thinker in the Enlightenment tradition. Thus his lifelong devotion to research in both the natural sciences and the humanities was supported by the delight that he took in observing signs of creativity, which he saw as traces of transcendence, as it were, as a window on to another way of seeing reality.

Jaspers was interested in the work of Vincent van Gogh, his appreciation of art encouraged by his father's pastime of painting watercolours. His family letters also suggest that he remained a loyal friend to Heidegger, who may be said to have relied on Jaspers' amazing breadth of knowledge as an educated art-lover, thinker and scientist. Jaspers understood how the medium of art, that is to say painting, may inspire thoughts or concepts that cannot necessarily be formulated with the rigour of a rational framework. At the same time, he was a devotee of the mental discipline that underpinned the formulation of concepts. The formulation of his philosophy of Existence – or, in German, *Existenz* – was such that this particular word ran like a golden thread through his works. Jaspers' concept of *Existenz* implied openness to an otherworldly realm, though this need not suggest that his philosophy is an esoteric work far removed from the problems of daily life.[5] Nor can his notion of *Existenz*, given its strictly ethical character, be said to have affected his admiration for Heidegger's standing as a thinker. However, Heidegger and his pupils seem to have stolen the limelight from Jaspers who made a point of criticizing a literary or aesthetic approach, as opposed to his own representation of a moralistic approach to philosophy.[6]

A former student of his, Jeanne Hersch, who first encountered Jaspers in Heidelberg when she was an eighteen-year-old student of German, was later to describe in her essay for the *Festschrift* in celebration of his seventieth birthday in 1953 how she was urged by a fellow student to attend one of his lectures. In her reminiscence, Hersch concluded by stressing that Jaspers' personality was equal to the stature of his works: 'You saw a man who depended upon truth – and on the truth alone.'[7] His life can be seen in this biography to have been dedicated to illuminating the implications of truth with reference to the guiding light of reason. What this general introduction to Jaspers' life does not attempt to define is Jaspers' understanding of 'truth' – a concept that he explored in the vast body of his published and posthumously published works of philosophy. Using the family correspondence as a basic source of reference, this biography instead seeks to illuminate the connection between Jaspers' life and works.

In a Translator's Note that he included as a preface to the authorized English translation of Jaspers' *Philosophy* that was first published in 1969, E. B. Ashton posed the question: 'What sort of language fits the principle of inconclusiveness? The obvious first answer is a painstaking insistence on leaving nothing unqualified, and Jaspers' writings do contain a stream of meticulous and-yets, whereases, and on-the-other-hands.'[8] Ashton faithfully translated *Philosophy* and several of Jaspers' most important essays, such as *The Question of German Guilt* (1976), into English, and Jaspers endorsed those translations during his lifetime.[9] Ashton's fundamental question about the sort of English idiom that fits Jaspers' German prose now reads as an understatement of the perplexing nature of his task. He rendered Jaspers' *Philosophy* into an English that some experts have regarded as potentially misleading.[10] In letters to his parents and his younger sister, Erna Dugend, Jaspers was accustomed to discuss some of the concepts of his *Philosophy*. These documents suggest that his German prose employed words in a quite literal sense, whereas the English idiom all too often conveys an impression of flexibility. What matters here is that Ashton's premise, that Jaspers made all things equal, seems to place Jaspers' works in English on a level that could be described as too theoretical. Naturally, Jaspers' *Philosophy* must be left to the expert scholar to solve the riddle of how to read a work that is written in a highly abstracted register of language through which shines the light of Platonic thinking. For the biographer, whose task is the narration of Jaspers' life story, it is helpful to assume that there is no single or prescribed approach to the stated aim of illuminating aspects of Jaspers' published works of philosophy within the context of his life.

An examination of Jaspers' life gives another opportunity to consider why, in a congratulatory letter to his son on the occasion of his twenty-fifth birthday, Jaspers' father highlighted what he remembered as the happy coincidence of his eldest son's birth with the first signs of spring: 'Spring inside and outside!'[11] At that time of his life, Karl Jaspers had succeeded in passing his state entrance examinations to practise medicine. His father's letter of birthday congratulation therefore recorded his admiration for his son's achievements in unusually lyrical terms. Yet adversity was strewn across their path, though Jaspers' strength of character helped him to master the severe and permanent restrictions that a lung illness, bronchiectasis, imposed upon his physical capacities. When his marriage proposal to Gertrud Mayer, the only surviving daughter of a devoutly German Jewish family, was accepted, he enjoyed the bonus of his wife's natural impulsiveness and warmth of heart.

By late September 1910, when Jaspers' marriage took place, it was no longer certain that he belonged to the rational world of psychiatry, the discipline to which he initially devoted his energies. Nor did his career as a young scientist – strictly speaking, his six years of training as a medical doctor – necessarily detract from his devotion to works of philosophy. He had explored and admired Spinoza's *Ethics* (1677) and Kant's *Critique of Pure Reason* (1781). Yet his schooldays had been overshadowed by his headmaster's Prussian militarism and the frequent interruptions to his education due to the illness. The support of his family and his father's unshakeable example were vital, as Jaspers explained in his memoirs. He began to write these memoirs in the late summer of 1937, only months after the Nazis retired him from his professorship at Heidelberg University. He worked on them as though he were continuing a long letter to his family and he mentioned a glimpse of a windmill, a picture that he seemed to associate with his first reading, at about the age of seventeen, of Spinoza's *Ethics*:

> With the view across the pastureland and the windmill – already feeling my life's possibilities threatened and fallen victim to a melancholy with the cares of the world – I read, to gain strength, Spinoza. My grandmother did not understand much of these things, but she was pleased, and praised me for my studies and for a thousand small things that indirectly raised my self-confidence, so that I returned home again with fresh courage.[12]

This allusion to the landscapes of Jaspers' home in north Germany shows his continued fascination with a visual correlation of words and pictures. He repeatedly discussed such a correlation in his letters to his father, letters that could be said to have provided an essential thinking space. Jaspers' family letters were not literary masterpieces, but they acted as the locus where his ideas took shape, as it were, through his reflections and associations of images. In this case, for example, the still sails of a windmill seem to have been connected with Spinoza's idea of the individual as a free agent. By the same token, the correlation of the picture and the idea of the individual's existence under the 'species of eternity' was not exactly an early sign of Jaspers' future career in philosophy. This particular reference to the open fields surrounding his grandparents' smallholding in Heering in the vale of Butjadingen emerged during a process of remembering that an early, unconscious rebellion against the circumstances of his illness appeared to have heightened his awareness of a need to find the meaning of life.

When Jaspers began his first, unpaid employment as a voluntary assistant in the Heidelberg Clinic of Psychiatry, he did not confine himself to research in the natural sciences. He was already working within the terms of philosophy, even during his training at the clinic. His personal ambition and his research as a psychiatrist had already merged in a good-natured friendship with Ernst Mayer, his wife's younger brother. The opportunity for debate that drew Jaspers into the Mayers' company, just as it formed the basis of everything that he admired in Max Weber, was established on a level of trust that Jaspers was wary of claiming for his acquaintance with Weber. His close connections with the Mayers helped him overcome, to a degree, what his father called unavoidable family traits of rationality and abruptness that were part of their Fresian heritage.[13] The family relationship that suffered most on this account was arguably Jaspers' with his younger brother Enno, whose pleasure-seeking ways offered such a profound contrast. Although Enno's suicide at the age of forty-two cannot be connected in any sense to the *de facto* breakdown of the brothers' relationship, nonetheless the deep sense of failure that Jaspers felt in respect of his brother highlighted a frustration with his inability to explore any other route than the tranquil path of the thinker.

This quiet life of contemplation that was so advantageous to Jaspers' health was not undisturbed. His story is characterized by surprising and even devastating developments. If Jaspers overcame personal crises, such as the suicide of his younger brother, he was chivvied along and encouraged to greater achievements by his devoted wife Gertrud. It was not by accident that he planned to give the works of Immanuel Kant as a first Christmas present to her. He considered Kant a seminal thinker and was already persevering with the study of Kant's philosophical works while training as a psychiatrist. It was Kant who introduced the element of humanity into Jaspers' work as a scientist and thinker.[14] What Jaspers achieved in his approach to thinking may be mirrored in his attempts to reach a deeper level of communication among family and friends. At times he succeeded; at other times he failed. Jaspers' journey through life could be called a series of navigations in truth that record his experiences and reflect the peace and security which he enjoyed with his wife and which, together, they hoped might endure within and beyond their lifetime.

Norderney 2/4 91 Kessel

PART I

Decisions and Realities

Enjoying now the light,
now the shade, all only play,
all sea, all midday, all time without aim.

Friedrich Nietzsche, 'Sils Maria'[1]

1   *A Classical Education*

IN OLDENBURG, WHERE KARL JASPERS WAS BORN on 23 February 1883, the changing attitudes that shape the fabric of civilized society were all but sheltered from view.[2] During these years of Bismarck's Germany, political life was in flux, for modernizing the regions into a federal, secularized and unified nation appeared to exacerbate disagreements among political parties which – apart from the higher authority of Emperor Wilhelm I – could have been scrutinizing Bismarck's policies of social and cultural integration.[3] By way of contrast to the country at large, Jaspers' family home was a haven of tranquillity. His family loyalties were to the rural hamlets of Jever and Heering, the north German villages where his father Karl Jaspers (senior) and his mother Henriette Tantzen were born; their families had lived in the region for several generations.[4] Karl Jaspers senior was a politically engaged member of the community, a liberal at heart, who enjoyed a comfortable, upper-middle-class lifestyle and earned great respect by fulfilling various administrative duties in the local community, such as protecting the countryside that he loved so well. He also served as an executive director of several companies, including the glass-making factory that was under the directorship of his younger brother Fritz.[5] Among his other civic offices, he counted the chairmanship of the local town council and he accepted the honour of being elected as a representative to Oldenburg's regional parliament (Landtag).[6] However, he refused repeated nominations for a seat in Bismarck's national parliament, the Reichstag, in

Berlin. Moreover, his healthy disrespect for emblems of institutionalized authority extended to his view that religion, or the Protestant Church, was much overrated, especially at times of crisis.

Jaspers' father did not intend his critical views of religious life to influence the attitudes of his offspring, Karl, Erna and Enno.[7] Jaspers himself was confirmed in the Protestant Church at the age of fifteen.[8] Like his father, he was wary of the impact, in practice, of Christian teachings. In this as in other matters, the father's sceptical attitude became a role model for the son. Karl Jaspers senior was a living reminder of the family's roots; and as if to renew the family's ties with the region, rather than the nation at large, when he married Henriette Tantzen he gave up his military service as a well-paid local official and took a position in the local savings bank, the Oldenburgische Spar-und Leihbank. His skill at managing money ensured his family a stable income and a prosperous albeit unostentatious lifestyle. An annual dividend of 9 per cent was paid out to the bank's customers and Jaspers' father never charged more than 5 per cent interest on loans.[9] His successful career as the bank's general manager lasted from 1896 until his retirement, at the age of seventy, in 1921.[10] By that time, both his sons had enjoyed the benefit of a university education, each in their own way thriving upon their liberal milieu. Whereas Enno, the younger of the brothers, tested both his father's patience and standards of self-discipline, Karl was only too aware of his father's influence, even though he saw that the challenges of his own generation were markedly different from the cares of his father's world.

The experience of Napoleon's sweep across Continental Europe was not quite within living memory of the Jaspers family. Jaspers' grandparents were not born when Prussian soldiers arrived in 1806 in the Grand Duchy of Oldenburg as part of Prussia's resistance against Napoleon. The defeat resulted in the so-called 'mediatization' of the regions, when the old order of small states and kingdoms was dissolved and the consciousness of unity slowly developed into hopes for a parliamentary future.[11] Karl Jaspers senior could remember an old rifle that his father had kept on the family farm in Sanderbusch. This heirloom was a token of Jaspers' grandfather's participation in the revolutionary year of 1848, when he served as a soldier in the civil defence.[12] In keeping with family tradition, Karl Jaspers senior was a confirmed patriot. That is to say he preferred the independence of his cherished homeland as opposed to his region's nominal inclusion in Bismarck's unified German Reich. The family's experience of living on the outside and looking in on political life from the nation's periphery was doubly reinforced by their love of local geography and the landscape itself.

The region of Lower Saxony where Jaspers spent his youth was geographically remote from Prussia and its flourishing capital, Berlin. The coastline near Oldenburg reaches from the North Sea to the Baltic and is flanked by a cluster of offshore islands – Norderney, Spiekeroog, Wangeroog, and Helgoland to the far north. Several of these islands were chosen as the family's summer-holiday destination, where in the company of his father Jaspers watched the sea merging into the heath, marshland and sandy dunes that eventually join with the lowlands of Holland.[13] The prospect of venturing forth into unknown territory was planted as an idea in Jaspers' mind as an early consciousness of freedom that was not so much an accidental influence as an experience that shaped the character of his youth. If he grew up under the impression that it was natural to act in this way as a free agent, his behaviour at school was destined to conflict with the solid conservative opinions of his headmaster, whose views interfered with many of the qualities of independence and openness towards others that Jaspers had come to expect among his family. His school life directly contrasted with the stable home environment where he began his education with his sister Erna, whose natural timidity led to her schooling being continued under the guidance of a private tutor.[14]

From an early age, Jaspers was free to roam the countryside, since his father also managed hunting grounds near the family's home and on the offshore island of Spiekeroog. When he reached grammar school age, Jaspers' training in the humanist canon that included the Greek and Roman languages and their ancient civilizations was to strengthen his sense of belonging to a cultural state of learned libertarians. Some of the principal educators of his youth were Goethe and Schiller, and it was not uncommon, as his mother was later to testify, for him to borrow books about philosophy from his local library.[15] He avidly read Spinoza and Kant. Perhaps the works of these thinkers stimulated his consciousness of a life of pre-ordered harmony, while promising a world outside his family's unimposing, red-brick house on the corner of Bismarckstraße 12 and his local grammar school, the Großherzogliches Gymnasium in Oldenburg. If Jaspers' schooling could be called classical, as in his learning from the humanist canon, he was to respond to his education by experiencing a change of heart about the focus of his interests. He carefully pondered over his choice of future career. In a sense, the change of approach, which will be explored in detail later, owed much to his early encounter with Kant's thinking. In another sense, Jaspers' contact with his family merits closer attention, not merely because of his affectionate concern throughout his life for his parents, his sister and his younger brother. These deep feelings for his family surface in his correspondence. In the absence of telecommunication, it was common courtesy for relatives to exchange views among themselves. What took pride of place in Jaspers' family circle was the correspondence, to which they resorted with the regularity of clockwork.

It was Jaspers' mother who was largely responsible for fulfilling this family duty, and her letters united the branches of her family scattered across the region and beyond.[16] Henriette Jaspers' letters conveyed few substantial details, let alone idle gossip about her son Karl's constantly evolving critical abilities, but they went far beyond the call of maternal duty as she exchanged with her relatives news about their events and experiences – sometimes several times a day. She managed to receive and impart news about the private lives of her correspondents without appearing to interfere or to judge. She preserved, too, the countless virtually illegible student letters that Jaspers sent to his parents when he was an undergraduate. In 1929, Henriette Jaspers meticulously typed out these letters in order to present them as a birthday present to Gertrud, her daughter-in-law.[17] The letters shed light on the manner in which Jaspers gradually gained independence from his close-knit family. At the same time, they recorded how his mother was the ideal partner with whom from the start he rehearsed a process to which he was later to give the name 'existential communication'.[18] It may seem far-fetched to suggest that Jaspers' conception of communication was evolved with his mother in mind, especially given that his mature thinking about communication developed in quite different circumstances. Yet Jaspers constantly confided in his mother both during his school years and as a student when he wrote in detail about his experiences. She was his earliest and most trusted correspondent. Henriette Jaspers showed the sort of integrity, discretion and empathetic understanding of Jaspers' aims that proved significant for him in later life. The scores of letters that she preserved gave expression to the possibility that Jaspers' mature ideas about communication developed because of their letter writing that was symbolic of the family's conduct and loving quality of his upbringing.

Jaspers' early childhood was, however, overshadowed by a kind of melancholy that derived in part from the family's northern roots and in part from circumstances beyond the family's control. The earliest sign of this air of gentle concern with which Jaspers' parents attempted to shield their eldest son from the force of circumstances may be detected when Jaspers, aged only three, accompanied his parents on their first holiday excursion as a family to the island of Spiekeroog. The short vacation was intended to cure the symptoms that Jaspers' father described on a holiday postcard sent to his wife after her earlier return home: 'Kally [as Karl was known] is quite lively, but he is still gurgling, coughing heavily in the evening, and only sleeping a little. I think that the "cure" has generally done him good, especially for his breathing. We will probably have to continue the bathing and as to the rest we will have to wait and see.'[19]

Family holidays were invariably designed to help the ailing Kally. As a grammar school pupil, Jaspers was accustomed to spending some of his summer holidays at a boarding house on the island of Norderney (see Ill. 1). A quiet resignation emerges from the surviving letters that he sent his parents in Oldenburg. The bright and youthful tone of the following account, for instance, is occasionally marred by his determined effort to forget the effects of his ill health:

Norderney, 10 July 1898

Dear parents,

Today a whole week of our holidays is now already over. That is a shame, but I am glad that in 3 weeks I can come home again. I have brilliant conditions here. Fräulein Busch says that I already look much fresher. My cough has not completely disappeared, though. In the daytime, I hardly cough at all, but Fr. Busch says that I have been coughing during the night. Every morning and evening I get milk in which salts from Ems spa are dissolved. It tastes disgusting and helps, I think, not one bit. Yesterday, Fräulein Busch's sister, Hedwig Busch, who manages the kitchen here, had her birthday. I have never seen so many flowers as she got. A whole room was filled up. Yesterday evening, I was with W[illy] Salfeld and Fridow Schneider on the beach, to see the sun go down. It was beautiful. The sun completely dipped into the sea, not a cloud was on the horizon. Today, I want to go bathing again. If I feel good afterwards, as I always have until now, I will bathe again tomorrow. What I actually miss on the beach is a travel blanket that I can wrap around my legs. The wind, as it is now, makes it quite necessary. I tried to wrap my coat around, but then I am too cold above. W. Salfeld has brought a blanket. I need the same as well. W. Salfeld wants to play tennis with me, if you think that it is worthwhile, please send me the rackets and 2 tennis balls. If not, though, it does not matter. I cannot easily have my photographs developed here; it would be too expensive. If you agree, I would quite like to buy one of those chairs for lazing in, the sort that can be folded together, it costs 2.25 [Marks]. I thank you affectionately, dear Mama, for your kind letter. It is too nice of you to write to me every day and you give me great pleasure. I can naturally not manage for the whole 4 weeks with 150 Marks. The boarding house alone costs 180 Marks. Besides, I have so far spent circa 32 Marks. […] I think it is best if you send me another 150 Marks, after eight or 14 days. Whatever I do not need, I will bring home again and then I will not be in difficulty. We want to go bathing now.

Fond greeting,

Your Kally[20]

At fifteen years, Jaspers was striving to overcome unpleasant coughing fits, severe catarrh and regular bouts of influenza. His mother, too, had noted these symptoms as signs of a mystery illness.[21] The ailments never disappeared completely, whether in the sea air or thanks to homespun remedies. The severe nature of his illness and an effective method of treatment were not identified until sixteen years later, when, as shall be seen shortly, he was about to read law at Freiburg University.

In the meantime, life continued as normally as possible. In summer, Jaspers joined his family's excursions to Spiekeroog and Norderney, and he occupied long, light evenings with cycle tours across the marshy plains near Oldenburg.[22] In autumn, the hunting season was marked by a family cele-bration for Karl Jaspers, senior, whose birthday fell on 1 October, when he would frequently disappear to hunt on grounds that he had partly acquired in order to raise his son's downcast spirits. But Jaspers was unable to find strength to fire his hunting rifle, and he was later content for his gun to be given away to one of his father's acquaintances. In the winter months, he went ice-skating on the frozen lakes near his grandfather's smallholding in Heering.[23] He also spent summer holidays touring the barns with his grandfather to inspect the livestock. The family's involvement in politics ran alongside their other activities throughout the seasons. Jaspers' uncle Theodor Tantzen, only five years his senior, was to become Minister President of Oldenburg, travelling as far afield as Weimar during the years of the republic. Jaspers' parents followed Tantzen's speeches in the local press, and they read no less eagerly about Max Weber whose family and political ambitions largely corresponded to their patriotic and democratic principles.

Karl Jaspers senior watched the civilized values and financial stability that he had carefully established for his family rapidly deteriorating during his lifetime. The sheer industry of Jaspers' father and his uncles, Fritz, Louis and Diedrich fulfilled the family's expectation of unbroken material prosperity.[24] For the duration of his schooling, however, few visible signs emerged of the money troubles that, on more than one occasion, confronted his father with the prospect of financial ruin. The family's wealth had been accumulated in the days of Jaspers' great-grandfather, Johann Friedrich Jaspers.[25] When Karl Jaspers senior came to inherit, his father's legacy had dwindled. Not that the family silver had been plundered by extravagant living, even if Jaspers recalled in his memoirs with considerable affection and good humour how much his grandfather enjoyed the smart villa that he had built for himself in Jever: 'In this house I felt in the most noble part of Jever. My grandfather behaved accordingly, walking in the evenings to the local public house, always wearing top hat and gloves.'[26] When Jaspers' grandfather died, at the age of sixty-nine, the family rallied round in resignation. The widowed Louise Jaspers continued under the impression that her inheritance was intact, whereas she was protected from knowing about the decline of the family inheritance by her sons' hard work and business activities.[27] The self-restraint and dignity that radiate from this fragment of Jaspers' memoirs faintly resembled Thomas Mann's first novel about the decline of the Buddenbrook clan, a story that Jaspers read with fascination at the time of its first publication in 1901.[28] The discreet letters of affection that were exchanged between Henriette Tantzen and her future brothers-in-law, Fritz and Louis Jaspers, suggested, too, that Jaspers' father had every reason to anticipate a fulfilling and harmonious marriage. He wrote as much to his future wife: 'Only a little more than 3 months, until we both begin the happy part of our lives.'[29]

When the marriage took place, on 26 October 1881, the match met with approval on all sides. Henriette Tantzen's parents were close to the farming community in Butjadingen; and Jaspers' great-great-grandmother, Helen Sophie Drost, was also from farming folk, near Jever. Contrary to expectations, the future held no pastoral idyll. Their rural lifestyle proved more or less a relic of former generations. Furthermore, when the prospect of bankruptcy descended upon Jaspers' family, due to circumstances surrounding Enno's suicide in 1931, the financial instability of the 'founder' years towards the end of Wilhelminian Germany had been forgotten. Although the death of Enno destroyed the family's peace of mind, their solidarity was strengthened by the sense of loss.[30]

The family's closeness was nowhere more clearly illustrated than in the letters and diaries that Jaspers began to write while he was still at school. He did not seem to have been aspiring to literary success, an observation borne out by the relevant section of his school-leaving certificate: 'He read the Classics with good understanding and interest and he showed a satisfactory range of expression in both oral and written work.'[31] Jaspers' matter-of-fact style and the brevity and economy of his prose were constant features of his writing from his school years onwards.[32] This precise mode of expression also characterized his memoirs, in which he included many excerpts from his student diaries and letters. These sources cannot convey much factual information about his school years, but the handful of fragmentary letters surviving from this period show that his memoirs gave a faithful account of his experiences. This period of Jaspers' life appears to have been a time of almost abject misery. Inside and outside school, he was involved in perpetual conflict. This unwelcome aspect of everyday life was captured in Jaspers' anecdote in a schoolboy letter about a calamity that occurred at the boarding house on Norderney:

[Norderney, 9. VII. 98]

[Dear parents,]

Today I am not writing a letter, as I no longer have much to write. Yesterday we were in the dunes, where a squall blew up. We fled rapidly home. Unfortunately, as we climbed a steep sand dune my umbrella broke in two. It was turned inside out by the wind and three rods broke away. As the frame is very complicated and everything was linked together, the whole frame is probably going to have to be renewed. I now want to ask you, whether I am supposed to buy another umbrella, or whether I am to have this one fixed, which would be very expensive, or whether I have no need for an umbrella at all. Yesterday evening, Fridow Schneider from Hamlin arrived (15 years, quite nice). He has a room all for himself, even though he came later than I did. I am very well. Everything is brilliant. Willy Salfeld has improved himself as I wished. I now quite like sleeping in the same room, you have to get used to everything. Many thanks for Mama's card.

With fond greeting,
Your Kally[33]

Jaspers hinted at a slight decline in confidence, a degree of vulnerability, or even a preference for loneliness. Yet these hints were concealed in his letter under the pretext of seeking advice about the cost of repairing his broken umbrella. This rare example of his insecurity while he was away from home is implicit in the account he provided in his memoirs of the ongoing battle of wits with authority, as personified by his headmaster Herr Steinvorth.

Jaspers' relationship to Steinvorth was complicated by the mystery surrounding the appropriate diagnosis of his illness. If his spirits were dampened by the effects of his unknown condition, his sensitivity towards others was heightened in a way that alienated him from his peers, whose robustness and good health naturally excluded them from feeling a similar level of isolation. The keen awareness of the possibility of different perceptions of reality that could be seen as part and parcel of daily life meant that Jaspers focused on matters of lesser importance that appeared frequently to have crossed his path. Among these matters of lesser value were the rules and regulations that his headmaster devised in order to ensure the smooth organization of school life. For Jaspers, such rules became targets of unbridled opposition. Steinvorth insisted on maintaining an old-schoolboy network of 'house' groups that Jaspers perceived as an unacceptable form of militarism that was especially misplaced at school. He mercilessly ridiculed the militaristic style of Herr Steinvorth's school rules as relics of an outdated type of social prejudice. His anecdote presented an emotionally charged account of his experience after voicing his opposition towards the spirit of the sixth-form house groups that he remembered by the names of Obscura, Prima, and Saxonia. Sons of senior government officials, officers and wealthy individuals belonged to the Obscura; sons of the professional middle classes were members of the Prima; and the lower-middle classes, farmers and tradesmen, were members of the Saxonia. Jaspers was to have joined the Obscura, but because of his intellectual and artistic interests he was invited to join the Prima. He refused to join any group, and he was eventually permitted to consort with the house groups as an 'independent'.[34]

The sixth-form house groups could be seen as forerunners of student fraternities that Jaspers could later have joined at university. He was opposed to the spirit of such privileged associations, which he regarded as inappropriate indications of social position. He was unwilling to participate in such arbitrary groups, though they could have prepared him for the transition from school to the world of a freshman student. Another clash of views with Herr Steinvorth reportedly occurred before Jaspers left the sixth form. On this occasion, he defended his refusal to recite a formal leaving speech in Latin, on the ground that the Latin class as a whole was incapable of delivering such a fluently phrased speech. Lastly, on his obligatory visit to Steinvorth before he left school he was greeted by his headmaster's cutting remark: 'Nothing can become of you anyway, because your illness is an organic fact of life!'[35]

This aggressive comment curiously underscored one of the chief benefits of Jaspers' rebellion against Steinvorth. His headmaster's words even high-lighted a particular virtue of the grammar school education: Jaspers learned to assert his independent status and to remain faithful to his principle of refusing to submit to higher authority. At school, he discovered how to negotiate for his position of independence in relation to those superficial appearances that he saw as reinforced by an absence of merit; and he confronted social and other types of prejudice with a well-thought-out strategy of survival. When survival counted for everything, social airs and graces mattered little. Jaspers' desire was to comprehend what left a delicate layer of appearances intact. He tried to distinguish what was perceived as tradition from a genuine historical case. His desire for knowledge later became a pattern of critical questioning.

As Jaspers strove to gain certainty about his position in relation to his education and upbringing, his objective approach was reinforced, at every turn, by the rational debates with his father. In each of the arguments with Steinvorth, for instance, especially for opting out of sixth-form house groups, Jaspers gained his father's full support. At the same time, however, Karl Jaspers senior pointed out the limits of his personal influence, and he warned of an unpleasant outcome if Jaspers were indeed to defeat his headmaster's authority. A compromise was also reached with Herr Steinvorth, because in any case Jaspers' frequent illnesses alienated him from most of his classmates. Perhaps for that reason, he developed a virtual obsession with art history and began to collect postcards, paintings and other pictorial mementoes. His interest in art was particularly stimulated by his father's hobby of watercolour painting. His father's landscapes and seascapes demonstrated a way of representing life through the medium of art that brought the shape of reality into focus, by ordering things into a state of possible harmony. If Jaspers preferred not to discuss, in his mature works, a critical conception of the fine arts, this approach was consistent with his admiration for his father's painting. The pleasure that he derived from observing his father's paintings, added to his father's strong personal influence, suggests that the traditional character of his classical education hardly contributed to the unprecedented change of heart that intervened and overturned his immediate plans for the future. In his childhood, Jaspers was free to explore the countryside near his home. He had grown up studying the appearance of natural phenomena. It seemed as though he sensed other possibilities awaiting his discovery and perhaps he even dreamed, too, of exploring the deeper meaning of life that was constantly represented by his awareness of the visible presence of the ocean.

2 *Young Scientist*

IN LATE APRIL 1901, after travelling south to enrol as a student of jurisprudence
at the University of Freiburg, Jaspers left his student lodgings, conveying to his
parents the news of an unforeseen change of plan: 'My current address is as
follows: Badenweiler (Black Forest) Diatetic Clinic (Villa Hedwig).'[1]

Jaspers spent what was to have been his first semester of law studies
convalescing at Dr Albert Fraenkel's clinic in the spa town of Badenweiler. He
had scarcely enrolled and attended a seminar in Roman law[2] when he followed
his father's advice to visit Dr Fraenkel, a close family friend.[3] The diagnosis of
his illness came about when Fraenkel concluded that Jaspers' condition was
bronchiectasis. The illness was discovered, almost by chance, when an interrupted train journey from Freiburg to Badenweiler left Jaspers stranded at
Müllheim, some four miles from his planned destination.[4] After walking on to
Badenweiler, Jaspers arrived in a breathless state. Fraenkel insisted upon an
immediate examination; and from his temporary accommodation at the
Europäischer Hof hotel in Freiburg, Jaspers reported to his parents:

Badenweiler, 27 April 1901

My dear parents,

[...] Herr Dr Fr[aenkel] thinks it necessary that I give up my
studies next semester and undergo a thorough health 'cure' to

convalesce and recuperate.[...] This sort of 'cure' will certainly not be cheap, but I think that Papa's funds will permit it when my health is at stake, that is, when my entire later life is at stake.[...]

I am no master of German style and I neither comprehend nor believe in the need to describe something in a more pleasant light than it is. For that reason, I wrote quite openly to you, but I can assure you that after all that Herr Dr Fr[aenkel] has told me (and he has promised to be quite open) this is nothing to be upset about, rather, I must be happy that the cause of my frequent illness has at last been discovered and can be treated.[...] We were used to seeing lung infections in every case as a fatal illness. That is clearly a quite mistaken view, if no tuberculosis, as with me, can be detected. I too had quite a shock at first, but I soon allowed myself to be advised for the better.

You will send me a telegram to the Europäischer Hof, so that I can quickly be clear about where I should go and in case Prof. Bäumler advises the same, I can settle myself in Badenweiler.

With fond greeting,

Your Kally[5]

At this critical time, the incidental questions of finance and the disappointing interruption to Jaspers' first semester of law studies were not foremost considerations. Dr Fraenkel alerted Karl and Henriette Jaspers to the urgency of their son's condition by sending them a separate account of his diagnosis, in which he strongly supported Jaspers' immediate convalescence:

B[adenweiler], 27. 4. 01

Dear Herr Jaspers!

In the middle of the week, we had the pleasure of seeing your Karl here for the first time.

I noticed that the small hike up from Müllheim had exhausted him and that he was short of breath for a long time. I could therefore not resist the temptation of determining the cause of this.

The examination showed that it is a case of illness to the left lung, which is combined with secretion and reveals the tendency to shrink and heal up in one place. The microscop[ic] examination of the secretion confirms previous results that it is <u>not</u> a case of tuberculosis. Probably, the start of the affliction lies a long way back. The tendency to fever and 'influenzas' during early and recent years is connected with the lung injury.[...] These changes provide a compelling explanation for the poor state of nourishment and his current unsatisfactory condition.[...]

Badenweiler ranks at the top of the list of small health spas that come into contention for such a 'cure'.[...]

I am sorry to be the cause of your intelligent, dear son's disappointment at postponing his studies and to send you these reports, but it seems my duty as a doctor and a friend to take action.[...]

I await your decision and remain with amiable greetings to your lady wife.

Yours faithfully,

Fraenkel[6]

Perhaps the memory of having himself contracted tuberculosis, an experience that interrupted his own career as a doctor only a decade previously, had led Fraenkel to underscore his faith in the advantage of Jaspers remaining in his care in Badenweiler.[7] The implication of his diagnosis was clear, although it was not obvious that Jaspers was at death's door. Tuberculosis or not, he was not expected to live for much longer than his early thirties. For the next year, at least, his academic study was an ad-hoc affair of salvaging what could be retrieved from the initial plans. His bronchiectasis was an incurable condition, borne out by Fraenkel's estimation that the causes dated from Jaspers' early childhood. The left lung was perforated to such an extent that Jaspers felt secondary, 'compensatory' effects upon his heart. A few days after having received Fraenkel's letter, Karl Jaspers senior sent a telegram to his son's hotel: 'pleased that cause of complaint discovered gladly in agreement with everything that you do, telegraph result of baeumler's examination, here all well papa'.[8]

Jaspers remained at Fraenkel's clinic in Badenweiler and submitted to a drastic 'fattening' diet (*Mastkur*) to help him gain weight. At eighteen, and weighing only 123 pounds, relative to his height of six foot one Jaspers was by present-day standards severely underweight.[9] After one week's convalescence, he reported a modest weight gain to 130 pounds.[10] By the end of the first month of treatment, his weight was gradually returning to normal.[11]

The summer months of May until mid-July 1901 were spent in Badenweiler at Fraenkel's clinic where Jaspers endured various treatments, such as lying at an incline, with his head below his feet, to clear the lungs of unwanted secretions. He also submitted to massages, continual bathing and cold rubs.[12] His letters show the good grace with which he accepted all this, yet the régime of lazing about in deck chairs, eating well and taking the Black Forest air interfered with his desire to experience other things. Jaspers began a pro-gramme of private reading and art work. He requested several books from home – a popular journal of art history that he subscribed to as a school pupil called *Kunstwart*, Hermann's lexicon of Roman law and several philosophical works, Paulsen's *Introduction to Philosophy* and the pocket-size Reclam edition of Spinoza's *Ethics*.[13] His desire for amusement also led him to resurrect earlier plans for drawing lessons for his first Freiburg semester,[14] but he gave up his attempt to practise sketching in Badenweiler, when his art teacher failed to live up to his expectations. Jaspers' father continued as a chosen partner for discussions and as a source of trusted advice on the subject of how accurately to represent the appearance of nature:

Badenweiler, 21. V. 01

Dear Papa,

I enjoy sketching a lot, but the teacher is no good. Yesterday, I made a free-hand drawing of an old oak tree. I captured the tree-trunk quite well, but I could not reproduce the foliage accurately, so I asked the teacher if he would not mind showing me. He now drew, nearby on the same paper, leaf for leaf. The whole tree would have ended by taking up several cubic metres. I told him that. Then he drew leaf for leaf, smaller. That became a load of scribble, I told him that as well, after which he was incapable of demonstrating it for me properly. He only used a couple of sentences to explain it to me in words. Also, the lesson costs 3 Marks. I have had three lessons; I will probably give them all up and sketch on my own.[...]

Fond greeting to all!

Your Karl[15]

In early June 1901, during the Whitsuntide break, Karl Jaspers senior ended his own health cure in Bad Kissingen, where he was recuperating from what was later diagnosed as a grumbling stomach ulcer. On his return journey to Oldenburg, he visited his son in Badenweiler. A plan was formed for their joint excursion to the art gallery in Basel, where Jaspers' father wanted to show him Arnold Böcklin's paintings.[16] On Fraenkel's advice, however, their visit was cancelled.[17] By way of compensation, Jaspers' father ordered a set of paints to be forwarded to Badenweiler.[18] He also sent a book of instructions about watercolour painting and directions for his son to improve his technique:

Oldenburg, 14 June 1901

Dear Kally,

[...] I put together the drawing utensils. Mother has sent them to you. Besides, I still hope to send you a number of colour tubes – I mean fifteen – directly from the manufacturer. I ask you, once you receive them, to send me a list of the tubes, by name of the colours, so that I can check the bill and pay.

The Chinese ink is in the box of colours. To rub it in, I have included a <u>small</u>, porcelain palette that you can easily take into the open air. I recommend that you transfer the prepared Chinese ink into the metal lid of the case, out of which you can paint with ease. You can, though, paint directly from the porcelain palette. You already know the tin box for water with the detachable bowls at both ends.

I have used the small board as a drawing board in the open air; I have attached a box of pins for fixing down the sketchbook. It is very comfortable for painting watercolours.

I could, unfortunately, not obtain a block of <u>watercolour</u> paper here.

Instead of Chinese ink, you can also use sepia, but with Chinese ink you can create much finer tones.

In the handbook for watercolour painting you will find a record of all the colours that have been sent to you. The names, though, do not always sound the same. In one place that I have earmarked you will find under the printed names some names that I have written alongside. [...]

You must study the handbook repeatedly and with care; I have introduced several sheets on which I have made colour studies. In bad weather, I recommend that you make similar studies, which can be very instructive.

In case I can give you advice from here, I suggest you ask.[...]

Fond greeting to you!

Your Papa[19]

Reporting that he had received his father's instructions, Jaspers copied a list of the watercolours that had arrived, including sepia, cobalt blue, French blue, indigo, black, Naples yellow, Krapplack pink, madder brown, Indian red, light red, burnt Siena, umber and burnt umber.[20] The colours seemed to represent the happy prospect of diverting his attention to the more pleasurable pastime of painting. Yet several months were to pass before Jaspers could begin in earnest with his law studies. In mid-July, with the permission of his doctors, Fraenkel and Bäumler, the specialist consultant in Freiburg that he sought out on Fraenkel's advice, Jaspers travelled homewards, stopping en route to visit an art exhibition in Darmstadt.[21] His destination was Norderney, where he continued his convalescence by the sea.[22] In mid-October he returned, via Helgoland and Hamburg, to Heidelberg, where he was able to begin the legal studies, which lasted for one year – an incomplete summer term in Freiburg, a winter semester in Heidelberg and a summer semester in Munich. During that year, Jaspers was struck by the idea that he should change to a different career. Indeed, it appears that something of a spiritual revival took place after Fraenkel's diagnosis of his illness.

On the further advice of Bäumler, Jaspers stayed for the entire month of August 1902 in the small Engadine hamlet of Sils Maria. The mood of this excursion contrasted with the shock he had experienced the previous year in Badenweiler upon learning the true nature of his illness. A cloud of energy seemed to hang in the air during the few weeks that he enjoyed in Sils Maria. Jaspers attempted to conceal his sentiments from his parents about the Alpine location that he was seeing for the first time. Gradually, however, the revival of spirits produced a change of heart about his course of study and his preferred future career.

The intoxicating mixture of excitement and inner change was perhaps reflected in the title of his memoirs, 'Destiny and Will' (*Schicksal und Wille*). This title suggests that Jaspers' life experience was represented by a map upon which his ambitions were sketched out, as it were, to be directly equated with particular events throughout his life. The specific reference to 'destiny' and 'will' in his memoirs may not have suggested such a retrospective account of his life experience. The term 'will', a Schopenhauerian word, is rarely encountered in Jaspers' family correspondence. In his first semester of study in Heidelberg, he briefly referred to his reading of Schopenhauer's *The World as Will and Representation* (1818).[23] In letters from Italy the following spring, as shall be seen, he overcame his initial enthusiasm for Schopenhauer's philosophy, whose removal from world affairs in a climate of pessimism had appealed to Jaspers' tendency to brood on life in his preferred isolation. That mood of introspection was redundant in the context of Jaspers' Italian journey – the Schopenhauerian 'will' implied a world-view of artistic contemplation that he began to regard as worthy of careful reconsideration.[24] The title theme of his memoirs may have owed something to his arrival in Sils Maria in 1902, when events unfolded with a certain momentum. At least, these aspects of change may be noted in the first letter that Jaspers sent his parents from his Alpine village:

Sils, 1. VIII. 02

Dear parents!

[...] When the clouds sweep across the high, bare mountains, where not a trace of human activity is to be seen, you believe you are present when the planet was formed in prehistoric times. The impact is above all always a powerfully impressive and terrible one. While looking at the sea imparts satisfaction and calm thanks to its orderliness and regularity, a quite opposite atmosphere emerges in this landscape, where the arbitrary and the disorderly reign among jagged forms and rugged masses. It is almost decadent to revel in that climate. Many will find it uplifting to feel man's insignificance in front of the ugly mountain giants, but you can feel this in a noble way on contemplating the endlessness of the sea beating on shore in a regular pulse of waves, or under the star-bedecked sky where you at least suspect an idea of the orderly. Here, you resist being subordinated by what seem to be the arbitrary forces of nature. You would dearly like to tear down the peaks soaring impertinently to the heavens. The landscape has a beauty similar to the representation of the giants in Wagner's *Ring* – summits that stand against wind and clouds seem to show less the persistent power of virility than man's defiant and shameless nature – like Böcklin's dragon in the Schack Gallery or the giant Polyphemus in Homer. It seems telling that Nietzsche is supposed to have spent five years here. My condition is <u>excellent</u>.

Fond greeting,

Your Kally[25]

Jaspers' encounter with the mountain landscape in Sils Maria led him wholeheartedly to rejoice at having arrived in one of Friedrich Nietzsche's favourite places. When he sent his reflections to his parents in Oldenburg, Nietzsche was perceived as a provocative author. Indeed, scarcely a decade previously, in the introduction to *An Essay on Aristocratic Radicalism* (1889), the Danish philosophy professor and literary critic Georg Brandes had noted: 'Friedrich Nietzsche appears to me the most interesting writer in German literature at the present time. Though little known in his own country, he is a thinker of a high order, who fully deserves to be studied, discussed, contested and mastered. Among many good qualities he has that of imparting his mood to others and setting their thoughts in motion.'[26]

Brandes was alerted to Nietzsche's writings partly through his acquaintance

with Lou Andreas Salomé, and he was among the first to take a serious interest
in Nietzsche's works and to regard their profound historical critique as the
mark of a great thinker. Jaspers sensed that quality in Nietzsche's works and
was eager to inform his parents of his personal impression of Nietzsche's
connection to Sils Maria. A faint polemical undertone to his comments
suggested that he especially admired the way that Nietzsche lived and expressed
his metaphors, as in *Thus Spoke Zarathustra* (1883), whose central idea of
'Eternal Recurrence' was inspired by Nietzsche's arrival in Sils Maria in 1881.[27]
By concluding his letter on a reassuring note for his parents, Jaspers checked
his enthusiasm for the Alpine scenery, hinting that even if the climate
whispered self-indulgence he was not tempted to engage his appetite for
adventure. Instead, he preferred the sea and the familiar coastline near
Oldenburg to the Alpine landscape. For all its imposing appearance, Jaspers
compared the scenery in Sils Maria to other examples of artistic representation
on a monumental scale. He then counted Wagner's music, Arnold Böcklin's
romanticized paintings and Homer's tale of Odysseus' encounter with the
Cyclops giant, Polyphemus, among examples of an aspect of the human psyche
that he preferred to observe at a safe distance.

In Sils Maria, Jaspers seems to have been impressed by Nietzsche's appeal
to the modern reader through the aphoristic forms of his literary works, as
though these forms were an intimation of a radically different perception of
reality that Jaspers deliberately represented in a critical light. His careful
account of such examples of artistic temperament was in contrast to his rather
carefree reaction to the nature that he observed and studied. His letters back
home confirmed his favoured topoi of the sea and open horizon as symbolic
manifestations of Kant's mode of thinking – monotonous and perhaps rather
dull by comparison to Nietzsche. Yet it was also in Sils Maria that Jaspers
glimpsed what he came to regard as his vocation. He recognized his calling so
intuitively that his unspoken ambition may have confined his interest in
psychology to the days of his youth, an assumption that may be compared with
Jaspers' later diary note on Nietzsche and his lecture preparations discussed
below.[28] In August 1902, Jaspers did not express such possibilities in as many
words. Yet a metamorphosis gradually transformed his outlook on life, and the
effects of his change of heart were more profound than superficially they
seemed.

Jaspers' decision to study medicine required him to adopt a new official
identity. He was obliged to substitute his former image as an aspiring law
student for the earnest outlook of a young scientist. That outward change of
status may have continued to influence his career for years after he had

completed his training as a medical doctor, that is, the six years from 1902 to 1908 that corresponded to his research activities and practical experiments in the natural sciences. The beginnings of Jaspers' new image survive in a photograph taken in Sils Maria (see Ill. 6). The picture shows a profile of him as a young man standing between two scholars, Professor Fano, a physiologist from Florence, and Professor Cornelius, an art historian in Freiburg. Jaspers befriended these scholars whose intelligent conversation he appreciated. The picture of the experienced scholars and the tall youth in their midst has a light-hearted atmosphere, with each of the participants in this photograph swearing a kind of 'hippocratic' oath to 'the spirit of science', as indicated by the open pages of a book. By accident or design, this book was placed in Jaspers' hands. This jovial pledge appeared lively enough. Yet Jaspers was serious about this gesture of respect towards the reputation of the scientist. Upon his return from Sils Maria, he devoted himself to convincing his father to lend his continued financial support to his decision to train as a doctor of medicine.

Jaspers needed to persuade his father that his association with the law faculty, for almost three semesters, had been an error of judgement and that he still intended to pursue an academic career. Dr Fraenkel's influence was delicately exploited in an extraordinary letter, several pages in length, in which Jaspers marshalled his arguments to persuade his father to accept his proposal.[29] He decided to use this letter as a prompt, in order to defend his views in person. His letter was rhetorically accomplished and rudimentary elements of a thesis can even be detected in the finer details. He pleaded his case as though he already intuitively grasped the psychological implications of his illness. Fraenkel ultimately emerged as his saviour from what Jaspers described as his 'miserable schooling and miserable teachers'.[30] Indeed, he claimed that the idea of beginning scientific work in earnest had crossed his mind only after he came into contact with Fraenkel. The pathos of that argument was offset by the persuasive line that his sudden decision to choose a course of study in the natural sciences was not to be misinterpreted as the action of an irrational hypochondriac.[31] The business of lawmaking was to lose out to a philosophical incentive that he identified as the wellspring of a scientist's authority. At the same time, Jaspers emphasized for his father's benefit that he regarded the discipline of philosophy as a world apart from the scientist's vocation. He described the possibility of a career in philosophy with an aura of hope, so concealing his ambition and uncertain talent.

Aged only nineteen, Jaspers extolled the rewards of empirical research. In this written presentation of his views, he set out a practical focus for his scientific ambitions. Yet his arguments and ideas later developed, as we shall see, with specific reference to relevant ideas in philosophy. As an aspiring candidate for a doctorate in medicine, Jaspers saw a scientist's vocation in the light of this perception: 'The investigation of the human body is the foundation of all other knowledge about the human psyche, as well as the study of illnesses in terms of their causes, effects and possible healing.[...] You not only learn about whatever is visible to the naked eye, but also about how the most minute forms of life come into being.'[32] Jaspers' determination to devote his energies to the study of medicine was clear. He was obliged to suggest that the three semesters of research in the humanities had not sufficiently challenged his powers of concentration. If his commitment to that particular branch of investigation in the humanities was not altogether abandoned, he had nonetheless transferred his allegiances to the practical activity of a scientific researcher with a view to carrying out observation, analysis and experimentation. Inevitably, he had to sacrifice some of his former interests in the arts in general if he was to qualify as a doctor within the relatively short (and compulsory) space of six years, or twelve semesters. His pleas about beginning a new career in medicine were successful: without further ado, his father agreed to finance his studies.

Jaspers' first semester of medical studies in 1902 began in Berlin. Yet he soon found that his daily journey from lectures to lodgings was physically exhausting. His old friend from near Oldenburg, Fritz zur Loye, made fun of his choice of lodgings, which were situated one hour from the university.[33] For the summer semester of 1903, Jaspers decided to relocate to Göttingen University, where he studied for the next three years. Fraenkel's treatment of the bronchiectasis meant that Jaspers had to commit himself to a rigid and restricted working routine that was intended to prolong his life. He learned to organize his working day into five or six hours of study, by commencing work around 8.30 a.m. and continuing until lunch time, when several hours of rest were required following a ritual exercise of coughing, in order to clear the bronchial system of secretions.[34] In the afternoons, Jaspers worked on a sofa, later relying on a reading device to hold the weight of the books. This combination of iron discipline and effective time management was put to good use in Göttingen. During the holiday periods, he conducted experiments at his parents' home. As a further mark of his father's generosity, he obtained permission to convert a small room in the family home into a chemical laboratory. This makeshift laboratory was even equipped with basic chemical compounds and experimental equipment.[35] Jaspers was accustomed to preparing bacteria cultivations, and he practised for anatomy lectures so as to keep pace with his fellow students by means of a programme of organized truancy. He often gained his certificates of study without even attending the lectures.[36]

Jaspers' programme of research and practical work incurred considerable additional costs, which could not have been met without his father's ability to underwrite the purchase of medical textbooks and other equipment, such as an 'atlas' of anatomy, a skeleton and a microscope.[37] Jaspers' mother reassured him of his father's readiness to continue investing in his medical training: 'Papa is in total agreement with the purchases that promote your studies, you might like to buy a new atlas and also a new skeleton. Papa said that all study aids are money that is well invested and I also think it is very nice for you, if during your studies in your room you have the skeleton before your eyes.'[38]

The arrival of the skeleton was jubilantly announced: 'The skeleton is in my student room as a sign of nature; I use it a lot [...].'[39] At the end of his first semester of medical study, Jaspers requested permission to purchase a microscope, as recommended by his professor, and as possessed by Fraenkel during his medical training. Jaspers' suggestion was that his parents might give him the microscope as a Christmas present, so that he could use the equipment during his Easter vacation: 'My wish would then be: a microscope for 270 Marks with the necessary utensils, approx. 300–320 Marks and in the course of the next year or more, an oil immersion for 100 Marks.'[40]

At his parents' home, Jaspers had access to a telescope, so that he could observe the stellar constellations. He also dabbled in geology, studying a small collection of rocks and minerals.[41] During the summer holidays of 1904, his father arranged a work placement on the zoological station on Helgoland, through a personal connection with the station's director.[42] His room was in the lighthouse with a view across the open sea.[43] While he joined the occasional excursion out on to the high seas, his contact with other researchers inspired him to continue his private studies in the station's library. After three years of medical training (six semesters), Jaspers passed his first-stage examinations with 'summa cum laude', and the excellent results arrived on his twenty-second birthday, 23 February 1905.[44]

Despite such a positive start to his medical training, Jaspers was already conscious of a dilemma, or a mind-game, that could be regarded as a lingering consequence of his change of faculty from law to medicine. This conundrum may not have been as profound as it appears upon first inspection, although it seems significant enough to shed light on his motives for deciding to change his programme of study. What can be reliably stated is that Jaspers deliberately chose to follow one avenue of investigation in the sciences as opposed to the other route of study in the humanities. At the same time, his scientific activities could be regarded as a welcome reprieve from his initial decision to train as a lawyer – a career for which his father had trained and which his younger brother Enno later practised. Jaspers' zoological studies on the station at Helgoland, as well as the experiments that he conducted during vacations and the opportunities he had to peer at life through the lenses of the microscope and telescope could equally be treated as a distraction from the chief focus of his interests: namely, to learn about mankind in the humanist sense. In this respect, it is interesting that Jaspers inscribed on the inside page of one of his Göttingen diaries, for the year 1904/5, the following words: 'Jeder kann nur eine Seite des Menschen darstellen, aber den Begriff davon haben, was der ganze Mensch sei'.[45] A rough translation of Jaspers' proposition may read as follows: 'Anyone can describe only one side of man's nature, but should possess an idea of what the whole man may be.' This motto may have been inspired by Goethe's *Elective Affinities*, a novel that Jaspers was reading about the time that he kept his diary.[46] In *Elective Affinities*, Ottilie's diary included a passage that is strikingly similar to Jaspers' rendition of Goethe's words. Assuming that the slight alteration in wording did not arise because he was quoting from memory, one plausible explanation for his rendition could be that he had adapted Goethe's original sentence to suit his own needs. What Goethe wrote was: 'Dem einzelnen bliebe die Freiheit, sich mit dem zu beschäftigen, was ihn anzieht, was ihm Freude macht, was ihm nützlich deucht; aber das eigentliche Studium der Menschheit ist der Mensch.'[47] ('The individual is free to occupy himself with whatever attracts him, with whatever gives him pleasure, with whatever seems to him useful: but the proper study of mankind is man.'[48]).

In one respect, Jaspers' alteration of Goethe's message rather simplified his reading. But even if the different wording derived from misremembering, his particular rendition of Goethe's observation remains revealing, because it veiled the finer distinction of Goethe's description of the humanity of mankind. Jaspers had aspired to a Goethean – that is, poetic or intuitive – appreciation of mankind as the best way to understand man's humanity, and his personal motto could therefore have implied that he was in two minds about the challenges of his vocation as a scientist. Indeed, by choosing his motto from Goethe's novella, Jaspers hinted that he was as open-minded about Goethe the poet as about Goethe the scientist.[49] At this time of Jaspers' career, his unique way of appropriating Goethe's words to suit his personal ambitions was perhaps intended as a light-hearted criticism of *scientists* for being generally too rationalistic in their attempts to comprehend the object of their research, namely, mankind itself.

Another plausible way of reading Jaspers' motto is to regard it as a reminder note to keep his options open. At any instant, his health might have deteriorated to become an ultimate obstacle with the power of permanently upsetting his plans for the future. It was imperative for him to choose a vocation that he could hope to fulfil within the constraints imposed upon his physical capacities. His fragile health meant that his stamina for performing to the best of his abilities was always in question. A detailed analysis of the symptoms and effects of bronchiectasis upon an individual, which Jaspers supplied in his memoirs, hardly conveyed the precarious nature of his situation during his medical training. This report about his illness was carefully screened to omit personalized references to his experience.[50] His approach was largely because of his altruistic wish to help other sufferers to live with this condition. His memoirs may therefore have lent credence to the idea that his illness was an imposition that he easily overcame. His desire for objectivity projected an image of his capacity as a psychiatrist to distance himself from his personal experience and to turn a clinically trained eye to the task of highlighting the possible methods of treatment for other bronchiectasis patients.

Although the clinical style of Jaspers' memoirs clearly fulfilled a vital purpose, his desire to assist others, the memoirs do not necessarily fully portray his experiences during his training as a young scientist. Since the memoirs set his enthusiastic approach as a young medical student in relief, it is important to consult a fragment of another of his Göttingen diaries, in which he began to reflect upon his illness in a way that reveals the reverberations of the shock inflicted by Dr Fraenkel's diagnosis of his condition. Jaspers' diary note, entitled 'About My Existence 1904',[51] is a complementary illustration of his memoirs, in which his schematic report about bronchiectasis was included. This diary note is cited here not as a revelation about Jaspers' suffering, but rather to indicate the subtle contrast of tone in the diverse sources about his illness. This contrast highlights an essential message, that Jaspers' diary reinstated the experience of illness with regard to his dignity as a patient; and the objective tone of his memoirs may be read as clarifying the painful honesty of this diary extract:

> If I once imagine that I were to be born as my parents' son, then the result would be that I must be dead long since. As it is, I am counted, only artificially, as an ailing plant among healthy ones and the success is that, due to conditions making the ailing plant's survival in a vegetative state possible (virtually any other than this artificial state would mean extinction), the ultimate appearance of the ailing plant is almost the same as the healthy one. The uninformed observer may therefore be led astray, to a wrong opinion about the ailing plant.[52]

The expressive capacity of Jaspers' language in this diary fragment, part of an unfinished letter to his father, provides a rare glimpse of his sensitivity towards others and his desire to conceal the suffering caused by his illness. In his clinically fashioned memoirs, he provided a dispassionate chronology of his illness prefaced by the cursory remark that 'What I experienced and what I did is mainly only to be understood by seeing a certain nuance, when the facts of my illness are in full view.'[53] He again employed the metaphor of the plant in a brief reference to 'vegetative life' in the context of the individual's attitude to sickness; and he underlined that for a patient to succumb to a passive state of accepting illness was to harm the individual sense of dignity.[54]

The comparison of Jaspers' physical state of health in the diary note to a form of vegetation showed his overall approach to illness. His capacity to shift his thoughts from consciousness of sickness to a focus on relative health was unusually sharp. Jaspers may have experienced his illness as a radical break with everything and everyone around him, yet he rarely communicated that experience to his fellow human beings. Whether read together or apart from the relevant section of his memoirs, this particular diary extract offers a poignant insight into his experiences in 1904. At that time, he clung to life by the finest of margins, which he turned into a metaphorical description of life. Yet his capacity for rational analysis led him to adopt the right attitude towards the illness, so that few, except perhaps for his close friends and family, were aware of its considerable impact upon his daily life.

As miraculous as Dr Fraenkel's diagnosis of his condition had been, Jaspers was virtually obliged to study independently of his peers. If his Göttingen years were productive in the sense they gave him a period of stimulation, maturity and growing independence, they could also be described as something of an inner rebellion against his isolation from all but a few friends. His sensitivity to the experience of the illness restored not only the dignity of his reaction, but his personal integrity. His friend and mentor Dr Fraenkel was quick to notice these aspects of his resilience to his diagnosis which he regarded as a measure of a precocious and rare intellectual talent. By the summer semester of 1906, Jaspers decided to relocate to Heidelberg University, which he suspected would be best for his health and so would provide a boost to his spirits in readiness for the crucial and demanding final stages of his studies.[55] Fraenkel offered to lend him a new piece of equipment, a blood-pressure gauge. He also devised a plan for Jaspers to work at Heidelberg's Clinic of Psychiatry, whose director, Franz Nissl, had agreed to supervise his research project. Jaspers gladly accepted. After several months' research, he realized that his project was unoriginal and therefore largely redundant. By this time, however, he had developed an interest in forensic medicine. He set aside the blood-pressure measurements that he had begun to make for his initial research and wrote home to his family with a request for any anecdotal material his family possessed about homesickness. He wanted to include the material in a new piece of work, to which he had already given the preliminary title 'Homesickness and Crime'.[56] Apart from this development of his scientific work, when Jaspers arrived in Heidelberg his way of life began to change for the better. His minute circle of acquaintances, which hardly extended beyond his closest friend Fritz zur Loye, was expanded by an irreplaceable friendship with a fellow student, Ernst Mayer. Like Jaspers, Mayer was in his tenth semester of medical studies. If Jaspers' liberation from the illness had required a mental *tour de force*, his intellectual talent and great sensitivity alone could not entirely have absorbed the shock of learning of Fraenkel's diagnosis. What sustained the revival of his spirits that had begun in Sils Maria was Ernst Mayer's perceptive decision to introduce his friend to his sister Gertrud. As a direct result of the Mayers' companionship, Jaspers' life was about to be happily transformed.

3　'German Student'

WHEN JASPERS BEGAN HIS LAW STUDIES at Heidelberg University in 1901, the town basked in its status as home to a wealthy liberal milieu of the educated bourgeoisie (*Bildungsbürgertum*). His family belonged to the civilized, upper-middle classes, and he was admirably qualified by his background to integrate into the bedrock of educated society. In attire and appearance, he personified the conscientiousness and civility appropriate for his proposed career as a lawyer, yet he was to evolve into an unlikely rebel during his undergraduate years. He made constructive observations about his peers and, eventually, had the chance to forge many genuine and lasting friendships.

From the start of his university career, Jaspers thought critically about his inclusion in student life, an approach that was at odds with his outward appearance as a member of a privileged stratum of society that tended to benefit from a university education. In that respect, Jaspers followed in his father's footsteps. Indeed, he agreed to study law in order to accommodate his wishes.[1] Like his father, Jaspers decided not to join the student fraternity.[2] His intellectual disposition now strengthened his former opposition to collective associations, such as his schoolboy rebellion against the house groups. As a freshman student, Jaspers preferred the peace and quiet of his own company, and this self-imposed isolation might have remained an enduring feature of his young adult life. But fortunately for him, Heidelberg was every bit a replica of his parental home, except that its location in the Neckar valley was different from the open landscape and low flatlands of rural northern Germany. Its unique atmosphere was captured in the opening verses of Hölderlin's poem 'Heidelberg':

> Long I have loved you and wish, for my own delight,
> I could call you Mother and give you an artless song,
> You of my native land's cities
> Known to me, the most rurally beautiful.
>
> As the bird of the forest does over mountain peaks –
> Over the river, where gleaming it passes your site
> Lightly and strongly the bridge vaults,
> Noisy with coaches and men.
>
> As though sent by gods, once an enchantment transfixed
> Me upon that bridge as I was walking by,
> And the alluring distance
> Shone for me into the hills,
>
> And that youth, the river, travelled on to the plain,
> Sadly glad, like the heart when, too full of itself,
> To perish lovingly
> It casts itself into the currents of time.[3]

Jaspers transferred his private world to Heidelberg, which was to become his second home from 1907 onwards, from the start of his final year as a medical student. In this southern climate, he began to realize all the possibilities of independent scholarship, and he was to make known what he later called 'Heidelberg's spirit'.[4] What he had in mind was less a lyrical quality in the landscape, as captured in Hölderlin's poem, and more a unique kind of spiritual strength, a way of fostering an atmosphere in which it is possible to concentrate on particular intellectual aims.

The sense that in Heidelberg it was possible to fulfil those aims was to sharpen a motivation that Jaspers had only cautiously expressed to his father in late summer 1902, when he had declared his wish to work as a scientist. His cherished goal, he had said then, was eventually to work towards a career in philosophy. In Heidelberg, Jaspers was free to explore his goals, thanks to its intellectual climate, a climate in which he detected an opportunity for scholarly dedication as though it was written into the landscape itself:

The spirit, as released from *terra firma*, supranational, above the state, alive within the university, is carried by numerous individuals. Whoever would like to belong also makes his request through his life and work, through the way he approaches involvement, yet without the prospect of any authority being present that might guarantee or dismiss his request. Unbeknown to each individual, everyone decides by his doing, whether he is included or excluded. Some of those who were here only temporarily have become citizens of Heidelberg by virtue of their secret invitation. Many have sensed a living fire here that casts its light into the world. They allowed a spark from that source to fall into their life, to glow until the end, to question their purpose and to spread happiness. In Eichendorff's words: 'So hatten sie's in Träumen wohl gesehen/Und jeder blickt's wie seine Heimat an/Und keinem hat der Zauber noch gelogen.' ['So had they seen it in their dreams/And each looked upon it as his home/And the magic deceived none.'] Whoever intends to refer to this spirit will find that it is denied him. Whoever wants to evoke it finds that precisely then it disappears. It seems freely to reveal itself, only to fall utterly and completely silent again. But is that 'genius loci' not visible in the landscape, the ruined castle, and the town as a cipher of this rural place that has a captivating visual quality, even if one's thought cannot follow it?[5]

Jaspers' decision to enter the university meant that he actively participated in a spirit of idealism that, during his lifetime, he encountered as a mind-set in pursuit of excellence, as devised in Wilhelm von Humboldt's blueprint for establishing the university in Berlin at the turn of the nineteenth century. If the checks and balances of Humboldt's historic inauguration of humanism as a pillar of his proposal for the German university facilitated higher learning for the offspring of the well-to-do, Jaspers gained a great deal from the Humboldtian system, insofar as he was engaged throughout his life as an ambassador for humanity and tolerance in the quest to understand mankind. When at the conclusion of his career as a student he joined the ranks of unpaid lecturers, he became part of a privileged group that was relatively free to conduct research. His material well-being was taken care of by his father's generous promise of financial support throughout his education. Despite his nominal membership of liberal circles, he adopted an objective view of those figures in authority whom he encountered as a student; during his first semester of study, for example, he frequently displayed this objectivity about personalities in the university. Yet his approach was also accompanied by an aloofness that surpassed the detachment resulting from his schoolboy rebellion and the isolation prompted by his independent studies as a young scientist.

In a light-hearted yet determined manner, Jaspers objected to his enrolment ceremony as an exaggerated form of reverence for university professors. In one of his earliest letters from Heidelberg, he humorously portrayed the rigmarole of that ceremony and offered his parents some whimsical observations about the university Rector's participation:

Heidelberg, 28 October 1901

Dear parents!

Our solemn celebration of our enrolment on Saturday turned out to be utterly ridiculous. All the students sat quite still and respectfully in a hall that was, by the way, quite beautiful, when the Rector entered with a procession. He gave a very stuttering, silly address (naturally he was a theologian) and then every single student went up and wrote his name in the register, for which he received a certificate of enrolment. There followed a general walking about, for which the Rector assumed a most worthy and celebratory expression. We could well do without such stupid formality, which is also probably supposed to impress us. [...]

Fond greeting to him [Enno] and you from,

Your Kally[6]

The trappings of the ceremony could hardly match Jaspers' ideas about his purpose in entering the university. Impatient though he was with the formality of the occasion, he intended to gain the most from the opportunities at his disposal.

Jaspers' timetable of study for his first semester at Heidelberg University was initially based on a weekly tally of twenty-five hours of lectures and seminars. His schedule was filled with a total of seventeen hours of law lectures and a supplementary eight hours on other topics, including a seminar on Arthur Schopenhauer chaired by the best-known professor of Heidelberg's philosophy faculty, Kuno Fischer. In addition, Jaspers planned to attend a lecture course about Richard Wagner delivered by Henry Thode, who held the first chair in art history at the university; and a seminar on experimental psychology presided over by Emil Kraepelin, who was the author of one of the first general compendiums of psychiatry.[7] When Jaspers listened to some of Fischer's lectures, his main thought was that he had arrived in a world of learned men. He felt humility and pride,[8] delighted that the institution appeared to oblige its members to move on a different plane of reality.[9] He did not bestow such respect upon the academics themselves, but rather enjoyed exposing the comical side of the famous professors at their lectures. For instance, Fischer fell out of favour after Jaspers had attended only a few lectures, for he decided that because of his fame, the man was a slave to professorial vanity.[10] He transferred his allegiance to the lesser known Thode, the highly respected Professor of Renaissance Art.[11] For Jaspers, Thode's lectures became 'the highlight of the day.'[12]

An additional advantage in attending Thode's lectures on Renaissance art was that they helped prepare Jaspers for his planned visit to Italy during his first Easter holiday in 1902.[13] His defection from Fischer's lectures may also have been justified by the need to reduce the number of hours pencilled in on his timetable. Although Jaspers responded enthusiastically to the opportunity to attend lectures in any number of fields of study, the certificates of study (*Scheine*) for his first Heidelberg semester show that he managed only a modest version of his original plan.[14] Because he was not inclined to accept at face value the authority of his lecturers and professors, his ideas about the tasks to be fulfilled in the university developed in accordance with his wide experiences as a student of many of Germany's most eminent seats of learning. His decision to change both the location and choice of undergraduate study led to his 'general' studies at the universities of Freiburg, Heidelberg and Munich, followed by five years, or ten semesters, of medical training at the universities of Berlin and Göttingen. He then returned to Heidelberg, where his university career had properly begun, in order to complete his final year, or twelfth semester of medical studies.

Jaspers encountered a number of Germany's leading men of science, not least during his time in Munich in 1902 when he attended Lujo Brentano's lectures on national economy. In Göttingen, he noted that he had been unaware of Edmund Husserl's presence during the early period of his medical training around 1904. However, it was in Heidelberg that Jaspers came across many of the professors who were famous in their day, and he later began to consort with a host of gifted scholars, such as the national economist Max Weber, perhaps best known as a sociologist and the leading light of his generation. At Weber's Sunday-afternoon receptions, as shall be seen later, Jaspers was also to meet many other young scholars, including the poet and internationally respected specialist in German literature Friedrich Gundolf, Georg Lukács and Ernst Bloch.[15] Whether or not Jaspers' flirtation with law studies was the foundation for another close friendship that was developed with Gustav Radbruch is an open question.[16]

In view of Jaspers' encounters with so many leading scholars, it is perhaps not surprising that he held scientists in high regard. He admired the idea of an intellectual aristocracy and believed that the scholar could afford to be magnanimous, and adopt an attitude of chivalry and nobility.[17] His objection to mediocrity in the scientific field was not, as his student experiences might suggest, prompted by elitism. What he hoped to achieve was the maximum benefit from the university both for himself and for others. The desire to deepen his knowledge was shown by the ambitious nature of his initial programme of study at Heidelberg University. His ability to assert himself as a student was complemented by his inclination to reject, almost out of hand, involvement with a cult following or disciplehood to a figure or an idea, unless the purpose of that following were rationalized and objectively analysed. In a later conversation with Hermann Glockner, Jaspers accepted that, through his association with Ludwig Klages' study of graphology, he had come into contact with the George Circle, [18] and underlined the doubts he felt about the way in which the poet Stefan George required a specific kind of adulation from his young followers.[19] What Jaspers respected, in the context of such involvement, was an individual ability to reflect both upon the principles of the chosen group and the desire for membership. He may have implicitly endorsed a Weberian view of the scientist's vocation – perhaps he had earned a mistaken reputation as an aristocratic thinker, especially when he later carried out his own professorial duties from 1921.[20] This attitude must be distinguished from his perception of the individual as a leader 'type', for his examination of the question of leadership was an important element of his approach from the very start of his undergraduate career. His response to authority in general was founded on a similar instinct to scrutinize the status quo as represented by the 'establishment' – whatever its complexion or ideological nature. That ability to maintain a critical distance from others was a vital asset during and prior to the Nazi takeover in 1933.

Jaspers' preference for isolation as a student was conditioned by his hope of finding the sort of friendship that would correspond to his high moral principles and personal standards of excellence. Friendship was to be established on the basis of equality. Though that hope was fulfilled when he married into Gertrud Mayer's family, the chances of his obtaining this genuine partnership that he longed for as a freshman student must have seemed slender. The ideal form of Socratic dialogue was possible with his close family and his friend Fritz zur Loye, who shared his Oldenburg roots. Jaspers' father, too, established an essential pattern for his son's ambitions; and Jaspers rarely contested his father's authority. Karl Jaspers senior was one of the key figures in shaping his son's approach. The pattern had been established during childhood, and Jaspers' desire to seek advice from his father as an objective partner quickly developed into a need to seek his constant approval in respect of the progress he was making. This feature of their relationship may help explain the clarity of the descriptions in Jaspers' memoirs of arrival in the university towns of Heidelberg and Freiburg. His family initially was intended as the target readership and the visual quality of this comparison is striking:

> My knowledge of Heidelberg was necessarily restricted to what I saw and heard in the streets, on the pathways and in the café. The remarkable thing is that despite that, from the first day onwards, Heidelberg affected me as an atmosphere that was intellectual and noble down to the landscape itself. The traditions of the town dating to the Romantic era, the memories of the Palatine region, the castle and the old baroque houses, the River Neckar with the Old Bridge – all of this was not a sufficient reason. An overarching work of art was missing. The university buildings were old and modest. The landscape at the beginning of the Neckar Valley was, to be sure, of incomparable, noble beauty, something in the style of Claude Lorraine. The soft lines of the hills, the greatness of the horizon, the rushing sound of the Neckar plunging from the hills on to the plain at the Hackteufel, the gothic bend of the line of the streets, viewed from the quietly over-growing old Castle grounds, all that had something unnerving about it which grew from the depths of time and from a distance. But nothing is adequate to explain that I felt myself welcomed by a 'genius loci', to which I was not yet in any sense devoted, yet whose presence did me no end of good. Freiburg had delighted me; it possesses much greater beauties than Heidelberg, for the Minster is unique and the hills of the Black Forest are more serious and meaningful. The clear mountain water constantly flowing in all the streets adds a charm – and yet Freiburg was something local to me, whereas Heidelberg breathed something universal, German and European. I had not the least inclination to return again to Freiburg. In Heidelberg, so it seemed to me, the 'spirit of the town' makes one open to others, while in Freiburg, the atmosphere was enclosed in a local security. It was as if those who participated in intellectual life were also, in Heidelberg, floating one metre above ground (as I then expressed myself).[21]

This faithful record of Jaspers' early experiences of Heidelberg's 'genius loci' as a timeless, spiritual reality gains greater significance from the fact that, at this time of his life, he was beginning to enjoy a new-found sense of liberty from his parents' home and their Oldenburg life. In his first Heidelberg semester, Jaspers enjoyed a variety of bachelor entertainments with Fritz zur Loye.[22] The friends indulged in a regular programme of theatre- and concert-going in nearby Mannheim. Jaspers heard some of Wagner's *Ring* cycle, the 'Rheingold', and the 'Ride of the Valkyries', and he declared himself not so averse to Wagner as he was to be the following summer in Sils Maria. As he told his parents after zur Loye's early death in 1916, his friend had been a music lover.[23] Perhaps, zur Loye persuaded Jaspers to attend these performances of Wagner's opera. Yet Jaspers also attended of his own accord talks about literary and artistic subjects arranged by a student society. He renewed his attempt to attend drawing classes, although he regarded his efforts as overshadowed by his father's.

Driven by his persistent desire to win his father's good opinion, Jaspers was not so much oblivious to political events as unmoved by their effects upon his everyday routine. He regarded the political activism of his fellow students' protest against a British politician, the then foreign secretary Joseph Chamberlain, as no less futile than the public unveiling of a monument to the German Emperor, Wilhelm II.[24] The dedication of this monument earned everyone at university an official day's holiday, as Jaspers recounted in a letter: 'Today there was a big hullabulloo here due to the unveiling of a monument to Kaiser Wilhelm. Even the Grand Duke was there. The monument is so bad that people were joking about a rumour that it was from the department store Tietz. The lazy professors naturally made the announcement that the monument was who it was supposed to be and lectures were cancelled.'[25]

Jaspers' ambitious study programme implied, too, a duty to prepare for Kuno Fischer's seminar by reading Arthur Schopenhauer's *World as Will and Representation* (1818). His perusal of Jacob Burckhardt's cultural histories of Italy (*Der Cicerone*) for Henry Thode's lectures on the Italian Renaissance also suggested that he was as cloistered within the world of the university as the professors whom he mocked for interrupting lectures to participate in public ceremonies.[26] An additional measure of his immersion in the task of learning was his willingness to embrace novelty.

Upon his arrival in Munich for what was to be his final semester of law studies, Jaspers was flirting with a Bohemian set that lived and worked in Munich's Schwabing district.[27] Through his friend zur Loye, he met the young unpaid lecturer Ludwig Klages, who was well connected in Schwabing's literary world.[28] Jaspers' interest in Klages' research into graphology may have obscured the fact that Klages was associating with

Schwabing's literary clique, whose members included Otto Gross and Else Richthofen, intimates of Max Weber's circle.[29] Jaspers' father carefully followed his son's accounts from Munich, noting their contents with increasing disquiet. Jaspers wrote about his encounters with a young novelist, Hélène Böhlau, the daughter of a respected Leipzig publisher. Böhlau had written a number of fashionable novels and Jaspers had described her as 'a young lady who is the picture of beauty and whom one does not suspect in the least of dabbling in writing'.[30] His family responded to this report with varying degrees of interest and concern. On the one hand, Jaspers' mother wrote that Böhlau's short stories appealed especially to his sister Erna and herself.[31] On the other hand, Jaspers' father made discreet enquiries into Böhlau's marital background (she was married to a man whose first marriage had not been annulled). This prompted him to advise his son to treat this literary circle with more than a degree of caution:

Kissingen, 11 May 1902

Dear Kally!

[...] In the last few days, I have browsed through: 'The Marshalling Yard', 'Mothers' Rights' and 'Semi-Animal!' I must say, that I cannot regard the tendency of her books as decisive, even if she [Hélène Böhlau] deals with delicate subjects. She is not to my taste, she writes in a much too boring style for me and her opinions leave room for error. As I said, I do not regard her books as immoral, but at best, they are unhealthy in their feeling. All in all, I would like to ask you to be quite careful in the circles that meet up there and, to be exact, to respond to the opinions that are aired there with calm and untroubled criticism.[...] I never had the opportunity to mix in those kind of circles and I can imagine that it might be quite interesting. But be careful! I would prefer you to enquire some more about the people in Munich.[...]

   With fond greeting,
   Your Papa[32]

When Jaspers realized that his matter-of-fact descriptions of Hélène Böhlau's literary circle had alerted his father to probe further into his reports and essentially to veto this group on account of moral scruples, he emphasized the scientific purpose of their meetings:

Munich, 13. V. 02

Dear Papa,

[…] How nice it is for me to feel that I can discuss everything with you and expect an unprejudiced opinion. Now, in relation to the affair itself, there is something curious. The lady, whom I took for H. Böhlau, since she seemed to stand out amongst the others due to her engaging and intelligent conversation, is not her at all, but another, whom I had already noticed as unpleasant because of her self-important manner on philosophy and her intrusion in the conversation. By the way, I have not read anything by her yet. My last letter must have been very unclear, for you to suspect me of joining a circle of artists or an authors' clique. It is only a <u>philosophical</u> evening and, in particular, students of philosophy are present. If the circle were decadent, demoralizing or unhealthy in any way, I would have just as miserable an opinion about that sort of thing. We discuss the philosophical subjects of space and time, parallel aspects of the psychic and physical and free will, among other things. I need to inform myself as little about that as anything that I can judge for myself by using my own intuition. You can be quite sure that I have not fallen into bad company there; and also, I can say without exaggeration that I have occupied myself enough with philosophy not to fall victim to arbitrary new insights without questioning them. […]

Fond greeting,

Your Kally[33]

Jaspers defended his involvement with the Schwabing literary circle with sufficient force for his comments to reveal a certain frustration with his father's intervention. Karl Jaspers senior had formed an unflattering idea of the private lives of Hélène Böhlau and her second husband, a converted Jew called Friedrich Arndt, who adopted the alias Omar Al Raschid Bey. However, Jaspers further hinted that it was during his contact with the Schwabing world, and especially through his acquaintance with Klages, that he first noticed the difficulty of applying certain theoretical principles to specific problems. It seems that Jaspers caused something of a stir when he agreed to attempt a reading of the hand-writing of a group of friends at his Munich lodgings.[34] Yet he completed this session without reference to any of Klages' principles. Jaspers at once realized that his generalizations about their personality traits were perceived as prophetic visions. He claimed that the experience alerted him to the pitfalls of what he later objected to as the pseudo-scientific approach of Freud's psychoanalysis.[35]

Whether Jaspers' limited experience of the artistic and, as his father thought, potentially immoral world of Munich-Schwabing was enough to colour his attitudes towards psychoanalysis is difficult to verify. What is clearer is that Jaspers' response to his father about his experience of the literary and philosophical groups in Munich is to be taken at face value. From the beginning of his undergraduate studies, Jaspers cast a discerning eye on the company of his peers. In Heidelberg, too, he appears to have remained so much on his guard that he refused to join any student fraternity.

Jaspers' impatience with his fellow students' repeated attempts to lure him away from his solitary afternoon walks to Heidelberg Castle was profound. He felt no inclination to join in with a beer-swilling community of privileged scholars – a lifestyle that Nietzsche and Max Weber had enjoyed in their time. His thoughts on the student fraternities in a letter to his parents betrayed a slight irritation, for it occurred to him that he attracted unwanted attention from his fellow students owing to his forlorn-looking state:

> Each afternoon I have taken a ride up to the castle and sat for 1 or 2 hours at the Scheffel monument. It is magnificent there and if you look at nature for some time, you have a regular feeling of contentment. Yesterday, I was disturbed unpleasantly by a few members of the fraternity who introduced themselves to me near the monument and wanted to recruit me by putting up a fight. I naturally got rid of them quickly, but all the poetry was gone with the customary formalities. I can, by the way, imagine how such a poor fox in my situation easily comes to the point of joining in the activities, due to lack of company, if he does not have my happy disposition of also quite enjoying being alone.[36]

The chequered history of the student fraternities in general, especially in their role as nationalistic agitators, at least since the gathering at the Wartburg in 1817, when 'unGerman, reactionary' books were burned, the Code Napoleon among them, eventually led to repressive action by the authorities.[37] In the case of Heidelberg the liberal sentiments of the fraternities' nationalistic creed also developed into a positive contribution when several hundred members of Heidelberg's fraternities joined the demonstration in an endeavour to establish democratic rights for professors and students at the 'Hambach Festival' in 1832.[38]

Jaspers saw the fraternities or *Burschenschaften* as a relic of the noble student Corps, manifested in names like 'Franconia', 'Wingolf' and 'Teutonia', whose tradition in Heidelberg predated the gradual politicization of fraternities in the turbulent period after the Karlsbad Decrees of 1819 and before the attempt at parliamentary revolution in 1848. During his student days, Jaspers preferred to observe, rather than to participate in, the clubby atmosphere of the fraternities. In this way, he reaped the rewards of his chosen isolation. Seen in a positive light, his exclusion from this aspect of student life acquires undue prominence against the backdrop of his family correspondence, which was symbolic of his belief in communication as evolving hand in hand with personal relationships. In a less positive light, his exclusion from companionship with his peers created the difficulty of deciding when to share his preference for a state of solitude, that is, a preference for being left alone with his own reflections and thus transforming it into the basis of enduring friendship. Whether or not that difficulty of deciding whom to trust with one's innermost thoughts contributed in any sense to the introductory paragraph of his seminal essay on 'Solitude' (1916), which he wrote as an unpaid lecturer of psychology more than a decade later, is an open question.[39]

But it is striking that when Jaspers' essay was written his liaison with Gertrud Mayer had replaced the seclusion of his days as a freshman student. While he differentiated in his essay between a state of solitude as a necessary form of instruction about the individual personality and a state of isolation that is potentially ambiguous, it is the curious interpenetration of these aspects that makes his analysis of the individual situation noteworthy. In this opening section of the essay, the emphasis placed on the notion of 'self' is unusual:

> To say 'I' is to be alone. Whoever says 'I' establishes a distance, draws a circle around himself. To give up solitude is to give up myself. Solitude can only be present where individuals are present. Wherever individuals are present, though, there are twin aspects: desire for individuality and therefore a drive *into* solitude; and suffering out of a sense of individuality, and therefore the drive to break *out* of solitude. In that case, what always counts is not so much to be an individual, as to feel and know oneself as an individual.[40]

What is unexpected about this introduction to Jaspers' essay is the emphatic and repeated references to the 'self', which echo his own perplexities at the time, implicit in his determination to come to terms with Dr Fraenkel's diagnosis of his illness. The illness can be seen as a barrier to consorting with his peers that caused him to retreat within himself. By the same token, that act of withdrawal also allowed him positive insights. His situation provided a unique chance to reflect upon life. His capacity to endure long periods of isolation from others was a way of developing a solitary and, by association, individual standpoint to life. Ultimately, however, that standpoint appears to have been based on the experience of knowing the 'self' by overcoming periods of intense loneliness. To discover at such times that he could decide not to trade in the positive aspects of isolation for friendships that could be hollow and meaningless was an assertion of individual freedom. Joining in the activities of others may not anyway have guaranteed permanent friendships. The isolation that Jaspers sought since his school days and during his time as a freshman student was to lead to profound intuitions about others' motives. To mention his later analysis of solitude in connection with his student experiences is not necessarily anachronistic, for this analysis seems symbolic of his determination only to settle for the sort of friendship that was to transcend his state of isolation.

Setting aside the psychological implications of Jaspers' commentary on the 'self', which are referred to in a later chapter, his analysis suggests how familiar he was with solitude as a positive and enriching experience that he integrated into his life in search of the dimension of the other.[41] That quest for otherness implies a perception of solitude as an open invitation to intellectual stimulation and dialogue, albeit an invitation that is extended tacitly. Hence it can be supposed that at the moment when Ernst Mayer first caught sight of Jaspers on one of his practical medical courses in Heidelberg, he had been struck by their encounter. Mayer also sensed Jaspers' determination to act in a way that was not necessarily predictable, given the latter's social milieu and upbringing. Mayer later told him in a letter that when he first saw him enter the operating theatre, in his tenth semester of studies at Heidelberg, he had instantly thought to himself: 'The first German student who meets me.'[42] When Jaspers responded in kind to Mayer's friendly advances, untroubled by their religious differences – Jaspers Christian and Mayer Jewish – the idea that his desire for seclusion might have imposed a barrier between them proved irrelevant. Mayer was to become one of Jaspers' closest and most loyal friends. As the period of Jaspers' self-imposed isolation drew to an end, it became clear that his career as a 'German student' was as much an exercise in tolerance as a search for moments of solitude with a promise of enduring friendship.

4 *Italian Postscript*

IN FEBRUARY 1902, several months before he travelled to Sils Maria and while still contending with the aftermath of Dr Fraenkel's diagnosis of the previous spring, Jaspers made plans for a journey to Italy. He even began to take Italian lessons.[1] A first journey abroad, via Switzerland, was mapped out so that no part of the route included more than seven hours at a single sitting. The dusty train carriages and rigours of travel could otherwise have exacerbated Jaspers' condition, but the sights and sounds of Italy promised the sort of stimulation that he had organized for himself in Badenweiler.

Before the journey could take place, Jaspers was compelled to write a series of letters in which he unfolded his scheme for depriving Fraenkel's principles of their rational basis. Fraenkel had ordered that Jaspers' available holiday time was to be exclusively reserved for recuperating, preferably in the purest possible air, such as in a mountain resort like Meran. Jaspers appealed to his parents' emotions by promoting the educational purpose of an Italian journey. His aim was to assert his ideas about the successful treatment of his illness. One line of argument was to suggest that if he were to cancel his trip he might never see Rome, because in later life he would have to contend with too many distractions and the chore of earning a living.[2] After considering the effects on his son's health of an arduous train journey followed by demanding visits to galleries and museums, Karl Jaspers senior sent him a telegram giving permission for his vacation to commence.[3] On 2 March 1902, Jaspers left

Heidelberg for Lucerne.[4] He carried with him a letter of credit from his father, authorizing him to withdraw money in Italy as and when he needed it:

> You can gladly obtain a letter of credit, which you seem to prefer. As you will be taking money with you at the outset, it need not be for a very great sum; on the other hand, I prefer not to have it made out for too small a figure from the Deutsche Bank – our own bank does not have direct links everywhere. I think, therefore, 2,000 Lire = 1,600 Marks. No extra costs will be incurred for that sum. The validity lasts until 1 July of this year, even if you return much earlier. Where do you want to be registered for credit? In Rome, of course, but in other places as well?[5]

Jaspers' first port of call was Milan, before leaving for Genoa, where he spent three days; via Pisa, he continued on to Rome, then Florence, and finally, more than a month later, he arrived in Venice, returning to Munich via Verona. Karl Jaspers senior financed this journey to the tune of 1,120 Marks, as Jaspers later calculated after his arrival in Munich. This was a considerable investment, yet it was sufficient to pay for all the rail travel, for accommodation in various guesthouses, and for the purchase of mementoes, including antique coins and over 200 photographs.[6]

If the travel itinerary was a princely reward for having asserted an independent opinion of bronchiectasis as a physical rather than an intellectual collapse, the magnitude of Jaspers' determination to be respected by his father, as well as by his friend, Dr Fraenkel, as the best person to consult about his own well-being, revealed an unexpected degree of liberty at his disposal. Jaspers undertook his excursion, initially, against the advice of his favourite doctor, though with his father's consent. That he made the journey at all at this stage signified a growing awareness of his ability to meet his immediate superiors on their level. In contrast to the battle with his headmaster, Herr Steinvorth, whose structuring of the grammar school according to militaristic principles had given rise to his crusade against the school rules, Jaspers' questions about the basis of social and intellectual status, as well as his observations on professorial authority in Heidelberg, could not have taken a more different turn. He integrated into his surroundings in Italy in a less awkward fashion than he had done as a freshman student. What was genuine about his impatience with the adoption of social convention was his objectivity about the intrinsic privileges of wealth and social station such as his own family enjoyed. This is not to say that his student letters from Italy were unmarked by those signs of privileges, such as the financial means to organize his journey with attention to ease of travel and comfort. Nor was his critical perception of mediocrity and prejudice to cease. As he crossed the Swiss-German border, he harboured a certain prejudice about the superior beauty of the Black Forest. Yet he greeted his first real glimpse of the Swiss Alps with delighted approval, which he developed into a commentary for his parents on the open and tolerant atmosphere of Swiss, French and Englishmen all in conversation with one another. Lake Lucerne, with the nearby Alpine peaks of Rigi and Pilatus, seemed closer to his heart than his later description of Sils Maria.[7]

The satisfaction he felt on arriving in Milan, where he admired the beggar on the street for the finest detail of his dress, or the attractive features of Italian girls, whose overall appearance he found to exceed the attractiveness of girls in Oldenburg by ten to one, was in the same vein as his concession to Italy as the land of 'beauty' and 'art'.[8] That concession was revealing. Jaspers' fascination with aspects of life that he found difficult to convey with customary aloofness underlined the subtle change of approach. His Italian letters can be treated as a postscript to the private conversations on art that he continued to enjoy with his father. Those conversations were, as far as they can be deciphered from Jaspers' personal correspondence, sufficient to enable him to develop an idea of his aims. In that sense, his appreciation of art was a personal concern, not a theoretical issue, even if his philosophical ambitions, as shall be seen later, were implicitly assisted by reference to this part of his personal life.

In the chief cities of Italian Renaissance culture, Jaspers was confronted with the impact of his reserved lifestyle as a conscientious German student. His experience of these sites of cultural and aesthetic significance was as much his own way of bidding farewell to a particular atmosphere in Germany that he associated in his letters with words such as longing, pain of the world, weariness, certainty of salvation (*Sehnsucht, Weltschmerz, Überdruss, Gewissheit der Erlösung.*)[9] He appropriated such influences, as he suggested, from his reading of Schopenhauer.[10] By contrast, what Jaspers experienced after his first full day in Rome, when he lingered at the Pincio to catch a glimpse of Michelangelo's dome in the shadow of the setting sun, was a new understanding of the effect of beauty on an individual's senses.[11]

That understanding was different from what Jaspers alluded to in his letters in his repeated exclamations about the incomparable beauty of Renaissance art, paintings, sculptures or classical architecture. His commentaries were largely unspecific and underlined that his purpose in visiting Rome at this time was less academic than to enjoy art, as an extension of his conversations with his father. When he returned to Munich, he noted that he looked upon his surroundings in a new way: 'Italy was, for me, the start of winning the world – while before Italy, I lived almost wholly in an abstract sense without the world.'[12] Hitherto, his approach to the study of mankind, for all his expression of dedication to the human subject in his selection of a motto from one of Goethe's works, had hardly coincided with any enthusiasm for the artistic aspect of creativity. Rather, his hypothetical arguments for becoming a young scientist focused on the application of scientific method as a source of understanding mankind's unique status. Those arguments were developed into his idea of his vocation as scientist following his return from Sils Maria in 1902. It is surprising that so few descriptions survived in Jaspers' Italian letters of what he thought about such sites as the Sistine Chapel, which he visited in Rome, but this may be because he needed to discuss his experiences in person. Jaspers listed numerous visits to four art galleries, his return to the Vatican museums five times, and a second visit to the Forum Romanum, yet his preoccupation was that of a cultural tourist, whose keenest interest was to discover the reality of ancient culture for the first time. His visits to the Via Appia Antiqua, the thermal baths of Caracalla, the Colosseum and Villas Este, Farnesina and Borghese, as well as a brief excursion to the Campagna, demonstrated his thirst for novelty, guided by his copy of Baedeker. His arrival in Florence could not dampen his enthusiasm for the wonders of Italian Renaissance art, but his thoughts increasingly turned homewards.[13] His visit to the Uffizi Gallery was scarcely reported, for with the journey almost exactly six weeks old, and peering across the lagoon from the Lido in Venice, Jaspers remembered the coastal landscape near Oldenburg that loomed in his imagination as more vivid than and far superior to this beautiful setting.[14] What he tried to convey to his father was his experience of the colours of Venice:

Venice, on the Lido
13/IV/02

Dear parents,
[...] The city of Venice is very picturesque and run down, you have the feeling that if the foreigners were not here, it would soon be quite deserted. If you want to go somewhere, you climb into a gondola; there is not a horse and no clatter of carriages in the whole of Venice. How pleasant that would be for Papa; in any case, I have often thought in Italy how nice it would be for me and for you if you were here with me.[...]

Due to the crowd in the inn, I was not able to sit for longer and after a walk on the beach I drove back to Venice and I then took a gondola on the lagoon, to see the sun setting. It was not more beautiful than in Norderney or on the Feldberg, but it was quite different and also magical because of the marvellous array of colours. A beautiful study about that is supposed to be captured in Goethe's *Italian Journey*.[…]

Fond greeting from

Your Kally[15]

The fleeting reference to Goethe's *Italian Journey* in association with Jaspers' observations about the beauty of the colours in Venice emphasized the importance of his father's involvement, not merely in his appreciation of art, but in the entire period of his early life.[16] Jaspers' journey to Italy had been a watershed, since at no time was he more earnest about changing his isolated situation than when he experienced a cathartic release from his school days in Oldenburg and the regimental rigour that he was obliged to adopt from the start of his undergraduate career due to his poor state of health. While he preferred to view the sights of Rome in his usual solitary manner, his journey had demonstrated independence from his illness and his family in a way that motivated him to embark on a different way of living. Outwardly, his pilgrimage to Italy had hardly disrupted his daily routine, since apart from his experience of the wonders of Italian art, his semester in Munich-Schwabing passed uneventfully.

PART II

Devotion, Duty and Family Ties

It is then in a noble soul that is found the true harmony
between reason and sense, between inclination and duty,
and grace is the expression of this harmony in the
sensuous world.

Friedrich Schiller, 'On Grace and Dignity'[1]

5 *Gertrud Mayer*

MONTHS AFTER MEETING GERTRUD MAYER for the first time on 14 July 1907, Karl Jaspers was officially engaged. Gertrud launched a prolific correspondence from the home of her cousin Julia Gottschalk.[2] She forwarded to Jaspers a carefully fashioned analysis of a date when her friendship, as she called it, might be seen in another light: 'Your whole life long, I will accompany you, almost certainly, as a loving friend, perhaps – and let us hope for it – differently.'[3] If the status of Gertrud's friendship was temporarily elevated, this was because of her unspoken aspiration to be recognized as Jaspers' wife. The decision to marry was taken at such speed that not even her family was informed. The wedding, a quiet affair, took place on 29 September 1910 – neither Gertrud nor Jaspers' parents attended the ceremony. A portrait of Gertrud Jaspers on her wedding day is one of the few surviving photographs of the occasion, celebrated at a Berlin registry office in the city's Zehlendorf district, where Gustav Mayer, Gertrud's eldest brother, lived with his family [Ill. 13]. Mayer acted as chaperone to his younger sister; and his wife Flora played her part in ensuring that the wedding was not postponed indefinitely.

Gertrud endeavoured to hide the news from her parents for as long as possible, but the secrecy was neither deliberately deceitful nor out of the ordinary, since she first withheld news (her parents were the last to know of her engagement) because of Jaspers' appalling health. In July 1907, Jaspers' family contemplated that he might never live to celebrate his thirtieth birthday.[4] Such dismal life expectancy raised serious doubts about Gertrud's future. If, as expected, she were to become a young widow, Gustav Mayer was determined for her pension rights to be arranged in a satisfactory manner, or at least in a way that would not compromise his existing family obligations.[5] With the cloud of uncertainty hanging over the couple, Jaspers mentioned Gertrud in the briefest of paragraphs in a sprawling, virtually illegible letter to his parents. At length, he listed his duties at Heidelberg's Clinic of Psychiatry, adding a cautiously optimistic note that he felt 'a certain human interest for a twenty-eight-year old lady, Fräulein Mayer'.[6] His matter-of-fact remark, especially the way he noted Gertrud's name in the same breath as that of his student friend, Ernst Mayer, made it seem as though he were deliberately making her sound anonymous. The information he supplied seemed to show that her life resembled one of his own psychiatric patients' medical histories: Gertrud was four years Jaspers' senior and had experienced the effects of mental illness in her family when her youngest sister Ida had been the victim of a nervous breakdown. Such facts were noted in Jaspers' letter alongside conventional details of their meeting through Ernst Mayer.

A matter of weeks after having introduced his sister to Jaspers, Ernst noticed that she was freely corresponding with his friend using the German familiar *Du*.[7] His concern was that Gertrud's good name might appear to have been tarnished by her rapid departure from the polite German *Sie*. Indeed, he was alarmed that his sister should have dispensed with the decorum that, socially, was to be expected of her. Gertrud was obliged to reveal the nature of her friendship, stressing that her contact with Jaspers was within the bounds of common decency. The modest and private nature of their liaison seemed to tally with Jaspers' gratitude for having met Gertrud at all. He noted her strength of character as a well-spring of the change of fortune that overwhelmed him on the July day when he had accompanied Ernst Mayer to Gertrud's lodgings at Klingenteich 4 near Heidelberg's castle:

> Unforgettable when, accompanied by her brother, I first entered her room! She sat at a large desk, arose, with her back still towards the visitor, she slowly closed a book and turned toward us. I followed each of her movements, which, in her quiet clarity, without artificiality or conventionality, unconsciously seemed to express the essence of purity, the nobility of her soul in her (very) appearance. It was as if self-evident that the conversation soon turned to the basic questions of life, as if we had already known each other for a long time. From the very

first hour there was between us an inconceivable harmony, something never expected to be possible.[8]

Gertrud made visible the beauty of life's possibilities. Jaspers had assumed that such an encounter with the happier side of life was beyond his grasp until he had embarked, as an undergraduate student, upon his journey of discovery to Rome and Florence. Their friendship released Jaspers from his solitary lifestyle. Their secret engagement meant that their relationship was a matter of seizing moments, as and when they presented themselves, but such opportunities for privacy only arose from attending to reciprocal needs that were constantly evolving. The knowledge that they might have missed a unique chance to steer their lives along a common path led Jaspers to interpret his destiny as a source of their meeting. His view was not so much romantic as based on the idea of a collision between time and eternity, as he later represented his memory of their first encounter:

> It was as if lightning had struck, and something had been decided in one moment for all time: that persons met each other in this world, who, as it were, fused together within the phenomenality of time as if they had always been bound together. Well, these are metaphors. No one can know how it really was.[9]

The air of mystery that surrounded their meeting was brought about perhaps as an act of self-defence, since Jaspers' recollections of this occasion seemed to say that the hand of fate alone could not ensure Gertrud's presence in his life. Their speaking out about their friendship may have betrayed a trust that could disappear as quickly as Gertrud had appeared in the first place. It is therefore difficult to state for certain when, and in what setting, their official engagement actually took place. What seems attractive about a surviving description of Jaspers' exhilarating journey with Gertrud is a quality in his account of a particular excursion that points to this occasion as the likely moment of his marriage proposal. Driving out together in an old landau, towards the picturesque hamlet of Neckargemünd, they travelled along the banks of the River Neckar, with the forest of the Odenwald in their sights, so that the journey, not the travellers, became a special feature of Jaspers' illustration:

> We took an excursion, at the quickest tempo, along one bank of the River Neckar and returning along the other, occasionally allowing a stop, climbing out, looking about and then travelling on. The mood of

elation, the rapid journey, the pleasure in the world and its beauty turned the distance between us, forbidding the slightest touch, into an erotic quality that we endured, without talking about it.

We spoke out, [declaring] that we were, without willing it, connected to each other. In that sense, we got engaged: we never wanted to let go of one another, even if marriage were never to become possible.[10]

The idea of being on the way to an unknown destination whose ultimate goal was tacitly understood appears to suggest that, having signed and sealed their decision, and with neither side overcoming their integral personalities, the distance between them turned into a symbol of fidelity and mutual trust. If Gertrud entered into the spirit of Jaspers' proposal, she kept their Neckargemünd pact a jealously guarded secret. Members of her family who knew about the engagement were either informed, or else they discovered by chance or by ingenious guesswork. Ernst Mayer suspected that his introduction resulted in a friendship of which he wholeheartedly approved. Gustav Mayer learned of it because of Gertrud's holiday with his family, shortly after her first meeting with Jaspers.[11] Julia Gottschalk, virtually a sister to Gertrud, suspected that something had occurred when Gertrud had visited her. Jaspers' mother knew; and she saw the hopelessness of Gertrud's situation, pouring her sympathy into a letter for them both:

And Kally said to me: Whatever life that I have had together with Gertrud Mayer, the world may see and know about it, mother, and in the future it will also be like that, as is proper and good for us both. You cannot take the proportions of my life by the usual measure and if it cannot be a lifelong connection with Gertrud, then it has been a great happiness for me to have grown acquainted and to have loved her dear soul.[12]

In view of their uncertain prospects, the engagement brought few changes, no relocations and hardly any visible change of plan, except for greater formality at every turn. Ernst Mayer left Heidelberg the year after Gertrud's engagement, to continue his medical training in Berlin; Gertrud stayed to prepare for her *Abitur* or school-leaving certificate; and Jaspers continued to write home as though Gertrud belonged to a circle of young scientists with whom he associated. Then, at the end of 1908, he took a position as an unpaid assistant in the clinic of psychiatry.[13] Gertrud's presence was a positive contribution to his routine, for her friends, her cousin Julia and other feminine faces were added to his circle of acquaintance. Evening meals at his lodgings on Heidelberg's Bergheimer Straße, near the clinic, became a convivial affair. All the same, Jaspers was mindful of the formality of his relationship when he wrote to his parents: 'With G. Mayer I am not entertaining much, as we almost always say "adieu" after the evening meal.'[14]

Notwithstanding that formality, Jaspers' engagement improved his lifestyle. Gertrud's disciplined studies in Latin and Greek flourished and, in turn, her diligent attitude towards her work positively influenced his research. Initially, her ambition had been to study philosophy, for she had attended Heinrich Rickert's lectures in Freiburg, where she came into contact with Rickert's pupil Emil Lask. Her acquaintance with Lask, who followed Rickert as an unpaid lecturer to Heidelberg, was instrumental in Jaspers' introduction to Heidelberg's Philosophical Seminar. While training as an unpaid assistant in the clinic of psychiatry, Jaspers attended Lask's lectures and seminars on Immanuel Kant.[15] Whether Lask's Kant seminars made a difference to the character of Jaspers' work is not our primary concern, but it seems that Jaspers was opposed to Lask's exposition of Kant, largely because of the failure of Lask's reading to overcome his association with Rickert.[16] Heidelberg's philosophical tradition, as represented by Lask's connection with Rickert and Wilhelm Windelband, was not destined to lead to the fulfilment of Gertrud's intellectual activities. After presenting a résumé at one of Windelband's seminars,[17] she decided to discontinue reading philosophy and to concentrate instead on history and politics. She, thus, asserted her independence from Jaspers, although she was familiar with these other subjects, as well as national economy, because of her father's preoccupation with politics and her brother's work as a social historian.[18] Her interests were not only prosaic, for she introduced Jaspers to the poetry of Goethe, Novalis and Hölderlin. Although he enjoyed reading Goethe during his Göttingen years, he had not yet developed a taste for the poetry. If Gertrud conversed with Jaspers about Goethe, she emphasized the solace she found in the beauty of his language. To read Goethe's *Iphigenie* was a way for Gertrud to confront her anxiety about the future. Yet, she declined to become too involved in interpretations of Goethe's poetry, in favour of persuading Jaspers that their Sunday afternoon leisure should include a joint perusal of Goethe's autobiographical work *Truth and Poetry*.[19]

As a result of her influence, Jaspers began to focus on poetry with animated fascination, writing to his parents: 'At the moment, I am reading, as much as time allows, Dante in a wonderful new translation with Frl. Mayer. We are studying it with the help of notes and historical essays. It is incomparably magnificent. However, we are still in "Hell". You need a lot of preparatory work, in order to gain the right understanding and enjoyment. But then it is not difficult at all.'[20]

Jaspers' desire to study Dante's *Divine Comedy* signalled the progress he had made in appreciating the poetry due to Gertrud's influence. In her company, his outlook became brighter and closer to others than ever before. Gertrud's involvement in arranging his leisure time introduced a distraction of beauty into the rationality of his scientific world. Her presence also placed a question-mark over the status of his investigations, since she could not always appreciate the logic of his theoretical puzzles, although she was determined to eradicate his tendency to an arrogance based on rational superiority. If their engagement was formal and socially acceptable, the friendship was flourishing within. Appraisals of the early years of their partnership are rare, but Enno, Jaspers' younger brother, occasionally mentioned his impressions of his brother's choice. Gertrud met Enno when he arrived in Heidelberg in 1909, to prepare for a first semester reading law. His words of praise revealed the effect of her personality on others. Moreover, he addressed a potential obstacle to his brother's marriage that Jaspers never mentioned, namely, Gertrud's Jewish background. Enno alluded to the question in the interest of learning more about his future sister-in-law: 'Frl. Mayer [...] A delightful young girl! (Excuse the harmless expression for such a serious individual.) She looks like a twenty-two-year-old, rather Jewish type, very pretty and clever eyes, very knowledge-able. That is the superficial impression that I have gained so far, it will grow deeper, after close acquaintance.' [21]

Gertrud's upbringing provided another strong motive for secrecy, since her father, David Mayer, was the head of the Jewish community in their home town of Prenzlau.[22] She feared that he would never consent to her marriage; and indeed he signalled to her only months before her wedding that it was his duty to remain loyal to 'certain demands' that his Jewish faith placed upon him as a senior member of the religious community.[23] As for Jaspers, he seemed unconcerned about their different religious backgrounds, for he was not convinced that the Church was a plausible representative of the values that had shaped his upbringing. That Gertrud belonged to a devout, Jewish family was hardly an obstacle for him; and even if Enno's remarks were an exception, they were merely an expression of his natural curiosity. Prenzlau, where the Mayers came from, was a provincial town in Brandenburg, about one hour from the capital, Berlin. Gustav Mayer's family chronicle revealed their sense of belonging to respected Prussian society. The family was granted a letter of protection in 1698.[24] With the regal patronage of the Prince Elect who granted them their status before his coronation as Friedrich III, or Friedrich I of Prussia, they enjoyed special privileges; and, living outside the ghetto, were perceived as equal to, yet different from, their German counterparts. An anecdote about an act of heroism performed by Gertrud's great-grandfather, Joseph Mayer, illustrated that difference, for Mayer was reportedly shot in the leg by a French soldier, having disobeyed orders to provide neither food nor water for the retreating Prussian army after the rout by Napoleon at Jena and Auerstadt in 1806.[25] This piece of evidence about the Mayer family's solidarity with their Prussian roots was an exception, however.[26] Their name was less associated with politics than with the business acumen of Gertrud's grandfather Ascher Mayer and her grandmother Henriette Hirschberg. Since 1828, the family business of wool traders and wholesalers had borne the name of the founding father, Ascher Mayer.[27] Gertrud's parents, David and Clara Mayer, were respected not only on account of their relative prosperity, but also for their devout observation of Jewish religious practices. If Gertrud was anxious about disclosing to her parents her engagement to a North German, Lutheran-Evangelical doctor from Oldenburg, it was because she feared her liaison could jeopardize her father's reputation. Although the pressure to conform to her family's expectation was not as great as she feared, she revealed her engagement only six months before her wedding, so it became vital for Jaspers to help her to resolve her quandary about when to break the news to her father.

At the height of Gertrud's inner conflict, Jaspers included a telling footnote in one of his letters to her, to highlight how the prospect of their union was intrinsically linked to his view of its significance. In the main body of the letter, he wrote: 'Ethically, I am indifferent to the whole matter. Marriage is no object to be achieved as a self-fulfilling and final end. If you once say to your father that you love me and if you do that openly in front of him, you are nowhere in the wrong.' Here he keyed in this footnote: 'Towards me, I feel from your side neither right nor wrong, no duty, only love.'[28]

This personal statement is relevant to the unfolding story of Jaspers' marriage. For him to insert such a note in a letter was to outline a particular view of what he called 'ethics' in relation to the wider significance of their marriage contract. In that sense, his perception of marriage appeared un-orthodox, for he all but rejected the contract as a conventional sign of values that he rather preferred to dispense with. For him marriage was more than an idea to be equated with a formal or worthless term such as 'ethics' – though unless their marriage were based upon some form of 'ethics', the ceremony itself could be seen as redundant. The framework of his discussion looks like an elaboration upon Kant's *Grounding for the Metaphysics of Morals* (1785), insofar as his note was anachronistic, with Jaspers fashioning his ideas upon a perception of virtue that appeared to present itself in the manner of utopian idealism. The idealism was implicit in Jaspers' suggested reorientation of 'ethics' – a means, perhaps, of alleviating Gertrud's anxiety about the likely severity of her father's reaction to the news of her engagement. His idealism was quite forward-looking, for by casting aside 'ethics' as nothing more than a meaningless symbol of conventional values, he was free to consider their marriage apart from conflicts that might have arisen if his father-in-law had indeed vetoed his daughter's marriage. His note accords with the way in which marriage often featured in his philosophical work, although he frequently omitted to state that 'ethics', as in Kant's appeal for an individualistic rule of thumb that has compelling validity, had long since ceased to be a contingent influence upon his approach to thinking.[29]

Jaspers jettisoned the term 'ethics' at a time when many uncertainties impacted upon his future. Yet how did he connect his moral principles with the public projection of his partnership that later became a model for his thinking? Perhaps an answer lies in his defiance of interferences that contradicted the idea of harmony within their marriage. The rift that Gertrud anticipated from her father's hostility to a son-in-law who was not Jewish threatened their future. When Jaspers chose not to emphasize marriage as an end in itself, he presumably rejected a conventional perception of their liaison because he thought the existing framework of values lacked meaning for them, or because he saw their purpose as breathing new life into outworn patterns of behaviour, or perhaps even because the negativity of their initial experiences drove him to defend his private world as a model to be shown to the world at large. To veil from the public gaze the extent of the disharmony obscuring the inner beauty of their friendship was important if such negative aspects were to be overcome. No wonder Jaspers saw marriage as both a delicate balancing act and a source of miraculous support. Indeed, when he later reiterated his views in his retirement lectures on 'Ciphers of Transcendance' (1970), he implied that marriage was a sacrosanct entity literally 'made in heaven'.[30] If he meant that marriage was without earthly comparison, perhaps his motive was to idealize the insularity of his married life. Were disagreements ever to feature within the Jaspers' marriage?

Jaspers' intervention in Gertrud's crisis may seem heartening, but it is insufficient to explain how their marriage evolved into a paradigm of communication as a 'loving contest' that was a focal point of his perception of his philosophical achievement. In reality, there were difficulties in the way of their marriage not just because of Gertrud's concern about David Mayer's reaction, but also because of uncertainty about the future prompted by Jaspers' health and the resulting precarious nature of Gertrud's financial position. The money matter plagued the timing of Gertrud's marriage, and Gustav Mayer saw the wisdom of solving that issue before deciding when to tell their father. Indirectly, he collaborated with Jaspers' father, who was in a position to underwrite funds for Gertrud's pension if only they could be mustered. Enno Jaspers provided evidence of the peculiar suitability of the two candidates. Although Gertrud was not quite the match that he expected his brother to make, he regarded her as a breath of fresh air; and, moreover, his deep affection for Gertrud radiated in one of his early letters:

Heidelberg, 27 April 1909

Dear parents,

[…] Fr. Mayer is physically completely run down. She is working like a horse and for the moment she is ruining her nerves with it. However, after the exams, in her and Kally's opinion, she will recover again very quickly. She is a splendid young individual. It is too difficult to describe her. She is completely different than I thought. More emotional intelligence [*Gemüt*] than one-sided intellect, she is truly feminine, but seems very clever. She has endured a lot. Her contact with Kally is purely on a friendship basis. Nor does she describe it differently. Once, e.g., she said: 'If I had married your brother, which now no longer comes into question, etc. …' She judges Kally's body exactly as K. himself. […]

Fond greeting, to Erna as well

Your

Enno[31]

Enno wondered whether Gertrud's *Abitur* were not a test of her friendship with his brother, but he concluded that her motives were not the decisive factor. Her ability to mix with others in their world made her a better prospect as Jaspers' wife than a candidate whose purely intellectual character could have made her socially inept and tiresome. That Gertrud's countenance was worldly, not just wise, appears to have come as a relief to Enno, whose suspicion about her capacity for withstanding emotional upheaval was all too justified.

Several years before meeting Jaspers, Gertrud was involved in a sentimental friendship with her sister Ida, her cousin Julia and a young Jewish poet, Walter Calé. This circle was shattered by Calé's suicide in 1904, when he shot himself with a revolver. His death, at twenty-two, destroyed the high-spirited relationship between the girls, sustained though it was by devotion to each other and by joint studies in poetry and philosophy. The reckless nature of the friendship became evident when Calé grew unable to identify his favourite muse, whether Gertrud, Ida or Julia.[32] Shortly before Calé's suicide, however, Ida Mayer, an artistically gifted soul, suffered a nervous breakdown and was confined to a sanatorium where she died years later.[33] In a fragment of one of Calé's surviving letters, he styled Gertrud as his muse: 'I forget you, like one forgets a ring, a very dear ring that one wears on one's finger – because it is always with you.'[34] Yet in the very next sentence he presented Julia as closer to his heart. The almost Kleistian twist to Calé's tale lies in that fantasia on his several muses, because the imaginary life that was so intense led him to mistake their real for ideal identities – as if the Romantic loss that was part of his world became magnified into the most acute of ruptures. The consequences are to be surmised from Calé's undated, distraught letter to Julia Gottschalk, which survived as a copy made in Gertrud's hand:

> My dear Julia,
>
> When you receive these lines, I am no longer living.
>
> The one reason lies in the many disappointments and in the exaggeration of everything in me.
>
> The other: that I committed a great betrayal of your trust that you will hear about. My life is broken, it is worth nothing. Forget me!
>
> I have two requests: Burn everything of mine, if you can.
>
> And do <u>not</u>! come on my account to Berlin. I don't deserve it.
>
> Accept this last greeting, companion. How difficult that all is. I wish you a good life.
>
> I have, when I loved you, truly loved.
>
> Walter[35]

If Calé perceived Gertrud, in a fantastic sense, as Julia's alter ego, his final note implied that he translated their friendship into a unison of the cousins. Such deep sensitivity cultivated emotional paralysis, or an inability to separate dream from reality. When Gertrud informed Jaspers about her friendship with Calé, she emphasized the impulsive side of their allegiance that focused more on poetry, philosophy and art than on any awareness of their destructive influence upon each other.[36] With Calé's suicide, Gertrud and Julia became closer. Though Calé himself distorted their relationship, he perhaps captured something about the warmth of their personalities. What Enno called Gertrud's *Gemüt,* or emotional understanding, was intensified in a romantically susceptible side of Julia's personality. As a result of her close friendship with Gertrud, Jaspers got to know Julia, and his affection even surfaced as cautious words of praise: 'I like her the best of all Gertrud's relatives. She is really human, not in a striking way, but on our level, and serious from the deepest part of the soul.'[37] Julia's involvement in the Calé calamity fascinated Jaspers because of his interest in psychological puzzles. If she were receptive to problems buried within the Romantic consciousness – Calé's note suggested that she possessed that capacity – Jaspers was not interested in her seductive character, but rather intrigued to know her mind. As a gesture of sympathy for Julia, who was training to be a doctor, he sent his parents instructions for his old skeleton to be delivered to her at her Heidelberg address.[38]

The untimely end to Gertrud's friendship with Calé marked her release from her family in Prenzlau, for she requested her parents' permission to nurse Ida, who was first incarcerated in a sanatorium near Frankfurt, Königstein im Taunus. Her departure from Prenzlau was a step towards independence, for her decision to leave home, initially thanks to Calé's influence, compelled her to understand the hardship caused by psychiatric cases. By nursing patients on wards, she learned to appreciate that the Calé episode might have had graver repercussions for herself and Julia. Her experiences marked out her capacity to understand Jaspers' distinction between those used to suffering and those apparently indifferent. Gertrud's tendency was, especially in dire circumstances, to depend upon texts, whether from the Bible or Goethe's poetry. When she successfully completed her *Abitur,* in 1908, she decided not to pursue her ambitions, either making a personal sacrifice in favour of Jaspers' talents or out of a stronger desire to work behind the scenes. Initially, her opportunity to shape his career was naturally limited by the financial constraints that delayed their marriage. When Flora Mayer announced that her mother, Frau Wolff, wanted to make a donation to Gertrud's pension fund, Gertrud was in possession of three thousand Marks.[39] First signs of optimism emerged in Jaspers' jovial remark about the warmth of Gertrud's personality as an attractive way of depriving her relatives of their money, as the prospects for their wedding had improved, though no date was to be fixed until David Mayer's approval had been guaranteed.[40] Yet Jaspers was anxious for legal measures to guarantee Flora Mayer's donation and to convince Gertrud's father of his suitability as a son-in-law. In a letter of gratitude to Gustav Mayer and his wife, he mentioned his 'sudden fear' that his future father-in-law might confuse his father's inclusion in negotiations as a sign that Gertrud's future was in the balance: 'With only a short time until 29 Sept. [his wedding day] you can well understand my concern about causing a delay by any misunderstanding in relation to a remark of my father. I will, like you, breathe a sigh of relief when we have everything behind us. But for me, I believe, it is more difficult: it is horrible to have the feeling of always appearing as the one making demands, when a fairytale happiness is being <u>given as a gift</u>.'[41]

The interesting feature of these developments shortly before the marriage was not necessarily the help given by Jaspers' or Gertrud's family and friends in the preparations, but Jaspers' virtual exclusion from the practical arrangements in the weeks before the wedding. However gallant or self-sacrificing his gesture may seem, his absence from these negotiations affecting his future was not just out of concern that his skills as a communicator were inadequate. Gertrud's intervention was the first sign that she would be organizing their domestic affairs, for she expressed a wish that Jaspers should arrange for his father to supply a reference on his behalf.[42] A formula for the financial arrangement that Gustav Mayer and Karl Jaspers senior worked out enabled them to break the news of the secret engagement in Prenzlau. The care Gertrud took in establishing trust between her father and her future parents-in-law had an unexpected outcome: 'Now that my father is also initiated into the secret, he is reacting as I never dreamed.'[43] She was astonished by his contribution of a generous dowry of ten thousand Marks.[44] A month or so before his wedding, Jaspers hurried to Berlin where, for the first time, he met Gertrud's six brothers and her cousins Paul and Ernst Gottschalk. Gustav Mayer requested a guarantee of Gertrud's pension from Jaspers' father in the likely event of Jaspers' premature death.[45] Had Gertrud become a young widow with a family (in the event she proved unable to have children), she would have retained the full rights of legal inheritance. Karl Jaspers senior guaranteed a full four thousand Marks as her pension for a future date when he would be able to pay this amount and Gustav Mayer agreed to these provisions.[46] Days before their wedding, Jaspers scribbled notes to his relatives, such as his grandmother and his uncle Theodor Tantzen, letting them know of the plans.[47] Scarcely one month after registering for their betrothal in Berlin, and two months after Gertrud had told her father of her engagement, the couple were married.

When arrangements were all but concluded, congratulatory messages passed between the families, and Karl Jaspers senior referred to the test of conscience that he supposed his counterpart, David Mayer, to have wrestled with; and he highlighted his family's deep affection for Gertrud.[48] In response,

David Mayer revealed how he had taken his decision to give his approval for his daughter's marriage:

Prenzlau, 27 Sept. 1910

Esteemed Herr Jaspers,
Esteemed Frau Jaspers,
You have highly delighted us with your endearing letter and the friendly lines of your honoured lady wife.

It took a long time before our Gertrud revealed herself to her parents and confessed that she had given her heart and found herself in love with a man to whom she not only devoted herself, honestly in love, but whom she valued and honoured. Indeed, as you, Herr Jaspers, correctly note, I had to strive hard within myself to find approval. There were no prejudices for me to overcome as I know myself free of them, but striving with principles based on deeply rooted piety towards my ancestors, whom I could not desert. Now I took facts along with me and I could meet the young couple and bestow a father's blessing from a faithful heart. May our dear children, who now approach their true union, be granted happiness, harmony, health and constant contentment, to the greatest joy of the parents on both sides. That is probably the joint wish that we harbour for our children. I have heard from my Gertrud and from all sides only good and dear things of you and your trusted family, and the time will not be far off when we can become acquainted and exchange our views.

My daughter will, hopefully, I firmly trust her, always endeavour, with a child's love, to receive and earn the affection of the parents of her husband.

With respectful, and if you permit, esteemed Herr Jaspers, with cordial greetings for you, your highly esteemed lady wife and all your family,

Yours respectfully
David Mayer[49]

6 'In the Clinic'

After the completion of his medical state entrance examination on 18 January 1908, Jaspers began work as a medical trainee in Heidelberg's Clinic of Psychiatry.[1] His position allowed him time to write and prepare a defence of his doctoral thesis on 'Homesickness and Crime' (1909). By mid-April, he was complaining that, while he appreciated his freedom to delve into patients' case histories, his traineeship was deficient in one respect that jeopardized his ambition to become a psychiatrist. His training excluded a vital aspect of the psychiatrist's occupation: 'The biggest mistake of this clinic is that you learn no therapy. Mostly, a sort of therapeutic nihilism is worshipped here. However, it is not that bad in the sense that if you are good at diagnosis, the therapy represents the easier part. For diagnostics, I could not have better instruction than here, because of the amount of material and the very critical, scientific approach that prevails in the clinic.'[2]

Although Jaspers frowned on the standing of therapy in Heidelberg, he recognized the research standards, as pioneered by the former head of the clinic Emil Kraepelin and the present director Franz Nissl, as sources of inspiration. His view that research alone was not enough to enable one to practise in psychiatry was rather eclipsed by the illness that prevented him from realizing his ambition, regardless of the training he acquired. He enjoyed particularly amicable relations with another assistant, Hans Gruhle, from whom he benefited in terms of both clinical experience and theoretical knowledge. Nevertheless, his preference was for contact with patients, and he noted that it was impossible to collect detailed knowledge from the sofa.[3]

Jaspers' twin objectives of maintaining the high calibre of research and his commitment to patients manifested itself in the pattern of his doctoral thesis. This work was a classic scientific study of criminal activities but it revealed his skill in explaining specific cases, a skill that led him into the field of forensic medicine. On several occasions, he prepared expert reports about cases that he later presented in court.[4] Aptly enough, his thesis was published in Gross's Archive for forensic science, news that he reported to his parents with pride.[5] Parallel to his doctoral research, Jaspers also began several projects based on analysis of patients' medical histories. While he applied himself enthusiastically enough, he called his doctoral thesis 'a boring, quite impersonal work' that was far too tedious for his parents to read.[6] Instead, he recommended they look at his other projects which he saw as potentially innovative, for he began to inspect IQ ratings, or so-called intelligence tests; these he saw as qualifying his studies for recognition as the work of a modern scientist. What was modern about his work was the specific focus on the individual case. To that end, he scoured patient records to improve his understanding of the healing process. That knowledge was to be applied in accordance with the psychiatrist's vocation. Yet, for all his interest in clinical practice, after successfully defending his doctoral thesis in early December 1908,[7] he was obliged to abandon his ambitions because of the practical demands of the work. By the following February, he had nonetheless progressed from the lowly rank of medical trainee to an equally uncertain status as an unpaid voluntary assistant, though he had not wholly given up on his idea of becoming a psychiatrist.[8] Under Franz Nissl's supervision, he arranged to research in the clinic's library.[9] At times, whenever colleagues were absent or unavailable, he undertook duties in the day clinic. Yet he bitterly regretted his incapacity, physically, to complete the rounds of patients. After one year as an unpaid assistant, he laboured under the impression that he was tolerated as a resident outsider. When a paid assistantship became available, he regretted that he would be passed over in favour of a young doctor who could easily fulfil the role.[10]

In silent frustration, Jaspers' imagination reinforced his impression that he was required to work twice as hard just to be accepted by his peers and his immediate superiors. Because of these perceived disadvantages, he forged ahead to modify his research on intelligence tests, dating from his time as a medical trainee, into fully fledged *Referate*, or in-depth oral presentations of findings that were revised for publication. He confided in Gertrud that his work fired him with enthusiasm to continue his evaluation, which he still regarded as a laborious task: 'I'm in the hot seat due to my work on intelligence tests. I have an enormous amount to do.'[11] His research coincided with the founding of a journal of neurology and psychiatry. The journal's managing editor, Alois Alzheimer, was in contact with another editor, Karl Wilmanns, who became Jaspers' contact in Heidelberg, arranging for publication of his scientific articles. Jaspers was fortunate, as regards progressing from his unpaid assistantship, for he was able to publish two of his earliest investigations on jealousy and IQ tests in the very first May 1910 editions of Alzheimer's journal.[12] A typical feature of his writings, which perhaps explains his early success, was their combination of conventional literature with an independent approach. The unusually illustrative or visual dimension of his work also shifted the onus from description, observation and analysis to meticulously prepared assessments of empirical material, painstakingly evaluated on grounds of merit. Such was the fluent manner in which he manipulated his material that his attention to detail soon reaped rewards. His reluctance to rule out even a minute fragment of patients' biographies enabled him to superimpose a theoretical slant upon investigations that were otherwise empirical. His growing confidence in the originality of his research led him to recommend his contributions to his parents: 'I am sending you my work on jealousy. If the intelligence test piece was merely a talk, then the core of this work is, in my opinion, original. I consider the work rather valuable at least, as by far the best of my previous studies. The biographies caused me a great deal of trouble. They are selected from a vast store of material that I worked through in vain.'[13]

To count as original, Jaspers' investigations had to be regarded as contributing a particular idea that was still to be discovered within his specialist field, but his research was not necessarily original, for his time-consuming interviews, his reports of patients' comments in biographies, were merely part of a complex process. To select relevant material and to connect it to a model versatile enough to provide the hypothetical basis for analysis was a laborious task. The detail provided specialized knowledge that was often to be set aside as irrelevant. What Jaspers could reasonably expect to show as results amounted to little more than a coincidental pattern of correlations between symptoms and causes of particular patients' histories, whose cases he happened to scrutinize if they came his way. His doctoral thesis, for example, relied upon a previously unpublished case history of Apollonia S., the case of a young girl who drowned a small child in her care, a tragedy that Jaspers followed in its every detail in order to illustrate his thesis about a possible link between crime and homesickness. The case history was used by permission of Karl Wilmanns.[14]

In effect, however, the pattern of Jaspers' results compelled him to plead for caution within his field of therapy, for he identified how a psychiatrist becomes involved in a process that is complicated by a temptation to seize upon causes, whose severity may have emerged from different sources. In that light, his task seemed self-defeating, for his conclusions invariably urged caution, suggesting that he perceived his specialist field as in disarray. He repeatedly emphasized that symptoms of marital breakdown, chronic jealousies, criminal activities, arson (as in his doctoral thesis), hallucinatory experiences or schizophrenia might not reveal actual causes of problems, but instead highlight a tendency among psychiatrists to believe in scientific explanation as foolproof solutions. The message of his investigations was that results of individual cases often indicate individual answers; and he attempted to explain how his basic questions showed, in these cases, the limitations of a scientific approach. Perhaps his collected papers on psychiatry were over-shadowed by a conflicting view of the therapist's ability to provide foolproof solutions to such cases, for Jaspers' most formidable opponent worked in psychosomatic medicine.

The discipline of psychoanalysis that Sigmund Freud established when Jaspers was beginning his academic studies was a source of inspiration. Freud's *Interpretation of Dreams* (1900) contrasted with Jaspers' style of 'back-room interview' with patients, so that Jaspers' writings seemed unclear, especially his conclusions, which although fluently phrased, lacked Freud's rhetorical flair.[15] Freud, not Jaspers, gained recognition for his pioneering work, in keeping with modernity's agenda, of overcoming social taboos about sexual morality. If Freud released an uncharted realm of unconscious desire, fear or irrational longing into the domain of the trained therapist, Jaspers seized his chance to learn about Freud's creative spur, which he regarded as equalled by French psychiatrists, especially Pierre Janet.[16] Jaspers was brightly optimistic about the chances of his work being able to compete with that of such eminent scientists for innovative research. He also thought that the discipline of psychiatry was crying out for a systematic clarification of current thinking. He turned to Wilhelm Dilthey's interpretation of the human sciences, which rather blurred the distinction between the philosophy of history and psychology in a way that Heinrich Rickert outlined in his delineation of the formation of philosophical concepts. By contrast, psychiatry was marked out as an 'exact' science, differentiating it from the rather contradictory status of empirical research. In that context, Jaspers turned his position as a resident 'outsider' in the clinic into a bonus, using his relative freedom to attend Lask's philosophical lectures and pursuing diverse influences in order to obtain an independent standpoint in his research. He borrowed the essence of ideas, especially those of Edmund Husserl and Max Weber, as a launching pad for his own. He was a scavenger who picked others' brains and channelled their thought processes into his order of thinking, adapting the vocabulary of the day to his empirical research.

Jaspers' approach was not to transform contemporary ideas but to appropriate the essentials, and so to learn more about the limitations of practice in his discipline. This involved the skilful creation of a tableau of salient ideas, in application to relevant notions in circulation, adapting their essence for his specific purposes. His growing disagreement with Freud, for instance, was more profound than an internal debate among different psychological schools. In Heidelberg, a popular rumour circulated that Jaspers was a 'Freudian', a confirmed disciple of Freud's psychoanalysis.[17] The rumour contained a grain of truth, although Jaspers' interest in Freud's early work was rather polemical, as he indicated to Gertrud in a telling note about his attendance at a scientific talk. Apparently, he made a point of behaving in a contrary and disruptive fashion: 'A short presentation on Freud. Myself, as a barking dog.'[18] Jaspers was not destined to dismiss Freud's work indefinitely, especially given his plan creatively to adapt others' thinking for his own purposes, but he was disinclined to accept Freud's exposure of the unconscious realm.

Jaspers' friendship with Hans Gruhle led to their indulgence in what Jaspers called 'psychological evenings', private meetings after hours that, at least from Jaspers' viewpoint, were to have been explorations of the limitations of psychology: 'In the clinic, nothing is new. I am working on a report about an epileptic patient. Our psychological evenings are well under way. Even in the mornings, discussions often take place.'[19] Jaspers credited Hans Gruhle as the source of inspiration for a critical breakthrough in his research. He remarked to his parents that, after an evening of arguing with Gruhle about a 'principal question' on which they disagreed because (according to Jaspers) Gruhle had not grasped the point of his argument, he had a flash of inspiration and decided to write a 'programmatic essay'.[20] Shortly afterwards, his essay on 'The Phenomenological Approach in Psychopathology' (1912) was published. This was a set piece analysis of Jaspers' main objectives. His key word was 'phenomenology', a reference to a highly condensed version of his ongoing research for the book that Julius Springer had commissioned him to write in July 1911, a compendium that was to be a guide for doctors and students in training.[21]

When 'The Phenomenological Approach' was published in the spring 1912 edition of Alzheimer's journal, a draft version of what was to be Jaspers' first book was already publicly available. The essay was a forerunner of this work and as such it was a subtle marketing exercise, for it simplified the book's systematic ordering of a web of ideas drawn from Jaspers' reading of Dilthey and Husserl, Rickert and Weber. 'The Phenomenological Approach' highlighted one essential point of the book, insofar as what Jaspers called 'understanding psychology'[22] might explain psychiatric questions to a limited degree. He clarified this matter as a two-way process: first, 'phenomenology' was a descriptive practice by means of which a psychiatrist could assess patients' communications, as derived through interviews or scrutiny of their biographies; and, second, 'phenomenology' was a process of understanding the patient–doctor relationship. That vital relationship was regarded as integrated into the task of therapy. In other words, Jaspers used phenomenology as a generic term (a term that he also further clarified as 'genetic understanding', and thus as 'understanding psychology' in cross-section seen as what he called in 'longitude').[23] To investigate that perception of the confidential context of clinical practice was to clarify the repertoire of tools available for connecting a psychiatrist's perception of the causes of patients' afflictions and the patients' need for understanding and an open exchange of information. Jaspers' book *General Psychopathology* (1913) was a revolutionary contribution, in that psychiatry thereby became established within psychopathology by virtue of the increased clarity about the psychiatrist's task. Above all, Jaspers implied that the discipline of psychiatry was confronted with a responsibility to recognize its limitations and to respect the confidential nature of patient interviews.

While he was in the final stages of preparing to submit his book to Springer, Jaspers provided an interim report for his parents revealing that his supervisor Franz Nissl had spontaneously interviewed him about his future, underlining the fact that he ought to consider taking employment. Nissl proposed to recommend Jaspers either to Emil Kraepelin in Munich or to Alzheimer in Breslau, in order for Jaspers to complete a *Habilitation* thesis, which Nissl regretted he could not supervise because there was not enough opportunity for Jaspers to continue to work in the clinic.[24] Nissl's response to Jaspers' book acknowledged that his contribution outclassed contemporary studies available in the field, even the existing compendium of psychiatry by Emil Kraepelin.[25] The final proof corrections of *General Psychopathology* were returned by early June 1913 to Springer in Berlin.[26] By early July, the book was at last available, at a price that was reasonable for a work which presented a fresh approach, by not adhering to any particular psychological school.

The spectrum of Jaspers' sources enabled him to argue that the capacity for explanation – whether in natural sciences or in the humanities – was, on the one hand, an arena of unlimited opportunity and, on the other, a field of limited potential. Thus a scientist's ability may be measured in proportion to his capacity to penetrate a realm that cannot ever be seen in its entirety: '*Understanding is limited and explanation is unlimited.*' Jaspers elaborated upon this motto as follows:

> It is a mistake to suggest that the psyche is the field for understanding while the physical world is the field for causal explanation. Every concrete event – whether of a physical or psychic nature – is open to causal explanation in principle, and psychic processes too may be subjected to such explanation. There is no limit to the discovery of causes and with every psychic event we always look for cause and effect. But with understanding there are limits everywhere.[27]

The task was therefore to overcome the limits to understanding, yet not to surrender the credentials of the psychiatrist and lose sight of one's vocation. Jaspers' thesis was that his branch of science was only just learning to appeal to a researcher determined to grow acquainted with relevant discoveries, by using both theory and practice in inner illumination of their purpose. His own contribution was his straightforward use of ideas for empirical objectives. Thus he provided an eloquent critique of Edmund Husserl's *Logical Investigations* (1900), even though he was inclined to give a simplistic-sounding answer to Husserl's essay on 'Philosophy as Exact Science' (1911).[28] Even before Jaspers' essay on 'The Phenomenological Approach' was published, Husserl had apparently hailed Jaspers' psychiatric studies as evidence of his discipleship. Several months before Jaspers published his essay in the spring 1912 edition of Alzheimer's journal, he informed his parents that he had received a letter from Husserl, and he forwarded it to them, explaining its context with considerable pride:

Heidelberg, 20/10/11

Dear parents,

[…] I am enclosing a letter that Husserl wrote to me in response to my work. Husserl is one of the first, if not the first, philosophers active at present. He is, above all, working on logic. I partly applied in my work a method that he practises. We speak of 'phenomenology'. I had modestly written to him that his <u>individual</u> analyses seemed very convincing to me, but that I actually had no clear idea of what, in fact, phenomenology is – that was intended as an attack, for I believe that he himself does not know. I am writing this so that you understand the reference to <u>my</u> letter in his letter. I was very pleased with his letter, even if it is rather paternal. But the fact that Husserl, who is the first and best able to judge in this field, recognizes my work, is worth a lot to me. [...]

    Fond greetings,
      Your Kally[29]

Jaspers had hardly intended to invite such gratifying admiration from Husserl, because he treated the older scholar's philosophical investigations rather as he had treated Freud's *Interpretation of Dreams* (1900); cautiously recommending Freud's pioneering work while rejecting his approach.[30] An alternative model that Jaspers admired was represented by Max Weber, in whom he saw something essential worth striving for in a psychiatrist's attitude to his task. He also experienced the wrangling dispute in Heidelberg among so-called Kantians and Hegelians, in the shape of Heinrich Rickert's philosophy of values, and the histories of philosophy by Kuno Fischer's successor Wilhelm Windelband.[31] While Jaspers strove to order his empirical study within a theoretical framework, he recognized, through his contact with Heidelberg's philosophers (which Gertrud especially advanced), that the clearest treatment of his study of the doctor–patient bond was not to be gleaned from psychology. If Dilthey's dictum – 'We explain Nature, we understand the soul'[32] – provided Jaspers with a foundation for what, with a nod to Weber, he called 'understanding psychology', his main aim was to preserve a calm atmosphere that might equally have derived from his study of Kant's philosophy.[33]

Jaspers put forward his picture of the ideal psychiatrist who is prepared to throw himself into the process of analysis. He relied upon the doctor–patient bond being open to question, but that precondition was evidenced by his good-humoured account of his personal interview with Edmund Husserl. At the end of September 1913, after checking on his uncle Fritz who was undergoing treatment after an operation in Bonn, Jaspers stopped in Göttingen and took the opportunity to seek out Husserl. He complained rather ruefully to Gertrud that Husserl and his assistants were all 'Jews', that there was a certain appeal in their fine manners which, as he ironically remarked, could not detract from the triviality of their conversation – with the notable exception of Husserl's.[34] Husserl's entourage was, according to Jaspers, interested in a fundamentally different picture of the world, an observation which suggested that Husserl with his scientific approach was delightfully unaware of the relevance of Jaspers' aims. Jaspers' interest in Husserl's second volume of *Logical Investigations* was hardly superficial,[35] for his purpose was to extract the quintessential message from Husserl that he believed could improve a psychiatrist's depth of knowledge. Indeed, the psychiatrist's problem was essentially his craving for knowledge in his claim to understand another's words. What Jaspers extracted from Husserl's notion of 'intentionality' was a principle that words and meanings are all, on some level, subjected to trans-position by individual preference.[36] He knew from personal experience how a patient's intentions may actually diverge from his doctor's ideas about his therapy. In *General Psychopathology* (1913), he highly recommended students of psychiatry to adopt what he called a 'phenomenological' approach to their field of work.[37] The doctor was to be trained to apply interpretational methods to his cases,[38] on condition that he might turn the tables upon himself. Hence, the psychiatrist is not only the subject in control of the process, but a legitimate target for self-reflection.

In a similar vein, Jaspers' disdain for Freud's therapeutic practices may be traced to his idealism about the doctor–patient bond.[39] He initially acknow-ledged the hypothetical benefits of Freud's research, which he called, in tacit approval, 'as-if understanding', but he subsequently used that formulation to suggest that Freud and his followers were engaged in a kind of pseudo-therapy.[40] To claim that the 'libido' provided an explanatory apparatus that could be used as a blanket rule for understanding extreme pathological cases was an attractive message for Freud, especially in an era when society was modernizing. For Jaspers, though, Freud was barking up the wrong tree. Freud's psychoanalysis could hardly be a viable basis for society to treat severe cases like schizophrenia. Jaspers warned that such cases could not be explained away, as Freud did, by noting the split of the personality into the 'ego', the 'id' and the 'super-ego'.[41] In subtle mimicry of Freud, in his later essay on 'Solitude' (1916) Jaspers simply listed cases of individual identity as 'the social ego', 'the man-of-the-moment', 'the impressionable ego', the 'performance-ego', the 'body-obsessed-' or 'the sexual ego'.[42] None of these character types, however, was found in this analysis to correspond to the development of a stable, let alone of a 'noble', personality. What Jaspers called the 'heroic' type of personality also represented a pattern of behaviour that showed a capacity to endure a level of solitude transcending the present situation in order to obtain freedom of expression and thought.[43] The individual who achieves his potential freedom in this way cannot seek refuge in the crowd of human society, especially not within religious communities. What emerges instead is a perception of the character 'type' whose dearest wish is the intimacy of a dialogue situation that develops in this essay almost as a counter-model, a negative way of describing one's personal involvement in a merely intellectual friendship. If this rational enterprise was made to founder by the inclusion of such a personalized element, or by particular emphasis on the equality of two personalities that Jaspers sees as a prerequisite for his model of a 'loving' state of communication, his contribution emphasized a moral aspect of breaking through to a model of communication. His idea implied a new possibility of overcoming potential inequality between individuals through the intensity of communication. The Socratic model of dialogue alone could not suffice to render his study of solitude as a practical solution to what he had initially expressed in the introduction to his study as the 'tautology' of individuality and solitude.[44]

In this short essay, which incidentally was published posthumously, Jaspers included an acknowledgement of the Freudian split of the 'conscious' from the 'unconscious' self, insofar as his inclusion of Freud's 'I' and the 'id' can be regarded as an early and rather compelling 'anti-Freudian' setpiece. He also turned these elements of Freud's categories in upon themselves, to the extent that his chief concern was not to argue against Freud, but to illuminate the redundancy of those various personality types in his study of an individual's identity. A key aspect of his analysis of 'Solitude' was that he had achieved a formulation of his model of 'loving contest', a model that he referred to in this instance as 'the contest in the state of love' (*der Kampf in der Liebe*).[45] His approach to his own definition of the engagement of the personality in a communicative context was to be based on a quite different paradigm than the isolation he chose to maintain as a student. One essential feature of his mature paradigm of communication, as outlined in this essay, was that it was based on accepting the dignity and integrity of the partners concerned. 'The instincts', as he observed in further clarification of his ideal, 'are analogous, whether the individual submits to a leader, a master, a Catholic Church, or a powerful ruler. Ultimately, he no longer desires to be an individual, but merely a part. His principle is in contrast to the individual who first wants above all to remain or to become himself, no matter whether this self is only a grain of sand against a rock. That manner of principle must appear to the other individual, as a kind of proud arrogance, as the ultimate evil.'[46]

Jaspers was later to include a vehement critique of Freud's contribution in his book about *Man in the Modern Age* (1931), a slim and highly significant work that he published in a quite different context. His arguments were expressed as part of this book's cultural critique of modernity, and he included a sharply critical characterization of Freud's psychoanalysis alongside Marxist and racial theory. Freud's approach was therefore presented less favourably than the comparatively benign and good-natured tone of ideas that Jaspers had first adopted in *General Psychopathology* (1913). The rejection of Freud's work as a 'pseudo-theoretical' line of enquiry conformed to the 'existential' manifesto of Jaspers' book about modern man, in which Freudian therapy was seen to turn the individual into a 'puppet of his unconscious' and as depriving modern man of his basic dignity.[47] This presentation of Freud's psychoanalysis could be seen as a distortion of Jaspers' earlier work, in the sense that he later objected to Freud's approach as blinkered, insofar as it ignored the scientific foundation of his task as a therapist. At the same time, it could also be said that Jaspers too overlooked in his later work his previously positive relationship to the theoretical status of psychosomatic medicine. *Man in the Modern Age* (1931) may have elevated Jaspers' status to that of an intellectual critic in the early 1930s, but the reader of that book may have been unaware of the extent to which his *General Psychopathology* had been indebted to Freud's pioneering research.

In the earlier part of his career, Jaspers concluded that Freud omitted to calculate for weaknesses inherent in his approach. The rationale for his cautious criticism was that he aimed to restore the patient's dignity. In his reading of Freud, his concern was that the individual's dignity could remain stranded upon the shore of the unconscious. In voicing these tentative thoughts in his first book, he fulfilled a latent ambition that he had referred to for the first time when he decided to study medicine in 1902. He combined scientific passion with philosophical depth. The sense of achievement was evidenced in an emotional letter of June 1913 in which he explained the personal dedication of his *General Psychopathology* to his father:

Heidelberg, 20. 6. 13

Dear Papa!

[...] I will not send you such a book again so soon – if I can ever repeat it another time – and it is indeed the result of my scientific work up to now. It could be a lot better, to be sure, but I am <u>relatively</u> content; and I know that there is no other book on the subject that might be nearly as good. This comparison to other books on <u>psychiatry</u> is not saying much, since psychiatrists are good for nothing and it is easy competition with them on <u>scientific</u> grounds.

I have dedicated the book to you, dear Papa. It is in no way a conventional dedication (such as is usual with doctoral theses, but not for such works). Actually, I would like to send you, like this one, a philosophical book, in which I formulate the 'world vision' [*Weltanschauung*] of trust in our reason, in which I feel myself so at one with you, yet without falling into the trap of philistine mindlessness [*Stumpfsinn*] that is typical of a so-called 'enlightened' non-believer. Yet I fear I won't live long enough to finish it. That I have you and Gertrud is a piece of good fortune that only few people enjoy – it makes the misfortune of my illness seem slight, even though it distorts my 'public' life and success.

A second point, in addition, dear Papa, is that I feel myself inwardly related with you in my basic views, as soon as I compare them with the views of others among my friends; although the formulations and structures that we gain in life are naturally different between us – we indeed belong to two generations. [...] Therefore, I ask you, dear Papa, gladly to accept the dedication. It means more to me than all the joy that I can give you with a public success.

Fondest

Your Kally[48]

Jaspers' *General Psychopathology* (1913) represented a particular scientific agenda of its own. The purpose was to avoid restricting the scope of the ideas in this book to a singular impression of individual experience. Jaspers' first book was a breath of fresh air, since he displayed an ability to order ideas without compromising the overall basis of the work to any one view. The practical relevance of this work, given that he had been commissioned to write a compendium for students, was an issue raised by his mother. Henriette Jaspers had not been forgotten in the above-quoted letter of explanation, but in a separate letter written to her on the same day, Jaspers revealed his unconventional approach to the status of women in a realm that might otherwise have been expected to be confined to men:

Heidelberg, 20. 6. 13

Dear Mother,

You have always, throughout your life, put yourself in such a moving way in second place. I know: you agree that I dedicate the book to Papa, although I could just as well dedicate it to you or Gertrud. [...] My dedication to Papa, though, includes a feeling that I could not have in relation to you women: namely, a feeling of manly friendship that has never been granted me in my life and that I have felt intensely from time to time in an otherwise so distant relationship to our Papa. [...]

Gertrud and I lead a beautiful life. She has such an unbelievable understanding and such intimate love for me that it is often a mystery to me. Such a life must still bear more fruits.

Many intimate greetings,

Your Kally[49]

Jaspers hardly relegated feminine influences to a subordinate status.[50] Gertrud was no silent muse, for her contribution ensured the basic equality of the partnership. Jaspers might maintain a façade of man-to-man dialogue, but his mother and wife were deeply involved in establishing the solid and stable foundation for his public life. Their influence was not confined to conventional clichés about the distribution of roles for women and men, even if Karl Jaspers senior's response did underline his generation's attachment to patriarchal duty. Jaspers' father observed his own lack of talent for expressing feelings and he noted his gratitude that his son had understood the reasons for his reticence and given him great pleasure with the book's dedication.[51] Henriette Jaspers saw the compactness of Jaspers' book as a particular bonus, although the work itself remained rather inaccessible to her.[52]

Jaspers' first book was nonetheless to underline a common link between their generations, a link that is rather less obvious in the English edition of *General Psychopathology* (not a translation of the first edition). The English text may be read as a blueprint of Jaspers' aspiration to write a philosophical work, for the shift from the early to the middle part of his career – that is, over the interval of almost two decades that separated the appearance of his debut work in 1913 from the publication of *Philosophy* (1932) – was less a scientific development than a natural progression towards philosophy. His *Philosophy* particularly influenced his 1942 revision of *General Psychopathology* through what he called 'the philosophical illumination of Existence itself'.[53] The original idea of *General Psychopathology* was its systematic ordering of the bond between doctor and patient. In essence, Jaspers' approach was 'anti-Freudian' and he expressed in that sense his heartfelt plea for patients' dignity. He had experienced this sort of respect for his humanity in contact with Dr Fraenkel. Not that Jaspers' doctor was the archetypal representative of what he came to advocate as a model of a doctor's dealings with his patient. Yet Jaspers saw the possibility of a role reversal between doctor and patient as a foundation of their mutual understanding:

The most vital part of the psychopathologist's knowledge is drawn from his *contact* with people. What he gains from this depends upon the particular way he gives himself and as therapist partakes in events, whether he illuminates himself as well as his patients. The process is not only one of simple observation, like reading off a measurement, but the exercise of a self-involving vision in which the psyche itself is glimpsed.[54]

Dr Fraenkel's support of his progress from his first unpaid employment in the clinic was underlined by his attendance at Jaspers' inaugural lecture on the 'Limits of Psychology' in December 1913.[55] Jaspers' book had been entered as a *Habilitation* thesis for psychology, and his text was therefore under review by Wilhelm Windelband, the acting director of Heidelberg's philosophy faculty.[56] The obstacles to its being accepted as a qualifying professorial thesis were considerable, because his medical qualification seemed to disqualify his book, unless he were quickly to complete a dissertation in philosophy. In addition, psychology was not established as a discipline in the philosophical faculty at that time. As Jaspers' mother reported to his father, who remained in Oldenburg due to illness, the important thing was not Windelband's opinion of Jaspers' book, but their curiosity to know what Max Weber thought of it. Jaspers wrote rather ruefully to his father that, although he was now accepted in the academic community, his inaugural lecture was merely the starting point of a post that was nearly, though not quite, enough to pay his living expenses: 'Now I am a lecturer. Everything else is fairly irrelevant. Mother has sent a very extensive report.'[57]

7   *Max Weber*

IF JASPERS DEFENDED THE RIGHT to distinguish Max Weber's personality from his works, the sincere discretion he showed towards the sociologist was motivated by his need to determine the limits of Weber's control over the pattern of his academic life. Weber was one of Jaspers' most influential mentors. To pretend that Jaspers ever doubted the basis of Weber's intellectual authority seems questionable, yet this may clarify whether Weber had greater or less influence over Jaspers' career than Jaspers' private conversations with his father. Jaspers had dedicated his first book to his father, as has been shown, because he valued their common aims in pursuit of tolerance. Not only did the idea of sharing hopes with his father's generation offer a peculiar support for Jaspers, but the power of his father's approval transcended any material success that he might achieve on the basis of his academic endeavours.

The distance in years between Jaspers and Weber was barely two decades, and in terms of their approach it was not clear to what extent they obtained or desired harmony. That question was a feature of a penetrating account of Weber's personality that Jaspers sent to his parents several years before his first book was published. When Jaspers met Weber, he was still an unknown, unpaid voluntary assistant supervised by Franz Nissl in Heidelberg's Clinic of Psychiatry. He was aware that cultivating relations with him could overcome his uncertainty about the direction of his future ambitions, whether he aimed to achieve success in the field of psychology or philosophy. To be accepted by

Weber on equal terms was a delicate if not impossible aim for Jaspers to fulfil at that time. Whenever he sought an appointment with him, he was encouraged by Gertrud's friendship with Weber's wife Marianne. If Gertrud urged Jaspers to accept Weber's invitations, he shyly evaded them. When he did call upon Weber, he usually arrived together with Gertrud.[1] Otherwise, he went in the company of his colleague Hans Gruhle, as he reported along with some first impressions of the aura surrounding Weber's personality:

Heid[elberg], 27. 2. 10

Dear parents!

On Friday, I was with Gruhle at Max Weber's. [...] I already knew the man by sight and more specifically from his writing. I really like him a great deal. He is a rare 'man' among learned scholars and completely enthusiastic about the value of reason as such. His talent is magnificent. At least, he is the most intelligent man to whom I have so far spoken, person to person. [...] I have a general antipathy towards spiritual and intellectual people. Those whom you get to know do not exactly inspire you to trust them personally, they are unreliable, vain, excitable individuals who are ruled by their emotions. They lack manly, solid and determined characteristics. Max Weber is completely different. He captures at first sight a man's trust. Only one thing causes a little anxiety. Often you notice an aroused expression pass across his face, his eyes become peculiarly piercing and you fear that at any moment he might become nervously ill just like he was once for almost two years. It is as though a mighty will is constantly wrestling to control a nervous system that is going to become agitated. The battle is not to give a trace of this away. His wife has a fine manner and soothing effect on him. You notice that he owes her a great deal. Their marriage seems to be a good one. [...] I was, the same as every time, asked in a very friendly manner to call again and simply to telephone to fix an appointment. But I doubt whether I belong in that circle. The people are too clever. I think that I have nothing to offer.

Fond wishes,

Your Kally[2]

This spontaneous account of what was probably one of Jaspers' first meetings with Weber provided clear evidence of a desire to strive for equality.[3] From the beginning, Jaspers recognized that Weber's presence was an implicit challenge to his generation. If his respect for Weber's abilities rivalled his admiration for his father, he also knew that Weber was the one personality with whom it was worthwhile to compete. He became fascinated by the progress of their discussions, for even to speak of progress in that regard was tantamount to being admitted as Weber's equal. At the start of their acquaintance, however, Jaspers was conscious of his inferiority. Although he believed that he had a realistic chance of gaining his respect, their friendship, as he informed his parents, provided little scope for direct influence. He stressed this difficulty in his memoirs:

> Max Weber I did not encounter as a friend, for to friendship belongs equality. To be sure, he behaved toward me entirely as if I were his equal and would not have done otherwise. But my respect before the greatness of this man was such that I felt shy before him. There were some exceptions … It happened that, in conversation, we did battle with each other on the level of equals. These were very serious questions. In such conversations there was perhaps a slight hint of beginning friendship. Even today, I would be too indiscreet if I were to talk about it.[4]

Privately, Jaspers revealed the trouble he faced in contending with Weber's towering authority. He showed that he was also in two minds about the stability of Weber's personality. His main incentive was to improve the range and breadth of his knowledge and he courted Weber's company in the hope of finding an opportunity to discuss with him his fledgling scientific research. Jaspers admired the words that flowed so readily from Weber's pen. In response to Weber's *The Protestant Ethic and the Spirit of Capitalism* (1904), for instance, he tried to model the style of his psychiatric papers on Weber's discursive approach.[5] Over time, however, he realized that it was impossible to emulate Weber; and, influential though Weber may have been as a mentor, not only did Jaspers' instincts conflict with his personality and general disposition, but the focus of his research in the clinic nominally required him not to stray too far from concentrating on the investigation of empirical questions.

Jaspers' striving to be recognized by his peers as a therapist enabled him to keep an open mind about the empirical focus of his work. His affiliation to research in psychology went against the grain of emulating Weber's rationalistic approach. In this respect, however, a stronger influence for Jaspers appears to have been those conversations with his father. In particular, the direction of his discussions led him to reflect upon the sort of activity that bore little direct and obvious connection to the development of his scientific research. The letter that Jaspers wrote to his parents shortly after the publication of his second book explains how his father's paintings were as much an influence upon his capacity to express his perception of life as his audiences with Weber had been:

Heidelberg, 13/6/19

Dear parents,

[…] I often think about you both when I think of the most essential thing that – indirectly – I wanted to express in my book. Whenever I look at Papa's watercolours, which I often consciously do day by day, then I feel the same thing in them. You can, after all, say the same thing with concepts as in art. Yet that is only comprehensible to people with the same nature and then only if the receptiveness is present for the particular medium that, in itself, is indifferent. I would not like it at all if you were to read my book. That would be a terribly tortuous thing. As a precondition you anyway need a certain knowledge of philosophical concepts. But I am not at all sad about that. For I feel that we have the essentials in common. And Papa succeeded in many paintings in a much purer way than I. For Papa, so much is immediate and unreflected, simply taken for granted, something that he rather just has in his existence, that I first search for. [...]

Fond greetings,

Your Kally[6]

Having grown accustomed to receiving the undivided attention and constant advice of his father, Jaspers confessed to have gained from his influence at least as much benefit for his intellectual work as contact with his peers and superiors, such as Max Weber, in his academic environment. The significance of his father's art was again underlined later that year when Karl Jaspers senior sent a number of his paintings to his son as a Christmas gift:

Heidelberg, 25/12/19

Dear Papa!

Your dear present – which you attribute to Mother and for which we have her to thank as well – was a great and wonderful surprise yesterday evening. I look at these pictures with great love and also many, partly melancholy thoughts of Mother and you, which without exception show me the world of happy childhood memories in the mirror of your soul. [...] At your age, most people easily become small-minded, they show the unpleasant characteristics that they always had, only even more clearly, and they are involved in everyday trifles with an inadequate kind of agitation. Your pictures radiate for me the other side of growing old that is certainly not new to me, the calmness and clarity, which has been acquired in long, inner battles that have little to do with knowledge or reasoning but that traditionally is and deserves to be called wisdom.

You prefer not to have anything explained about the value of your paintings and you call them, all too modestly, your 'productions'. I am also not an expert in works of art, but I am pleased when I notice a feeling and sense it striking a chord within me and then I call the picture good. That is the way it is with your pictures. For me, they are so true to life, quite apart from the external clarity and care with which everything is done and ordered. I could list a great many specific details: the wonderful perspective and depth of the pictures, the unmistakably soothing proportions of the ordering, the glowing white sand of the dunes in the quite dark weather of the pictures, the forms of trees and shrubs, just like they are on Spiekeroog, partly fully grown, partly forced and stunted, and the leafless, dead branches eerily streching into the air, the black sea or the narrow strip of water gleaming far behind the mudflats, partly the surge and turmoil of nature in the wild, then the calm sense of peace again (in Heering), or the Italian beauty of form (especially in pine trees). Every picture tells me something. Quite apart from the personal feelings that make the pictures so valuable to me, I believe that an expert would also soon recognize the skill and craftsmanship of the drawing technique. You can see that you have had proper instruction and practised and that you have accomplished this painting, like everything that you have begun in your life, with the same thoroughness and discipline.

The tendency to stylize and the characteristic emphasis of primitive forms that partly derives from their production according to sketches and not in the open air makes Afra Geiger see the pictures as 'remarkably modern'. She was also entirely enthusiastic. For us, they will always be a delightful possession. [...] It is a wonderful Christmas time!

Your Kally[7]

The consciousness of structure and form that is unusually clarified in the fluent ordering of ideas in Jaspers' second book, entitled 'Psychology of World Visions' (1919), could therefore just as easily have followed from conversations with his father about these paintings as from contact with Max Weber. Jaspers admired Weber's methodology of 'objectivity' as a convincing pattern for himself to adopt in his quest for transparency and clear expression of ideas. His intentions, as he described them to his father, indirectly conflicted with Weber's 'objectivity', for in an interesting appendix to his book, Jaspers included an analysis of Kant's doctrine of ideas. In that section of his analysis, he was not dismissive of an artist's capacity to harness intuitive elements supposedly foreign to the systematic ordering of theoretical ideas that was a hallmark of the main body of his book. By adding a study of Kant's *Critique of Judgement* at the end of this book, a study that had originally been prepared for one of Emil Lask's Kant seminars,[8] he highlighted the need for caution in associating his thinking too closely with that of Max Weber.

In this light, the implication of Jaspers' book rested easily with his desire to emulate his father's example as a painter. What his father could express was similar to what Jaspers sought to communicate indirectly to his readers by means of philosophical concepts. In the quest to express his concepts as a work of philosophy, it seems that he strove to compete with his father's example. His academic work was in that sense also a work of art and a way, too, of extracting himself from Weber's influence.

If a quality of Jaspers' father's paintings, as indicated by the response of Gertrud's close friend Afra Geiger, a young student of Jaspers, was that they could be called 'modern', the paintings were not 'modern' in terms of their subject matter.[9] Jaspers' emphasis on the 'truth' of the sentiment and the clarity of the feeling in his father's paintings seems doubly important. He was later to come into contact with the productions of mentally ill patients, for he was acquainted with the Prinzhorn collection in Heidelberg, an extensive collection of around five thousand paintings, first exhibited in 1922.[10] He also referred to his knowledge of this collection by Hans Prinzhorn at his former place of training, the Heidelberg Clinic of Psychiatry. The Prinzhorn collection was a further point of comparison for a study of paintings by Vincent van Gogh that Jaspers published in 1922, as we will see in the next part. With such contemporary influences in mind, the landscape paintings of Jaspers' father were not merely situated in a world apart, the world of Jaspers' childhood, but in a sphere of consciousness that was removed from parallel developments in the professional world of modern art. The paintings by Otto Dix, Max Beckmann and Georges Grosz, for instance, were an expression of anguish at the desperation unleashed during the four years of the First World War.[11]

On the outbreak of war in 1914, Max Weber's significance as one of Jaspers' closest personal friends was confirmed. He was a fount of insider knowledge about the development of a conflict that Jaspers observed closely from the outset because, as we will see, his brother Enno joined up to fight with the infantry in the first few days of the war. When the full extent of the suffering on all sides gradually became clear, Jaspers' opinions of Germany's situation and the purpose of its involvement in the conflict were largely based on what he knew of Weber's thinking. The following note to his parents is characteristic of his many accounts of Weber's perception of Germany's controversial policy of unlimited submarine warfare, a policy that the Chancellor Bethmann-Hollweg had reluctantly reintroduced at the start of February 1917: 'Max Weber is now basically optimistic. But you notice that the submarine war and America go against the grain. He hopes, however, for success. We are all hoping the same. After only 3 months, we will gain a feeling in Germany for the way the thing is going. And if the thing does not succeed, then we must make the quickest possible peace and, to be exact, peace *à tout prix*.'[12]

Jaspers' interest in political developments was again connected to his family's moral support for Weber. His reluctance to discuss politics in his public lectures was a matter of family loyalties as much as devotion for him. The way in which Karl and Gertrud Jaspers' friendship developed with Weber had been a source of pleasure for Jaspers' parents that had been mutually reciprocated when Marianne Weber had taken the opportunity to speak to Jaspers' mother when she was giving a speech in Oldenburg on behalf of her proactive campaign for womens' rights.[13] Henriette Jaspers provided a close description of Marianne Weber's appearance and concluded in a letter to Jaspers that she was a 'delightful personality, so feminine, and everyone found her pleasant when she spoke in a lively way and laughed in such a friendly manner'.[14] Karl and Henriette Jaspers later encouraged his plan to write a monograph about Weber; and his father even suggested minor modifications to its introduction, as well as advising the inclusion of a short biography.[15] Meanwhile Jaspers relied on Weber for news about the 1914–18 conflict to help soothe his family's concerns about his brother's safety.

When Jaspers joined a political club at the university, from which Max Weber was debarred, he hardly intended to become a mouthpiece for him. He explained to his father that he was the club's only junior member without a full-time professorship. Otherwise the membership included full professors of history, Hermann Oncken, and law, Richard Thomas, and the historian Karl

Hampe.[16] In their company, Jaspers was cautious about divulging material to which he was privy because of his close acquaintance with Weber. Nevertheless, he used those occasions to speak at the club in order to develop an independent appraisal of the conflict. His views resembled Weber's critical articles about the progress of the war in the *Frankfurter Zeitung,* but he laboured, too, under fears for Enno's safety. In the year of a speech that he delivered at the political club, published posthumously as 'Political Moods',[17] his brother was in Flanders, where he had been posted as a reconnaissance pilot. Jaspers appealed in this speech for Germany's politicians to prevent an unnecessary continuation of the conflict, an appeal that coincided with some of the most daring activities Enno undertook during the war. His opinions were not exactly pacifist, but they were progressive. He called for the 'political animal' to rule out ideological attitudes, an indirect reference to the Bolshevist revolution in Russia, which he repeatedly noted in letters to his family with increasing alarm. This speech highlighted the need for a minor revolution in German national policies, for in it Jaspers speculated that politicians could break free of nationalistic policy-making if only they were to accept the responsibilities of their office, though the word democracy was not used exactly in the same decisive sense that Thomas Mann was to use it in almost a year later in his essay, 'Reflections of a Nonpolitical Man' (1918). Jaspers noticed the perplexed response of his audience: 'Yesterday evening I held my talk about "Weltanschauung in politics" at our political club. They were very positive, I should give another talk, but I had the feeling that nobody quite understood what I meant. When I heard other people repeating my words, it sounded as though they were talking a foreign language.'[18] Jaspers' speech resembled the idealistic language of his second book about the 'Psychology of World Visions' (1919). In both of these works, Jaspers expressed a vote for freedom. In the speech, a dialectical flow of ideas depicted a rich interpretation of what he called 'political moods'.[19] Most notably, in the context of a global conflict, he used the opportunity to represent an alternative viewpoint to partisanship, by referring to what he called the 'double standards' of private and public morality as an example of the beneficial exploitation of arguments in British parliamentary debate – an indirect compliment, perhaps, to parliamentary democracy.[20] Such comments symbolized what he saw as the basic human predicament of the time: 'Our opponents are in the essential facts human beings like we are, their suffering and our suffering is the same thing. We are all guilty.'[21]

In the lectures Jaspers gave after the outbreak of war, especially from 1916 onwards, he devoted his attention to the systematic analysis of a pattern of options (to be defined in ethical terms in Weber's major speeches for a series of talks on 'the life of the mind as a vocation'). The subject matter of Jaspers' lectures coincided, to a certain extent, with the approach followed in Weber's talks. Weber's first talk, *Science as a Vocation* (1917) was held in Munich in November 1917 and his later speech, *Politics as a Vocation* (1919), in January 1919. Jaspers received a personal copy of these speeches upon their publication in 1919. What struck a chord with his own work at that time was essentially Weber's highlighting of ethical principles as a measure of the calibre of Germany's intellectual tradition. In his second book, Jaspers described the need to overcome what he called the 'shells of fixed doctrines': 'You could call it a psychological world vision [*Weltanschauung*] if the psychological dimension that is only communicated in objective and generally valid forms were not at the same time to be regarded as the least essential.'[22]

A precise analysis of Weber's influential speeches is not possible within the present context, except to note that his definition of 'ethics of responsibility' (*Gesinnungsethik*) in his speech *Politics as a Vocation* (1919) appealed to Jaspers' hope of steering his work towards philosophy as opposed to psychology. In his book, Jaspers wrestled with the task of organizing his thoughts into what he called 'prophetic' philosophy.[23] If the plausibility of identifying such a 'prophetic' vision of life was about to collapse on a devastating scale, he remained faithful to his book in the sense that he chose not to revise his comments about the atmosphere in which his ideas had developed. His book stood, as he noted in the preface to the fourth edition, as a commitment to 'the time of being under pressure and in need during the first war'.[24]

Several months after the war had begun, Gertrud described Jaspers' attendance at so-called 'cultural philosophical' evenings to her parents-in-law. From the end of 1914, he met up with the young Georg Lukács, Ernst Bloch and Max Scheler, so that for several years before Weber's famous speeches Jaspers was motivated to explore the philosophical angle that he had claimed as the true description of his first book.[25] At the 'cultural philosophical' gatherings, according to Gertrud's reports, the subject matter was 'metaphysics'. Jaspers' presence at these meetings was apparently to enable him to represent his 'negative results' for, as Gertrud explained, the real 'metaphysicians' at the meetings were so fired up by Jaspers' comments that they eagerly debated into the small hours.[26] Her descriptions of these meetings were, however, not kept up. It may be assumed that Jaspers drew encouragement from his participation in the discussions, from which he appeared to have derived confirmation of the philosophical direction of his future work. This opportunity for intellectual exchange attracted Karl and Gertrud Jaspers to Weber's Sunday-afternoon gatherings, where they also met many other scholars, such as Emil Lask, Georg

Simmel and Heinrich Rickert. The indispensability of Jaspers' bond of trust with Weber was forged not merely by such close contact, but also through his hope of enhancing in his own lectures and activities the reputation of German scholarship during the war years. His approach was fashioned, to a certain extent, on his admiration for Weber's contribution to science as a timeless influence. He felt compelled to consider his own way of honouring him, by striving to achieve an independent contribution to philosophy. Jaspers had received a number of favourable reviews of his book, 'Psychology of World Visions' (1919), which gave him grounds for believing that he might obtain a philosophy professorship. In view of Weber's helping hand in the past, as when he had convinced Windelband to open the doors of Heidelberg's philosophy faculty to Jaspers, it is likely that he expected to depend upon his support for years to come. Weber's untimely death, at the age of fifty-six, intervened at a most delicate and inopportune moment for him. When Jaspers found himself delivering a eulogy for Weber, his promotion, that is, the elusive 'call' (*Ruf*) to a professorship, had yet to arrive.

In mid-summer 1920, as Gertrud travelled with Julia Gottschalk to the Bavarian Alps for a short holiday, she postponed their departure from Munich when she heard of Weber's influenza. She suspected that his condition was serious and called at his address in the city, where she was ushered in by Else Jaffé.[27] She had stumbled upon what she told Jaspers was 'a house of death'.[28] As a qualified doctor, Julia instantly recognized from her descriptions that Weber's condition was grave. Gertrud's hurried accounts of the scenes in Munich informed Jaspers about Weber's condition even before news of his death on 14 June was announced. In Heidelberg, he was as close to Weber in his dying hours as he could be. Publicly, he greeted the news in virtual silence.[29] Privately, he conveyed what he thought the event signified for Germany and for the learned world in particular. When he agreed to deliver the memorial speech for Weber in front of students at Heidelberg University on 17 July 1920, his text contained details from his wife's experiences of the dramatic events only a month beforehand. The controlled rhetoric of the speech translated the emotion of the occasion into a courageous message to think ahead. Only days after the event, he wrote to his parents in Oldenburg:

Heidelberg, 16 June 1920

Dear parents!

You will have read in the newspaper that Max Weber is dead. He died of influenza. At present, few people are thinking about what that means. I feel as though I am paralysed, but at the same time I am enthusiastic in my love – in a quite impersonal sense – for this mind. He is the only philosopher of our time and I have no doubt that he will be recognized as such in future. The world seems like a changed place for me. We were so protected in our intellectual world because Max Weber's existence was a guarantee that 'greatness' is still attainable today. Now I feel that nobody is above me any more on an intellectual level and to me the learned world seems empty. [...] Now we lesser mortals remain and we have to find our place in science on our own merits. I feel now that a different responsibility falls to us. When the flame is extinguished, the glowing sparks have to be kindled.

What Max Weber last said to me as he left in the dark is like a bequest. He said in his friendly way about my last book, 'It was <u>very</u> worthwhile,' then he repeated twice in his habitual, emphatic manner: 'I thank you for the book,' and then: 'I wish you every further success and productivity.' Lastly he added: 'I will also comment on your book elsewhere.' Now he can no longer do that. But I have the feeling that he saw in me this sort of glowing spark and I want to strive with all my ability to achieve what I still can in philosophy – to use this general and vague word – and to try to explain in this field to the youth of today his ideas and works.

Those are the impulses that seize hold of you at a moment like this. But death is also near and the desire to make a difference in life, carried by the consciousness of the end and of the incomprehensible meaning of it all.

I enclose Gertrud's first letter for you, with a request, to send it back by return of post. She telephoned me the same evening with the news of the end. [...]

All good and fondest wishes!

Your Kally[30]

In his public tribute, Jaspers revealed his devotion in the novel suggestion that Weber was a philosopher. The idea was not only a keynote of the speech but a symbol of his sense of personal responsibility to Weber's memory.[31] In putting forward this interpretation he did not represent the views of his colleagues in philosophy. Heinrich Rickert, whose position of seniority as a full professor of philosophy meant that he was above Jaspers in the hierarchy of the university, was naturally critical of Jaspers' line. In many ways, Rickert's seniority depended upon rivalry with Weber; and their relations were further strained by personal animosity.[32] As is the custom with such rivalries in university life, Jaspers' acquaintance with Weber led Rickert to perceive him as a natural competitor. Gertrud anticipated that the loss of Weber as their mutual friend would enable Jaspers finally to come to terms with some of the personal animosity directed at him by Rickert. Jaspers did not dwell upon these animosities in his acknowledgement of Weber's contribution to intellectual life. He referred to his scientific work as being of the world, yet as something non-personal. Speaking so soon after Weber's death, he did not elaborate on the sources of Weber's 'greatness'.[33]

In his speech, Jaspers emphasized that Weber's authority called to mind examples of greatness in human history. He cited Hegel in support of what, in Rickert's view, could hardly have failed to be a controversial perception of Weber.[34] Jaspers was perhaps trying to provoke an emotional response from Rickert, since by linking Weber with Hegel's definition of the *Zeitgeist* – by ranking Weber as an all-seeing interpreter of the soul – he implied that his thinking was an incarnation of Hegel's 'absolute spirit' (*Weltgeist*).[35] His reference was a discreet way of configuring his personal view of Weber's authority: 'The philosopher is the heart in the flow of time, but he is not only this, for he is able to articulate what time has in store, to hold up a mirror against her, and while articulating her meaning, he is able to define time through the force of the mind.'[36] This rousing homage to Weber as a philosopher also carried Jaspers' audience to the core of his friendship. The rhetorical comparison with Hegel's work was secondary to the force of his argument about Weber as the key representative of modern life in all its fragility. If Weber's achievements were valid as a reflecting glass through which modern society could peer at itself, Jaspers regarded this function as offering a warning about the role of the intellectual. That was a motif of Weber's essay, *The Protestant Ethic and the Spirit of Capitalism* (1904), in which a comparative survey of northern European cultures, especially America and England, led him to identify incentives for capitalism accompanying the decline of spiritual values. His approach of seeking out comparable, yet not necessarily causal, explanations for religions and cultures was associated with his endeavours to establish sociology as a discipline.

This factor was not to deter Jaspers from his promotion of Weber's unfinished works as a philosophical system; and his task was not as onerous as it seemed. Upon his death, the fragmentary character of Weber's 'system' was an indisputable fact. To have taken such an interest in his works was perhaps a token of Jaspers' affection for Marianne Weber. Yet a principle was also at stake, one that became a feature of Jaspers' support of Weber after Weber's death: namely, his primary concern was discretion in honour of their friendship. When Jaspers spoke at Weber's commemoration service, he was at a crossroads in his career. He was hoping to obtain a full professorship, so that he could finally manage without his father's subsidies. Was it because Weber's death highlighted his own uncertainties about the future that he chose not to connect his public statements about Weber's personal life with his status as a scholar?

Jaspers preferred to highlight Weber's scholarship as a series of profound studies of the soul, epitomized by the way Weber revised and extended an important section of his sociology of religion to append a discourse on the passion of the soul. Jaspers indulged in a high-minded speculation about Weber's personal connection to these emotional issues, as when he used his memorial speech to express in front of students and colleagues his knowledge of what philosophy needed to achieve if intellectuals were to be believable. This sombre occasion was turned into an opportunity to speak about philosophy not just as the queen of science, but as the heart and soul of Weber's life. The lofty and emphatic dimension of this message transported Jaspers to the heart of a conflict of motives that Gertrud had first drawn to his attention after witnessing the death scene in Munich. It was then that she had expressed her belief in the danger of indiscretion in respect of Weber's memory.

If Weber were a philosopher of the standing to which Jaspers laid claim, the problem was for Jaspers himself to produce something in the field of philosophy that was not to remain in the other man's shadow. Jaspers was now confronted with a profound dilemma over his ambitions. After Weber's death, he was required both to express and to conceal his personal opinions in such a way as to make it appear that he overlooked a potential discrepancy between Weber's public and private life. This oversight, if that is what it was, seemed to haunt him in later life.[37] His persistent refusal to penetrate in public the possible grey areas of Weber's psyche suggested that he was deeply concerned about giving credance to a Weber 'myth', a distortion of the facts about Weber.[38] He acted as a loyal guardian of the sociologist's posthumous fame.[39]

The extent of Jaspers' determination to prevent Weber's private circumstances being aired in public meant that his own work, and that of Marianne Weber, could develop a distinctive but complementary assessment of Weber's legacy. In 1932 he published a brief yet comprehensive appraisal of Weber's life and times. He had difficulty finding an appropriate subtitle for this book, as evidenced by the different versions he suggested to Ernst Mayer.[40] The stirring appeal of the chosen subtitle, with its stress on 'German essence', was partially reflected in one of three sections of the book that he devoted to a study of

Weber's political life. In the remaining sections, he characterized Weber as a scientist and a philosopher. He retained these three parts as separate aspects of his study of Weber's unpredictable life that he loosely associated with the volatile character of politics in Germany in the early 1930s. That association led one of Jaspers' doctoral students, Hannah Arendt, to express her concern about what she saw as a potential error of judgement in publishing the book on Weber. Jaspers' aims had nothing at all to do with the terror tactics that, only months after his book was published, confirmed the stranglehold of Nazi ideology on public life. His reluctance directly to analyse contemporary politics in his book on Weber led his brother-in-law Ernst Mayer to worry too about the work's obscurity.[41] Hannah Arendt had delayed her letter of thanks for her personal copy of the book because of her anxiety about the unspecified political implications of the phrase 'German essence'.[42] Her enquiry raised a legitimate question that Jaspers had privately considered at the time of Weber's death, when he had doubted the possibility of believing at all in 'greatness' and remained uncertain as to what the future might hold.

In his monograph, Jaspers returned to the thesis of his 1920 speech, by examining Weber's bequest as a philosopher.[43] An important difference in this case was that Jaspers himself discussed Weber's legacy in the knowledge that he had already published his own work of philosophy. If he portrayed his subject as a peripatetic yet supremely ineffectual politician, his reference to the débâcle of Weber's candidacy for the liberal German Democratic Party (DDP) in 1918 made the inclusion of his anti-Bismarck pamphleteering at this particular time seem futile.[44] The overall ineffectiveness of the liberals in Germany may have been a reason why Jaspers himself was a member of the DDP for only a few months in 1919.[45] The past included Bismarck's legacy. No matter how critically Weber represented Bismarck, his study of statesmanship contributed something to the definition of that ineffable quality of leadership – charisma.[46] What Jaspers had hoped to draw attention to in his monograph was that Weber's coining of the term 'charismatic leadership' referred to an ethereal greatness, as it existed in people's heads, regardless of whether the leader actually possessed his textbook definition of leadership.[47] Jaspers later conceded that Weber's definition of charisma was one of the three categories of 'leadership' applying to the state of affairs in Germany that became thinkable under Hitler,[48] though Weber perceived 'charisma' on the basis of an 'ethic of responsibility' that was entirely absent from the abuse of power under Hitler. When Hitler literally 'took over' as Führer in August 1934, he accomplished the deed by 'diabolic forces', by deviously sweeping aside the powers of the Presidency.[49] These executive powers were, ironically enough, the terms of office that Weber became involved in defining when he accepted an advisory role on the Weimar constitution and rationalized the Presidency, by bringing its powers into line with those of the Chancellor. When Jaspers published his monograph, there was a need to connect Weber's failure as a politician with Jaspers' attitude to Germany's future as a nation, especially since he intended, as he informed Hannah Arendt, to introduce a young, unsuspecting audience to Weber as the personification of patriotic loyalty to the nation.[50]

A problem with Jaspers' good intentions was that they seemed strangely removed from political affairs. His deep misgivings about Germany's future were clear to his close family, but they may not have seemed so clear to outsiders, even those such as Arendt in the privileged position of being one of his doctoral students. Another concern raised by Ernst Mayer was that Jaspers had decided to give the contract for his Weber monograph to a relatively small, provincial publishing house, Gerhard Stalling. He did this for the sentimental reason that the publisher was local to Oldenburg and had known his brother Enno. Nevertheless, Jaspers had misgivings about dealing with a lesser known firm as compared with Springer in Berlin or Göschen in Leipzig. Jaspers wanted to erect a monument to his deceased brother Enno, so he overlooked a series published by Gerhard Stalling which he regarded as 'emphatically right-wing' and 'intent on making money out of the word "nation"'.[51] He emphasized that he hoped his work would be considered a relevant study, in association with Weber's name and in silent sympathy for Enno, who had known and loved Weber's works. In September 1932, the draft manuscript of Jaspers' Weber book was completed.[52] Ernst Mayer was so opposed that he wanted publication halted, an act that, as Jaspers complained, would have meant abandoning the project because of the exclusivity of the contract. In a reassuring note to his parents, he confirmed that the book would proceed with some of the alterations that Mayer had suggested: 'But I do not share Ernst's opinion; I like the text and so does Trudelein. Now, though, I will probably do some finer work on the text and, in spite of Ernst's protest, then risk publishing the book. Of course, it would be bad if Ernst were to be proved right.'[53]

Jaspers believed that the risk of associating his name with the popular brand of nationalism was negligible, whereas Ernst Mayer was worried that such a calculation was unrealistic. The book could be purchased by a public whose readers supported numerous political factions, from patriots who might wish to retain the German monarchy to a group of national democrats, among whom Jaspers initially counted himself, albeit briefly, as a member of Friedrich Naumann's DDP. Jaspers' book could also appeal to an extreme right-wing group of fanatical Nazis who had manipulated Hindenburg's Presidency and, upon his death, assumed ownership of the Presidency, the Chancellorship and the nation at large. Jaspers' book, forwarded for approval to Marianne Weber, had to satisfy many needs, a requirement that seemed to be confirmed when Gertrud wrote to warn him that the proof copies were not at all what they had expected. When the package arrived in Heidelberg, a number of disturbing factors were noted, not least the lay-out of the title-page on which Jaspers' name was set in large type and Weber's hardly visible.[54] The minor amendments to the appearance of the first edition meant that Jaspers' name appeared in black, unobtrusive upper-case letters, whereas 'Max Weber' appeared in a larger, italicized script that was unmistakeably 'brown' and therefore conjured up the colour of Hitler's private army of so-called 'Brownshirts', the SA (*Sturmabteilung*). Jaspers suspected that his book had been manipulated, to accord with the Stalling Library Series ('Letters to the Nation'). He nevertheless believed that it was desirable for his book to be published. The work was not just about Weber's authority as an intellectual, but a reflection of the lack of such influential personalities after Weber's death. Weber had inspired others through his generosity and advice and had especially opened avenues for Jaspers, who also recognized the need to assert his reputation independently of Weber's influence. Although Jaspers now chose to associate his name with Weber, the discretion he showed about their friendship slightly obscured the degree of independence that he had already begun to assert during Weber's lifetime. His perception of Weber's influence was based on changing patterns at different moments of his life. If his later remarks about Weber seemed designed to revitalize the admiration of his youth, he also concealed his opinions out of respect for Weber's intellectual standing.[55] The closing sentences of Jaspers' *Philosophy* (1932) may have been intended as an emblem of his homage to Weber.[56] He endorsed critical assessments of his friendship with Weber that described Weber as a modern-day Socrates. However, he wanted his own ideals to live on after Weber's untimely death.[57] The pathos of Weber's last words about 'the true is the truth' (*das Wahre ist die Wahrheit*) was not to remain in tortuous self-contradiction, for even as she had loitered on the threshold of Weber's Munich residence, Gertrud had felt the weight of the sociologist's demise. And she encouraged Jaspers to restore higher meaning to the words Weber uttered as he took his dying breath.

8 *Enno Jaspers*

Enno Jaspers' aspiration for the lifestyle of a *bon viveur* was in direct contrast to his brother's iron discipline and daily régime. Enno was boisterous, whereas Karl was calm and composed. Enno enjoyed extravagant living, whereas Karl's illness narrowed his chances of a successful career and spread uncertainty over the future. No less intelligent than Karl and Erna, Enno was easily the most reckless of the three, squandering his pocket money, when Karl always saved something. In a small pocket book, dating from Jaspers' fifth form, he meticulously recorded a log of income and expenditure for March, April and May 1898. According to his record, Jaspers had given ten Pfennigs to Enno (on 19 March) and yet his account still showed an end-of-quarter profit.[1]

Jaspers saw a side of his brother's personality that he found potentially wild. He later noted five principles that he employed to govern his behaviour towards Enno. These principles, recorded in Jaspers' 1903 Göttingen diary, did not so much prescribe his actual dealings, as provide an indication of the brothers' relationship at that time.[2] Three of these principles, in particular, seem relevant, since their high moral tone makes them sound irreversible. The first was that Jaspers should moderate his rationality that he described as a potential obstacle to their friendship. He compared his approach with his younger brother's happy-go-lucky ways. His second was never to expect anything of his brother that may have been unpleasant for him. Jaspers described his own habit of appearing schoolmasterly as potentially problematic, but hoped that he could nonetheless be seen as a role model for Enno. The fifth principle introduced an unfamiliar note to Jaspers' record, because it showed that he regretted his icy reserve that merely concealed his underlying envy of Enno's pleasure-seeking ways: '5. No expression of any form of revenge.'[3]

A third party was occasionally necessary to keep the peace, and Jaspers saw his sister, Erna, as a vital intermediary. Erna's influence was calming and reassuring. His feelings about his sister's diplomatic talents were recorded in another sketch, dated around 1905, when Jaspers was in Göttingen and still preoccupied with his medical studies.

> <u>Karl</u>, more of a philistine, awkward, alienated from the world (eminently increased due to his illness). [...] All the same, ethical preferences. [...]
>
> <u>Enno</u>, needs more enjoyment, less awkward, loves the world, high spirits. [...] A need for education is present, but fades into the background by comparison with other preferences. [...] A need for change. Preference for exaggerated action. Little self-discipline, lets himself go a lot. All these character traits are also developed in Karl, only to a lesser extent.
>
> <u>Erna</u>, forms here, too, an intermediate link between the two extremes, only the kind of link that far exceeds the value of both brothers. Her tender organization [and ...] her feelings are throroughly developed, deep and reliable.[4]

In some respects, his observations on the brothers' different psychologies appear superficial, but they underline an early interest in psychology, as well as revealing how unusually close they were. Academically, Karl's results were most promising. Although Enno's school-leaving certificate was competent, he seemed destined for a path of action. A factor in the tragic developments later in Enno's life was his ineptitude for those morally defined principles that governed his brother's outlook. When events took a turn for the worse with a spiral of bad luck, imprudent money deals, the loss of several jobs, and three broken engagements, the impact of Enno's calamities was such that Karl could not rescue his younger brother from an ultimate disaster of two bankruptcies and a likely cocaine addiction.

Jaspers' chronicle of his relationship with Enno and Erna shows how he saw Enno as his alter ego, as though his brother's fun-loving, energetic qualities were potentially reflections of his own goals, if only his vitality had not been thwarted by illness. The brothers' solidarity was a particular aspect of their early correspondence that began when Enno started his first paid employment as an apprentice bank clerk at the offices of Carl F. Plump & Co. in Bremen. During his first sixth months there Enno initiated an extended conversation with Karl, to expose the emotional straitjacket that his elder brother wore in order to protect himself. In seemingly good-humoured reports about his apprenticeship, Enno challenged his brother to liberate himself from the panzer of his deep reserve, by demanding the kind of intuitive empathy that he supposed to be an essential ingredient for Jaspers' intellectual life. Enno's impatience to progress clearly fell on sympathetic ears; and this part of his comic letter underlines the tedious nature of his experiences for his brother:

Bremen, 20 March 1907

Dear Kally,

[...] My job is the most boring task thinkable: it consists of: 1) paying money in, 2) cashing in money, 3) running to the post office and the central bank and 4) copying and registering. The first three of these types of activity only test the muscles in your legs and the fourth requires that you do not quite fall asleep from all the running about, but to show any understanding is always totally unnecessary, at times, even troublesome. After half a year, this activity is over for me, but then it is not going to get much more interesting. The entire job of a bank clerk lastly consists in copying from one piece of paper to another. [...]

Friendly greeting,

Enno[5]

In response, Jaspers described Enno's slow progress as relative to a particular stage, not to the whole of an individual career. He sympathized and referred to the challenge of obtaining his doctoral qualification and his early contact with patients in the clinic of psychiatry in Heidelberg.[6] Whilst Enno developed the conversation in a style of camaraderie, Karl took his brother's questioning seriously. After several months of his apprenticeship, Enno complained that Jaspers' letters were superficial, motivated even by a misplaced sense of duty.[7] Enno wanted to explore their different perceptions of trivia and entertainment, and alternative distinctions of obligation and pleasure. His accusations about his brother's insensitivity and deep withdrawal within himself intensified.

Bremen, 5 July 1907

Dear Kally,

[...] You are now in the happy position of always being able to replace descriptions of personal things with general observations. In that way, you always manage not to force yourself to write about personal matters and to give free rein to your preferences and capacities. If you then write that you did not experience anything personal, that is foolish. It is a pleasant feeling to describe oneself as in need of pity and to believe it, when in reality, it is quite wrong, but in general, one should not persuade oneself of that sort of thing. Your body prevents you from doing a lot of things, but to conclude a lack of personal experiences from that does not seem justified to me.

Next time more!

Friendly greeting,

Enno[8]

A fiery exchange of views ensued between the brothers. Enno hoped to grow closer to his brother by drawing Jaspers out of himself. Firstly, Enno suggested that his brother had an impoverished conception of personal experience. In brief, he accused Jaspers of using his illness as an artificial defence to avoid direct personal contact with others. Enno's emotional and rather unjustified accusation struck a nerve when he called Jaspers' existence an artificial shell, an alibi to conceal from others the true nature of his experiences. Secondly, Enno's identification of Jaspers' capacity to generalize in a rational way about subjective experience implied that such generalizations were convenient summaries of all manner of personal whims, likes, dislikes and prejudices. Jaspers designated personal matters as universally valid, a supposition that Enno regarded as frustrating for an opponent, such as himself, who sought common ground and tried to develop an independent standpoint. Enno received a seven page, double-sided response in which Jaspers already showed his ability to develop a speculative line of argument using his personal experiences as a starting point, albeit a line of discussion that was lightened with the telling admission: 'You have caught me in one of my most sensitive places'.[9]

Jaspers' illness could give rise to endless discourses on the nature of subjectivity, yet the difference, as he explained in his letter, between significant and trivial personal experiences (*Persönliche Erlebnisse*) amounted to their effect on the individual. The depth of an experience could only truly be identified as a personal source through the manner and level of reflections: 'A human being only has personal experiences when these are in accord with his purely intellectual and emotional temperament.'[10]

Enno was an important interlocutor for Jaspers' interest in definitions that transcended psychological facets of experience. Indeed, he noted that to represent another's experience accurately was not to explain that experience, unless such explanations underwent deeper reflection about the source of another's motives. Jaspers appealed to Enno to show greater sensitivity in a way that undermined Enno's accusation about his brother's approach:

> To be sure, I did not want to describe myself in my last letter as in need of pity. Rather, it is a drive, a desire to be understood which makes me talk so often and repeatedly about my illness. If I then find such an answer and opinion, as in your present letter, a sting of pain goes through my heart to be so misunderstood.[11]

This theme in the brothers' conversation was developed when Enno later attended a talk in Bremen on Wilhelm Wundt's experimental psychology. Enno returned to the initial point of his dialogue by venturing his idea of psychology as a creative force because of its application to problems of national economy and politics.[12] At that time, Enno was considering a future career as a lawyer and he looked upon the bonus of university training as a way of appropriating what he called 'world vision' (*Weltanschauung*), a word that he mentioned as if to question his brother's opinion of whether he were ever likely to achieve his goals.

Jaspers readily applauded Enno's idealism. He reassured his brother that if he were to maintain his critical approach to his further education, he would quickly achieve his ambitions. As to the relevance of psychology, Jaspers concluded on a cautiously optimistic note, representing the discipline as a starting point, yet endorsing his views with a quotation from Kant. The schoolmasterly tendency that Jaspers had warned himself of in his personal notebook is now evident in his copying for Enno the entire paragraph §60 of Kant's *Anthropology from a Pragmatic Point of View* (1798), the second half of which reads as follows:

> Young man! Cherish and enjoy work; renounce all pleasures, not to abstain from them, but as far as possible, always to keep them within sight. Do not dull the senses to this prospect by an early life of pleasure. At a mature age you never regret abstinence from physical indulgence

and even these sacrifices will guarantee you a bonus and contentment, which are independent of chance or the laws of nature.[13]

Initially, Enno may have heeded his brother's advice about moderating his unbridled behaviour. Towards the end of summer in 1909, Enno decided to defer his university entrance to read law, and before he completed a year's obligatory military service, he chose to spend several weeks in Bournemouth, in order to improve his command of English.[14] This visit also proved an ideal opportunity for Enno to indulge his love of sailing. The late English summer inspired his appreciation of the fading grandeur of an Edwardian gentleman's lifestyle, as he wrote to his parents:

[Bournemouth], 14 August 1909

Dear parents,

Today I was on the Isle of Wight and to be exact, in Cowes. [...] The town itself is only small and enclosed towards the seafront by very attractive villas owned by English Lords and rich people, but its reputation is from the *Royal Yacht Squadron*, similar to the German *Imperial Yacht Club*, whose entire flotilla is in harbour here. For the last few weeks, a big regatta has been held off Cowes, in honour of the Tsar who is staying; and, as well as the English yachts, lots of French and Dutch vessels were also in anchor. It was a pretty sight to see them all. The countryside here is wonderful. White chalk cliffs rise in a steep incline straight from the sea; and they look amazingly beautiful next to the blue water. The woods collide with the chalk cliffs directly onto the sea and nature provides such a view as I have never seen. [...]

Fond greeting,

Your Enno[15]

Enno readily adapted to his new routine. 'Every morning at eight o'clock I take a dip in the sea, 9 o'clock breakfast, 1.15 p.m. lunch, 6.30 p.m. dinner, every afternoon at 4 o'clock, afternoon tea.'[16] The leisurely atmosphere of his excursion was evident during his first visit to London, when he joined an omnibus tour of the city and visited several landmarks – the Tower of London and St Paul's Cathedral. Enno was fascinated by the British monarchy and military history. He noted cultural differences between the countries by comparing the architecture of St Paul's to that of Cologne Cathedral. He applied for admission to the 'Stranger's Gallery' to witness a session of

Parliament in the House of Commons. His animated London descriptions would contrast with Jaspers' apprehensive appreciations of life in the metropolis in late August 1925, when he stayed for several days in Bloomsbury with Gertrud and her cousins, Julia and Ernst Gottschalk.[17]

After his short journey to England, Enno continued to complete the year's military service in Oldenburg. He then began his legal training, initially in Heidelberg, where he benefited from his brother's connections in the intelligentsia. A series of introductions, such as to Jaspers' friend, the professor of law, Gustav Radbruch, could not deter Enno's relocation to Bonn University, where he completed his official state entrance examination for law in February 1913. Karl's continued messages of support for his brother now took on a deeper significance. At the start of August 1914, Enno was boarding a train in Oldenburg that was bound for France. On the day that Britain declared war on Germany, 4 August 1914, Jaspers wrote:

Oldenburg, 4. 8. 14

Dear Enno,
    My longing for you is great. I would always like to say something brotherly and dear to you. But we cannot do that sort of thing. Only an instinctive trust in fate that you are going to return to us in good health permits life still to seem possible. If only I had the strength to go with you, so that we could help each other! I am full of love for you.
    Your Karl[18]

Enno was not involved in the frontline, 'Schlieffen' manoeuvres that marked the German surge into Belgium and France. Nor was he involved in the 1915 battle of the Marne, although he was originally sent to the Marne with the infantry. A quiet air of concern prevailed in the family, as Jaspers revealed in his letter only a few days after Enno's departure: 'Not long after you had left, we collected Papa. Papa and mother were walking separately [?] and they were both in tears. But they both have courage and do not believe anything other than your quite definite return to us.'[19]

As a wave of enthusiasm for the war swept across western Europe in the wake of Archduke Franz Ferdinand's assassination in Sarajevo, the atmosphere of feverish excitement reached Heidelberg. The university professors signed a statement of allegiance to German science that Jaspers also signed because, as he explained to Enno, he wanted to place on record his view of German science as being far superior to any other nation's conception of academic excellence.[20]

His justification for signing this statement suggested an aristocratic, conservative viewpoint that could be regarded as being in keeping with his devotion to Max Weber. However, it is unclear whether his decision to join in the spirit of this declaration was truly a vote for the sentiment of the initiative, or whether he rather acted out of solidarity with Enno. Jaspers may have nominally rejected a British notion of fair play by signing up to the document, but he was well aware that the war jeopardized his lifestyle as an academic. As he wrote to Enno:

Oldenburg, 3. 10. 14

Dear Enno,

[...] Sometimes a point is made here of doing important-looking things: Germany's professors published a declaration that 'militarism' and the spirit of science are not to be separated and that we now all belong together. As I <u>now</u> inwardly emphasized that point, <u>I myself</u> have also signed. The declaration is directed against the English, who declared that German science and German militarism are to be distinguished from each other. The war is only to be waged against the latter of the two. I am filled with the idea that actual science only flourishes on a permanent basis in Germany. Anywhere else, individual greatness and only imitation of Germany is to be found. Nowhere is a 'level' of real science present. I would not like to belong to a foreign scientific organization. In view of the real possibilities, that becomes quite clear. [...]

Many fond greetings. I hope you are quite well!

Your Kally[21]

Jaspers' attitude of concealed panic, after receiving a call-up to an equivalent of the home guard, 'Landsturm ohne Waffe', shows in this context his nervous reaction about leaving the ivory tower of science.[22] He wrote to his parents in great agitation that if he were recruited for the home guard, his possible duties could mean physical labour of which he was incapable. He speculated that as a civilian with poor health, yet with medical training, he might contribute to the war effort in one of Heidelberg's clinics. To gain sound advice on the legal implications of his position, he turned to Max Weber who advised obtaining several doctor's certificates and volunteering for a desk job. Despite Weber's confidence that it was a formality to represent his case, Jaspers wrote home with renewed anxiety:

[…] It is terrible to be ill, but at such times, it is pathetic and depressing. The whole German Empire means nothing to me, I do not see a source of any kind of true enthusiasm anywhere: there is such a surge of desire that one would like to be part of that force; and instead of that, as a consequence of my whole life, I have miserably to lie my way through, in order to preserve my existence.[23]

Jaspers' position was exposed in the eyes of those who, like his own brother, were at war. His stance on the periphery of world events led him to warn of dangers ahead if Germany were denied success: 'In that case, it is necessary for mankind that we score a victory.'[24] Whilst Jaspers made no secret of his allegiances and his hopes for a German victory, his wishes and those of Gertrud were intrinsically humane. The occasional mention of Enno's division in newspaper reports permitted Jaspers to follow his brother's activities. By the end of September 1914, Enno had joined the cavalry. Having previous military experience, he served in an officer's rank. By January 1915, he was transferred to a company of engineers, whose main task was bridge-building in France.[25] Many of Enno's letters survive only as copies that his mother forwarded to Jaspers in Heidelberg. It was clear from these that Enno's talents and abilities both intellectual and physical, and his appetite for adventure were put to good use. Later that spring, Enno was involved in the fighting in western Galicia.[26] At the end of September 1915, the brothers were briefly reunited when Enno returned for a few weeks' leave and visited Heidelberg. Barely a year into the war, Jaspers noted how the human cost was taking its toll on his brother's well-being. Indeed, he was already devising a joint plan with him that, when the war finished, Enno should rest his nerves in Heidelberg for several weeks.[27]

While Enno was confronted with the reality of war, Karl's activities were confined to the university. He attempted to transmit from his academic surroundings an objective and encouraging view of Enno's situation. Their mutual dismissal of Friedrich Naumann's *Mitteleuropa*[28] was supported by Jaspers' favouring Jacob Burckhardt's histories, and he also recommended that his brother read Goethe. Jaspers included in a parcel of books for Christmas a copy of Goethe's *Campaign in France* (1792), which as he wrote to Enno, 'interested us as a source of comparison for now – so to speak, as a daily report and record of events in 1792. Perhaps, you may like to read it in spare hours, especially as places in the Champagne region partly appear that are now mentioned a lot. How comfortable a war was in those days!'[29]

Jaspers' attempt to guide Enno through his direct experience of the conflict was consistent with his ambitious programme of research, which was perhaps even begun as a way to justify what he referred to in a letter to his sister as his 'luxury existence'.[30] Jaspers' second book, the 'Psychology of World Visions' (1919), mirrored his detailed research into Kierkegaard's and Nietzsche's works of philosophy at a time when the civilian population was increasingly feeling the harsh impact of the war. Jaspers' lectures began to be frequented by a more modest audience that reflected the decline in male students. Gertrud reported some statistics to her parents-in-law at the same time as mentioning, quite exceptionally, an anecdote of Heidelberg gossip:

[Heidelberg], 18. V. 15

Dear parents,

[...] Kally is very well; I am happy about that. His seminar is well attended, up to now the statistics have been as follows:

Young men	Girls
11	19
17	22
11	24
13	29

You see that the female attendance is growing. That is unfortunate – they look all too stupid. I am waiting for the teaching fees to be paid. Recently, at the Bismarck commemoration, I heard the following discussion between two female students.

The first: 'Yes, he is terribly tall, I often see him on the Hauptstraße, he looks strange there because of his height.'

The second: 'Jaspers is supposed to be important.' The first: 'Yes, he is probably the most important man whom we now have here.'

You can imagine that I liked to hear that. Kally would be quite angry, if he knew that I am writing that to you. I will confess my guilt to him afterwards. It is also fun for you though.

When you hear from Enno, we will also hear of it?

Fond greetings,

Your Gertrud[31]

In early 1916, Enno announced his decision to experiment with a new stage of his military career: he volunteered to train as a pilot. In response, Jaspers wrote an impulsive letter in which he expressed concern:

Heidelberg, 24. 3. 16

Dear Enno,

I just received your dear letter. For me, it is naturally at first a shock – we are so spoilt to be able to think of you without worry; yet, I have no right to such feelings, that is clear to me at once. Your way of writing so simply and without illusions about the realities did me good. I love the manliness in you that is so far from me and yet that I feel so closely. [...] I believe in your good star in your destiny: from my whole heart I wish you great achievements, but also, that you remain alive and active for the achievements of peace.

You are indeed a man who takes himself seriously enough not to risk something that makes no sense. Your voluntary action makes me want to rejoice, if your volunteering as a pilot were not so laden with danger. It makes me suspect that you are going to feel your life fulfilled by concentrating your energies on your performance (some people also talk of a life's 'work'). In our safe world of activity, we know nothing about such fulfilment.

Forgive me, dear Enno, that I answer your simple letter in so many words. It is easier for a man of action to be less emotional.

Fond greetings from your
Kally

Gertrud is on her travels to Prenzlau, I am sending your letter on to her.[32]

After several months' flight training, with lessons in meteorology, surveillance and photography, Enno's mission as a reconnaissance pilot began.[33] At first, he was posted to Flanders, but in early autumn 1917, Henriette Jaspers forwarded the information that they had received in a telegram of Enno's having been wounded.[34] His mother read the telegram as a stroke of good fortune, summing up Enno's news as the best they could have hoped for: 'We are quite happy. How easily the shot could have hit his head!'[35]

Several detailed letters passed between Heidelberg and Cologne, where Enno was sent for an operation on his leg, as Karl informed Enno about the likely medical consequences. The treatment was a success.[36] But Enno's convalescence lasted for several months; and the war was more or less over for him. The concern for Enno's recovery meant that a number of issues went unnoticed: Enno found little contentment in civilian life, for he was unable to succeed in any area where he could gain social esteem; and, moreover, he seemed not to be able to sustain any relationship, bound by legal or contractual terms, whether of a personal or professional nature.

A first sign of Enno's predicament was his careless use of money that Jaspers estimated led him to borrow a total of 1,600 Marks, half of the sum from himself and his sister. He concluded: 'As long as there is war, we cannot refuse him. When he is facing death a man must decide for himself what is right.'[37] In peacetime, however, the family's attitude was different. Enno re-established his career as a lawyer and worked for a year with a respectable local firm. After his father's retirement in 1921, he progressed to a co-directorship in his father's bank, from January 1922, until the end of 1925.[38] But even Karl Jaspers senior's reputation as a prudent banker could not save Enno from the collapse of his first joint venture in Spring 1926. Enno's association with a Dutch company, Indag, (the Industrielle Disconto-Aktiengesellschaft) had encouraged him to retain only temporary employment at the bank, in order to establish himself as a high-flying businessman.[39] By early 1926, Enno was living in Berlin where he occupied a spacious apartment in the leafy Dahlem district and he had acquired a new fiancée from the landed gentry. Countess Charlotte von Arnim, a 31-year-old divorcee was apparently well matched with Enno in terms of experience and also met with Enno's hopes for a prosperous future.[40] Enno's parents' approval was restrained and during a visit to Berlin, Henriette Jaspers by no means appeared certain that Enno's new and second engagement would be sealed in marriage.[41] Within a month of announcing this engagement, Enno's marriage prospects deteriorated when he was hounded by debt. The size of his debt perhaps reflected the instability of the economy in the 1920s. (After hyperinflation and the Stresemann re-negotiation of reparations under the terms of the Versailles Treaty, the situation in Germany stabilized.) Nevertheless, Enno's negotiations to purchase shares, to the tune of 14,000 Marks, seem to have been based on an overoptimistic assessment of Indag's likely returns.[42] Enno's deal with the company was not sufficient to cover a serious debt claim, for by 1 July 1926, he planned to pay off 40,000 Marks. The debt was managed by his father's intervention when Karl Jaspers senior made 4,000 Marks available as a loan and donated another 25,000 Marks from the sale of rural property (a 'Heidehof'), with the plan to release a further 50,000 Marks during that year.[43] Apart from the financial emergency, Enno had to leave his flat in Berlin-Dahlem, selling the expensive furniture, and postponing his plans for marriage indefinitely. His hopes for recovery were such that he believed he could soon obtain a new position in a different bank and, indeed, a job offer emerged with the prospect of relocation to Weimar. The family rallied round, although a comment made by Henriette Jaspers underlines their concern and desire for prudence: 'I have told him everything so clearly, how important the money is for the family, so that Papa now said that I should no longer speak about it.'[44] Enno was given the benefit of the doubt; but without his own money, supported by his father, he was obliged to move to Göttingen, where his lifestyle was restricted to a single room in lodgings and an occasional theatre or cinema visit.[45]

Upon returning to Heidelberg, in late September 1926, after several weeks convalescing on the island of Wangerooge after a serious health scare, Jaspers sent his parents a thirteen-page report on Enno that he posted from Cassel. Jaspers' highly analytical account was laced with direct quotations from Enno's conversations that may be taken out of context, since this letter can read as a series of maxims, making it possible to appreciate Enno's reckless attitude to money, but to see, too, his depressive state of mind. The essential factor of Jaspers' account, on page eleven, emerged in a telling example of Enno's attitude to money:

> Enno is complaining about too little money.
>
> I: 'But Papa is paying special expenses, like travel; and for living costs the money must be sufficient.'
>
> Enno: 'For that, I also travel in a noble fashion. In Weimar, I stayed in the best hotel.' To my astonishment, he replied: 'Yes, but that is necessary. If the people were to notice that I have no money at all, then everything is finished. If they happen to ask after my hotel, or even send me into a hotel, then it must be first class.'[46]

The analysis leaves little doubt about the brothers' differences over money. Nonetheless, Jaspers could not help adding that he felt sympathy for Enno's case and he emphasized that his brother's comments were not to be taken as his basic attitude towards life: 'However, these phrases are confidential. On the whole, he speaks objectively, sensibly – you hardly notice that phantasy, when you devote yourself to Enno in conversation.' Jaspers also showed his particular concern that the family could alienate Enno. On the penultimate page of his report, he described a disconcerting aspect of Enno's behaviour:

> I have no other need than to love Enno. Yet I also fear not only for, but of him. He cannot do anything with himself and is seized by a greed for

entertainment, activity and adventure that are only to be satisfied with financial means that are considerable. All childishness, good nature and lack of formality is, as I must see Enno, shot through with a ceaseless and egocentric striving for money for consumption, not for money as a foundation for living and for the future, but simply for money that he calls 'dirt'.

Jaspers' half-ventured suspicion that something significant was happening in Enno's life was reflected in Enno's unnatural optimism about new projects: 'I feel myself in mind and body so fit and capable of achieving as I have never done in recent years. And this feeling of strength at least gives me confidence, without my being able to rest such confidence in concrete things.'[47]

By the end of November 1926, Enno's hopes for a career in finance were set aside in favour of his becoming a lawyer in Hamburg. The possible causes of Enno's mood swings transpired in a confession that he took cocaine. His mother knew about the affair and had decided to conceal it from his father and uncle, Theodor Tantzen.[48] As the family's concern grew, in the final six months before Enno's death, he underlined how he had overcome his habit with repeated denials to Jaspers' requests for honest information.[49] Enno's procrastinations about his actual financial position caused Jaspers to write him pleading letters in which he laid out the family's case for no longer rescuing Enno from his difficulties as they had in 1926.[50] Jaspers offered to refer his brother to the clinic of psychiatry, on condition that his brother authorize him to help and agree to the process of treatment for his addiction. If necessary, Jaspers offered to finance his brother's recovery in a guesthouse in a rural environment, to avoid his money being used to purchase more cocaine.

In early February 1931, Enno was in dire financial straits. He requested help from Erna for an additional 4,000 Marks to be forwarded to an unnamed lady, together with a further 2,000 Marks for down payment before 2 March, information that led Jaspers to take the matter into his own hands, writing to his sister that he thought they should refuse the 2,000 Marks, but should provide, in the meantime, 50 Marks to be supplemented by an additional three payments of the same amount. Such payments were to ensure that Enno did not descend into starvation and that he could continue to run his practice in Hamburg: 'Enno will declare his whole life long that, whatever happens, it is always us who are guilty of ruining his glowing prospects. That ought not to provoke us.'[51] If Jaspers' instructions appeared harsh, his actions followed an entire year of attempts to extract accurate information about Enno's lifestyle.

On 8 March 1931, a telegram arrived in Heidelberg. The day beforehand, Enno had poisoned himself:

Oldenburg, 8/3/31

Our dear Enno, yesterday evening at 10 o'clock, was gently laid to rest, without a fight, at his own will. He had been here since Thursday night. You must not come because of your health, a cold East wind and lots of influenza. I will write at length today. We are quite calm. We are coming to see you in May. Papa Mother.[52]

In a letter to her youngest sister, Anna Heddewig, Henriette Jaspers described her sense of relief at Enno's return to the family home, a gesture that enabled her to reconcile herself to his action, by watching over him for several hours in a way that earned Enno's thanks.[53] The only visible sign of Enno's torment was an embittered and faintly melodramatic letter that he left for his brother.

Oldenburg, 8. III. 31

Dear Kally!

[…] So I am at an end. At the moment, I am making use of the powder that I once mentioned to you I have in my possession. The 'family' will later reconsider its position, look seriously and be genuinely shattered, and will admit that all 'guilt' is on my side, that all family members wanted the best etc. And in the end the old farmer's instinct that covets gold can only discover: the man is dead; the ducats are saved.

Fare well.

Your

Enno[54]

It is difficult to separate Enno's fate from the aftermath of the First World War whose effects took their toll on his health and meant that he bequeathed an estate of sizeable debt that was managed by Erna's husband, Eugen Dugend.[55] Jaspers was powerless to act. He was unable to attend his brother's funeral because of his mother's fears for his health and consoled only by Gertrud's presence on his behalf. Several days after the funeral, in the company of Eugen Dugend, Gertrud attended a memorial service for Enno and wrote to Jaspers how closely she had watched over his brother's final resting place: 'I thought: "You are dust and to dust you return." [...] And somehow he feels perhaps <u>accepting</u> that our picture of him is transfigured.'[56]

PART III

Artistic Associations

There is something infinite in painting – I cannot explain
it to you so well – but it is so delightful just for
expressing one's feelings. There are hidden harmonies or
contrasts in colours which involuntarily combine to
work together and which could not possibly be used in
another way.

Vincent van Gogh[1]

9 'Ordinarius' in Heidelberg

DEPRESSION, INSTABILITY AND CRISIS coincided with Jaspers' climb to fame in the university. By April 1917, the United States of America had entered the First World War and as the domestic situation in Germany deteriorated, food shortages became severe.[2] A formal resolution of Jaspers' academic position had already occurred the year before war broke out, when the success of Jaspers' first book paved the way to his appointment as an unpaid lecturer in psychology. The regulations concerning this matter allowed for Jaspers' *General Psychopathology* (1913) to be accepted as the *Habilitation* or professorial thesis for psychology.[3] This meant that Jaspers qualified to lecture in the philosophy faculty, even though he was a doctor of medicine. By a twist of fate, his *Habilitation* was registered as qualifying him to teach philosophy.[4] The Dean of the philosophy faculty, Professor Carl Neumann, informed the education ministry in Karlsruhe that Jaspers' qualification was for psychology, with his appointment, alone, being in the faculty of philosophy.[5] To honour the terms of his appointment, before his promotion to an associate professorship (*Extraordinarius*), Jaspers advertised lectures in psychology. In reality, however, he began an intensive programme of research in philosophy.

In one sense, Jaspers' application for an associate professorship in 1916 was already premature. It was considered unorthodox in ministerial circles for lecturers to apply for promotion before gaining at least six years' experience.[6] If Jaspers' promotion were approved, he could overtake other candidates in his field, and thus, he could become a full professor faster than the system allowed. By November 1916, Jaspers' promotion from unpaid lecturer to associate professor was definite. His contract was to teach, one two-hourly lecture course in psychology each semester. This position carried a weekly teaching fee of 200 Marks, but Jaspers was now eligible to be considered for a full professorship.[7]As if to reflect this wider aim, the focus of his lectures gently shifted from 'the psychology of religion' (in the winter semester, 1916–17) and the 'psychology of world visions' (summer semester, 1917) to seminars on Kierkegaard and Nietzsche (winter and summer semesters, 1918). These lectures were supported by Jaspers' systematic studies of Hegel and Nietzsche, begun in early 1915. If his encounter with the classical works of German philosophy appeared to follow rather late in the day, it has to be seen in the context of his beginning to concentrate, with greater determination, on philosophical as opposed to strictly psychological sources.[8] Jaspers' book provided the evidence of his capacity to digest and order a wide variety of sources, for his 'Psychology of World Visions' (1919) contained continual references to the poets, Goethe and Schiller, as though their works were used to put the German Idealist tradition in perspective. The poetry placed Jaspers' sweeping survey of different periods of experience and knowledge in the context of a tradition from Kierkegaard and Nietzsche, but if he described the outcome as 'prophetic philosophy',[9] he knew that the daily experiences of his readership were far removed from the humanitarian ideals of man in harmony with nature. At that time, the political situation in Germany was such that the quality of life dramatically deteriorated.

A slight delay between the timing of Jaspers' lectures and the publication of his book may have obscured the fact that this book especially represented a bright view of scientific tradition, even though the ethos of this work appeared difficult to distinguish from the air of consternation about Germany's future. Jaspers agreed with Max Weber that the good of the country was hardly served by prolonging Germany's image as a military aggressor. If his private comments on politics were coloured by the rhetoric of war, his concern, in solidarity with his brother, was with the timing and conditions of peace:

Heidelberg, 12/7/17

Dear parents,

    [...] Grand politics is not exactly encouraging. It is clear that the idea of 'forcing England to her knees' is ridiculous. A status-quo peace is the only solution. If the government says that openly, as Erzberger wants, <u>perhaps</u> that can mean something to enemy nations. Unfortunately, the matter is only poised so that they will find other reasons to beat us into submission. Yet an attempt has to be made soon with the formula: 'no annexations', at least, so say the instincts of a growing number of people and you cannot claim they have lost their nerve. We have to have peace, no matter how. Enno is now of this opinion as well, even if he adds, quite rightly, that we cannot form an opinion based on knowledge of the actual situation.

    Fond greetings,

    Your Kally[10]

Jaspers was reflecting the mood for peace that was circulating in the German Reichstag by July 1917. A politician of the catholic Centre Party, Matthias Erzberger, was amongst the first openly to criticize the government policy of unlimited submarine warfare. The confusion over the politicians' ability to construct an agreement that boosted the country's morale yet without losing face to the outside world was clear when the German Chancellor, Bethmann-Hollweg, was voted out of office because of his support for peace. If Germany were to escape defeat by 'enemy' powers, as Jaspers' letter implied, it was clear that everyone would be utterly demoralized by the harshness of the peace conditions. Jaspers reflected upon his chance to air his opinions when he recounted his experiences at the political club, shortly before the appointment of the new Chancellor, Prince Max von Baden on 3 October 1918:

Heidelberg, 8 October 1918

Dear parents,

    […] On Tuesday, two days before Prince Max took office, we held our political evening. I proposed the possible alternative: either to accept Wilson's 14 Points (that means giving up Alsace-Lorraine, or at least the chance of losing it). If the offer is accepted we save our existence. Or: the offer is refused; then we would need all the strength we still possess and a battle <u>can</u> perhaps still save us, precisely because we did our utmost beforehand to offer peace. At that, a storm of indignation rose against me. 'A peace offer now would be a mistake. A refusal would completely ruin morale. Our chances were not nearly half as bad, etc.' A few days later, when everything turned out just as I suggested, I thought it seemed strange. I can hardly wait to see what

these national-liberal supporters have to say next time. Now they will surely find everything in order and perfectly natural. [...]
    Fond greetings,
    Your Kally[11]

Another cause for concern, especially for liberal intellectuals, among whom Jaspers may be counted, was the general fear of an uprising in Germany like the 1917 October Revolution in Russia.[12] A radical wing that broke with the Social Democratic Party, for which Jaspers confessed to his father that he had voted in 1912 in preference to the National Liberals,[13] had split itself into a group of activists and formed the German Communist Party on 31 December 1918. The leaders of this group, Karl Liebknecht and Rosa Luxemburg, promoted the idea of workers' direct action even before the war had ended. The presence of a new mood that their so-called Spartacus Group reflected was felt in Berlin when the Spartacists' call for a general strike to commence on 11 November 1918 actually plunged the German capital into chaos. The proclamation by Philipp Scheidemann, from the window of the German Reichstag building in Berlin on 9 November 1918, of the end of the monarchy forced Kaiser Wilhelm II to abdicate and flee to Holland.[14] Scheidemann's declaration of the republic enabled the Social Democrats to restore stability at a time when the country could have been on the brink of Communist revolution.[15] The Spartacists had already formed an alliance with the Leninist, Karl Radek, so that fears of a Communist uprising were not exaggerated. This concern was confirmed by the experiences of Gertrud's eldest brother, Gustav Mayer, whose private residence in Berlin's Zehlendorf district was stormed in a midnight raid by a unit of government soldiers, searching for Radek himself.

An army officer posing as a member of the Spartacists sought to befriend Mayer, who admitted that he had contacts with Radek. The officer, Wendland, who arranged to lodge for the night in Mayer's house, proved to be connected to the raid. Gertrud was implicated in the episode. Hours before the raid had occurred, her brother had been dictating a letter to her that his wife, Flora, was writing down when Wendland had interrupted them. Gertrud recorded the event in an animated letter to her parents-in-law:

[Prenzlau], 9. II. 19

Dear parents,
    [...] In the middle of the night, at 3 o'clock, the maid was awoken by loud knocking at the front door. As she could not find the keys so

quickly, she went to the veranda and asked what was the matter. Soldiers shouted up to her to open the door at once, or else they would hammer the doors down. She went to Wendland's door and found him, together with his friend, fully dressed and now they began to shout at her rudely. Instead of waiting for the key, the soldiers used clubs to bash down the entrance door and the front door. About 20 or 30 soldiers with hand grenades and revolvers stormed into all the rooms, smashed all the panes in the glass doors, etc. They held a revolver to my brother and sister-in-law, who had hurriedly dressed and stood freezing, and they kept on shouting: 'Radek is hiding here, we want him, tell us where he is.' They would not believe my brother's explanations. [...] Whilst they separated husband and wife and searched the house, they seized, as incriminating material, a piece of paper from my brother's papers on which the name 'Liebknecht' was written. Of course, it was the father, Wilhelm Liebknecht, which the ignorant leaders did not know and they claimed my picture – the one that is pinned near Kally's sick bed was a picture of Rosa Luxemburg. It was no use explaining. Even the children were not spared and the search continued under their beds with revolvers, etc., looking for Radek. They did say, though, that the children were not to be afraid. [...] Finally, they found the letter that was being written to me that evening and wanted to read it. My brother refused and said he would show it to the judge but not to this mob of saboteurs. [...] But that is enough.

Fond greetings,
Your Gertrud[16]

The material damage to Gustav Mayer's property was one thing. The shock and sheer audacity of the break-in, as Gertrud reflected it, was another. Amidst this upheaval, Jaspers' personal fortunes began to improve, since the chance to influence public attitudes on all manner of subjects fell his way.

The positive echo to his lectures continued, even after the interest in his inaugural lecture at the end of 1913 had died down.[17] Nonetheless, a disproportionate quota of female students, as reported on by Gertrud, continued to participate in Jaspers' seminars which Gertrud and Marianne Weber also attended.[18] Jaspers' popularity as a lecturer was not to be dissociated from his role as an educator. A change in his lecture style reflected his growing confidence, especially after the publication of his second book:

> I have <u>tried</u> to introduce a big change to my lecture style, that is, on the morning before the lecture I immerse myself in the subject of the lecture, then I speak freely and the progression of my thoughts largely depends on the moment, so I can turn my attention more immediately to the listener. In that way, the lecture becomes a lot livelier, but it is also more binding [?] to the word; and my audience seems much more attentive than it was before. The hall continued to fill up during the first weeks and I can be quite satisfied with the attendance. However, I do not know how effective I am.[19]

Perhaps the experiment with a free lecture style, developing a thought, word for word, led Jaspers to contemplate writing another short book on ethics that was to have contained his thoughts on the final questions of life, 'as though, in the work, I could express my better self, as a measure of how little I am worth'.[20] This later plan was never carried out, but it seems to have coincided with Jaspers' humanist ideal to strive for rank, not as a personal goal, but as a sign of a flourishing education system. A professor in a system of 'Ordinarien' was effectively an ambassador in Humboldt's sense, according to whom educators were empowered not just to serve the community like knowledgeable diplomats, but to contribute, with a sense of honour, to something enduring, noble and greater than the individual self. The desire for public notoriety, or the need to strive for distinction in the eyes of his colleagues may not be entirely discounted from Jaspers' ambitions, since he was perceived by those who remembered him as an over-zealous guardian of rank and, moreover, as one who jealously protected personal authority.[21] Yet such literal deference to status could also be a by-product of a system that perpetuated the belief in professors as 'aristocrats' and, as such, as individuals who were necessarily to be distinguished from the crowd by virtue of their station. As a student, Jaspers rarely showed unquestioning reverence towards some of his professors. Authority, élitism, aristocracy may be connected to a literal interpretation of Humboldt's system, but Jaspers accepted the humanitarian tradition in order to promote the diverse interests of teachers and students that he believed were to be free of manipulation and to enhance creativity, originality and equality of learning.[22]

Meanwhile, the challenge of lecturing in unheated auditoriums and the increasing food shortages directly affected him when he was struck down by a progression of the bronchiectasis that obliged him to recuperate from malnutrition.[23] As the economic climate deteriorated and inflation increased, Jaspers decided to turn whatever additional income he derived from stocks and shares – managed mainly upon his father's advice – into a longer term invest-ment: namely, he would protect his earnings from depreciating share values and government efforts to finance the war by investing in books.[24] A bequest of his uncle, Fritz Jaspers, who died at the end of December 1917 leaving a personal fortune of around 300,000 Marks, was, however, not available until 1918.[25] Jaspers' father offered to support the book acquisitions; and he contributed 2,000 Marks for the purpose.[26]

The family involvement in the acquisition of Jaspers' personal library was gradually reflected in the type of his book orders. Whereas he first restricted his acquisitions to standard editions of Fichte, Hegel and Schelling,[27] he decided to order more valuable and expensive books from his wife's cousin, Paul Gottschalk. Nearly a decade before the war broke out, Paul Gottschalk had the good fortune to locate his business in America and, even after the outbreak of war, he attracted major orders from Yale, Princeton and other American university libraries.[28] Gottschalk's antique book-selling business continued to flourish during the war so that Jaspers' father was instructed to settle the bills through the Disconto-Gesellschaft, one of the major German banks that was then located in the same place that Gottschalk chose for his bookshop, Unter den Linden in the heart of Berlin.[29] Although the book acquisitions were also looked upon as a reference library for Jaspers in case his health were to prevent him from leaving the confines of his own four walls, the library became a family heirloom and, by September 1917, he estimated that it was too valuable to put a price on.[30]

The acquisition of this library more or less coincided with the pace of Jaspers' promotion. His chances of success improved, too, in line with the fortunes of his second book. From 1 April 1920, as successor to Hans Driesch, Jaspers was appointed to an officially planned professorship (*etatmäßiges Extraordinariat*) for philosophy.[31] For the first time, his position guaranteed an annual salary of 3,900 Marks.[32] Gertrud hinted to her parents-in-law that now they felt financially secure.[33] At the time, she calculated that, given the financial instability of the country as a whole, their situation could hardly be expected to improve, even if Jaspers were to soar to the pinnacle of his career prospects like a 'professor, remote from the world in his robe of success'.[34] Gertrud's classic understatement of their hopes for the future revealed how keenly they anticipated Jaspers' promotion once the war ended. However, it was impossible to predict when that promotion might be. The process of obtaining a professorship depended on offers arriving from other universities. Again, Gertrud speculated that if such an offer, a *Ruf,* were forthcoming, they could hardly depend upon the state of Baden's education authority matching a promotion from outside their region.[35] If Jaspers were successful, he would most likely be obliged to leave Heidelberg.

When Heinrich Rickert published a learned review of Jaspers' 'Psychology of World Visions' (1919) in the well-known journal *Logos*,[36] Jaspers could hardly conceal his delight. To his parents, he confessed that the prospect of Rickert's review being seen as an inverted compliment for his achievement was a boost for his work: 'He [Rickert] felt himself, indirectly, in his philosophical existence very much in question in my book. And this criticism is meant to show that, in principle, I am completely wrong. […] Rickert's pupils see it as a sign of highest recognition that Rickert devotes a whole essay to me, as he has never extended that honour to any book before. For the moment though, the result is meant to be destructive!'[37] Jaspers was inclined to feel gratitude for Rickert's attention, since although he regarded Rickert's review as prejudicial, the review highlighted the difficulty of an objective analysis of what Jaspers meant by the concept of 'world vision'.[38] Privately, Jaspers also seemed irritated that Rickert's critique might have jeopardized his chances of promotion. After a year waiting in suspense, he confessed to his parents that he felt 'justified' in expecting a position to emerge in Heidelberg.[39]

By early January 1921, the first edition of Jaspers' second book had almost sold out.[40] Jaspers was eager to make 'stylistic' changes to a new, second edition, although he had no plans to revise the content.[41] In early spring 1921, Jaspers received a *Ruf* from the University of Kiel and, shortly afterwards, from Greifswald University. Two offers of promotion in rapid succession increased the likelihood of a vacancy being made available in Heidelberg. Jaspers recalled that his friend and ally, Dr Fraenkel, had persuaded him to steer his own path to success. In Dr Fraenkel's view, Jaspers would do well to advertise to his Heidelberg colleagues his positive reaction to the climate in Kiel that was not so damaging to his health as they perhaps imagined.[42] A confidential note from Gertrud to her parents-in-law revealed how considerable advantage was derived from the convenient timing of Jaspers' promotion offers. Towards the end of May 1921, Gertrud mentioned the outcome of their unofficial visit to Berlin where Jaspers had been told by education ministry officials handling his case that if he were to accept the position, his professorship in Kiel was definite.[43] Gertrud's desire to remain in Heidelberg merely increased but Jaspers was more positive: 'I was received with great respect in Berlin. They obviously want to win me and have a curiously high opinion of me. The "intrigue" has apparently done no harm. If I now give a sign that I want to go to Kiel, then I will receive the "*Ruf*" to go at once.'[44]

All the same, the timing of Jaspers' response had to be carefully managed.

On 8 June 1921, Jaspers wrote to the Dean of Faculty in Heidelberg to inform him of his *Ruf* from Kiel, – just as he claimed the official news arrived of his appointment in Greifswald.[45] The tactics worked in his favour. At the end of June 1921, Heidelberg's *Ruf* materialized. Jaspers was awarded a personal chair in philosophy at Heidelberg University from 14 October 1921, as successor to Heinrich Maier.[46] His appointment as an 'Ordinarius' for philosophy came into effect on 1 April 1922.[47] The relative speed of Jaspers' advancement from an unpaid lecturer in psychology to a personal professorship in philosophy sprang from the opportunities at his disposal to communicate with many like-minded and differently disposed individuals. His career was also advanced by privileged access to Max Weber. Equally, his friendship with Ernst Mayer and his membership of various groups – the political club, the informal, so-called 'metaphysical evenings' – had been platforms for Jaspers to rehearse his rapidly evolving ideas that were later to be reflected in his philosophy.[48]

10   *Paris, Sicily and Vincent van Gogh*

A PROFESSORSHIP AT HEIDELBERG UNIVERSITY was not enough to record as a lifetime's achievement so far as Gertrud was concerned. With Jaspers' reputation in mind, she planned a study tour of Sicily and commented to her parents-in-law: 'A philosopher in modern times has to stay alive and not freeze in the narrow world of an armchair existence.'[1]

Jaspers was at a distinct disadvantage, for his illness made contact with foreign lands and cultures difficult to organize. The assistance of Paul and Julia Gottschalk enabled Gertrud to persuade him to go to Sicily. The touring party met in Munich on 19 March 1922.[2] The journey ended in early May, so that prior arrangements were necessary for a delayed start to the summer semester, but with the security of his professorship in Heidelberg, Jaspers could now afford to apply for a week's study leave.[3] In Naples, Paul Gottschalk was to have arranged an appointment with the Italian philosopher Benedetto Croce. If Jaspers' interview with Croce came about, no record of their meeting survives.[4] Jaspers was, however, at ease with the thought of a *Ruf* from Naples University: 'I feel unbelievably well here and I would – if there were such a thing – immediately accept a "*Ruf*" to Naples – or perhaps rather not?'[5]

Jaspers' letters from Sicily illuminated why Gertrud enticed him away from Heidelberg. Their study tour highlighted the benefits of stimulating even the most contemplative of minds by the kind of activity that comes from seeing things for oneself. At this stage in his life Jaspers' appreciation of his own ambitions as a philosopher was coming to light. Indeed, he already felt as if he could achieve something new after his speech at the political club in 1917 which had demonstrated his ability to project ideas beyond their historical contexts, a feature of the densely illustrated 'Psychology of World Visions' (1919).

At the same time, Jaspers was able to translate his systematic approach into what he called 'understanding psychology.' For several years before his second book was published, his wish was to develop his project, 'understanding psychology', into a philosophically engaging piece. The ambivalent nature of this project points to an earlier fragment in his 1905 Göttingen diary about Nietzsche's rank as a psychologist. Whilst he was training as a medical student, Jaspers had pondered the meaning of Nietzsche's visionary figure of Zarathustra. Although the diary note hardly compares to Jaspers' mature thinking about Nietzsche in the early 1930s, Jaspers' essentially 'anti-psychological, attitude to *Thus Spoke Zarathustra* in the context of his own work in this period is noteworthy. His diary reads as follows:

27/28. 1. 05

I recently read Nietzsche's 'Zarathustra'. The book left me completely astonished; after all the complaints about Nietzsche, I was not expecting much and I was highly surprised to read a glowing, and in every detail, a significant achievement by a great poet. The poetic effect struck me more than anything else; the wonderful pictures and visions that are described in such a wonderfully fine way so that every word has its great meaning: I felt mightily impressed. The purely philosophical content, as far as it is possible to base a judgement in terms of comprehension, is not of great importance to anyone who is not of an intelligent frame of mind; all judgements are sure to be heavily one-sided, but if you do not consider them as statements of absolute truth, but rather as an expression of specific emotional states, you will find them to be of great meaning. Nietzsche seems to me to be a great psychologist, his pure descriptions of psychological conditions and processes are very accurate and moving and even in those statements that seem to be most incorrect, I find confirmation for Lipps's intuitions about the individual's striving for release and for self-perfection.[6]

A subtle shift of focus between psychology and philosophy, as exemplified in Jaspers' youthful and enthusiastic response to Nietzsche's *Thus Spoke Zarathustra*, strikes a chord with the pattern of a transition in Jaspers' work that became evident when he published a pathography of *Strindberg and van Gogh* (1922) that first appeared in a series of psychiatric papers. This book was one of the few works that Jaspers published after his promotion to a full professorship. The question as to why he chose to publish such a psychiatric portrait of August Strindberg and Vincent van Gogh is particularly interesting, considering that his critical appreciation of an artist's perception of reality was restricted professionally to his training in medicine, his knowledge of psychiatry and his experience as a lecturer in psychology. That question can be clarified to a degree by noting the nature of his experiences in Sicily.

Indeed, it might be said of Jaspers' descriptions that his time in Sicily approached the sublime. Nature, as it intercedes in the text of Jaspers' undated picture postcard from Syracuse, provided an instance of an unchanging force of time against which the universe seemed imprinted ever more vividly upon his imagination:[7]

> Dear parents,
>
> Fond wishes will have to suffice for the moment. We are using every hour of our short time. In warm sunlight, with a pleasant breeze, under lemons and mango fruits, everywhere numerous lizards, the clearest air, the stars quite bright as near to the horizon as you can see – and in all this, the magnificent antique ruins of this city where Plato wanted to establish his philosophy – it is so beautiful that you grow quite still. Tomorrow, on to Taormina, then to Girgenti, then Palermo. A card can reach us there.
>
> Fondest greetings,
> Your K.[8]

After Syracuse, if not before, a release from everyday concerns occurred and the journey seems to have precipitated a change of mood. It was not, however, the source of the same sort of spiritual renewal as in his younger days in Sils Maria. This journey was, rather, a reminder of his purpose as a thinker, and he renewed a conviction that it was important not to be bound by transforming personal experiences into mirror images reflected in thoughts, but to release the abstract character of thought through inner action and to strive to suspend, if possible, categories of time.

Jaspers' study tour was a taste of freedom, as he confided to his parents.

His experience was in proportion to his ability to see beyond his lifelong predicament: 'It is true that what is actually impossible – for me, as an ill person, to travel about like this can now be made possible.'[9] This level of experiencing freedom of thought and action was also a focus of Jaspers' monograph *Strindberg and van Gogh* (1922). He remained decidedly hostile towards August Strindberg, in particular, because of the delusions that he had identified as underlying the breakdown of Strindberg's marriages.[10] In the case of van Gogh, however, Jaspers became obsessed with the paintings that undoubtedly appealed to his appreciation of simplicity and honesty. His analysis of Strindberg and van Gogh and, to a lesser extent, the poet, Friedrich Hölderlin, was virtually unprecedented.[11] Already, as he had laboured over the manuscript of *General Psychopathology* (1913), Jaspers had pondered the case of Vincent van Gogh. His firm belief in the psychiatrist as a humanist had been paralleled by a scrupulous regard for van Gogh's artworks, a sense of esteem even, which struck a chord with his interest in the descriptive powers at the psychiatrist's disposal. Jaspers' problem was not to determine whether a psychiatrist's powers of interpretation were sufficient to visualize causes of psychopathological disorder, but whether such powers were adequate to establish a method of understanding the complexities of specific cases. That philosophical matter was precisely what troubled him when he first saw van Gogh's paintings at an exhibition in Bremen, around Christmas 1911.[12] Perhaps, the selection of approximately fifty paintings by van Gogh that Jaspers then saw was a reason why he took a direct interest in the work of the Impressionists. At any rate, he had interrupted his work on the manuscript of *General Psychopathology* in order to visit Paris; and together with Gertrud, he arrived for a first stay in this city in spring 1912.[13]

Their visit to Paris turned into an information-gathering exercise on what Jaspers called the 'new style of French painting', or Impressionism.[14] In the Louvre, they had hardly discovered any paintings by the Impressionists. Jaspers' comments on nineteenth-century French salon painting proved that he was baffled by this particular selection of art: 'I do not know what forms the impressive quality. Delicate colours, gracefulness on the one hand, cool objectivity on the other, these are not enough.'[15] At the museum in the Jardin du Luxembourg, they found the paintings they had hoped to see:

> After searching for a long time amongst boring, academic paintings,
> we at last found the hall with the Impressionists: Manet, Monet,
> Pissarro, Renoir, Sisley. This tasteful and very objective style of

painting is not close to us, although we had a meaningful insight and we greatly admired the work. The whole genre of modern art in Germany – the Secessionists, Liebermann etc. take their inspiration from this style – so they say.[16]

During a privately arranged visit to the Durand-Ruel collection (Durand-Ruel was a Paris art dealer who had briefly tried to sell ten van Gogh paintings before the turn of the century), they perused at leisure the Impressionist paintings.[17] Jaspers made no specific reference to any work by van Gogh. As he explained to Erna, they found the paintings they had seen not to their liking: 'Everything is purely aesthetic, tasteful, artistically moving, even if an idea (I mean a deep feeling, not a thought) is effective in all of that, it does not actually come anywhere near to our feelings.'[18] Towards the end of September 1912, however, Jaspers' quest to see the 'new style' of painting that truly moved them was rewarded. Almost at the end of its run, Jaspers visited the International Art Exhibition in Cologne.[19] The question that presented itself about descriptive capacities in his psychiatric work was no longer academic; it had captured his imagination.

The phenomenon of van Gogh's art inspired Jaspers with all the passionate intensity of a serious artlover. At the Cologne exhibition, he viewed a cross-section of Expressionist paintings. He saw works by artists living at the time, as well as a retrospective on the 'controversial artwork' by Vincent van Gogh, Paul Cézanne and Paul Gauguin.[20] The works on show were owned and donated by 'German, Swiss, Hungarian and above all Dutch collectors' and the paintings included, as the exhibition catalogue boasted, 'over one hundred paintings alone by that great Dutchman, whom we proudly count amongst our race and whose works form the centrepiece of the exhibition.'[21] Van Gogh's paintings attracted Jaspers like a magnet. He saw numerous early sketches, *The Potato Eaters*, the later landscape paintings and still lifes, paintings representing van Gogh's interest in Japanese prints, and numerous self-portraits and figures. In total, Jaspers had the opportunity to view 108 paintings by van Gogh in the same location.

Amongst one of the earliest exhibitions of van Gogh's works in Germany was that organized by Paul Cassirer, managing director of the Berlin Secession from 1901, and brainchild of the third Secession exhibition in May 1901, when five van Goghs were exhibited.[22] The Cologne exhibition that Jaspers attended in 1912 was one of the first comprehensive collections of van Gogh's paintings to be shown in Germany, after the major Amsterdam exhibition of van Gogh's work in 1905. In Cologne, Jaspers took detailed notes about many of the

paintings that he later used as supplementary material for his pathography –
when he visited the exhibition, van Gogh's correspondence with his brother
was not yet published.[23] When the letters were published, Jaspers could
compare his notes with van Gogh's correspondence. In that way, he identified
a rudimentary transition in the paintings he had seen. He still ruefully
complained about the inadequacy of the materials at his disposal.[24] Despite his
avowed lack of expertise, he presented in his book his ideas on van Gogh's art
as a surprisingly tolerant critic:

> The Philistine habit of using the term *ill* in a derogatory manner or of
> considering its entry into the association of ideas as something
> lowbrow blinds a person to a reality which we can grasp today only
> casuistically and which we are not at all able to interpret. Indeed, its
> formulation causes us difficulties, presumably because we are caught
> up in limited categories of evaluation, and in an intellect which still
> keeps us bound, while we feel that it will resolve itself in favour of one
> which is more all-embracing, freer and more flexible.[25]

Van Gogh's paintings were neither cast aside as decadent, nor was the artist
branded as a corrupter of morality. His style of painting was said by Jaspers to
open up new vistas that were unheard of, unknown, and perhaps hitherto
unseen. The paintings were to be viewed as a potential liberation from narrow-
minded horizons of the well-to-do and thoughtless middle class. Jaspers
wanted to use the pictures as some sort of ideal image to describe pathological
cases at a level at which the descriptions would be taken seriously. Van Gogh's
art opened up new vistas on the disposition of artists and creative thinkers, and
Jaspers' purpose was to discover something unique and irreplaceable through
the medium of these paintings. He needed to determine how van Gogh
brought the subjects of his art to life. With his basic knowledge of drawing
technique, he recognized, in particular aspects of van Gogh's handiwork – the
brushwork and use of colour – visible traces of something that he now saw as
synonymous with van Gogh's style. The 1888 crisis, when van Gogh moved out
of the *maison d'artiste* that he shared with Gauguin in order to recover in the
sanatorium in Arles was a period of heightened creativity, a period that Jaspers
compared to the artist's nervous affliction that he, characteristically, hesitated
to name as schizophrenia.[26] During this period, van Gogh produced his most
famous paintings. Amongst the exhibits that caught Jaspers' eye were, for
example, *Wheatfield with Reaper*.[27] Jaspers was fascinated by the deterioration
of brushstrokes that produced an increasingly irregular pattern of curves on

the canvas.[28] What was new in this, as in many paintings of the period, was van Gogh's ability to permit something to exist through the sheer expression itself. The 'Expressionism' that Jaspers discovered was neither a fabrication of art, nor a gesture of abstract thought.

Van Gogh's painting anticipated a gesture that Jaspers strove to articulate and he discovered an astonishing influence in van Gogh's artworks that was of interest for his own work:

> It is as if a last wellhead of life should fleetingly come within sight, as if the hidden 'Whys' of all life had found here an immediate basis on which to resolve themselves. For us, this is an emotional trauma which we could not endure for long, upon which we would gladly turn our backs, and which we find for a moment relaxed in some of van Gogh's great works, although we cannot endure this either for a long time. It is a trauma which does not easily lead to the assimilation of what is foreign, but which demands the transposition into a different form, which is acceptable to us. His world is terribly exciting, but it is not our world.[29]

The artist's utensils, as the only traces of his handiwork, were for Jaspers the origin of van Gogh's art. Jaspers' fascination with the brushwork and the use of colour highlighted such elements as though the tools themselves were artefacts that actively brought forth van Gogh's paintings. The artefacts were invisible. Therefore, they were a contradictory source of inspiration for what Jaspers read as van Gogh's representation of a new kind of spirituality.

In great contrast to Jaspers' response to van Gogh's paintings was that of Martin Heidegger in his later Frankfurt speech, *The Origin of the Work of Art* (1935).[30] What Heidegger had then set in motion by mention of 'peasant shoes' seemed a red herring. His work could be read as creating a mere topos or an abstracted vision of creativity that he interpreted as the 'ontological' character of truth that brought forth the essence of the painting: 'Van Gogh's painting is the disclosure of what the equipment, the pair of peasant shoes, *is* in truth.'[31] In this sense, Heidegger suggestively turned the domain of art into a theoretical field strewn with a tantalizing promise to unveil what Jaspers, as a member of the viewing public, had earlier discussed as the freedom of the artist to paint. Jaspers saw this creative freedom as a source of the 'new style' just as much as van Gogh's state of mind.[32]

Van Gogh saw a creative possibility in every form of life, yet his models were reduced neither to caricatures nor to mere topoi of the various locations where he painted. From the standpoint of the psychiatrist, an altogether different aspect of these paintings presented itself. Jaspers acknowledged this aspect as the reality of art, as a form of freedom with power to unveil a new way of seeing things. Such openness to the medium of art suggested Jaspers' ability to respond to creative originality and leave the psychiatrist's chair. Van Gogh's paintings depicted a choice not dependent upon this or that way of life but on something that Jaspers saw as reflected in the artist's experience, whose meaning he further questioned: 'Do we actually believe, surrounded by the medium of a highly intellectual culture, by our own unlimited desire for clarity, by our duty to be honest and accordingly realistic, do we believe in the genuineness of this resolving depth, in this awareness of God, only as the property of these mentally ill patients?'[33] Here was a genuine hope for the future, as if Jaspers had recognized the possibilities for his own work. During and after the 1888 crisis in van Gogh's life, the artist painted still lifes and the 'most beautiful floral paintings'.[34] For Jaspers, these paintings (see p. 108 and Ills 17–19) showed that, in a sublime sense, the human spirit was alive. This essentially spiritual vitality was translated into a painting as the domain of the artist, Vincent van Gogh, whose ability was to have elevated his subject, whether a landscape, an object, a figure, or a painting of sunflowers into the dimension of art. The subjects of van Gogh's paintings endured as 'figures', yet they were neither reduced, nor distorted by the time that elapsed until their artistic rendition was accomplished.[35] Instead, the figures retained their life-like appeal through what van Gogh called colour 'composites'.[36] Whatever the transition from concrete to abstract, or from nature to colour, the original form could be seen as it was, despite the fading presence of those observations that brought forth the transitions as art.

Although van Gogh's work was one step removed from the task of the thinker, the problems the artist experienced exposed a parallel difficulty for the thinker of how to describe an original form or conception of life without corrupting, amending or in any sense undermining the quality of what was first experienced. What van Gogh achieved by transferring his observations of life on to his canvas hardly compared with Jaspers' developing theory of *Existenz*. Yet in a certain sense, the subsequent expression of Jaspers' philosophical concepts had their own essential beauty, even though Jaspers insisted in his approach to his theoretical work that the medium of art, as with the use of colour in a painting, cannot be incorporated into the abstracted vision of life. He needed to find an alternative way to rise to the challenge of striving for inner freedom from life's predicaments:

Situations like the following: I am always caught in situations, I cannot live without conflict and suffering, I cannot avoid guilt, I must die – these are what I call 'limit situations'. They *never change*, except in appearance. There is *no way to survey them* in existence, no way to see anything behind them. They are like a wall we run into, a wall on which we founder. We cannot modify them; all that we can do is to make them lucid, but without explaining or deducing them from something else. They go with existence itself.[37]

The dimension of art that van Gogh represented in the figures of his paintings was later to be developed into Jaspers' philosophical creed. That creed was an illumination of the individual's capacities in relation to his ability to reflect on life's higher objectives and achievements. In the process of defining his approach to those objectives, Jaspers' visit to the 1912 Cologne exhibition was a profound jolt to the conscience, an unforgettable experience that showed him that it was possible to encounter something new yet not to narrow the field of his vision to a single interpretation of the novelty. The quality of the interpretation would establish whether his endeavour was to open or to restrict his work to an expression of observations – mere art criticism – or a philosophical theory of life. Jaspers believed that the manifold implications of individual experience remain intangible. That intangibility means an opportunity is lost to describe the implication of individual situations once they are directly considered with respect to terms of art. By the same token, art was an inspiration for his philosophical conception of life.[38] In particular, the simplicity of those paintings that he viewed by Vincent van Gogh was a source of the beauty and freedom that he genuinely admired.

11　*Martin Heidegger in the 1920s*

When Karl Jaspers invited Martin Heidegger to pay his first of many visits to Heidelberg, he informed Gertrud who was with her family in Prenzlau,[1] that he had sent Heidegger '1,000 Reichsmarks for travel money'.[2] The money had been Gertrud's, received as a gift from her cousin, Paul Gottschalk. In early September 1922, Heidegger arrived and Jaspers informed Gertrud that her money was being put to good use: 'We are now hard at work philosophizing'.[3] The Jaspers' generosity towards Heidegger was reflected in the personal sympathy that Jaspers felt from his younger colleague when they met for the first time in Freiburg, on the occasion of Edmund Husserl's birthday.[4] As Jaspers noticed Heidegger's support for his criticisms of authority and bureaucracy in the university, he became brightly optimistic about a friendship developing. For Jaspers, Heidegger's presence meant enjoying the companionship he had sought since student days. Yet the contact between the thinkers, formed through the compatibility of their work, became strained when Jaspers began to wonder whether he could rely upon Heidegger. Jaspers' doubts would cause relations to falter. In the heyday of the 1920s, however, the opportunities for Jaspers to talk with Heidegger were frequent. Any uncertainty in their friendship – that, with hindsight, may be detected on both sides – resulted not from a clash of ideas but of personality.[5] When Heidegger initially wrote to Jaspers to acknowledge his hospitality, the former remarked upon the 'style' of his reception in Heidelberg and how he had appreciated

Jaspers' 'prosaic' company.[6] Heidegger noted, with a hint of surprise, how friendship had stolen upon them in what he called an 'unsentimental, savoury step'[7]. Jaspers read into Heidegger's comments a glimmer of hope for their future cooperation and replied: 'In the philosophical wilderness of our time it is good to experience that we may trust in one another.'[8]

Convinced of their loyalty to each others' ambitions, Jaspers proposed a journal that he wanted to call: 'Philosophy of our Time, critical journals by Martin Heidegger and Karl Jaspers'.[9] Jaspers seemed to relish the thought of Heidegger's cooperation, for he had surprisingly esoteric ideas about their journal becoming an act of faith in the public realm. The publication, to which both were to have contributed at whim, might have attested to how alive the humanist spirit was in the Weimar period. Yet, Jaspers wanted to oppose the 'school' tradition, and he observed that once they had their fill of polemicizing against the façade of academic philosophy, they could lay the journal to rest. The only drawback was that Heidegger was not yet a full professor. In office as a full professor himself for barely half a year, Jaspers' attitude seemed rather high-handed. Heidegger, still an unpaid lecturer at Freiburg University, gained increasing popularity – as former pupils, Hannah Arendt, and Hans-Georg Gadamer, testified – because of the technical brilliance of his lectures. Less than a year after Jaspers' planning of their journal, Heidegger was promoted to an associate professorship at the University of Marburg.[10] All the same, Jaspers initially refused to entertain the thought of their names appearing together in print, until Heidegger's rank was officially clarified. In private, Jaspers jokingly mocked Heidegger's deference towards his official title: 'Now that we have long since established a "philosophical" relationship, you will surely not insist on calling me "Professor"? Or do you place so little trust in me?'[11] Perhaps, the question also applied indirectly to Jaspers, who retreated behind his title, whilst voicing doubts about the type of friendships that were possible within the university.

As an outsider in a system that prided itself on scholarly excellence, Jaspers was without a 'pupillage' to add to his name. The mixed blessing of Jaspers' scholarly freedom was his chronic lack of connections. Jaspers gained none of the potential benefits of being under the wing of a mentor, whereas Heidegger was obliged to show the gratitude that was to be expected of his associations. Jaspers was not as suspicious of Heidegger's public dedications to Rickert, Husserl or Max Scheler, as he was concerned about their sincerity.[12] The question of whether Heidegger was an opportunist, cultivating his connections by strategic dedications of his books was a sensitive issue for Jaspers, eager, no less, to see himself flanked by Heidegger, who was to have supported his polemical stance against university tradition.

Behind the scenes, Gertrud, the financier of Heidegger's first visit, was one of the keenest sponsors of this friendship. Jaspers' discussions with Heidegger gained her tacit approval. She assumed that the talents of the one were indispensable and complementary to the abilities of the other. Furthermore, she believed that if Heidegger were to see through the looking-glass of scholarship, he would find Jaspers his equal, more than able to educate him. The question whether or not, because of Heidegger's contemplative approach to thinking, he was bound to be suspect in Jaspers' eyes is a matter for speculation. Gertrud wrote: 'It is Heidegger's nature only to research with his mind on philosophy and religion. He is a scholar and a philologist, but he cannot represent anything systematically in his thought.'[13] It was she, however, who made this meeting of minds a reality. She saw their encounters go from strength to strength. Once she ceased to believe in Heidegger and withdrew her moral support, it necessarily became difficult for Jaspers to continue his friendship.

Heidegger's ability to anticipate Jaspers was never sharper than at the start of their friendship when he wrote a resounding critique of Jaspers' second book, 'Psychology of World Visions' (1919).[14] In June 1921, Heidegger personally sent Jaspers a copy of his review that arrived, rather inconveniently, at a time when Jaspers was contemplating the second edition of his book, published in 1922 with cursory amendments. Later, Jaspers complained that Heidegger's review was 'boring' and 'unfruitful'.[15] It is plausible that at that time he was inclined to reject the review out of hand, since his agenda was to oppose the philosophical tradition that Heidegger claimed to have overcome in his review of Jaspers' book.[16] Heidegger acknowledged the breathtaking scope of Jaspers' research in a letter to Heinrich Rickert: 'This book must, in my opinion, be fought in the severest manner, precisely because it has so much to offer that Jaspers has learned from everywhere and because it appropriates a trace of the times.'[17] Jaspers worried that his failure to engage with the content of Heidegger's review might be seen as a personal affront.[18] It is unclear whether he was interested in intensifying their dialogue, for he was disturbed by an aggressive tone to Heidegger's review that he considered a sly misappropriation of trust. Heidegger's thoughts were expressed in an aggressive manner that merely intensified Jaspers' suspicions of his sincerity towards their joint aims.[19]

Heidegger's critique culminated in the sharp observation that Jaspers' concept of 'limit situations' was not a standpoint drawn from a survey of tradition, but a method that Jaspers formulated in a wholly unsatisfactory manner, oblivious of the philosophical dimension of his work.[20] Heidegger accused Jaspers of grasping at 'surrogate' notions of '*Weltanschauungen*'.[21] He reduced the formal level of Jaspers' book to a 'basic aesthetic experience', whose implication he proposed more cautiously: 'This is not to say that Jaspers means to "represent" an "aesthetic" world vision. I know nothing about that.'[22] Heidegger had pinpointed an issue that was key for Jaspers.[23] Jaspers would have liked to create a cosmos of ideas, just as easily as his father painted a picture. Yet his task was to order ideas, not merely on a formal level, where figures represented an imaginary system of personalized or subjectively defined 'world visions', but on a higher level still, where figures he envisaged corresponded to something other than an imaginary space – something like an ideal plane of reality where characters are possibly free individuals. As if to underline his disapproval of Heidegger's criticisms, Jaspers wrote in his personal copy of the second edition of 'Psychology of World Visions': 'The new edition is unchanged. I cannot revise the book without writing it from scratch.'[24]

Jaspers refused to entertain a deeper level of dialogue with Heidegger. But Heidegger was persistent, responding more placidly to a copy of *Strindberg and van Gogh* (1922) that he received from Jaspers.[25] Heidegger's criticisms shifted to an open discussion of a discrepancy that preoccupied him at that time, a discrepancy that became his favourite question of the rift between 'life' ('essentia') and 'existence' ('existentia'). In these terms, Heidegger endorsed Jaspers' pathography as connected to the question of Being.[26] Heidegger noted that one of the aims of Jaspers' study of Vincent van Gogh was a pressing need to decide upon the categories used for describing the phenomenon of schizophrenia. For Heidegger, however, this was not a problem of spirituality, a line of thought that Jaspers pursued with his seminars on Kierkegaard and Nietzsche. According to Heidegger, either they were to take their role seriously and to engage in philosophy as scientific research, or else they were to resign their thoughts to the products of 'scientific individuals' whose concepts lacked precision and whose reactions emerged on demand.[27] Heidegger admitted that seeing things in the direct way that fascinated Jaspers was virtually unknown territory for him. His own knowledge of van Gogh was based entirely on the artist's personal correspondence.[28] In contrast, Jaspers' perception of artistic creativity was related to the freedom that he saw as a goal of his thinking. Heidegger proposed that he and Jaspers inaugurate what he called a 'community of contest' (*Kampfgemeinschaft*), for the similarities of their projects were such that each was concerned with the status of mankind and, hence, they remained, in terms of their work, close counterparts.[29] Jaspers accepted the spirit of Heidegger's offer, inviting him on several occasions to Heidelberg, to test what the idea of their friendship meant in practice. Indeed, he warned Heidegger that he intended to take his proposal seriously: '*Should* a contest prove necessary at some time, then it should be a *contest*.'[30] What Jaspers may have meant by his rather emotional plea about their friendship as a battle for hearts and minds was central to his developing ideas about the dimension of 'contest' not purely in terms of conflict.

In July 1923, Jaspers commented on the ludicrous pace of inflation when he announced to Gertrud that Springer's fee to publish his essay, *The Idea of the University* (1923), was 5½ million Marks, yet this amount was merely sufficient for a short period.[31] Inflation was not at its peak, but the following year, the Mark lost value so rapidly that barrow-loads of banknotes were consigned to the shredder.[32] In January 1923, the Jaspers moved into a house that was around the corner from the university. Their relocation came as a relief to Jaspers who praised Gertrud's organization of their removal – from across the river Neckar – and only wrote to his parents once the domestic upheaval was over: 'Address: Plöck 66. Indeed, of agreeable brevity!'[33] Their new Heidelberg address radiated an atmosphere of civilized education or *Bildung* that appealed to Jaspers, although his residence also fulfilled their urgent need for hygienic facilities to make it easier to cope with his illness. Taking stock of his new surroundings, Jaspers underlined his dependency on a proper location in order to accomplish his work and his sense of satisfaction at being close to the university appeared to inspire him.[34]

A matter of months after their relocation to Plöck 66, Jaspers was preparing a programmatic essay in which he cast a critical eye upon the role of the university in Weimar culture. Jaspers' *The Idea of the University* (1923) caused a first false note to sound in his 'community of contest' with Heidegger. Jaspers heard a rumour that Heidegger had commented on his essay as one of the most 'trivial pieces of all trivia today'.[35] He later recalled having confronted Heidegger about his alleged remark, only to be met by a vehement denial that, as Jaspers observed, sent Heidegger into a flurry of agitation because of Jaspers' even-handed dismissal of the rumour.[36] So many of his personal memories were in the background of his essay,[37] but it was unlikely that sentimental reasons alone were to permit an alleged comment to be taken so seriously. As a student, Jaspers established a code to discriminate against personalities whose appearances were seen to interfere with Humboldt's *universitas* – personalities who offended the idea of the university by exaggerated opinions of their self-importance. Such character-types were implicitly downgraded in Jaspers' estimation. The occasions when he revised his essay – after the war in 1946 and in cooperation with Kurt Rossmann in 1961 – suggested that his ethos of personality was as strong as ever, despite the changed contexts in which his essays were re-released. The symmetry of the subsequent revisions of Jaspers' text highlighted his understanding of tradition as historical,[38] yet only insofar as German science could be seen to merit and, indeed, to withstand critical treatment. Jaspers' idea of tradition was founded in this context upon something timeless that was inherent in his notion of historicity, and also a realization of the need constantly to refresh knowledge of the past in the present. The change that overcame his perception of the university in Weimar culture was his willingness to reverse his earlier opinions. In view of his readiness to support German science as a nationally incomparable system at the outset of the First World War, he now more or less rejuvenated his career as a young scientist, when he had placed faith in independent activity as a counterbalance to a purely contemplative outlook. This youthful creed was reproduced in Jaspers' essay as a statement that rather summarized his perspective as a medical student: 'The world is not the platonic philosopher's state.'[39] That the phrase should have reappeared in each version of Jaspers' essay suggested that he felt anxious to convey a point about standards during this period.[40]

This essential message could have been a popular one, if Jaspers had not meant to suggest, too, that intellectuals preferred to rest upon their laurels, without caring to think about what it meant to appropriate tradition in practice. Jaspers' concern was to alert the public to a potential derailment of the humanist project that he seemed to say was on the brink of a similar fate as Germany experienced at Versailles. Yet he was reluctant to sever links with the context of his own training.[41] That background was crystal clear in the new preface, 'The picture of the University', that Jaspers wrote in 1961.[42] By that time, he was living and working in Switzerland. He was obliged to concede that his 'picture' was virtually obsolete: the 'mass' system had overtaken Humboldt's ideals; the decline of the middle class had rendered the issue of funding critical; and even a general lowering of standards conflicted with the expectation, as in the Weimar period, that the university might again be rejuvenated as a place of higher learning.[43] Nevertheless, the introduction to the first edition of *The Idea of the University* (1923) ended with a rallying call that the decline of Germany's scientific tradition was not because of the nation's political or military defeat, but because of an absence of leadership. The Weberian tenor of this analysis highlighted how the university was failing generations of youngsters. Jaspers implied that intellectuals had all but abandoned education for 'surrogates', or shades of *Bildung*. He seemed to criticize the Hegelian idea of the mind (*Geist*) and knowledge (*Wissenschaft*) which he found parading as tradition. He worked, too, with a classical model of education that resembled Goethe's description of Wilhelm Meister's formation as an individual.[44] Each idea was dispensed with in favour of a Socratic method of learning based on what he called 'universal communication'.[45] Ultimately, Jaspers' vision of education was Nietzschean, and was of a place where the individual who was willing and able to communicate might come to the forefront.[46] Such elements of tradition would have a particular bearing on Jaspers' preoccupation with university reform in 1933, when his thinking, as shall be seen, seemed on a similar plane to that of Heidegger, with a singular exception that when the moment of truth arrived for the university under Hitler, Jaspers' appraisal was too honest to be used to prevent the radical destruction of science that ensued. What he saw in 1923 were characteristic traits of a capacity to distort the task of education in such a way that interfered with his instinctive feeling that individuals could sometimes talk to one another without anybody actually hearing what was being said.

One case that seemed to illustrate Jaspers' fears of slipping standards occurred when he confided to Gertrud that he had been asked to serve with two colleagues on a disciplinary committee, to investigate the record of a member of the philosophy faculty.[47] The case of Emil Julius Gumbel, an unpaid lecturer for statistics, propelled Jaspers into a position of administrative responsibility. Gumbel's controversial remarks on the Great War, at a political meeting on 26 July 1924, were reported in the local newspaper. He was summoned to account in the Rector's office, for his comments were perceived as a slander to the memory of war victims who were honoured in Heidelberg in a special memorial ceremony.[48] Gumbel issued a public apology for his 'unfortunate expression' and withdrew his remarks.[49] Nonetheless, the faculty of philosophy proposed to withdraw his teaching rights, a proposal carried by the University Senate, but not supported by the Ministry of Education in Karlsruhe. This attempt to suspend Gumbel failed.[50]

Jaspers' role in this case – voting against the motion of his colleagues – highlighted his dislike of the increasing politicization of university life and he sought to defend the institution against the intrusion of party politics. He also took into account that conditions for action needed to be maintained in accord with social and political parameters for free speech and truthful conduct. His bestselling *Man in the Modern Age* (1931) suggested that it mattered enormously to him whether the ideals of humanism and truth were maintained, but here again Jaspers' critique of declining standards in the university failed to account for a possibility that the collapse of academic freedom was analogous to a fundamental change of political attitudes. He did not realize the wider implications of his penetrating critique of university life until Weimar democracy had disastrously failed.

On a postcard of Heidelberg's 'Castle and Old Bridge' that Heidegger sent to Elisabeth Blochmann, at the end of March 1933, he again alluded to his view that Jaspers had been blissfully ignorant about the political climate in the early 1930s. Heidegger's remarks implied that he himself knew about politics and therefore had a deeper insight into the reality of what was happening. According to Heidegger, Jaspers had summoned him to Heidelberg to discuss the 'intellectual situation'.[51] Upon his return to Freiburg, Heidegger suggested that Jaspers was oblivious to politics. He implied that he understood how Jaspers could contemplate life 'without being touched by actual events – or even to know about them',[52] but complained that Jaspers was ignorant of the Greek world in a way that amounted to a disaster 'in the present world-moment of western events'.[53] According to Jaspers, when Heidegger visited him towards the end of March 1933, they had listened to Gregorian chant. Heidegger abruptly announced his need to return to Freiburg and Jaspers recalled his departure with the words: 'One has to join in.'[54] Jaspers' recollections were of their joint participation in a purely intellectual level of conversation.

Jaspers was inclined to think that Heidegger's Rectoral address in Freiburg on 27 May 1933 was part of a lengthier meditation, such as, perhaps, his own essay about the role of the university. He enlarged upon Heidegger's speech with cautious praise:

> Your grand design of placing the starting point in Greece has once again impressed me as a new and yet self-evident truth. Here you are in agreement with Nietzsche, but with the difference that one may hope that what you say will one day be actualized in a philosophically interpretative manner. This gives your speech its convincing substance. I am not referring to its style or compactness which, as far as I can see, make this speech until now the only lasting document of today's academic will.[55]

Jaspers' faltering acknowledgement of Heidegger's acceptance of the Rectorship in Freiburg in April 1933 concealed his growing mistrust of the intellectual basis and actuality of Heidegger's decision.[56]

As the 1920s drew to a close it was not Heidegger's *Being and Time* (1927), but Schelling, that had formed the basis of their conversations. Jaspers had first encouraged Heidegger to read Schelling when he sent him a copy of *On the Essence of Human Freedom* (1809) (*Vom Wesen der menschlichen Freiheit*).[57] At the time of their discussions on Schelling, Jaspers confided to Gertrud that he was growing impatient with Heidegger and had decided not to be moved by his stimulating conversation. Rather, he preferred to talk to Gertrud, whom he knew he could trust to contest his thinking, and to judge their conversations in the light of what they both believed in as the necessary questioning of the other's position in a process of communication.[58] Relations with Heidegger were cooling off.[59] A process of 'disenchantment' was in motion. Jaspers relied upon openness and honesty, a basis of their friendship that touched the core of his distinction between speech as conversation, as the ability to talk to one another, and speech as a literal unfolding of a thought before an audience in a lecture theatre.[60] What Jaspers promoted as communication was, indirectly, defined by the presence of a listening partner, like Gertrud, who habitually reminded him of his connection and responsibility to the public realm.[61] Whereas Gertrud was to be trusted, in private and public, Heidegger was not. The interruption of Jaspers' contact with Heidegger was in the nature of his demands upon their friendship as a form of higher, intellectual communication in which the sincerity of the individual personality was to permeate the exchange of views.[62] If Gertrud was the first to intervene, later preventing Jaspers from publishing a review of his contact with Heidegger, she hoped to remind him of that higher purpose.[63] At the moment when Heidegger, like all other intellectuals in Germany at that time, was exposed to the force of university reform, a decision on Jaspers' part not to have sought to discuss the state of affairs with him would have been a betrayal of trust that was out of character with Jaspers' respect for Heidegger's creativity as a thinker.[64] However, after visiting the Jaspers at the end of June 1933, Heidegger never visited them again.

Absences and Presences

For the eyes of the mind, by which it sees and observes
things, are the demonstrations themselves.

Spinoza, *Ethics*[1]

12   *Inside Nazi Germany*

IN HIS ESSAY ENTITLED *The Question of German Guilt* (1946), Karl Jaspers
wrote:

> Germany under the Nazi régime was a prison. The guilt of falling into
> this prison is political guilt. Once the gates were shut, however, a
> prison break from within was no longer possible. Any responsibility
> and guilt of the imprisoned which either remained or arose afterwards
> must always consider the question what they could do at all.[2]

A journal that Jaspers kept from 1939 to 1942 shows that he was already
considering the implications of 'guilt' several years before the Nazi dictatorship
was overthrown by allied forces. His diary entries and, as shall be seen,
Gertrud's letters to her brothers focused on the personal – moral and other –
inner dilemma of their survival. Karl and Gertrud Jaspers had agreed to
commit suicide if Gertrud's safety were in jeopardy. In moments of despair,
Gertrud believed that it was necessary for her to sacrifice her life, the only way
for Jaspers to continue his work. In his diary for 2 May 1942, Jaspers noted: 'My
philosophy would amount to nothing if it failed at this decisive point. Trust is
absolute at some point, or else it does not exist at all.'[3] By 1942 when so-called
privileged 'mixed marriages', that is, a childless marriage between a German
husband and a Jewish wife,[4] came under renewed pressure of persecution by

the Nazi élite, Jaspers made a note of the different *modi* of the guilt problem. The political dimension of the situation was described dispassionately in Jaspers' diary, but with a sense of urgency to determine in his own mind that every possible effort had been made to 'negotiate' with the Nazi authorities. Jaspers' dignity was not such that he was above attempting to intervene.

The diary shows the context in which Jaspers' decision to act in his best interests wherever possible was made. When Nazi legislation of 7 April 1933 was used to dismiss him from his professorship at Heidelberg University in the late summer of 1937, he tried to exploit all the possibilities he could in order to win respectful treatment. On 9 September 1942, he recorded: 'I myself want to have no guilt at all at our end, if it has to be.'[5] Jaspers was conscious of the fact that as long as he survived his ordeal, he was to remain accountable for his actions and yet, as he noted in his diary, he always chose to act instead of procrastinating, or waiting for decisions to be imposed by the Nazi authorities, whose responses could achieve nothing for the human dimension of his case.

Jaspers' position inside Nazi Germany can be appreciated in the context of one of the measured conclusions of the definitive version of Hitler's life: 'Generalizations about the mentalities and behaviour of millions of Germans in the Nazi era are bound to be of limited application – apart, perhaps, from the generalization that, for the great mass of the population, the figurative colours to look for are less likely to be stark black and white than varying and chequered shades of grey.'[6] Jaspers' actions on behalf of his wife's and his own sense of dignity were, however, largely halted by Hitler's takeover of power as Chancellor on 30 January 1933. Under the terms of the Enabling Act, Hitler dissolved the Reichstag and effectively installed a dictatorship.[7] Although elections to the Reichstag were arranged for early March, the Conservative ministers, especially the former Chancellor von Papen, were unable to stem the tide of Nazi control swelled by Hitler's skill in manipulating for his own ends public opinion on the death of the respected First World War hero, the aged German President Paul von Hindenburg. The day before Hindenburg's death on 2 August 1934, Hitler passed a decree that paved the way to his seizure of all executive power. As German Chancellor *and* President, Hitler styled himself 'Führer'. The German army was now required to swear an oath of allegiance to Hitler, whereas the army's loyalty had previously been sworn to Field Marshal von Hindenburg.[8] The civil service was also obliged to show loyalty to Hitler and, as a professor and state official, Jaspers was therefore compelled to pledge the following oath: 'I swear: I will be loyal and obey the "Führer" of the German Reich and Volk, Adolf Hitler, I will observe the laws and fulfil my official duties with conscience. So help me God.'[9]

Whilst on paper Jaspers signalled his loyalty to a state that was now synonymous with Hitler, the fact that he had accepted a different idea of public service under the democratic constitution of the Weimar Republic was meaningless.[10] The Weimar constitution ceased to be valid, because Hitler's seizure of power cancelled the sense of belonging to a region, a community, or any idea of spiritual life that had previously existed. Whatever privileges Jaspers possessed as an internationally respected academic, he attempted to use them to protect Gertrud from events that rapidly compelled her six brothers to take flight. All but one of Gertrud's brothers succeeded in leaving Germany for good before the outbreak of war. Jaspers' attempts to emigrate after 1933, as shall be seen, came to nothing. Karl and Gertrud managed to survive by leading a life that was increasingly restricted by Nazi laws that punished Gertrud, her family and many of their friends, either because they were Jews or because they held political opinions that were not recognized by the Nazi state. The idea of a Communist being behind the Reichstag fire on 27 February 1933 was symptomatic of the ruthlessness with which Hitler's enemies could be treated if a pretext to attack them were found.[11]

That Jaspers interpreted his pledge of loyalty to Hitler as literally as possible was a sign that he was highly alert to the imperative of behaving in a manner that gave the authorities no further pretext than his marriage to a Jewess as ideological grounds for persecuting himself and Gertrud. Their security depended upon a demonstration of 'reliability' and on not drawing undue attention to their situation. Karl and Gertrud Jaspers restricted their movements outside their home and reduced their social contact to a small number of trusted friends. They withdrew into a private world of study, of reading the works of Shakespeare or the Bible. They restricted their analysis of the political situation to conversations with trusted friends or correspondence with close family. Yet their own circle was gradually disappearing. By April 1933, Gertrud's youngest brother, Fritz Mayer, had lost his doctor's practice in Berlin.[12] Fritz and Ernst Mayer, as well as their cousin Julia Gottschalk, were all banned, as Jewish doctors, from treating state-insured health care patients.[13] The Mayer brothers were either deprived of their professions or else their livelihood was destroyed by the boycott of the family business.[14]

Gustav Mayer was already in England as an honorary research fellow at the London School of Economics and when Hitler came to power, he stayed in London and never returned permanently to his home in Berlin. Paul Gottschalk salvaged a major part of his wealth and bookselling business by relocating in 1933 to Wassenaar, near The Hague. Gottschalk assisted with the departure of Arthur Mayer, who left his position at the bank, M. M. Warburg

& Co. in Hamburg, to travel to Seattle, after first arriving in New York.[15] Ernst Mayer fled illegally to join his wife and son in Holland in 1938, first seeking refuge in Gottschalk's house in Wassenaar. Gottschalk had travelled to America on business, only months before the outbreak of war and his planned return was cancelled. He remained in America, returning to Europe in October 1945 with special orders of books for the American military.[16] For Ernst Mayer, survival meant going into hiding, and he was fortunate enough to make contact with Maria van Boven who hid him and his wife, with the help of the Dutch resistance, in her home.[17] Although Jaspers lost contact with Ernst Mayer, in early 1941, he sent money through their mutual friend, Robert Oboussier, a Swiss composer and conductor who returned to Zurich before the war, as well as through Helmuth Plessner in Utrecht.[18]

Gertrud had received a letter from her brother Heinrich, with a request for her to send a parcel that could weigh up to one kilogramme to Bergen-Belsen where he arrived in early 1944 with his wife, Jennie. They appear to have been held there for an unspecified period whilst awaiting the arrival of Germans in exchange for their long awaited emigration to Palestine.[19] As Gertrud informed Erna, her sister-in-law, she had sent her brother four parcels in total, with dried apple and a cake that she had baked, and her letter anticipated that her brother and his wife would soon be allowed to leave Bergen-Belsen that she stressed to Erna was 'no concentration camp, no work camp'.[20]

Within six months of Hitler's takeover, Fritz Mayer decided to emigrate to Palestine.[21] He interpreted the destruction of his livelihood as a symbolic sacrifice and wrote to Gertrud: 'I will give the news to you straight, but I ask that you hold your head high with me: it is also a deep blow to the soul to be violently excluded. However, that blow will be borne in the knowledge of the Jewish fate and in solidarity with all of those who innocently endure the same suffering!'[22] Fritz Mayer believed that Jews had no choice but to accept what befell them with dignity. He believed that all Jews were called upon to save themselves and unite under the banner of Zionism. His convictions influenced Otto and, eventually, Heinrich's, departures for Palestine.[23] Gertrud had hoped that her family's letter of protection of 1698 might have shielded them from Fritz's instinctive feeling that the situation for Jews in general would shortly deteriorate beyond measure.[24] She soon recognized that her family was trapped as she wrote to her mother-in-law:

As a philosophical individual, I <u>am not allowed to prioritize</u>! But I would never fight any longer against Zionism, as I used to. We had the very well edited newspaper, *Jüdische Rundschau*, which enticed me to believe in Zionism even with my uncontrollable pride. It was suggested that all those problems could be endured by comparison to this situation which can only lead to disgrace and bitter disappointment. Whenever I observe closely how terrible it looks for my brothers, how young people see every avenue blocked both here and outside – I become incensed once again. [...] Only now, I hear Kally's words again, even if I listen to his love and his pleading all the time to endure life. They do not allow Jews to put down roots and then they reproach them with their homelessness. I am glad that I always thought passionately about this question and that I never avoided it.[25]

Gertrud persuaded her second youngest brother, Otto, who was plagued by indecision about emigration, eventually to join Fritz a year after his arrival in Haifa and relocation to Tel Aviv.[26] Since Fritz Mayer's practice in Berlin was bankrupt, only the financial assistance of Heinrich released the necessary capital for the journey to Palestine.[27] Fritz, his wife, and their young son stayed at the Jaspers' house in Heidelberg for several days before their departure. Gertrud plotted her youngest brother's escape by making sure he visited Florence and Rome before arriving at the seaport of Naples at the end of October 1933.[28] A month later, Mayer reported their safe arrival in Tel Aviv and wrote of his plans for a new life.[29]

In Oldenburg, Jaspers' parents participated in the unfolding plight of Gertrud's family, since she frequently confided her feelings of anguish. The twist to the family fortunes took them all by surprise, for only two years previously, they had celebrated the success of *Man in the Modern Age* (1931), the 'Göschen' book. This book's popularity was beneficial to the launch of Jaspers' three-volume magnum opus *Philosophy* (1932), a work that was highly significant, not least because it marked Jaspers' first major publication since his monograph on Vincent van Gogh. The range and depth of the theoretical speculations in Jaspers' magnum opus, *Philosophy*, will be considered later in this section, to the extent that key ideas of that work were illuminated in Jaspers' private correspondence.[30] It was with the 'Göschen' book, the thousandth edition of a book series published by Walter de Gruyter in Leipzig, that Jaspers' name was once again in the public eye.

The overwhelming popularity of the book was because of its penetrating critique of modernity. The alert political commentator, Dolf Sternberger, later noted that at the time of its publication he had not realized that the clarity of Jaspers' 'Göschen' edition was a profound representation of the atmosphere of demoralization in early 1930s Germany.[31] Jaspers' family, too, admired his book's implicit endorsement of the liberal and democratic tradition that they ardently believed in. Karl Jaspers senior especially praised the clarity and tone of his son's work.[32] With this seal of approval from his father's generation, it seemed reasonable to assume that readers could generally be attracted to the underlying patriotic fervour expressed in this work for the nation's past. However, Jaspers' 'Göschen' edition was also released only months before the national elections reflected a worrying increase of right-wing fanaticism.[33] By the spring of 1932, Henriette Jaspers noted the National Socialists' presence in their hometown of Oldenburg: 'Perhaps, we are soon to have a Nazi government here.'[34] Only a year after *Man in the Modern Age* went into a fourth edition,[35] Jaspers' mother and sister paid a surprise visit to Heidelberg to celebrate his fiftieth birthday, on 23 February 1933. Jaspers' mother took the opportunity to reciprocate a similar tribute that Jaspers paid her three months earlier on her seventy-fifth birthday, by delivering a speech at a small party of guests, including Marianne Weber, who were gathered for the celebration.[36] The music arranged for a morning concert was a selection from Bach's Prelude in C, Beethoven's *Die Ehre Gottes aus der Natur* and Mozart's String Quartet in B.[37] Amidst such happiness about their family celebration and the fortunes of his book, Jaspers confided in his father that he was particularly anxious about the increasing support for the National Socialists. He anticipated that potential gains for the Nazi party during forthcoming elections would send the country on the road to a dictatorship that would be difficult to reverse.[38]

The parliamentary elections to the Reichstag on 5 March 1933 carried an ominous message that Hitler's consolidation of power was almost a certainty. The National Socialists polled a sizeable 43.9 per cent of the vote, but they were forced to form a coalition with the right-wing German People's Party (DNVP) that scored 8 per cent of the vote, so that, overall, a ruling majority prevailed.[39] Nowhere was a direct reference to an imminent collapse of German democracy to be found in Jaspers' most recent publications – not even in his book about Max Weber, 'Max Weber. German Essence in Political Thought, Science and Philosophizing' (1932) (*Max Weber. Deutsches Wesen im politischen Denken, im Forschen und Philosophieren*). When Gertrud caught sight of about forty copies of the 'Göschen' edition in a bookshop, an alarm bell sounded and she realized that this book's popularity may have reflected something of the fanaticism spreading like wildfire across the country.[40] Gertrud half suspected that readers could not only comprise the intellectual circles that they imagined to be in possession of Jaspers' works. Jaspers put a similar thought to the back of his mind when he chose, out of respect for Enno, to publish his Weber monograph with an Oldenburg publisher. Jaspers saw that the right-wing government, at that time, under Chancellor von Papen, was not the best, but the only hope of maintaining the rule of law at home and representing Germany's interests abroad. He was less certain, however, about the ability of Conservative politicians to deal with Hitler's SA (*Sturmabteilung*): 'In the question of armament it is first a basic matter of the government obtaining the approval of other powers for incorporating the SA troops, in some form of the military, into the armed forces and by that means to make Hitler fade into thin air.'[41]

Jaspers later felt compelled to connect his personal views on politics, aired so freely amongst his family, with his philosophical work, a response that he claimed as a direct result of his experience of Hitler's dictatorship.[42] That his opinions about politics seldom affected his published works of philosophy before Hitler's seizure of power makes it difficult to read the 'Göschen' book today because of its high-brow character. Jaspers' position appeared rather withdrawn from aspects that he portrayed. The detached tone of his book is, however, not entirely representative of his acute awareness of political affairs that is typical of his personal correspondence. His characterization of intellectual creativity serves as one of many possible illustrations of the tone of his critique.[43] His analogy with an ageless spirit of creativity, as handed down through the works of Shakespeare, was an element that contributed to the tragedy of modern man. For Jaspers, dramatic figures such as Hamlet or Edgar in *King Lear* were a reflection of the spirit of nobility and passion that was not necessarily to be found in contemporary life.[44] In this regard, Jaspers' views were in accord with his enthusiasm for first-hand impressions of what he described in his intellectual studies.

Over Easter 1932, the Jaspers visited Gertrud's family in Berlin. Paul and Julia Gottschalk, Ernst Mayer and Robert Oboussier (who worked as a music critic for Berlin newspapers from 1933 to 1938[45]), all attended a variety of the capital's musical entertainment – Brecht's *Three-Penny Opera* (with music by Kurt Weill) and Wagner's *Tristan and Isolde*. Jaspers was perhaps persuaded to participate, since he enjoyed the performances all the more in the pleasure of their company. Even Gertrud was surprised about Jaspers' curiosity, especially for Wagner:

That Kally was inclined to follow an entire performance of *Tristan* surprised me yet again. I am pleased the music means something to him. He was against the philosophy of Wagner and Schopenhauer. The tragic longing for death through love is against his ideas. I listened to a concert with [Otto] Klemperer and [Ernst] Schnabel who played a quite wonderful performance of a Beethoven piano concerto. We also had great enjoyment in the museums.[46]

The examples of music, architecture, sculpture, painting and poetry which were described by Jaspers in the third volume of his *Philosophy* or *Metaphysics*, were indirect reflections of his appreciation of the creativity of art being symbolic of an individual's ability to think.[47] To encourage individual reflection was equally one of the purposes of *Man in the Modern Age* (1931) that drove out of every nook and cranny supposedly pseudo-scientific theories which were held up as a mirror to reflect the crisis of the moment that was a failure of democratic leadership.[48]

Jaspers' typology of modern life appeared to characterize his text as Weberian in approach, as liberal and aristocratic in the sense of seeking to promote the calibre of 'objective' reflections on the contemporary situation. There was also a serious message on the subject of friendship as forming a positive basis for objective discourse.[49] Perhaps Jaspers' invitation to Heidegger to stay at his home on the eve of his speech to the Heidelberg students was so that he could examine the type of shadow that Heidegger cast over their friendship. Gertrud wrote to her parents-in-law that Jaspers was 'totally absorbed' by Heidegger's visit.[50] She was unnerved by Heidegger's presence, because she was to welcome him when he arrived, a thought that filled her with trepidation: 'Now I must say to myself: you are a lady from the Orient, they know how to cultivate hospitality! And I must simply be kind and keep quiet! Hopefully, I can manage it. It has to be that way for Kally and his friendship for Heidegger.'[51] According to Gertrud, Jaspers entered into detailed discussions with Heidegger about his speech, 'The University in the New Reich', given on 30 June 1933 in Heidelberg.[52] Heidegger spoke with militant veneration for the Nazi régime, rallying students by a vote for the future of higher education as élite training centres. There was no doubt about his support for Hitler.[53] The finer points of Jaspers' views at that time were depicted in a document, published posthumously: Jaspers' *How Can the Universities be Rejuvenated? Some Theses (1933)* was a draft proposal that he had prepared in July 1933 after unofficial meetings with colleagues at Heidelberg University.[54] At first sight, the *Theses (1933)* appeared sympathetic towards Heidegger, to whom they were indirectly addressed.[55] If Jaspers hoped that, with this proposal, he might jump on the bandwaggon of reform, the text of his ideas shows that he held grave reservations about the entire reform process that he uneasily anticipated would commence in Heidelberg over the summer. For that reason, he had written to his parents that he would not be able to spend the holidays in Oldenburg: 'I still, instinctively, have to be present in Heidelberg for every single moment, even during the summer holidays. We do not know what is going to happen. Perhaps, we will hear something important. And perhaps this autumn, very far-reaching restructuring of the university is to occur.'[56]

The Nazi reform of the university effectively installed the Rector as 'Führer' and removed democratic accountability from the faculties, whose deans were nominated by the Rector.[57] These reforms took place the day before Jaspers sent word of his 'Theses' to Heidegger.[58] Notably, it was due to Heidegger's actions as Rector of Freiburg University that the reform process began in Baden before it commenced anywhere else in Germany. In view of Jaspers' friendship with Heidegger, for which even Gertrud had expressed her determination to remain tolerant, Jaspers still seemed to think that he could rely on Heidegger's support for his reform proposals in the corridors of power.[59] That is one possible implication of the second of two additional notes that Jaspers included in a note with his draft proposals: 'I cannot do anything unless I am asked, since I am told that, as I do not belong to the Party and am married to a Jewish woman, I am merely tolerated and cannot be trusted.'[60]

The question of trust was a particularly delicate matter, since according to Nazi ideology Jaspers' position was significantly 'compromised' by his marriage to a Jewess. A reading of Jaspers' 'Theses', or his letter to Heidegger about the Rectoral speech, may supply a portrait of Jaspers as another intellectual inside Hitler's Germany who 'himself connected hopes to the national revolution in 1933 and read Heidegger's Rectoral address with goodwill'.[61] Although Jaspers was a loyal friend of Heidegger, his motivation to persuade Heidegger to become an honest broker for his alternative conception of university reform was genuinely fuelled by different considerations. If Jaspers' 'Theses' had been sent to Heidegger, it might have been intended as an indirect appeal to Heidegger to think about what he was doing. Heidegger's June 1933 visit coincided with anxious times for Gertrud, whose peace of mind was daily disturbed by news from her brothers in Berlin. Whilst Gertrud was already unwilling to trust Heidegger, Jaspers' 'Theses' included a turn of phrase that suggested he was as yet undecided: Jaspers' proposals appeared tentatively to coincide with certain sections of Heidegger's infamous Rectoral Address.[62] Jaspers did not send his 'Theses' to Heidegger. Speculation about his proposals that never saw the light of day therefore seems futile. Nevertheless, what is certain is the amendment in Jaspers' proposals to the spirit of his *The Idea of the University* (1923) that was implicitly represented in his proposed paper for reform: namely, Jaspers' *Theses (1933)* undeniably included an ominous paragraph about 'Labour Service and Military Sport', – the activities that the Nazis, including Heidegger, eagerly supported.[63] These activities had already been introduced in Heidelberg since early 1933. Jaspers' proposals mentioned the factors of *Arbeitsdienst* and *Wehrsport* in a separate paragraph, with a specific recommendation to exclude these elements from university education.[64]

What Jaspers proposed was rather his *The Idea of the University*, that is, his critical picture of scientific standards drawn up in the Weimar Republic, as a blueprint for his unpublished *Theses (1933)*. The theses were to contribute to a general mood of reform in a quite different set of circumstances when activities of 'labour service' and 'military sport' were *de facto* a part of university life. Jaspers' proposals relied on an outdated belief in the spirit of the university as 'truth-seeking' – a just goal for the scientific community.[65] He focused more sharply on sources of declining standards – he was especially concerned about the situation in medicine, an example that was his point of departure.[66] He feared that the overall poor achievement of scientific standards was beginning, gravely, to place in doubt the prospect of 'a true renewal of German science', that the danger of 'its irrevocable demise' was now plausible.[67] Nowhere in his unfinished document was a direct complaint to be found against Hitler.[68] Jaspers did not in principle object to the rationale given for reform, but he confided to his parents his views about the Nazi reform of the German university that, in Freiburg, Heidegger had taken a hand in promoting:

Heidelberg, 28 August 1933

Dear parents,
     Now a new university constitution has been drawn up according to the 'Führerprinzip'. The Rector is to be appointed by the Ministry; the Deans nominated by the Rector. No elections take place. As long as the faculties still remain intact, they are only to be given an advisory role – decisions are not voted upon. The earlier 'scholars' "republic"' [*Gelehrten „republik"*] is at an end. After my experiences of it, that suits me well enough, especially if I myself could become Rector, or another name that I trust just as much as myself! Excuse my high spirits! [...]
     Fond greetings,
     Your Kally[69]

To all outward appearances, the old system of privileges, or what Jaspers referred to as the 'scholars' "republic"', had served his career remarkably well.

Why should he have suggested to his parents that he had thought of taking over as Rector, a notion that was practically unworkable given his bill of health?

Any answer to this question seems at least double-edged, especially given the irony of Jaspers' remarks. Indeed, irony in this context is the one redeeming feature of his private opinion about the loss of the university's independence. The humanity of his response to his parents seems also linked to Gertrud's deep mistrust of Heidegger's actions as a Nazi party member, which meant that their connections were abruptly severed. Jaspers failed to respond to Heidegger's acknowledgement of his Nietzsche book in 1936.[70] As Jaspers subsequently concluded in his autobiography: 'I had failed with regard to Heidegger, who himself had been seized by an intoxication. I had not told him that he had chosen the wrong road. I did not trust his changed nature at all anymore. [...] In May [*sic*] 1933 Heidegger said good-bye for the last time. We have not seen each other again.'[71]

Even if Jaspers noted ironically that he would have liked to take charge in Heidelberg, he was, in general, overwhelmed by a sense of dismal failure about having maintained goodwill for the reforms. Here the tragic potential of his comments emerges in as much as he realized that it was too late to try to influence events. What remained for him was to accept the decimation of the university's reputation and to face a new reality: the voluntary withdrawal and enforced removal of his closest and most trusted friends, before he himself fell victim to the régime's purge of liberal or independent-minded intellectuals.

Jaspers witnessed the voluntary withdrawal of their longtime friend and ally, Dr Fraenkel, who was officially dismissed in August 1933 according to the 7 April 1933 'Law for the Restoration of the Professional Civil Service'.[72] They saw their friend, Alfred Weber, apply for early retirement – an application that was accepted from the beginning of August 1933. Weber's opposition to the Nazi takeover was self-evident when he ordered the Nazi 'swastika' to be removed from the flagpole of the Heidelberg Institute.[73] They saw another friend, the Heidelberg law professor Gustav Radbruch, withdraw from his lecturing duties because of connections with the Social Democratic Party – his withdrawal was accepted as retirement by early May 1933. Gertrud recorded the retirement, again on political grounds, of Jaspers' former boss and director of Heidelberg's Clinic of Psychiatry, Karl Wilmanns.[74] With sadness and relief, they watched Heinrich Zimmer and his wife, Christiane, daughter of the Austrian poet Hugo von Hofmannsthal, two of their last remaining friends in Heidelberg, emigrate to America in spring of 1939.[75] When Jaspers was due to travel to Groningen University as a guest lecturer in spring 1935, he weighed up the pros and cons of making such a journey.[76] There was the possibility of visiting his parents from Groningen and the chance to prepare for the lectures in a different atmosphere, as well as the prestige of the occasion: Jaspers' request for permission to accept the invitation included the greeting, 'Heil Hitler!'[77]

Jaspers' guest lectures in Groningen, from 25 until 29 March 1935, marked a change of approach, even though the thrust of his introductory lecture, *Reason and Existenz* (1935) was in the nature of his previous works.[78] The Groningen lectures were to be read as 'an entity that could be considered a whole'.[79] The lectures contradicted the view that philosophy prescribes a single route to truth, as though philosophers possess a key to wisdom. Simplifying and expanding the text of his lectures, Jaspers delivered a message about his purpose of adopting an anti-dogmatic approach.[80] In the lecture 'Truth as Communicability', he spoke for the first time about a boundary concept that introduced a further development of his philosophical work.[81] He made a finer distinction between 'Being' and 'Truth' and introduced what he called *The Encompassing* as a metaphor for his conception of mankind's aims and higher goals.[82] This metaphor reflected Jaspers' approach to thinking, without reference to dogma of any sort. In *Philosophy* (1932), Jaspers had already defined his concept of *Existenz*, in brief, a concept to elucidate the individual's situation in the context of mankind's capacity to achieve his aims. In the Groningen lectures, Jaspers continued his search for a bridge between a merely intuitive grasp of *Existenz* (such as he had begun in his study of van Gogh), and the capacity to reason. In that respect, Jaspers' metaphor of *The Encompassing* functioned as a vital hinge – a secret key to the key cabinet[83] – upon which the future of his work turned.

The future was to be represented by what Jaspers called his project of the 'Philosophical Logic', that is, one of the most extensive studies he ever wrote about the inner dynamics of communication and truth, a project that he effectively publicized in his lectures delivered in Holland. A key feature of the lectures was that Jaspers had changed his choice of words from *Existenz* to 'Reason', a change that happened to coincide with his increasing isolation. On Christmas day 1938, Jaspers informed his parents of the death three days beforehand of his doctor and their family friend, Albert Fraenkel. Jaspers was possibly amongst the last to have visited Dr Fraenkel.[84] When he reflected on his memories he felt a new hope for the individual's courage and power of reflection. In this spirit, he owed Dr Fraenkel a great deal, as he wrote to his parents:

Heidelberg, 25. 12. 38

Dear parents,

[...] As chance would have it, I probably had the last conversation with him [Dr Fraenkel], at 12 o'clock mid-day – he died at seven o'clock in the evening. After my conversation he is supposed not to have fully regained consciousness. During our conversation, he occasionally sank then he quickly came to himself and spoke sensibly, objectively, as usual. He was a very clever and good person. In medicine, he was immortal, due to his discovery of a therapy that has already given back to thousands, years of their lives – a treatment that was no chance discovery, but the result of decades of methodical research. That he received enquiries from all over the world about the application and introduction of the medicine was, during his last weeks, still a great satisfaction for him. That he had himself been no longer able to communicate his knowledge since 1 October caused him pain that he could scarcely overcome. He was in his element when he could help. That was denied him and death came as though it were natural once he no longer had this purpose to live. Some time ago, he gave his blood pressure gauge (the first of this kind that was built around 1909 and that he had owned since then and used to examine all his patients) to a young English doctor who had learned his methods – in a similar, though quite different way, to Papa giving away his hunting rifle since no one in the family could inherit it. It is a real source of pain to me that he is no longer with us. I not only have a great deal to thank him for personally, but I enjoyed talking to him from time to time. He was unusually clever, sometimes almost visionary in his recognition of connections and at the same time he was so sober and objective, just as a scientific individual is. He will be buried on Tuesday. I have ordered a wreath for you, I think a very nice one. We are sending a fine bunch of red carnations. He has earned that kind of luxury. [...]

Fondest greetings,

Your Kally[85]

Jaspers admired Dr Fraenkel not just because he was a brilliant researcher. He also remembered his doctor as a pioneer whose talent was that he knew how to apply the knowledge he acquired so that his presence was a service to those in need.

Little wonder that whilst Jaspers began to lose contact with many of his most valued friends, his longstanding interest in humanity (*Menschlichkeit*) broadened to a profound concern for the future of mankind (*Menschheit*).[86] Only days after the National Socialist 'Nuremberg Laws' came into force (the 'Law for the Protection of German Blood and Honour' classified Gertrud as an outlaw in her own state), Jaspers applied to the Rector of Heidelberg University for permission to travel to Zurich.[87] He mentioned in his travel application a number of topics that he planned to speak about in front of a private reader's club, the Hottingen Circle, in the main lecture theatre of Zurich university.[88] At the beginning of March 1936, accompanied by Gertrud, Jaspers travelled to Zurich, possibly with the hope of obtaining a university professorship there.[89] During their brief visit, he contacted Ernst Mayer's son, Albrecht, whom he was supporting financially to attend a private school in Zurich.[90] On 4 March 1936, Jaspers delivered his lecture about 'Radical Evil according to Kant'.[91] He investigated what was, in view of his family responsibilities, a cardinal question about man's propensity to commit evil.

Kant's essay, *Religion within the Boundaries of Pure Reason* (1793), was Jaspers' point of departure which he took to discuss a culture of evil that seemed to have infiltrated everyday life to the complete obliteration of moral decency. Jaspers reworked Kant's thoughts into the leading question: 'How do I find the respective, definite and morally right content of my action?'[92] Kant had attributed the source of evil to a turnabout that occurred by a revolutionary process (*Umkehr*) that he defined as 'Radical Evil'.[93] In agreement with Kant, Jaspers suggested that the chance for man to squander his freedom emerges when morality vanishes into thin air. However, he found Kant's explanation for 'Radical Evil' wholly inadequate. Kant followed an assumption that evil was explicable as a basic deficiency of metaphysical weight.[94] For Jaspers, the evil source was neither explicable nor comprehensible in Kant's sense, since he identified a threshold where human beings start to use foul, not fair means to accomplish their ends.

In this lecture, Jaspers seemed to suggest that the perception of this threshold of evil requires a particular insight into the complexity of human psychology. He turned the whole question about 'Radical Evil' on its head and found that no earthly jurisdiction is a moral guide for the individual who seeks a correct way of behaviour in Hitler's Germany. As Jaspers suggested in his diary, the outcome of his decision to remain in Germany depended upon his estimation of his chances of surviving the persecution of his wife and that meant that his philosophy was at stake.

13   *Nietzsche Lectures*

By June 1933, Jaspers forwarded Ernst Mayer samples of his manuscript about Friedrich Nietzsche. Mayer had requested to see the manuscript, but he began to voice doubts about becoming involved in the project.[1] Jaspers' comprehensive guide to Friedrich Nietzsche's life and works was completed by December 1935, but in spring 1934, Mayer already possessed a draft of the introduction.[2] Jaspers indicated that this part of the manuscript caused him trouble and he sought Mayer's advice: 'Here is the problem: I want to quote as exactly as possible, to let my ideas speak through Nietzsche, but it must be a text that reads in its entirety, as a smoothly flowing piece, without the reader tripping over the quotation marks.'[3]

Jaspers was convinced that it was necessary to reproduce Nietzsche in his own words and he wanted to elevate Nietzsche in the public estimation. However, too much quotation might defeat his purpose.[4] Ernst Mayer, for one, doubted whether this approach was appropriate and his suggestions provoked heated debate. Jaspers' perception of Nietzsche was steered by his desire to include exemplary material as the narrator whose voice was to fade into the background. The narrative was to place lengthy sections of Nietzsche's texts in blocks of finer print, visibly offset from the flow of Jaspers' arguments.[5] In an uncharacteristically dogmatic manner, Mayer objected to this technique because of its lack of literary finesse. The book's hackneyed presentation was governed by the work's content, but Mayer began to claim to know the content better than Jaspers himself.

From the start, Mayer took exception to the introductory chapter that he complained overlooked Wagner's music and Nietzsche's crisis after the break with Wagner.[6] Jaspers argued that his aim, and even his abilities, were such that he intended neither to analyse Nietzsche as an artist, nor to consider Nietzsche's attempts at musical composition: 'What you write on Wagner is <u>very</u> important. Yet since I cannot properly understand music, the presentation must naturally be reduced to Nietzsche.'[7] Instead of continuing their debate, Jaspers complained that Mayer read into his work the very things he planned to exclude.[8] Mayer provided feedback on a separate project, informing Jaspers that he was compiling his own manuscript, entitled 'Remaining Critique on Nietzsche', and he called it a 'matter of the heart' to arrange his thoughts on what he called 'philosophical language'.[9] Mayer complained bitterly that Jaspers' text was 'biographical intrusion' based on 'a biographer's mannerism'.[10] Mayer's most emotional accusation was that Jaspers' work ended in a 'dead-end of communication', although in one of his few positive comments Mayer conceded that Jaspers' book would nevertheless 'set the scene for existing interpretations'.[11]

The severity of Mayer's criticisms was potentially devastating. Mayer was Jaspers' closest and trusted associate; and he was just as intimately acquainted as was Gertrud with the progression of Jaspers' thinking. Yet his opinions on Jaspers' Nietzsche project were linked to the trauma of rescuing his family and doctor's practice in Berlin.[12] The contrast of their positions was stark, in as much as Jaspers was intent upon defending his authorial rights; whilst Mayer's whole livelihood was at stake. Their quarrel over Jaspers' portrayal of Nietzsche was enflamed by the Mayer family crisis. As Gertrud recognized when she visited Julia Gottschalk in Berlin, at the start of 1935: 'The question has no answer for the Jews. I am determined to withdraw from the world as it is and only to live with this knowledge and in the reality of the precious few – but stateless.'[13]

A late holiday in Scheveningen, Holland, was to have helped them to forget what was happening around them. The holiday was also to speed up the progress with the book – just as the lectures, *Reason and Existenz* (1935), that Jaspers delivered in 1935 as a guest lecturer in Groningen were connected to his work on Nietzsche. Looking forward to their late summer holiday in Scheveningen, Jaspers confided to his parents: 'We are meant to have rooms with a view over the sea; that is important.'[14] The holiday across the German border was an interval of peace and contemplation. Their stay at the Hotel Oranje, Scheveningen, complied with their need for leisure, diversion and relaxation with Gertrud's cousin, Julia:

Scheveningen, 22. 8. 35

Dear parents,

I am sitting on the balcony of our room with a view over the wide sea. The whole day you hear softly from afar the shrieks of the bathers, always reminding you of the joy of living that does you good if you are not amongst people. The sea is calm, no waves breaking at all, the sails are reflecting in the water as though you were in a sketch album. The beach is strewn far and wide with people. The sky is bright the whole day, the east wind (from land) is hardly to be felt. If you read the newspaper outside, the page does not move. That is quite unnatural weather and will certainly soon change. It is a nice start, especially when one is getting older and finds everything beautiful that nature shows as it is.

Trudlein [...] thinks that [bathing] is one of life's highest joys. Julia and I watched from the balcony (she stopped here in the room) before going out of the hotel in a bathing coat to the beach. [...]

The money was paid out to us and we have enough for the stay. But it is complicated with these travel currencies. Everything was arranged by the hotel. [...] Towards evening we are taking a walk by the water. [...]

Fond greetings,
Your Kally[15]

Several weeks after their holiday, the change that Gertrud had noticed as she wrote to her sister-in-law at the start of the year showed that, as she herself suspected and her youngest brother knew, the severity of the situation for Jews in Germany was irreversible. The Nuremberg Laws, 15 September 1935, dictated that Germans and Jews were forbidden to live in the same community. A package of regulations was advertised with the 'Law for the Protection of German blood and Honour', according to which marriages between Jews and Germans were prohibited. Henriette Jaspers' letter of congratulation for Karl and Gertrud Jaspers' silver wedding anniversary on 29 September 1935 was all the more significant:

[Oldenburg, 27 September 1935]

My dearest Gertrud! My dear, dear Kally!

I celebrate your silver wedding with my heart full of thanks and I wish you happiness on your further way through life! You, my dear

Trudelein, have brought so much sunshine, so much love into my life and I travel back in my memory – how Kally brought you home as his girlfriend, how your love to my dear son appeared illuminated in my heart and I felt that you also learned to love his mother! And through all the long years I see you as his most faithful companion, in joy and care and you both became irrevocably as one! Every day my thoughts accompany your beautiful life of work, in the deepest seriousness and in all difficulties that occur, dear Gertrud, your dear soul is strengthened by the support of your husband! May all cares soon be cleared. I cannot express what connects us both to one another, dear Kally. It is something coming from God, this love, that always sustains my soul with the same fire! Whenever I read your *Philosophy*, you are alive and near to me every day and I feel something eternal. May your health remain for you both and your life and activities be further blessed!

I shall soon write again and greet you both!

Your mother[16]

In his reply, Jaspers noted that his family's solidarity was needed more than ever before: 'I read it in your words, dear mother, which you speak for us both and in which you refer to your eternal bond that reaches into the beginnings of my consciousness as being the natural context of our life that is never in question and always present. That love for you was also a motive in my philosophizing and permeates the book *Philosophy* that Trudlein and I regard as our most favourite.'[17]

In spite of his family's support, however, the ongoing disagreement with Ernst took its toll. Mayer's cooperation with Jaspers was one of the few lifelines that he knew to be an unconditional source of assistance. For Mayer, to be included in Jaspers' Nietzsche project was to work through fears about pending excommunication from the culture of music and literature in which Mayer, like his sister and all her family, found security and a sense of belonging. When Jaspers notified his parents about his final preparations for his Nietzsche book, accepted by the Leipzig publisher, de Gruyter, he wrote that, for the time being, he was still a 'desirable author'. At the same time, he concluded on a worried note: 'We have great concerns for Ernst. The practice threatens to collapse almost completely. All members of the German Labour Front (*Arbeitsfront*) are called upon not to go to the Jewish doctor. It is felt in one blow.'[18]

Mayer's plight was part of the context in which Jaspers prepared his Nietzsche book. Mayer's objections seemed more relevant to Jaspers than those of later critics, such as the translator of Nietzsche's works into English, Walter Kaufmann.[19] Had Kaufmann's criticisms refreshed the temporary breakdown of relations with Mayer?[20] The radical political change in Hitler's Germany that dictated public behaviour was not applicable within Jaspers' family sphere. Scarcely two weeks after Hitler's takeover, Jaspers had confided in Ernst that Germany was on the brink of something that no one talked about openly. In uneasy, hushed silence, he sent Ernst a rare reaction to two of Hitler's speeches and he conveyed his resignation: 'We heard Hitler on the radio last night and again today. You know what is going on when you hear him.'[21]

Jaspers' instinctive understanding of what Hitler's seizure of power signified was reflected in his pedagogical intention to leave a narrative trail of Nietzsche's words in his book that illuminated a facet of the tradition of tolerance amongst Germans and Jews that was alive in the days of Lessing. Mayer in his desperation, judged Jaspers' *Nietzsche* (1936) an exercise in provocation, yet he ardently desired to believe in the continuity of tolerance that he was accustomed to experience in friendship with Jaspers. As if to reflect this atmosphere, Jaspers mentioned to Ernst that he occasionally read Goethe's maxims and reflections whilst studying Nietzsche's aphorisms. This change of diet, from Nietzsche to Goethe, was to prepare him for his task. As he wrote to Ernst: 'It is as though, from the strict discipline of seeing, for all its ghostliness, you arrive in the brightening illumination of light.'[22] Mayer's concession that Jaspers' survey was profound did not detract from his disagreement with the ineptitude of Jaspers' literary and narrative style. Jaspers' Nietzsche project cannot have failed to have alerted him to the fanatical change of mood in Germany. He later confided in Hannah Arendt that his Nietzsche book (his last major publication, as will be seen, before his 'early retirement'), was ignored by a Nazi 'co-ordinated' press.[23] Such apathy, he felt, should have alerted him sooner to what it meant to become 'an outlaw' in his own country.[24] Jaspers strictly defined a way to read Nietzsche, for he neither wanted to provide 'mere superficial contact' nor 'passive enjoyment of linguistic felicities'.[25] With Nietzsche, he sought to 'learn what is involved by dealing with the very thoughts that he had in mind.'[26] Jaspers' method of leaving everything open to question (*in der Schwebe*) made it difficult to avoid reassessing other hypotheses about Nietzsche's life. There is also the issue of the political intention of writing about Nietzsche at such a time.[27] It was impossible, as Jaspers stressed, to find a straightforward connection between Nietzsche's life and works.[28] His interest in Nietzsche's case had predated the summer semester of 1916 when he advertised his first lecture, 'Nietzsche as a psychologist'.[29] Contrary to the impressionistic account of reading Nietzsche that is to be found in his 1905 Göttingen diary, Jaspers' 1916 lecture was based on a detailed exploration of Nietzsche's life. The 'anti-psychological' tendency that emerged in the diary was especially harnessed for the lectures, for as Jaspers explained in a letter to his father, he had grown to regard Nietzsche as a philosopher of unparalleled rank.[30] Moreover, he intended to connect Nietzsche's biography with his doctrines, with the aim of discovering by what means Nietzsche's personality and conduct could be linked with the possibility of his production of such far-reaching and penetrating works. Jaspers noted further that his 'understanding psychology' would merely be promoted by his lectures; and he hoped to bring his work on psychology to a sensible conclusion, as long as he lived another ten years.[31]

Later, in his book on Nietzsche, instead of emphasizing harmony, Jaspers focused on the inherent disunity of his subject's life and published works. He argued that the riddle of Nietzsche's illness remained unsolved. His introduction to *Nietzsche* (1936) concurred with conventional views that the early 1880s was a turning point when Nietzsche's illness compelled him to exploit his creative ambitions. And he again conventionally dated Nietzsche's prolific creativity as a writer from Nietzsche's resignation from Basel University in 1879. Jaspers left the question of literary creativity undecided, but as a psychiatrist, he emphasized how Nietzsche's illness left scientific study in disarray. Nietzsche's illness could not account for the string of works that followed *Thus Spoke Zarathustra*.[32] Jaspers claimed his perception of creativity was the 'authentic Nietzsche'.[33] If Nietzsche's life were in such disarray that he became a philosopher, it was only natural to describe his illness as a state of heightened activity that could be called 'creative'. He exposed other, less plausible scenarios with a carefully worded synonym for illness that he called an 'unknown biological factor'.[34] Jaspers disowned the psychiatric background of his subject that he observed was never to supply a satisfactory answer about Nietzsche's illness. He gave Nietzsche's *Existenz* as the context for distinguishing Nietzsche's creativity as a thinker.[35]

In this specific light, Jaspers' analysis was unique and, though his book contrasted with Heidegger's Nietzsche lectures at the University of Freiburg in the winter term of 1936/7 ('Nietzsche: The Will to Power as Art'), his conclusions were on a par with Heidegger's thinking. Nietzsche's metaphors of the 'Eternal Recurrence of the Same', the 'Overman', or the 'Will to Power', are studied in the light of Jaspers' concept of *Existenz*, a concept that rather discredited a detailed inspection of Nietzsche's metaphors in any context other than seeking to understand their patterns of truth. Jaspers mentioned Beauty only as a self-fulfilling prophecy that all art is the product of the creator.[36]

Heidegger highlighted a discord between Truth and Art which he interpreted in the context of his idea that Nietzsche's biography was insignificant and insisted on an appropriate reading of Nietzsche's metaphors within a theoretical interpretation of Truth.[37] That assertion accentuated a problem with Jaspers' narrative which Mayer had raised: namely, Jaspers read Nietzsche's metaphor of 'Eternal Recurrence', as he wrote in his book, 'like a new ethical imperative, which demands that I measure everything I feel, will, do, and am by one standard: whether I accomplish it in such a way or, in other words, whether I can will that this same existence occur time and again. This imperative is a mere form, capable of receiving a limitless number of contents.'[38] This avowal to read a thought from Nietzsche's mind suggested that Jaspers believed he knew how to interpret the metaphorical form of Nietzsche's thought in a way that provoked Heidegger to a biting polemic against Jaspers' book. Heidegger read out Nietzsche's creative influence as a statement: 'Art is worth more than "the truth"'.[39] Moreover, he claimed Jaspers was deluded about the relevance of Nietzsche's biographical details:

> It is told how the doctrine of the 'Eternal Return' is decisive for Nietzsche yet, at the same time, he omits to mention that it was questionable for him, so, as a result, the unspoken conclusion emerges everywhere that the whole of philosophy is not to be taken seriously. Nietzsche's person is an exception, as are those people that were inspired by Nietzsche's person, instead of asking, why then, if this doctrine was already questioned by Nietzsche, it had to be questioned and what was actually questioned by that process and whether that is not also our question, namely, that of our western existence and our future.[40]

Heidegger's polemic was developed into his own reading of Nietzsche's Platonism.[41] That reading, first published in 1961, was personally endorsed in a preface that Heidegger later used indirectly to refer to the climate in which, like Jaspers, he also delivered Nietzsche lectures: 'Whence the confrontation (*Auseinander-setzung*) with the "Nietzsche matter" comes and whither it goes may become manifest to the reader when he himself sets off along the way the following texts have taken.'[42] According to Heidegger's version of events, it could be assumed, as Arendt chose to believe,[43] that he meant to apologize for his involvement in Nazi reform of the university system. Jaspers was less inclined to accept Heidegger's version and his bitter disappointment about Heidegger's silence when Jaspers was himself dismissed from his professorship left its marks upon personal reading notes inscribed in Jaspers' copy of Heidegger's Nietzsche lectures.[44]

In Freiburg, Heidegger appeared aggravated, though strangely impressed by Jaspers' *Nietzsche* (1936) that threw a kind of exclusion zone around Nietzsche's 'Will to Power', the unpublished works that National Socialist ideology tried to claim as its own.[45] For Jaspers, Nietzsche's posthumous works beckoned the reader into a labyrinth of neverending creativity. The message, as he identified it, perhaps, led nowhere. An issue that Jaspers highlighted in his book was whether Nietzsche's unpublished notes that were subsequently released as a single work under the title *Will to Power* were not beyond the grasp of reason. Jaspers emphasized the shaky ground of hypothetical studies that failed to identify the 'unknown biological factor' of Nietzsche's illness and he found such studies 'confusing'.[46] He warned about the suggestive power of Nietzsche's creativity:

> It might be said that this would reveal a spiritual creation and then immediately dismiss it as mere illness. In answer to this we may reply that we nowhere assert such 'identity' but, rather, that all we *know* of a person is always a particular aspect seen from one point of view and never the whole man; furthermore that the seeming and ever-puzzling change from one aspect to another, as though both were one and the same, points to the dark chasm into which we cannot penetrate.[47]

The possibility that Jaspers had supplied a prejudicial picture of Nietzsche in his book was at least implied by Heidegger's subsequent criticism of Jaspers' emphasis on Nietzsche's 'grand politics'. Heidegger placed Jaspers' work in the line of the cult following from Stefan George to the Nazi propagandist and Nietzsche interpreter, Alfred Bäumler.[48] Jaspers' *Nietzsche*, as it was first published, with countless quotations from Nietzsche's published and posthumous writings, included a coded warning that editions of Nietzsche's work were 'marred by deliberate omissions on the one hand and opinions and viewpoints on the other'.[49] Jaspers attempted to trace Nietzsche's arrival at the thought of 'truth' as 'error'. He highlighted the case of 'genuine' communication as being dependent upon personality: '*genuine communication* is only possible between people who occupy *the same niveau*'.[50] This idea was a central aspect of the communicative model for which Jaspers drew from Nietzsche's *Joyous Science* (1882): 'truth begins in twos'.[51] Jaspers' own 'anti-Freudian' analysis of personality types, described in his early essay, 'Solitude' (1916) highlighted a specific geometry that he now represented as a process of interruptions about Nietzsche's experience of 'Truth':

Community members are obliged to 'lie' in accordance with fixed convention. To put it otherwise, they must be truthful by playing the group's game with the conventionally marked dice. To fail to pay in the coin of the realm is to tell forbidden lies, for, on this view, whatever transcends conventional truth is falsehood. To tell lies of this kind is to sacrifice the world of meanings upon which the endurance of his community rests. Conversely, there are forbidden truths. This same threat to the continuance of the community is also counteracted by relentlessly preventing anyone from thinking and uttering unconventional but authentic truths.[52]

Nietzsche's thoughts rose to the rank of Nihilism. That rank was based on a shift of perspective that Jaspers called a 'new activity'.[53] To appreciate that decisive change was to connect with Nietzsche's understanding of pre-Socratic thought, a point in time that Jaspers called Nietzsche's arrival.[54] Thus, Nietzsche's crisis, in the early 1880s, led to an intensification of his poetic abilities.[55] The source of that discovery led to the 'path of living *Existenz* itself'.[56] To follow that path was to render Nietzsche's thoughts open to what Jaspers called a 'substratum',[57] or an essential route to make Nietzsche's life transparent and to render his thoughts accessible to reason. Nietzsche's profound inner change was a key focus of Jaspers' study.

Jasper's *Nietzsche*, in summary, was a radical psychological exercise, so to speak, a bid to undermine the prevailing force of dogma for philosophical ends. His preference was to see Nietzsche's metaphors of 'Eternal Recurrence' and the 'Overman' not as an act of 'Will', but as a statement of Nietzsche's faith.[58] In that case, though, Jaspers was famously inconclusive about whether Nietzsche's faith emerged because of the breakdown of his community of friends or because of his life experience. Indeed, he was reluctant to explore the significant turning point in Nietzsche's life: 'What happened to Nietzsche since 1880 must for the present remain uncertain. But the unbiased observer who has carefully studied the letters and writings in their entirety and in chronological sequence can, in my opinion, scarcely doubt that something incisive took place.'[59] For Jaspers, Nietzsche's life's journey foundered upon an event that conducted Nietzsche to a way out, or else, a solitary path, dictated not by communication, but by ever further retreat into a quest for metaphors.[60] The fact that Jaspers' *Nietzsche* banished a detailed interpretation of Nietzsche's metaphors meant that he was able to give his Nietzsche lectures and to publish their results in a turbulent political climate. More importantly, with his distinctive analysis of Nietzsche's personality, Jaspers succeeded in illuminating his subject's humanity. This was perhaps the singular achievement of the book: it was a courageous attempt to uphold its author's longstanding admiration for the dignity and nobility of the Nietzschean soul.

14   Keeping Faith

By the end of 1937, the Nazi state had excluded from office all civil servants who were married to a Jew.[1] After almost twenty years' service as a philosophy professor in Heidelberg, Jaspers was also retired, with effect from the end of September 1937.[2] The 'Law for the Restoration of the Professional Civil Service' invoked for his retirement stated: 'To simplify administration, civil servants can be retired even if they are still capable of service. If civil servants are retired for this reason, it follows that their positions may no longer be occupied.'[3] Jaspers informed his parents of the news, quoting parts of the law, as though he felt personally disgraced:

Heidelberg, 28. 6. 37

Dear parents,

Today I received my notification of retirement, according to paragraph six of the law of 7 April 1933, with no further explanation. (The law talks about 'in the interest of service' and 'to simplify administration' – the paragraph loses validity on 1 July). I know nothing yet about the amount of my pension and other consequences (whether I still count as an inactive professor and, so, whether I still nominally belong to the university or not).

It pains me a great deal, dear parents, to have to tell you about this end to my public career after what has actually been a long life when I have had only successes. I can continue to work on my own account. I will have to see whether I will still publish. That I <u>have</u> my work, with quite definite plans and significant lines of thought turns the fact into a new task: to work more intensely and quickly than is possible during lecture times. As long as we have to live, our life can still be productive. That I have to do without the youngsters is difficult. I received the letter two hours ago, ten minutes before the lecture. The students know nothing yet. They greeted me, as always, with the trampling of feet. At the end of the lecture, extraordinary applause broke out that – contrary to all custom – followed me far out into the corridor: I must have just given an impressive lecture. I have to do without this pleasure and without the feeling that I can spread sparks of interest amongst our German youth. The written text can never replace the spoken word. My talent is that I am able to speak, my only talent. Nobody wants it any longer and I am content with that. [...]

I will, I think and hope, continue to go about the world cheerfully – or at least, I will not be different than before.

You will tell the news to Erna, Eugen and Enno.

Fondest, your Kally[4]

Jaspers tried to contradict the pretext of his dismissal in a detailed appeal to the Minister of Education in Karlsruhe.[5] He quoted another paragraph of a different law that he claimed regulated university personnel.[6] He explained that the law of 7 April 1933 affected civil servants as a whole. If the different law were used, his retirement could be defined as 'withdrawal from duty' (*Entpflichtung*), a minor revision, yet an amendment that would have meant that he kept his rights, including a full pension. His status could have been that of professor emeritus. Along with his argument, he supplied a frank account of his health, observing that he was not able to sort and hold books for himself, remarking upon his physical incapacity when walking all but short distances, and finally, pointing out his need for domestic assistance at every turn. He set out the facts as reasons for the financial burden on his pocket. Officially, he mentioned that his personal disgrace might be alleviated by the revision he sought. Unofficially, his representation was to shield Gertrud from the thought that she was to blame for their predicament.

The Dean of the philosophy faculty, Ernst Krieck, supported Jaspers' appeal, even if his recommendation was coloured in a way that was un-favourable to Jaspers. Krieck suggested a propaganda advantage, especially in the foreign press, from broadcasting Jaspers' 'withdrawal from duty' on grounds of ill health.[7] Both their representations failed: Jaspers was married to a Jewess.[8]

Before learning about his removal from office, Jaspers had agreed to lecture at the Freie Deutsche Hochstift, in Frankfurt am Main, Goethe's birthplace and the Goethe museum. The director of this private academic foundation, Professor Ernst Beutler, emphasized his desire to keep Jaspers as a public speaker.[9] On this occasion, Jaspers' lectures, *Philosophy of Existence* (1937), were to persuade his audience to believe in the future, although he as much as suggested that mankind's existence was in peril. Jaspers talked about his approach to philosophy as though it were a drop in the ocean of the chance for philosophy to survive.[10] The keynote was whether what he called *Existenz* was to be heard as an appeal to a listener with an open mind, or as a dogma that mirrored the prevailing ideology in the country at large. He cloaked his ideas in a metaphor of *The Encompassing*:

> We always live, as it were, within a horizon of our knowledge. We strive to get beyond every horizon that still surrounds us and obstructs our view. But we never attain a standpoint where the limiting horizon disappears and from where we could survey the whole, now complete and without horizon, and therefore no longer pointing to anything beyond itself.[11]

This assertion of the individual's predicament in life mirrored the precarious position in which Jaspers found himself: his presence in Germany was a thorn in the side of the Nazi state that was not interested in hearing from intellectuals. His essay on René Descartes was still sanctioned for publication, but it appeared in a special issue of the prestigious *Revue philosophique* for the 300th anniversary of Descartes' *Discourse on Method* (1637) giving Jaspers one of his last opportunities to communicate with the outside world.[12] His Descartes interpretation was a detailed portrait of one of the fathers of modern science, a study whose specific assertions are characterized by Jaspers' vehement objection to Cartesian rationality which, to him, became *irrationality* because, so it seems, of the absence of experience from the method of investigation. Jaspers composed an ambiguous account of Descartes' standing in the history of philosophy that was also linked to his understanding of the special relationship between philosophy and science, something that is discussed below.[13] His essay needs to be read in the context of the times as an indication of how his work on Descartes seems to have made him even more aware of the implicit paradox of his situation in a state whose citizens, as stated in the Nuremberg Laws, were not accepted unless they could prove that they were of 'Aryan' race. Jaspers faithfully acquired the necessary information from his parents about several generations of his family's lineage, in order to satisfy the demand for proof of 'Aryan' ancestry.[14] If he harboured a particular reason to overturn Descartes' incentive for 'evidence' and 'certitude' as verifications of rational thinking, he, at the same time, called Descartes' *cogito ergo sum* a practice of doubting that could no longer be regarded as applicable to modern times and Jaspers gave a striking analysis of the basis of a separation of his philosophy of Existence from the rationalism of Cartesian thought.

Jaspers' skills as a psychiatrist were now called upon to avoid undue worry for Gertrud, and, indeed, his grasp of psychology was to play a vital role in his wife's survival. His strategy was one of vigilance in a state that could not be trusted – to maintain an inconspicuous lifestyle and so not arouse suspicion from any quarter. The deliberate policy of lying to protect oneself paid dividends, as Jaspers later explained: 'What we had to do was to act naively, to pretend no interest in the affairs of the world, to preserve a natural dignity (which still protected us in many situations), and if need be to lie without scruples. For beasts in possession of an absolute power to destroy must be treated with cunning and not as men and rational beings.'[15] Jaspers hardly breathed a word of this in Frankfurt. He seemed merely to reiterate what he had already talked about in Groningen – except that in Frankfurt he was more emphatic in his comparison of 'The Encompassing' to a distant horizon that he evoked as though no single dogma could obstruct the urgent need to be free. Yet he mentioned freedom as though it were already something unfamiliar. He spoke as though he assumed his audience knew about his *Philosophy* (1932), concluding by inserting the image of a prison into his final lecture that began with the analogy of 'myself' transposed into a realm called *The Encompassing*.[16] Perhaps, that analogy was based on what in the second volume of *Philosophy* (1932), entitled *Existential Elucidation*, he defined as his theory of 'limit situations'. This meant a kind of mortal imprisonment for the individual consciousness that strives to know what being free of mortality actually implies. The analogy that Jaspers gave was that of *Existenz*, as being caught between a perpetual antagonism of the beginning and end of time. If reality intervenes in this antagonism, the best efforts to alter the course of the future are doomed to failure, since only in the course of history, when one thing leads to another, can a chance arise to influence events: 'Reality is only in the present, and as such, historic, unrepeatable.'[17]

1. Souvenir of Norderney
(*Erinnerung an Norderney*),
1898. Karl Jaspers is in the back
row (second from the right)
with Fraülein Busch (four from
the right, second row down, in
the frilled jacket) and children
from the bording house.

2. Henriette Jaspers, 1879.

3. 'In no "house" group' (*In keiner Vereinigung*). Karl Jaspers is in the middle row, far left and Steinvorth, the headmaster, is to the far right. Jaspers lists the 'house' groups as 'Prima', 'Obscura' and 'Saxonia'. He formed his own group as an 'independent'.

4. The Jaspers family villa, Jever. Painting by Caspar Sonnekes.

5. *Rothsandleuchtthurm*
(Red Sand
Lighthouse),
watercolour by Karl
Jaspers, senior.

6. 'Oath to the Spirit of
Science' (*Schwur auf
den Geist der
Wissenschaft*).
Professor Fano, Karl
Jaspers and Professor
Cornelius, Sils Maria,
1902.

7. Gertrud Mayer and Karl Jaspers,
Marktplatz, Heidelberg, 1907.
Photograph by a mutual friend, Marie
Munk.

8. Walter Calé.

9. Gertrud with her father, David Mayer, *c.* 1904/5.

10. The Mayer family business, 'Ascher Mayer', traders in wool, Steinstraße 12, Prenzlau.

11. Gertrud with her younger brothers. Fritz is to the right and, to the left, probably Otto. Both Fritz and Otto emigrated to Palestine in the early 1930s.

12. Max Weber, economist and sociologist.

13. Gertrud on her wedding day, 29 September 1910.

14. Enno in uniform, 1916/17.

15. Karl and Enno Jaspers, Heidelberg, 1930/31.

16. Jaspers family portrait, *c.* 1917. Front row (*from left to right*): Karl Jaspers, Henriette Jaspers, Enno Dugend, Karl Jaspers, senior, Erwin Dugend, Erna Dugend. Behind (*from left to right*): Gertrud Jaspers, Enno's first fiancée, Gisela Basewitz (?), Enno Jaspers, Eugen Dugend.

17–19 (and p. 108) Jaspers saw these paintings at the International Art Exhibition in Cologne, 1912.

17. Vincent van Gogh, *Small Pear Tree in Blossom* (1890). (Courtesy of the Van Gogh Museum Foundation, Amsterdam/Vincent van Gogh Foundation.)

18. Vincent van Gogh, *The Bedroom* (1888). (Courtesy of the Van Gogh Museum Foundation, Amsterdam/ Vincent van Gogh Foundation.)

19. Vincent van Gogh, *Vase with Sunflowers* (1889). (Courtesy of the Van Gogh Museum Foundation, Amsterdam/Vincent van Gogh Foundation.)

20. Martin Heidegger, philosopher
and friend.

21. Plöck 66, Heidelberg. Karl and
Gertrud Jaspers lived here from 1923
to 1948.

22. Gertrud in Karl Jaspers' library.

23. Gertrud Jaspers, Certificate of the
Jewish Community of Heidelberg.

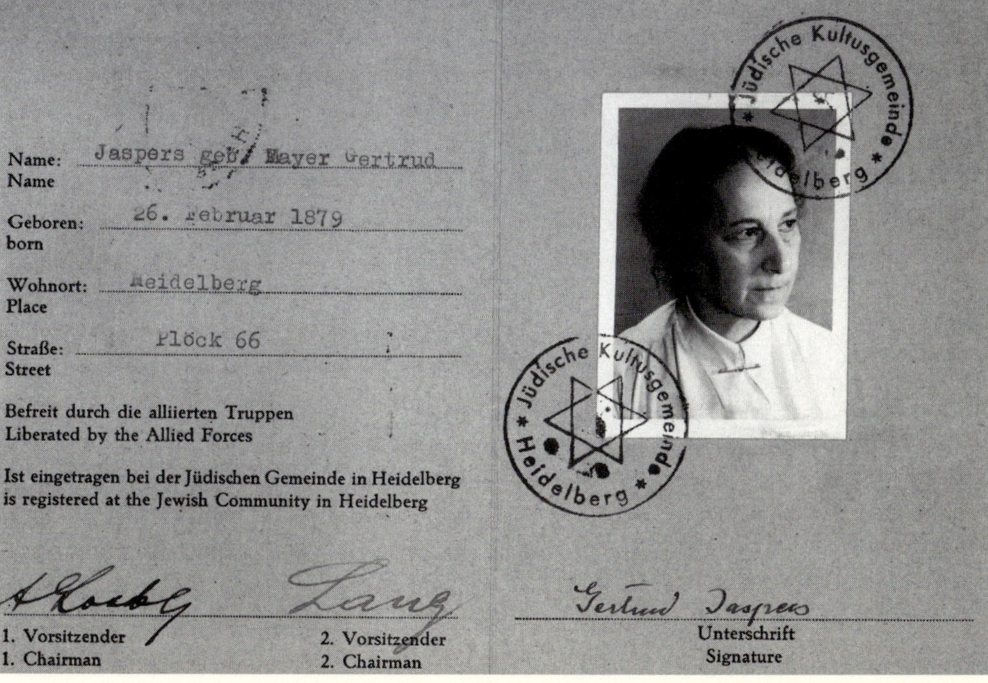

24. Gertrud Jaspers and
Erna Dugend. Norderney,
1930.

25. Karl Jaspers, senior and
Henriette with Karl and
Gertrud Jaspers,
Wangerooge, 1927.

26. Paul Gottschalk.

27. Gertrud and her cousin Julia Gottshalk.

28. Henriette and Gertrud.

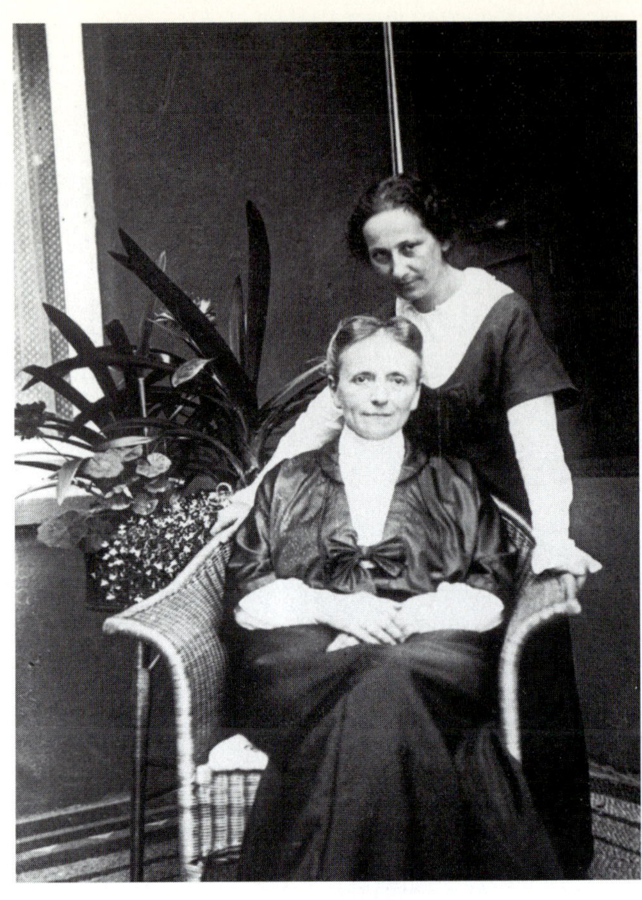

29. Karl and Gertrud Jaspers in
central Basel, Switzerland.

30. Gertrud with Ernst and Ella Mayer, Ausstraße 126, Basel.

31. Hannah Arendt, summer 1952.

32. 'View over the landscape' (*Blick auf die Landscaft*). Karl Jaspers, St Moritz, 1949.

If Jaspers' theory of 'limit situations' was meant to project a state of permanent disharmony, then what is theoretically defined as historical progress can never be achieved. Whatever appears in a state of permanence frustrates an individual, whose reality conforms to his *Existenz*, that is, he strives for harmony in the unity of his historical status that infers the achievement of freedom. Nobody can indefinitely control his relationship with the present. Hence, Jaspers was inherently suspicious about comparing the individual's situation with the status of authority:

> No matter how many steps he has climbed along the way to mature freedom, the honest individual cannot do without the tension between his freedom and authority; without it his way would seem uncertain and unstable to him. The contents of his own freedom clamour for confirmation by authority; or they clamour for resistance to authority; to prove themselves in that resistance becomes a sign of their possible truth, without which sign they would not be different from arbitrary and chance impulses.[18]

If authority takes hold of an individual's life, a sort of denial obscures what is possible in the future. Jaspers knew how fragile an individual's hopes may be because his younger brother, Enno, fell victim to a sort of denial that, ultimately, deprived him of his life. Jaspers' analysis of suicide in *Existential Elucidation* introduced a poetic notion of 'free death' (*Freitod*), as opposed to the concept of 'self-murder' (*Selbstmord*).[19] Enno's death left its mark on Jaspers' work, as can be seen from the introduction of Jaspers' analysis of suicide: 'Anyone who has ever experienced a suicide in his immediate environment will have learned, if he loves human beings and has a trace of psychological sensitivity, that not a single motive makes the event comprehensible. Always, a mystery remains in the end. Yet this is no reason to limit our endeavours to comprehend what can be known and determined empirically.'[20]

In his final letter, Enno had accused Jaspers and the family of failure to equate the monetary value of his debts with the cost of his life. Enno's belated cry for help underlined the complete breakdown of communication between the brothers. What made Enno's accusation strike home was not that Jaspers had had a hand in his father's refusal to underwrite the risky business ventures. Rather, the accusation made such an impression because Jaspers had fully expected his younger, healthier and active brother to survive him by many years.

At the end of 1926, Jaspers was obliged to take a sabbatical semester because he was recovering from a heart tremor that signalled a gradual worsening of his illness. Under the impression that he might never see Enno again, he wrote what was to have been a final letter, just as the fiasco of Enno's joint venture with the Amsterdam company came to light. Enno moved to Göttingen where Jaspers, now convalescing, forwarded him a copy of the letter that he had written in the likely event of his death.[21] According to this 'posthumous' letter, Enno's bravery during the First World War was praised as an immense source of admiration. Jaspers wrote that Enno's recent behaviour cast a shadow over their relationship. Whilst he was willing to speculate that his disagreement with Enno would have been swept aside at some future date, he was unwilling, not even for his brother, to alter his basic principle about how to overcome their differences: Enno needed to see the error of his ways. Enno was meant to repair the differences that temporarily caused the brothers to tolerate their uneasy estrangement. Jaspers underlined his position as follows: 'You know – theoretically from my book on "world visions" [*Weltanschauungspsychologie*] – that I do not believe in love as a possession, but only in love in communication and in loving contest. I hope intensely that the abyss of silence that has opened up between us is going to close again, whenever you can bear everything. It may take some time.'[22]

In possession of Enno's final letter, an unspeakable guilt lay on Jaspers' shoulders. Perhaps he should have revealed to Enno his own share of the blame for the lack of *loving contest* between them. Was Enno not deserving of the affection he felt? Or was Jaspers' idea of communication to have suspended that affection, out of selfish pride, and a need to insist in a most rational sense that Enno lead a modest lifestyle for his own good? The rational element of the brothers' relationship appeared to have prevailed, when what mattered most was to pay each man his dues in a way that was the right way for him. Jaspers certainly appeared to have modified his rationalistic views about his model of *loving contest* when he wrote to his parents that he was now able to respect the way in which Enno could have lived through what Kierkegaard called the split between a morally good and a passionately right way to live – Enno personified a life in pursuit of the elusive path of honour, seduction and pleasure.[23]

The relationship with Enno had failed, but who or what was to be blamed? The commonsense approach was to leave his brother's memory as an enigma. On the one hand, Jaspers could not transgress the threshold that irrevocably separated them. Moreover, it was unreasonable to expect that, as a survivor, he could imagine his brother's pain. On the other hand, a ceaseless enquiry was fuelled by a need to understand whether his brother's decision to end his life could not have been avoided, if his decision had been known about earlier. The agonizing problem no longer related to a temporary disruption of communication. The issue, as Jaspers clearly underlined in his philosophical study, was as follows:

> The unconditional source of suicide remains the incommunicable secret of the lonely individual. Any confessions left behind by suicides raise the question *whether by contemplating suicide, the individual understood himself.* Nowhere can we hear the unconditional resolve. We can only try to construe possibilities of suicide, aiming, beyond everything intelligible, not to understand but to elucidate its original unconditional source. The construction – which for an instant seems to make suicide intelligible, only to leave it an even more baffling enigma – goes as follows: *Existenz* in its limit situation despairs of the meaning and the substance of its being alive (*Dasein*), and of all existence. The thinking goes: everything passes away; what's the point of enjoying life if all things perish? Guilt is unavoidable. Looking towards the end, life is misery and sorrow throughout. All harmony is a mirage.[24]

The moral question surrounding suicide is shrouded in the mystery of the death, but the guilt that creeps everywhere is a task for the survivor to turn over a new leaf. Since a survivor cannot say or do anything to rescue a suicide victim from his decision to act, Jaspers concluded that he can only learn to live with his share of the guilt: 'With the fate of entanglement I am linked by compassion and by the pain of perhaps having missed a possible solution; but the sight of this transcendent fulfilment in nothingness makes me shudder. The question "Is it true?" remains disquieting in our ordered world.'[25]

The survivor's complicity in the event of a suicide is no more realistic than apportioning blame that may not be filed away or assuaged as a sin of omission in the religious sense. For Jaspers, the guilt of survival surpassed the moral burden upon an individual *Existenz*.[26] What intervened in this sense of void about survival was the language of Jaspers' *Metaphysics*, the third volume of his *Philosophy* (1932), which conspicuously intruded upon this part of his philosophical study of *Existenz*: 'If, for example, in "The Passion for the Night" death has since become familiar and even positive, so the return to life will be prevented by the surrender to an incommunicable transcendence.'[27] These terms from *Metaphysics* had been expressed in a letter that he wrote to Gertrud when she travelled to Oldenburg to attend Enno's funeral on his behalf. Enno,

Jaspers confided, had bequeathed in his last letter an open accusation about the family's guilt arguing from a completely different standpoint: 'He says it without apportioning blame, with the error of one with a "Passion for the Night".'[28] Although Jaspers refrained from referring chapter and verse to the relevant sections of his philosophy, his brother's last letter seemed to vindicate what he thought about the moral blame that he implicitly accepted for Enno's situation. By accepting that blame, however, all talk of morality was suspended. The suicide proved that his brother had already been living on a plane of reality where the way of the world was radically different, as Jaspers had written to Gertrud: 'Whatever this Otherness is, it is only present in death.'[29]

Perhaps, Jaspers' mother had also sensed the importance of Jaspers' voice when she wrote that she was particularly struck by Jaspers' *Metaphysics*, and specifically, his description of 'The Law of the Day' and 'The Passion for the Night':

Oldenburg, 7 Nov. 1933

My dear Gertrud,
  My dear Kally,
  […] I am reading 'Metaphysics'. Quite slowly. Recently, 'The Law of the Day and the Passion for the Night'. For me, page 109 is so moving: against the blind will for life is the light room of man [. . .] I accompany you daily on your ways. […]
  May Papa's and my fondest greetings reach you,
  Mother[30]

As Henriette Jaspers' letter implied, she read in Jaspers' study how blame that was transposed to a level of sheer survival suggested that a decision to live or die may appear removed from earthly jurisdiction, when the judge and jury remained a mortal being. Jaspers' philosophical analysis turned to Shakespeare's *King Lear*, to suggest a step towards mortality that occurs in the fullness of time: 'Men must endure/ Their going hence even as their coming hither. Ripeness is all.'[31] Jaspers' *Metaphysics* restored dignity to his brother, as his mother's letter suggests, because Enno's death was respected as his choice alone, a choice that his family found peace with because they knew that the tragedy was strangely consistent with Enno's experiences of war and peace. The vocabulary of Jaspers' philosophy seems to have collided so closely with his family's experiences that the intrinsically compassionate register almost transforms the original source, yet without creating an emotional attitude from that source. As facets of experiences supply an avenue of enquiry, so too, each avenue is filtered by a radical truthfulness that obscures the intuitive level for the activity of thinking.

The Nazis may have retired Jaspers at the pinnacle of his career, yet he continued his philosophical work as though his retirement had not taken place.[32] After Erna visited Heidelberg for several weeks in November 1937, Jaspers decided to write his memoirs.[33] As the text evolved in the months and years ahead, Jaspers' autobiography was not destined to become a conventional literary product. 'It seems to me,' he wrote to his parents, 'that the entire project is like one letter from me.'[34] His draft memoirs possessed what he liked to call a 'speaking', or 'symbolic' quality that he believed revealed sources of *Philosophy* to be his own experiences.[35] Henriette Jaspers wrote of the family's amazement at the scope of his recollection.[36] Whilst his mother promised to supply comments once she finished reading the text, his father corrected the phrases of the 'Platt' German dialect that were to introduce a hint of authenticity. Jaspers' memoirs were an exclusive retreat into a world of pure nostalgia. The only public engagement that he undertook after his retirement was a speech in Hanover, where he planned a rendezvous with Erna, who was then unable to make the journey.[37] The text of Jaspers' speech which he gave in 1938, *Nietzsche and Christianity* (1946) was perhaps a more effective barometer than his memoirs, 'Destiny and Will' (1967), about the direction of his thinking during the months following his retirement. Like the memoirs that Jaspers authorized Hans Saner to publish only two years before his death, the analysis of Nietzsche's attitude towards Christianity remained unpublished until after the war. The speech was a way to reflect the metaphor of 'The Encompassing' as another window to look upon the world.[38] It was largely a refinement of his full-length book about Nietzsche.

On the Night of the Broken Glass, 9 November 1938, Jewish synagogues were burned, Jewish property was destroyed and Jews were made to pay – on 12 November 1938, Field Marshal Göring issued a decree about the 'penance' to be exacted from Jews of German citizenship who were to contribute a penalty of one billion Marks to the German Reich.[39] Weeks before the terrible night of ransacking, Jaspers had confided in his sister: 'For some time, I have felt such a strong need for humanity from faraway, if the source shares our roots and is indeed related to us – and I always have the globe in front of me on my desk.'[40] Averting his gaze from the European continent, he ceased to believe that Germany automatically deserved a place amongst Europe's civilized nations. Aided and abetted by the Indologist, Heinrich Zimmer, he began to explore, from now onwards, the ancient cultures and philosophies of a different corner of the globe. Jaspers' research on Indian and Chinese philosophies and cultures continued alongside his project to write a 'philosophical logic'. In reality, however, Jaspers' life was confined to the four walls of Plöck 66 in Heidelberg. Only now and then was a fleeting glimpse to be caught of a tall figure in a dark overcoat and hat as Jaspers took his customary evening walk to the River Neckar (see p. 138).[41] Otherwise, Jaspers withdrew into reading tales from the *Mahabharata.* Transported to a remote point of history, he had abandoned all thought of a national arena for one located in a faraway corner of his globe.

15 Oxford Connections, Visitors and Loyal Friends

THE RELOCATION OF GUSTAV MAYER, from London to Oxford, at the end of 1938 provided an opportunity for Jaspers to think about emigration to England.[1] Mayer alerted the London-based 'Society for the Protection of Science and Learning' (SPSL) to Jaspers' case.[2] Heidegger's former assistant, Werner Brock, was also involved, collecting the necessary paperwork and references, and hoping that Jaspers would relocate to Oxford.[3] Brock had been in close contact with Jaspers since he emigrated to Cambridge in 1933.[4] He was keen for Jaspers' situation to be properly represented to the host universities in England.[5] Jaspers was tempted by the thought of leaving Germany for a civilized country where he could continue to work without continual worries for Gertrud's safety. The prospect of being invited to Oxford University even inspired him to take English lessons.[6] If a position had become available, it is likely that he would have accepted, although he was nervous about leaving Heidelberg, even for a short period. The thought of emigration to Oxford was associated with numerous hazards that made Jaspers see the idea of their relocation to another country as a difficult undertaking:

Heidelberg, 15. 1. 39

Dear parents,

It <u>can</u> be – and Julia thinks it probable – that I will receive an offer in Oxford in the near future. <u>Absolute</u> discretion is necessary, as all talk can disrupt university matters, and for other reasons. The offer would be surprising and a stroke of fortune. But we will not avoid the question whether we ought to risk accepting an offer for two years, without knowing for certain in advance where it will lead. If an extension were to be considered likely for us, I would be content. Almost nobody in our position gains a permanent position abroad. The people in Oxford are supposed to be informed about my illness. I would probably lose my pension (judging by similar cases: they do not permit you to move your residence abroad, which means losing the pension if you then do relocate). Yet the consideration will be to balance these two risks. The offer would be magnificent, like a fairy tale: I would <u>only</u> have to write my books. That is only possible in an aristocratic, conservative society. The income – we have no figures – would be modest, but probably sufficient for a healthy living. I hope you are well.

Fondest wishes to you all.

Your Kally[7]

Julia hoped that Jaspers would be invited as a guest professor to Oxford, where she would be nearer to Gertrud.[8] However at St John's College, Oxford, where the award of a grant was strongly supported by Jaspers' sponsor, the White's Professor of Moral Philosophy, H. J. Paton, Jaspers' case was rejected in favour of another candidate. All efforts to entice him from Heidelberg were thwarted.

The decision by St John's College not to sponsor Jaspers was not necessarily because his referees failed to recognize the urgency of his case. Rather, the SPSL was inundated with so many biographies of hardship that sufficient funds were not available to support everyone. However, there was a misconception about his philosophy. The attempt to arrange a guest professorship either at Oxford, or indeed, as Brock hoped, at Cambridge University, was frustrated by a communication problem. If the host failed to appreciate the language of the guest's philosophy, it was equally the case that the guest had difficulty with the language of the host. Heinrich Zimmer highlighted his difficulties with Oxonian English when he reported to Jaspers on his experiences after arriving in Oxford in spring 1939.[9] Raymond Klibansky had invited Zimmer to a meeting of the Oxford Philosophical Society where they had listened to a lecture on Plato's *Parmenides*. Although he could follow the general thrust of the ensuing discussion, Zimmer wrote to Jaspers that the way of expression in Oxford was 'quiet, nimble and floating'.[10] The SPSL issued a standard questionnaire for political refugees that Jaspers returned to London with a clear indication that if he did come to England, he was not sure whether his knowledge of the English language would be sufficient, although he was gaining confidence about his English-speaking skills and his responses showed as much: 'How well can you read English? – "quite well". How well can you speak English? – "not very much for the time being". How well can you write English? – "not very much at present".'[11]

Critical reception of Jaspers' philosophy in England had been marred by inaccurate translations.[12] But there was also a call for concrete resolution of his speculative language. A scepticism about continental philosophy had been implicit in some recommendations on Jaspers' behalf,[13] an interpretative blind spot that did not apply to the recommendation of H. J. Paton who especially highlighted the anti-dogmatic quality of Jaspers' work as directed against Hitler's régime.[14] However, the praise, on one side, for the descriptive capacities of the early period of Jaspers' work, and criticism, on the other, for the obscurity of Jaspers' language led to resistance to Jaspers' psychological approach.[15]

In Germany, there was speculation that Jaspers was about to leave the country. The rumour that he was to accept a guest professorship in Istanbul was rife in Berlin. Even before the Oxford plan materialized, Gertrud reassured her parents-in-law that the story (Jaspers' relocation would have been prohibited if it had been true), was without foundation.[16] Less idle was the speculation about which one of Jaspers' friends abroad could devise a successful plan to persuade him to quit the country. At least three further attempts were made to help – the first by Lucien Lévy-Bruhl in Paris[17] and the others from the University of Basel. It was not for want of trying to leave Germany that Jaspers remained, but that a favourable moment for his emigration never materialized. Jaspers was cautious about leaving the country, but it was dangerous for Gertrud to stay. She might now fall victim to the Gestapo that had already reacted to orders to transport Jews from Baden and Württemberg (apart from Jews in so-called 'mixed marriages' and foreign 'non-Aryans'), to the south of France.[18] If Gertrud were to be threatened by deportation, the Jaspers' suicide pact would have been put into action – they had hidden poison capsules in the bathroom cupboard.[19] Whilst Gertrud was relatively safe until 1943, the chances that Jaspers himself might not survive the war increased. His last trip abroad was at the beginning of August 1939.[20] In reply to a concerned enquiry about Gertrud from Gustav Mayer, Jaspers outlined his view of their position. He wrote that their category of 'mixed marriage' (that Jaspers also regretted was a marriage without children), provided them with four specific privileges, qualifying Gertrud as an 'exception': Gertrud was not required to hand over precious gemstones and valuable jewellery; she could remain together with her husband in their place of residence; she was exempted from compulsory membership of the National Representation of German Jews (*Reichsvereinigung der Juden in Deutschland*) that was established to promote emigration; and, in principle, she was permitted to accompany Jaspers to a health spa, if authorized by a doctor's note.[21] However, Gertrud was forbidden entry to a museum, theatre, cinema or other public place and whilst Heidelberg's tradesmen continued to deliver their domestic supplies, dealing directly with Gertrud, the Jaspers lived under a constant fear for her safety. Jaspers was deeply worried what might happen if he were to fall ill, a possibility that he nonetheless raised in his letter to Gustav Mayer: 'Every "exception" is unfortunately highly <u>questionable</u> to me (we have not discussed and not decided) what would happen in the case of my death. That is my great worry. It would be better if we had children (then the exception still applies, even after the husband's death).'[22]

Fortunately, Jaspers had purchased the rights to their lifelong tenancy at Plöck 66 some months before Hitler's takeover.[23] At least, Gertrud would not become homeless, even in the event of his death. Yet it was possible that at an arbitrary future date, they could be cheated out of their home. Their survival strategy had commenced during the early days of Hitler's régime when Gertrud preferred not to visit even their closest friends, in order not to endanger them. She reluctantly broke the rule to accept a tea invitation at the home of the theologian, Martin Dibelius, when their friend pressed Gertrud to make the effort: 'I am going to accept, though not without being timid.'[24]

Another exception to their restricted lifestyle was a short Easter holiday during April 1934 when they stayed in the spa town of Badenweiler, together with Marianne Weber (who drove them about the Black Forest).[25] In Badenweiler, Gertrud was able to bathe in the Roman spa waters. Jaspers commented to his parents that he was reading Goethe's *Italian Journey*; he now claimed to have recognized Goethe's attitude as open to works of art and architecture and he felt he could enjoy the narrative all the more, in comparison to his memories of Italy.[26]

The risk of association with Jaspers was great because of their 'mixed marriage', a factor that did not deter a steady stream of visitors who continued to arrive on Jaspers' doorstep. Their visitors included well and lesser known personalities: Marianne and Alfred Weber; the classical scholar, Ludwig Curtius; Heinrich Zimmer and his wife; Gustav Radbruch; a student friend, Wilhelmine Drescher; Maria Salditt; and, last but not least, a young lecturer from Leipzig, Hans-Georg Gadamer. Several of their guests who were especial favourites with Gertrud were Jeanne Hersch, at that time, a young lecturer of philosophy at Geneva University; and Renato de Rosa, a former assistant to Aliotta at Naples University. Gertrud enjoyed Jeanne Hersch's visits as those of an exemplary house guest who made few demands on Jaspers' time and always arrived with one purpose in mind – to engage Jaspers in conversation about his philosophy and to convey news about the reception of his work in France.[27]

When the German invasion of Poland precipitated Britain's declaration of war on 1 September 1939, Jaspers suspended all work completely. The necessity of preparing for war reached Plöck 66 – all the windows were blacked out, the cellar was turned into a makeshift air-raid shelter, the house was protected, as far as possible, against gas attacks.[28] Not satisfied with their safeguards, Jaspers purchased an old treasurers' chest to deposit 'the ton' of his life's work that he was, he wrote to his parents, determined to rescue in the event of their survival.[29] The general air of concern about world events led Jaspers to retreat further into his private world. His congratulatory message for his father's eighty-ninth birthday on 1 October 1939, contained a subdued and nostalgic note:

> The day was always a family day, from my earliest childhood, especially since it coincided with the change of the seasons and the start of the hare-hunting season. Actually, this day was marked by your absence, being away on the hunt and returning home in the evening with lots of hares. That is more than 25 years ago, but for my mood, at least, the memory of that belongs to this day.[30]

At this time, Gertrud typed two additional chapters of Jaspers' memoirs on student life (1901–7) and his notes on illness – she retrieved his almost illegible student diaries that were partially used as sources for the first of these chapters.[31] Perhaps, Jaspers saw this work as an interference with his research for the 'Philosophical Logic', since it is doubtful that his primary concern was ever towards the literary dimension of his memoirs. Rather, they were to be read aloud – a 'communicative' project.[32] Jaspers forwarded careful instructions to his mother that if she were to read the latest instalment of his text aloud to his father, she was to introduce each quotation as 'letter', with the given date, or as 'diary'; and likewise, she was to repeat at the end of a quotation, 'end of letter/quotation'.[33] In that way, Jaspers' memoirs became an extended conversation with his family, a fact that was all the more poignant when, scarcely two months later, on 24 February, his father died.[34]

In wartime, Jaspers could not travel to Oldenburg for his father's funeral.

Instead, he wrote a long speech to be read aloud at the funeral service. In certain places, the speech revealed characteristics that could have applied to father and son. Familiar Jaspers qualities were a preference for solitude that was tolerable because of a devoted wife; strength of character and uncompromising honesty; strong belief in the power of nature; truthfulness in place of allegiance to a religious faith; and yet, respect for the Bible's teachings.[35]

After his father's death, Jaspers' attitude towards their residency in Germany altered by degrees. He felt no obligation to stay, especially when, eleven months later, on the last day of January 1941, his mother died at his sister's family home in Oldenburg. He wrote that their mother's last letter had only arrived in Heidelberg at the moment that his sister telephoned the news that their mother had died, peacefully, in her armchair.[36] To comfort his sister, Jaspers reminded her: 'Mother [...] was the constant mirror of our life, she was interested in everything and every matter that affected us.'[37]

Two days after Henriette Jaspers' funeral in Oldenburg, he informed his sister that he was considering accepting an invitation from Basel University to work for several terms as a guest professor. The head librarian of Basel University Library, Dr Karl Schwarber, was the intermediary who forwarded to Jaspers the official invitation from the private foundation, the Freie Akademische Stiftung.[38] The Swiss invitation was the best prospect that Jaspers received for emigration. Yet as he wrote to Erna, they were reluctant to use the invitation as a way to leave Germany:

Heidelberg, 5. 2. 41

Dear Erna,

Our thoughts, my longing, our love meet daily. Yet today I do not really want to write.

Since mid-January, something is being discussed that we deliberately did not tell mother about because we wanted to wait and see the result beforehand. I have been invited for guest lectures to Basel, initially, for 2 years with 10,000 Swiss francs as an annual salary. Of course, all this is strictly confidential. I have already spoken to the Rector here. We do not want to 'emigrate' but to keep our home here, to try and secure all permits, as well as the permit for our return together to Heidelberg. That is probably all still very unlikely. In the end, presumably nothing will come of it. Now our friend, Gabriele, is travelling to Berlin and I would really like her to talk to Stephan, to get his opinion and advice. Can you send me his address and title, as quickly as possible, by return of post? I will give Gabriele a letter for her to hand to him personally. The Swiss are touching. By today's standards, the offer is fantastic, entry arrangements and all other difficulties are taken care of on the Swiss side.

Fond greetings to you all,

Your Kally[39]

Jaspers had applied for a special visa that permitted Gertrud, either on her own, or in Jaspers' company, to travel to Heidelberg during holiday periods.[40] The request for unconditional free passage between Germany and Switzerland seems to have been a result of advice from Paul Schmitthenner. Schmitthenner was more sympathetic to Jaspers than previous Rectors of Heidelberg University had been. Indeed, Jaspers requested an appointment with him for advice on how to present his Basel invitation to the Education Ministry in Berlin.[41] The private source of Swiss funds for Jaspers' invitation meant that his guest professorship in Basel was not to be treated as a chance for a permanent position. Therefore, he emphasized to the authorities that it would be beneficial for his research on 'philosophical logic', as well as for his studies on ancient cultures and civilizations to accept the Basel invitation. In his official letter to the Minister of Education, Jaspers persuasively illustrated the positive echo for his philosophy, especially Luigi Pareyson's *La filosofia dell'esistenza e Carlo Jaspers* (1940) that had appeared in Italy.[42] Furthermore, Schmitthenner's personal recommendation appeared a genuine vote for Jaspers' exit visa.[43] When Jaspers' application was rejected, several months later, he sent Schmitthenner a cordial note of thanks for his assistance.[44] A year later, the Basel invitation was renewed, but this time, Gertrud was refused an exist visa. Their hopes of emigrating during wartime now completely vanished.

The failure of the Swiss plan was followed by another piece of bad news. Jaspers hoped to publish a completely revised edition of *General Psycho-pathology* (1913), something that his publisher, Julius Springer, was keen to support because by now the book was out of print. Springer approached the Director of Heidelberg's Clinic of Psychiatry, to arrange for Jaspers to use the library facilities[45] and Jaspers finished rewriting the new, fourth edition of *General Psychopathology* by summer 1942. He was forbidden to publish the work because, in spring 1943, the Reichschrifttumskammer vetoed publica-tions.[46] Before the publication ban was enforced, Jaspers was able to finish an autobiographical essay that was written at the suggestion of Renato de Rosa who was staying with them. (Having discovered, upon his arrival in

Heidelberg, that Jaspers' lectures were cancelled, de Rosa remained and occupied the Jaspers' guest rooms in the attic of Plöck 66 until he had to return to Italy.[47]) By June 1941, Gertrud was typing the final amendments for Jaspers' essay, 'About my Philosophy' (1941), published in the Italian journal, *Logos*, translated by Renato de Rosa.[48] The Italian manuscript of Jaspers' essay was smuggled out of the country in a diplomatic bag.[49] The essay was one of the more coherent descriptions of the inner dynamics of Jaspers' work. In the months following his father's death, he mentioned to his sister that he was especially concentrating on a new project that he referred to as the 'universal history of philosophy', a project that he began by several weeks' preparatory reading on ancient history, civilizations and ethnology. He put the project alongside what would be published after the war as his 'philosophical logic'. He wrote to his sister of an introduction to his project in which he described the 'principles, methods and tasks' of a 'universal history of philosophy'. This project sounded as though it were indeed to become a third pillar of Jaspers' later works. (The first pillar had been his 'philosophical logic'; and the second was his portraits of the world's leading philosophers.) Jaspers wrote to Erna that his new ideas grew perhaps more by accident than design: 'I had a pang of hunger for material, gave up my work on the "logic" for a while, although I will soon return to it.'[50]

Jaspers' essay, 'About my Philosophy' (1941), provided several clues to the systematic purpose of the planned project on history that he had already mentioned in correspondence with Heinrich Zimmer.[51] His inspiration, as he wrote in his autobiographical essay, was for a gallery of historical achievement whose appropriation (*Aneignung*) was to be projected onto a world stage. The scenery or backdrop of that stage was to be comprised of three geographical locations, two of which, China and India, he was already researching with Zimmer's advice, and the third was in the West. Although Jaspers' text on world history is unfinished its ineffable quality of displaying ideas like a picture gallery is challenging: '*The Encompassing* that the world is as Being itself is represented (*angeschaut*), as though in a parallel gallery of world landscapes'.[52] The question of whether Jaspers' perception of global landscapes was born only of silent yearning to be anywhere except in Hitler's Germany or whether this project was in the systematic nature of his thinking is an open one.[53]

The timing of the investigations is of particular relevance in that Jaspers' project of the 'global' or 'universal' history of philosophy emerged when his future was at stake. The National Representation for German Jews in Berlin informed Jaspers that, due to new regulations for 'mixed marriages', he was forbidden to employ a German maid to help Gertrud with the domestic chores.[54] Jaspers appealed against the decision, in a similar way that he had pleaded against the terms of his retirement. He argued that, if his scientific work were not to be jeopardized, he was obliged to rely on domestic help. A flurry of letters passed to and fro, but an internal communiqué from the Gestapo to the Minister of Education in Karlsruhe outlined that Jaspers was either to divorce his wife or employ in his household a 'Mischling of the first degree' (*Mischling I. Grades*), that is, a person descended from two Jewish grandparents, but not belonging to the Jewish religion and not married to a Jewish person on 15 September 1935.[55] Another investigation by the secret police was ordered into the precise status of his privileged 'mixed marriage'.[56] Gertrud was in desperate danger. Clearly, their marriage was no longer filed away in Gestapo archives as one of the privileged 'exceptions' to the Nuremberg Laws of 1935, and new measures could be ordered at any moment.[57] Up until then, Jaspers had successfully appealed, using his contacts, to 'reliable' Nazis such as Paul Schmitthenner against all measures designed to deprive them of their basic rights. After October 1944, Jews in 'mixed marriages' were also being deported from Baden and Württemberg but Jaspers never ceased to shield Gertrud. On at least three separate occasions, after 5 October 1944, she went into hiding.[58] They were helped by Jaspers' former student, Theodor Haubach, who became a victim of his association with the Kreisau Circle and the 20 July plot to assassinate Hitler in 1944. Before his death, Haubach introduced Jaspers to another friend, Emil Henk, who had political connections with the Social Democrats and the resistance to Hitler. Henk's Berlin contacts warned him of the dangers for Gertrud, and, in the evenings, Jaspers accompanied her to the railway station where she was met by Emil Henk and taken to a secret hiding place.[59]

On 12 February 1945, Jews from Baden and Württemberg were collected for forced labour, sent to a transit camp near Ludwigsburg and deported to an unknown destination.[60] On 2 March 1945, in a desperate attempt to intervene on Jaspers' behalf, Paul Schmitthenner sought an assurance from the SS in Berlin that Gertrud would be excluded from any further measures against Jews in her region.[61] The Jaspers knew that the next deportation of Jews from Heidelberg was, otherwise, to have included Gertrud.[62]

PART V

Pictures of Humanity

Would a painter, in your view, be less expert because,
after having delineated with consummate art an ideal of a
perfectly beautiful man, he was unable to show that any
such man could ever have existed?

Plato, *The Republic*, V. 472d

16 *'Liberated by Allied Forces'*

A DIARY THAT JASPERS BEGAN only days before the Americans arrived in
Heidelberg recorded his version of events. As his attention turned from the
Nazi occupation to the liberation of Heidelberg, he was anxious for the
operation to proceed with the minimum cost to human life. As it was, there
was little fierce fighting:

30. 3. [1945]
[…] No electricity, no water, no gas. We are trying to equip ourselves.
A spirit stove will do for a short time. Water can be fetched from the
spring at the Klingentor. The young people are in the best mood. It is
magnificent fun for them to live like Indians, and they are bright and
active at the same time.

Then at eight o'clock Frau v. J. [Else Jaffé] arrived and reported:
this morning the Americans arrived on the Neuenheimerlandstraße,
they found all the bridges destroyed and stood in front of them with
tanks. They discovered the boathouse near the new bridge, took the
paddleboats and paddled across the river, landing at the grammar
school where they are stationed. They must also have arrived upstream
by the Neckar. They came into town by *Schlierbach* and are at the town
hall and in control there.

Frau v. J. came to congratulate us that at last our Trudlein is free: a moment without words. It is a miracle that we are still alive.[1]

Jaspers glimpsed several German infantrymen trying to hide in a row of trees behind his house, but their presence proved to be merely superficial as was that of the teenage boys, forcibly recruited to resist the capture of Heidelberg. As the young recruits were loaded onto a hay cart with old men, the prospect of victory for a well-equipped American army seemed a foregone conclusion.[2] Such actions to resist the inevitable merely prolonged the hour of the German capitulation. Jaspers captured the moment in his diary with the animation of a civilian, intrigued by the novelty of watching military manoeuvres at close quarters:

30. 3. [45]:
At 10 o'clock: the shooting begins again, in the west, not so near any more. But a sign that everything is not in order here yet.

People on the street say that the Americans are only present on the Neuenheim side of the river. In the *Plöck*, the Translation Institute and another building have hoisted a white flag.

11 o'clock: artillery fire, heavy and nearby, almost like yesterday. The occupation of Heidelberg is obviously not quite over. However: news just now that Americans are standing on Werder square.

I have just heard from the field hospital across the road: the American order is for everyone to leave the streets – anyone on the street is in danger of being shot at.

11.30: On the embankment behind the garden I see 6 infantry soldiers, one of them always taking cover behind the tree-trunks. Shots – back to the east. In the *Plöck*, in front of our house, 3 infantrymen are disarmed by an American and led away as prisoners.

In the afternoon: to the south of the river Neckar the town is occupied by a few soldiers that came from the west. A bridgehead with paddleboats is at the destroyed bridge to Neuenheim. The furthest command post reaches as far as the lazarette across the road from us in the *Plöck*. American soldiers, in pairs, are patrolling the length of the *Plöck*, around the library, towards the left. A police patrol unit with blue armbands has given the order to clear the streets after 6 o'clock, the town still has to surrender, battles are still possible.

Tonight, on the south side of the river, Heidelberg is without American or German military.[3]

These observations contrasted with a note of disbelief that when American reinforcements arrived a day later, the Gestapo drove out of town seemingly unimpeded.[4] Jaspers' distinction between the bravery of the incoming military and the cowardice of the fleeing Nazis was elaborated upon when he met Dr Edward Hartshorne, an American sociologist and expert on Max Weber and the German university.[5] Hartshorne assumed responsibility for the reopening of Heidelberg University and he suggested that Jaspers speak on key occasions, such as for the opening of the medical faculty when it was opportune to underline the enormous debt owed in Germany to the Allied forces.[6]

There is a gradual shift of mood in Jaspers' diary from suppressed elation to awareness that the Americans and the victorious Sixth Army, whose commander, Colonel Charles D. Winning was stationed in nearby Mannheim,[7] were part of a victorious occupation force. However, the Allies' common aim was for democracy and in the American zone, the policy of peaceful coexistence with the native population was underscored by General Eisenhower's instruction of 3 April 1945 that former Nazis who could be identified were to be turned in.[8] On the official day of Heidelberg's liberation Jaspers recorded, '1. 4. [45]: The capitulation of all power is total. It is like a fairytale, when you read the posters on the same walls behind which we have had to live for 12 years of utmost horror, then you see that the Americans, for the most part, make an impeccable impression [...].'[9] Jaspers' gratitude to the Americans was not offered out of politeness. His liberators had already added his name to a so-called 'White' List of twenty-five reliable partners to be trusted with the challenge of re-education after twelve years of dictatorship. According to the 'White' List, Jaspers was 'absolutely opposed to the Nazis'.[10] When several American officers visited them at their home, with greetings from Gertrud's eldest brother, Gustav Mayer, the Jaspers' gratitude towards the young officers turned into renewed confidence about once again being respected as German citizens.[11] By degrees, the fairytale appeared gradually to come true, for a series of coincidences signalled the likelihood of Jaspers beginning to lecture again after eight years of silence.

After the official closure of the university on 1 April 1945, several officers of the Counter Intelligence Corps (CIC) were despatched to the home of Emil Henk – Jaspers' friend and Gertrud's protector – for a first unofficial gathering of a small party of academics. At this meeting, the university's status was discussed, since almost all present had been deprived of their professorships under the Nazis.[12] When special agent, Thomas A. Emmet, invited the group to form a temporary advisory committee, an air of buoyant optimism circulated, as the committee members, including Jaspers, were authorized to reinstate university personnel and to plan to restart lectures as they saw fit. The party who were present at Henk's meeting, with the exception of Else Jaffé, were members of the committee, directed by the professor of theology, Martin Dibelius, and joined by a candidate for the Rector's position, Karl Heinrich Bauer. The temporary advisory committee quickly became known as the 'Committee of Thirteen' (*Dreizehnerausschuß*). In future, meetings were held at Jaspers' house, a piece of luck that saved his home from military requisition. Nevertheless, Jaspers became disillusioned by the fact that the university was not to reopen as quickly as he had hoped.[13] Perhaps, he was also disappointed that there were officers, albeit friendly, present at their meetings. For the time being, the library, the main lecture theatres and all the nearby buildings remained closed.[14]

The first few days of freedom were filled with receiving the steady stream of visitors who arrived at Jaspers' house – committee members, American officers, former colleagues and students. All were seeking assistance, encouragement and advice. Jaspers' time was monopolized by unprecedented activity. The day after the Americans entered Heidelberg, Gertrud wrote a detailed letter to Gustav and her sister-in-law, Flora, stating: 'We still cannot believe it, we are saved.'[15] Gertrud attempted to forget the past, but she mentioned here how her fear had reached new heights and that she felt compelled to take her life. She was facing something that, only a few months later, after the liberation of Germany on 8 May 1945, she claimed to be ignorant about when she confided to Gustav that the contents of the Allied news broadcasts about the concentration camps came as a profound shock. Everybody guessed something terrible must be happening, yet nobody '<u>knew</u>' what was taking place.[16]

Thousands of miles away, on another continent, Hannah Arendt studied the self same issue with her claim that 'the only way in which we can identify an anti-Nazi is when the Nazis have hanged him', uncannily echoed in Gertrud's letter.[17] What Arendt identified was a connection between acting and knowing, or cognitive responsibility and passive guilt, whereby she highlighted the difficulty of accounting for crimes against humanity committed in Nazi concentration camps: 'The number of those who are responsible *and* guilty will be relatively small. There are many who share responsibility without any visible proof of guilt. There are many more who have become guilty without being in the least responsible.'[18] The guilt question was not the focus of Gertrud's letter. She remembered how her fear of deportation had obscured the question. She experienced liberation as a reprieve from the perpetual fear of death. The realization that she was safe turned the question of blame into one of survival.

What Gertrud noted about a 'collective' form of denial in Germany was not so much based on psychology or morality. She related her feeling of survivor's guilt in a special tribute for Jaspers:

> My dear brother, my dear Flora,
>
> 1 April, Easter Sunday
>
> That I can write to you and do so openly! For the time being, that cures my sense of longing. For the last week I have not been able to concentrate, before that I was reading the volumes of Engels with great pleasure. Karl is happy and moved, he is older, but he already feels productive ideas coming again. He kept me – without him, I would have thought more and more of suicide. His soul daily endured everything with indescribable power of love. May the gift of my life be given to me, to live for him and to remain inwardly united with you, until death parts us.
>
> Your Trude.[19]

A statement that Jaspers mentioned in his philosophical autobiography recurs.[20] Gertrud recorded how Jaspers repeatedly consoled her with the words: 'I am Germany for you.'[21] This sentiment was not a moralistic statement about a good or evil side of Germany and still less an intentional identification with Germany as a whole. The expression voiced the kind of solidarity that had encouraged Gertrud to live. The attitude was supported by the idealism that motivated Jaspers' need for Gertrud as the one person who could encourage him to strive for higher aims throughout his life: her presence was a reminder of his purpose.

If these facts seemed relevant only to their engagement in 1907, Jaspers' devotion to Gertrud in her hour of need was a way of repaying a debt of gratitude that he felt he owed for her dedication to the daily ritual of his life. Throughout their lives together, in moments concealed from the public gaze, Jaspers' illness took sudden turns for the worse and, at times, his condition became life threatening. A note that Jaspers scribbled on 9 November 1930 during an attack of bronchial fever hardly reckons with recovery. Jaspers writes several, uncharacteristically haphazard instructions to his parents, or another, such as 'To my Trudelein': 'The book is yours'.[22] (Here Jaspers referred to his *Philosophy* (1932) which was then undergoing literary revision, guided by Ernst Mayer.) The note as much as says that Jaspers' own existence would have vanished into thin air, if Gertrud herself were ever to perish.

The reality of survival was also made clear in one of Gertrud's letters addressed to all six of her brothers, written when she feared that she was going to be rounded up by the Gestapo.[23] In this letter, dated 25 February 1945, she searches for an explanation for the Nazi 'forced labour camp', the reports of which remained unconfirmed. She could not forget how her brother-in-law, Eugen Dugend, an official directing administrative tribunals, had been forced to join the Nazi Party. Against his wishes, he had been registered as a member of the Party from 1938. He had opposed the boycott of Jewish businesses; and had sent parcels of one-thousand-Mark notes with his wife, Erna, or other visitors to Jaspers from Oldenburg, that were to save Ernst Mayer in hiding in Holland. Gertrud's account is compelling: 'One day the Party telephones him: "Herr President, we are surprised that you have not yet enquired about becoming a member in the Party." He [replies]: "I did not do so, because my past as a democrat is generally known." The Party: "Now, then you are herewith a member of the Party." '[24] Tragically their young friend, Afra Geiger, who had spent Christmas 1929 with the Jaspers' in Heidelberg, lost her life in Bergen-Belsen.[25] Such aspects of Gertrud's experience established a need to know how any of her friends and relatives could have survived at all.

Heidelberg escaped Allied bombing raids that destroyed most of nearby Mannheim, but the town was destitute – not even a shoelace was to be purchased.[26] It was little wonder that when Jaspers gave his first public speech for the reopening of part of Heidelberg University on 15 August 1945, he made their experiences of liberation the basis for his introductory remarks. The reopening of the university's medical faculty was also the occasion for the inauguration of the first post-war Rector of Heidelberg University, Karl Heinrich Bauer. The official ceremony for Bauer was followed by Jaspers' speech as a fully reinstated professor of philosophy.[27] During his retirement years, Jaspers' professorship had been occupied by the Nazi, Ernst Krieck, and afterwards, by Paul Schmitthenner whose professorship was now declared null and void.[28] When Jaspers was voted an honorary senator of the university (an invitation he had to decline due to his health), his status as a public figure was assured. The high moral tone of his speeches both impressed the Americans and would inspire Bauer to continue with his duties when he came under suspicion of previous involvement with the Nazis.[29] In his 15 August speech, 'Rejuvenation of the University' (1945), Jaspers tried not to provoke tensions and problems. The speech was printed in the first edition of a new journal, *Die Wandlung*, authorized and issued with a licence by the Americans, with Jaspers acting as co-editor in cooperation with Alfred Weber, Werner Knauss and his former pupil, Dolf Sternberger, who was editor-in-chief.[30] Jaspers' speech underlined that the terms of Germany's military defeat were to be accepted with good grace. The 'silent disappearance' of former leaders of the Nazi régime had made the act of surrender and the reorganization of Germany a fact of life.[31] With the benefit of hindsight, Jaspers gave a stark résumé of the lack of civil courage that he suggested had contributed to Germany's total capitulation:

> We were able to seek death when the crimes of the régime became obvious in public: on 30 June 1934, or with the lootings, deportations and murders of our Jewish friends and fellow citizens, when to our perpetual shame and disgrace the synagogues – houses of God – were in flames throughout Germany in 1938. [...] Thousands in Germany either sought death or were killed anyway because of their opposition to the régime. The majority of them remain anonymous. We survivors did not seek death. We did not go out on the streets when our Jewish friends were led away, nor did we cry out until they destroyed us as well. We preferred to stay alive on the weak, if justified grounds that our death would not have helped anyway. That we live is our guilt. We know before God, what deeply humbles us.[32]

Several months later, Jaspers began to lecture on the 'The Guilt Question' that he gently introduced to the audience of aspiring medical students as a reminder of how the National Socialists had tarnished the reputation of medicine by crimes against humanity.[33]

In his August speech Jaspers claimed to have used some thoughts that he had set down in his unpublished 'Theses for the Rejuvenation of the University' (1933).[34] Jaspers' *Theses (1933)* were first sketched with the medical faculty in mind, for even in July 1933, he hardly had a complimentary word to say: 'Things are at their worst in medicine where in the end everyone passes the examination.'[35] His ideas about the simplification of scientific standards over the years were based on a keen desire to see medical and philosophical faculties reunited in mutual awareness of their tasks. Jaspers' concern was – and he admitted his failure to communicate such reservations to Heidegger – that philosophy should act as a good conscience for the scientist. If practical activity were to become the basis of medical research instead of ideological thinking, the guiding light could be sought from philosophy. This anti-ideological message certainly figured in Jaspers' August 1945 speech when he was at pains to place a medical vocation within a clearer conception of humanity – a far cry from the blatant disregard for mankind, condoned under the Nazis' racial theory.[36] In the new climate, Jaspers emphasized *humanity* and *science*; and the occasion was not to pass without underlining his esteem for Kant: 'Man is always more than whatever can be known about him.'[37] These words could also have been a motto for Jaspers' essay, *The Idea of the University* (1923), a text that he revised during the months after the Americans' arrival in Heidelberg and for which he received approval for publication in the following year. Even so, Jaspers' message about philosophy and science left much to the imagination, for he concentrated largely on the outline, without necessarily filling in the details, although he was soon to make good that shortcoming.[38]

Jaspers chose to discuss a similar theme, that is, the status of German science, for a candid talk given on 11 January 1946 to inaugurate a series of open lectures by Heidelberg professors.[39] This talk corroborated the messages he disseminated on so many occasions after the American occupation of Heidelberg. His article, 'Answer to Sigrid Undset', published in the American newspaper, *Die Neue Zeitung*, on 4 November 1945, was part of the relentless criticism he raised about Germany's new situation, although the common thread that tied his texts together was their surprisingly positive outlook. With the claim of the Norwegian author, Sigrid Undset, that the reputation of Germany had reached an all-time low, Jaspers felt compelled to clarify the overall position, not least because of his experiences of the Nazi state.[40]

Jaspers' open lecture in January was given the symbolic title, 'About the Living Spirit of the University' (1946). This title was a deliberate reference to the motto, 'To the living spirit' (*Dem lebendigen Geist*), the words that Friedrich Gundolf had suggested adorn the space above the entrance to Heidelberg University's new lecture theatres, where the statue of the Olympian goddess of wisdom, Pallas Athene, was mounted on a pedestal above the portal. In 1936, these symbols of Humboldt's ideals were replaced with a large eagle, and the words 'Dem deutschen Geist' were inscribed above the entrance as an act of self-glorification that coincided with the university's 550th anniversary celebrations under the National Socialists.[41] In reference to these events, Jaspers tried to show how intellectual life had been brought to a standstill, since once the emblems of humanity were declared meaningless, the breakdown of communication in Nazi Germany had totally reversed the validity of Humboldt's ideals. A type of paralysis had gripped the community and even overshadowed the activity of the university in a way that Jaspers called an unforgettable disgrace:

> Instead of an intellectual community in loving contest, what emerged, on the one hand, was a wariness of the common ground of social cameraderie, and on the other hand, endless rounds of discussion consisting of chance opinions, vain self-promotion and sophistry.

Everywhere, a secret code of behaviour was valid: everything is still undecided; things are not to be taken so seriously. Conciliatory behaviour was the condition for being regarded as a decent human being.[42]

For the first time, Jaspers allowed his personal reflections about politics, a constant feature of his family correspondence, to see the light of day. Jaspers' lecture was a breakthrough. The pathos of the 'Göschen' edition was overturned in favour of terse, but embellished commentary. Jaspers talked about the moral lapse amongst intellectuals, as though Hitler had transfixed them, even to the point of betraying their ideals in a community whose reputation was to have been established upon laurels of truth. Had he been so immune to that cardinal sin of altering his suit of clothing to the requirements of the day? The question was not exactly the subject of a preface (*Geleitwort*) that Jaspers agreed to contribute to the first edition of *Die Wandlung*, but his text did suggest that those who survived, regardless of their social status, should consider how they had turned Germany into a haven for dictatorship. To start afresh, it was not enough to forget the past: 'A new beginning must be made. Whilst we begin to allow the transformation to happen and to lend it support, we hope to be on the way to that end, where we will again lay a foundation. We are revising everything so completely that we cannot even be sure of these foundations.'[43] Talk of 'transformation' was introduced as though Jaspers were only too aware of treading on eggshells. A hint of caution about the general situation also permeated Jaspers' new and characteristically short phrases: 'The individual is only himself, if the other is also himself. Freedom is only relative to everybody's being free.'[44]

In this way, Jaspers introduced a generation of readers to democracy and the responsibility that he accepted along with that role was mirrored in his 'Theses for Political Freedom', published in the June 1946 edition of *Die Wandlung*. In this article, he outlined an ethos of democracy as meaning participation and communication in a flourishing community. Yet it seemed as though his principles took precedence over political parties and the reality of establishing a new constitution: 'The decisive character of free circumstances is *belief in freedom*.'[45]

It was vital to Jaspers to replace belief in the forces of coercion with a new reality of democracy. He was struck by Hannah Arendt's essay, *Organized Guilt and Universal Responsibility* (1945), in which she pronounced that: 'Where all are guilty, nobody in the last analysis can be judged.'[46] That Jaspers accepted her thesis was clear from the way that he quoted verbatim from her essay in

'About the Living Spirit of the University': 'For many years now we have met Germans who declare that they are ashamed of being Germans. I have often felt tempted to answer that I am ashamed of being human.'[47] Jaspers persuaded the co-editors of *Die Wandlung* to publish a German translation of Arendt's essay in the fourth issue of the journal (April 1946). To a certain extent, he was already refining Arendt's political language into a compassionate lecture *The Question of German Guilt* (1946) that became part of a programme of studies, published for the winter semester of 1945/6. This lecture series was to coincide with the reopening of the philosophical faculty on 7 January 1946. In the second part of the lectures that were devoted to understanding Germany's intellectual situation, Jaspers included the problem of guilt. He especially sought clarification about the leading question: 'How was National Socialism possible?'[48]

The way in which Jaspers illustrated his theme in *The Question of German Guilt* was by a series of definitions on the penalty for active and passive involvement with the Nazis. He qualified these definitions by asserting that 'moral' guilt was an individual matter, whereas everyone who survived, when others had perished, continued to be involved in a problem that affected everybody, no matter where, no matter when. This legacy was 'metaphysical' guilt, a legacy that Jaspers designated as uniquely relevant for the future of mankind.[49] A precondition for considering this legacy was that human beings are treated as members of the human race, since only then are the concerns of one man to be considered as relevant to the next. Jaspers defined the legacy as follows:

> Metaphysical guilt is the lack of absolute solidarity with a fellow human being. It lingers on as an indelible claim, whereas a moral demand already ceases to carry meaning. This kind of solidarity is wounded, if I am present, wherever a wrong or a crime takes place. It is not enough to risk my life cautiously to prevent it. If it happens, if I was there, and if I survive where the other is killed, I know from a voice within myself: that I live now is my guilt.[50]

In defining 'metaphysical' guilt, Jaspers was seeking to understand the limitations of living in a world where humans were once accustomed, as in Nazi Germany, to treat their fellow men as though they possessed the right to act as judge and jury over another's life. If Jaspers implied that the Nazis had acted within a realm of earthly jurisdiction where otherwise the divine power of God holds sway, what he talked about as 'metaphysical' guilt did not relate to the individual's fate on judgement day.[51] The notion of a religious encounter was, so it seems, not what Jaspers had in mind. The reality of imprisonment had been their way of life in Hitler's Germany. Jaspers referred to this reality in his lecture, but Gertrud recalled her experiences whenever she talked about 'metaphysical' guilt as though the concept had entered their everyday conversations.

Gertrud was haunted by a permanent feeling of responsibility for the death of her younger sister, Ida. That was a burden Gertrud called 'metaphysical guilt before God'.[52] In the same way, no intercession could assuage the guilt of association with her young friend, Walter Calé, whose suicide coincided with Ida's confinement in the sanatorium and left her cousin, Julia, seeking eternal penance. Julia felt that she ought to have rescued Calé from his fate. Gertrud decided that it was futile to try and intervene. If survivor's guilt of the Holocaust was indeed to be called 'metaphysical', Gertrud also connected her sensations, in her letter of 25 February 1945, to the last lines of Shakespeare's Sonnet LXVI: 'Tir'd with all these, from these would I be gone, / Save that, to die, I leave my love alone.'[53]

What Jaspers called 'metaphysical' guilt appears not to have referred to tragedy in the classical sense, but was about the depth of the modern tragedy of survivor's guilt. In the modern world, there is no Aristotelean catharsis. The burden of survivor's guilt 'before God' may be overcome by liberation from the strings attached to the mortal state, since, in order to live, a survivor must turn his life into a daily 'metamorphosis'. This phrase in Jaspers' lecture implied that everyone is in the same boat when it comes to the urgency of survival. Yet it also seems that only the awakening of one's conscience may illuminate the fragility of this predicament: 'Those who were utterly powerless, outraged and in despair, yet who were unable to prevent the worst also took a step in their metamorphosis through their becoming aware of metaphysical guilt.'[54] Jaspers would come to regard his essay about survivor's guilt as the most misconstrued piece of his entire collected works.[55]

For the Jaspers the problem of survival, the issue that had dominated every waking moment of their lives, was now the least of their worries. Hannah Arendt, amongst others, sent a weekly shipment of care packets with medicine, diet supplements and luxuries that were impossible to buy in Germany. Publicly, Jaspers was now hailed amongst colleagues, in the local press and by Americans in Heidelberg as a figure commanding respect as a moral leader. When a renewed invitation was made through Edgar Salin at the end of 1946 for guest lectures at Basel University, Jaspers tried to postpone it. The offer was repeated in March 1947. Jaspers was in a quandary. He was obliged to apply for a whole month's holiday from his duties in Heidelberg at the end of June 1947. He was released from his duties for the guest lectures, after which he spent fourteen days' holiday in Switzerland. At the end of an eventful year, marked by the award of an honorary doctorate from the University of Lausanne, and the Goethe Prize on 28 August 1947, Jaspers received an offer of a full professorship at Basel University.

The relocation to Basel was so hastily arranged with the American authorities that the Jaspers did not even take leave of their friends. They fully expected to be turned back at the Swiss border, only to return, along with Jaspers' priceless library, to their old residence in Heidelberg.

17 Citizens of Basel

At the age of sixty-five, another chapter in Jaspers' life was about to begin. In the last few days of March 1948, with a permit from the American military authorities in Stuttgart to transfer his manuscripts and books, Karl and Gertrud Jaspers left Germany for good. They were transported in a Swiss chauffeur-driven car to Ausstraße 126, their new residence in central Basel.

The previous summer, Jaspers' book 'On Truth' (1947) had been published. A unique aspect of this work, which filled over one thousand pages, was that in one sense it was the outcome of research that continued in Heidelberg during Jaspers' 'retirement' years. In another sense, the work coincided with the Jaspers' change of location that gave a new impetus to his philosophical activities. Not that Jaspers' book was a direct sign of the ongoing transition in his life at that time, for the development of ideas that formed the book's contents dated from ongoing work and lectures that Jaspers gave in the mid- to late 1930s. In these lectures, Jaspers had first introduced the metaphor of *The Encompassing* as a particular conception of the shape of our reality, and thus, as a conception of being that merged, so to speak, into the background scenery of living for the present. 'On Truth' represented Jaspers' bid to articulate an ethical approach to life through the lucidity of his language of 'truth'.[1] That is to say that by showing that there existed a systematic pattern of interrelations amongst particular entities – such as 'life, consciousness as such, mind and *Existenz*' (*Dasein, Bewusstsein überhaupt, Geist* and *Existenz*) – he attempted to give an ethical study of freedom as a matter for the individual.[2] Jaspers' decision to change not just his place of residence, but the direction of his philosophizing in this late period of his life may be seen to illuminate what, with his metaphor of *The Encompassing*, he had compiled as a language of inherent entities relating to the truth. From the time that Jaspers had accepted the invitation to speak as a guest lecturer at the home of the Goethe Foundation in late September 1937, he had gone on record in his lectures, *The Philosophy of Existence* (1937), as saying that even philosophers, who may be expected to possess theories of truth, cannot undo errors of servitude and oppression. Jaspers' book about truth may also be read as an implicit statement of his opposition to Hitler. Since that statement could not be published during the period of Nazi rule, Jaspers was eager to see his work appear as soon as possible in the immediate post-war years.

The Jaspers' arrival in Basel marked a period of creative inspiration dependent upon the tried and tested model of their marriage.[3] Jaspers' philosophical work underwent subtle alterations, and a sense of rejuvenation meant he was able to separate his private life from the weight of expectations he felt bearing upon him. In fact, the pinnacle of Jaspers productive output coincided with his departure from Heidelberg. He felt a debt of gratitude to his Swiss colleagues, especially Edgar Salin, who organized his guest lectures, as well as his unassuming residence on the quiet street in the centre of Basel. As long as Gertrud accompanied him, Jaspers was ready to embrace the revival. The Jaspers' became citizens of Basel in June 1967.[4] But they had somehow been 'exiles' from Germany for some time before then. There were efforts behind the scenes to keep Jaspers in Heidelberg.[5] The Rector tried to persuade Jaspers to stay with a formal plea, endorsed by the higher Senate of the university. In one part of the Senate's message, the extent of their hopes and aspirations for Jaspers' work in Heidelberg was openly expressed: 'During the time when the university was re-established, you spoke for us and for German universities as a whole and, along with us, many people look on you as the man who embodies the highest western traditions for Germany. For that reason, we ask you to stay with us and to maintain the richest and deepest acclaim for your work at our university.'[6] It took the Jaspers' best efforts to dispel the view that their relocation had been a snub for Heidelberg.

This appeal for Jaspers to stay may have flattered his pride, and he certainly did not reject the support of what, in a letter of thanks for the Senate's statement, he had already called a common realm of the 'intellectual aristocracy of German-speaking universities'.[7] All the same, he announced his departure from Heidelberg in the local *Rhein–Neckar–Zeitung* just four days before he left. Interestingly, his statement contained a turn of phrase that he had used in his reply to the Rector in thanks for the Senate's approval of his remaining in Heidelberg which he had written several months previously: 'I remain a citizen of Heidelberg, wherever I may be.'[8] It may be, then, that Jaspers had already made up his mind several months before to accept Paul Häberlin's vacant professorship in Basel. All that remained for Heidelberg University was to print an official reaction alongside Jaspers' public statement that recorded 'painful regret' at his decision.[9]

Now, as before, Jaspers was concerned to ensure the high calibre of scientific activity that he wanted to encourage as a reality, not merely as an emblem of flattery to be used whenever it suited a whim or political agenda. The strain of managing his work as a public speaker and the need to maintain the privacy that gave space to his thinking may explain a growing resistance to the quiet lifestyle they had been forced to adopt to escape from the worst violence of Nazi terror. During Hitler's dictatorship the Jaspers had hidden away in Plöck 66, but they now appeared to be held captive in Heidelberg. The provincial mentality of their region was also the theme of an essay that Jaspers contributed to his co-edited journal, *Die Wandlung*.[10]

'On Biblical Religion' (1946) was written to communicate with readers whose faith in mankind was shaken by the experience of Fascist rule.[11] The essay resembled Jaspers' discussion of survival as an opportunity to reflect on the circumstances and need for restoring worldwide confidence in Germany's humanist reputation. These aspects had been magnified in a reader's letter, published in *Die Wandlung*, that quoted a memorable section of Jaspers' speech on the 'Rejuvenation of the University' (1945): 'That we live is our guilt. We know before God what deeply humbles us.'[12] The reader had used this fragment as a cleverly worded expression of doubt about the whole point of Jaspers' ideas, arguing that, in view of recent history in the Nazi period and Christian teaching, a spiritual renewal for Germany was impossible to achieve. In reply, Jaspers illuminated the sophistry inherent in the reader's letter, for to question spiritual redemption, he wrote, was futile, unless a thorough re-examination took place of the purpose of reading the Bible in times of crisis.[13] Jaspers' examination of this matter was no longer rhetorical, with the purpose of responding to the reader's sharp comments, but one of addressing an issue of faith, or a particular task of gaining awareness about the implications of the individual's truthful conduct.

To read the Bible in Hitler's Germany had been an act of verification about the hardship of surviving the inhuman face of a brutal régime. In that turmoil, Gertrud and Karl Jaspers found inner peace in the Old Testament prophet,

Jeremiah, in the Book of Job, and in Gospel teachings. Jaspers now discussed their Bible reading as a striving for inner redemption that was to be set apart from the complex theological question of interpreting the authority that the texts revealed. The Bible was therefore to be seen as one of the most important sources of present-day reality in the life of the reader, as he outlined in his essay:

> The world is not closed as creation, but an infinite entity for our recognition, with the open flank to its source in Transcendence. [...] The demands are on us: to recognize what is in the world as knowledge that is distinguished, objective and compelling – to seize whatever is unconditional in our historical *Existenz* as choice of the Good – to call to mind the multifaceted language of Being as the richness of its patterns in the play of the symbols as cipher of transcendence – to avoid all pretences that cloud the sober capacity for real knowledge and, at the same time, the everyday ethos of our life as *Existenz* – to preserve the possibility of what we can do and know by maintaining the limits, whose confusion makes our motives, as well as their contents, unclear and false.[14]

By co-opting the terms of *Philosophy* (1932) into his essay, Jaspers was not supplying jargon or a lifeless, technical vocabulary with which to preach an insight into the depth of life experience from the heights of his perception of higher meaning.[15] What Jaspers called Transcendence, or God, was in opposition to a dogmatic interpretation of Christian faith. His thesis about 'biblical religion' highlighted a need for the radical overhaul of doctrinal teaching in favour of an approach that Jaspers coined in his phrase 'philosophical faith'. This new departure in Jaspers' terminology and the later period of his work emerged from a conviction that no evidence for spiritual life may be gained through experience that is not sought from ethical enquiries, thus illuminating possibilities summarized by Kierkegaard in *Either/Or*. Jaspers' guest lectures in Basel in 1947, *The Perennial Scope of Philosophy* (1947), were based on his appropriation of Kierkegaard's notion of *Existenz*, refined and developed by Jaspers' notion of 'philosophical faith'. Jaspers implied, in the sense of 'faith', a pattern of inner redemption which could promote freedom independently of what, in Christian terms, would be a life of grace. His alternative was to seek participation in the activities of others, a view that was destined to collide with those of his counterparts in theology. Indeed, his complaint was that he found it difficult to discover the same level of involvement in his world as he was able to show towards the world of theological scholarship: 'No one who is in definitive possession of the truth, can speak properly with someone else – he breaks off authentic communication in favour of the belief that he holds.'[16]

Jaspers' thinking in this direction may have been one source of inspiration for his desire to become involved in intense debate with some of his new colleagues in Basel. The nature of dialogue that Jaspers sought was rarely achieved, except perhaps with Karl Barth and Heinrich Barth, and to a lesser, or greater extent, depending on the standpoint, with Rudolf Bultmann, in *Myth and Christianity* (1954).[17] In this polemical controversy about myth and revelation, published together with Bultmann's responses, Bultmann replied to Jaspers' conception of Christianity by highlighting his difficulty of communicating with Jaspers who spoke *ex cathedra*, whereas Bultmann sought a dialectical debate in the Socratic tradition.[18] A difficulty with the Jaspersian manifesto of 'philosophical faith' was that it was calculated to provoke disagreement amongst theologians, especially Bultmann with whom Jaspers contested the exclusivity of the Christian revelation whilst, at the same time, asserting his identity as belonging to the Protestant faith, and his identity as a Christian who considered himself guided by the Bible and the works of Kant.[19] In the ensuing public controversy between the two men, Jaspers invoked an argument for mythological language as a way of giving testament to sources of truth that were equally to be derived from the world's religions, not just from the Bible. Here his studies of the later works of Schelling are instrumental, especially on the mythology of the revelation (*Die Mythologie der Offenbarung* (1842)). These lectures informed Jaspers' argument about mythological language as a trace of truth, something he studied at length in his book *Philosophical Faith and Revelation* (1962). His contemplation of the late lectures of Schelling was in the manner of his belief in communication as something more intense than dialogue, as something moving beyond the Platonic dialogue towards a reflection of the personalities involved in what he called 'loving contest'. With this conception of communication in mind, Jaspers appeared to suppose that theologians should somehow automatically show a degree of sensitivity towards the dynamics of communication and truthful conduct, as he described in his *Great Philosophers* (1957), especially with reference to his portrait of Jesus. What fascinated Jaspers was Jesus' doctrine of love as designating exemplary conduct in word and deed.[20] Jaspers' desire for thoughts and actions to be harmonized in the context of an individual life experience was an aspect of his almost dogmatic insistence upon open and truthful debate between the disciplines of philosophy and religion. Nevertheless, to suggest that the Christian idea of grace or redemption through the forgiveness of sin was compensated for by Jaspers' notion of spiritual redemption through freedom was to highlight a tenuous link of Jaspers' model of 'loving contest' with his notion of 'biblical religion'.

That link literally depended upon an outside influence, as Jaspers admitted to Bultmann: 'In justifying himself through faith, insofar as I, as an outsider, connect anything at all with that approach, that believer is not a gift to himself in his own freedom of *nobilitas ingentia*, but he experiences divine grace in the forgiveness of sins. Here, I no longer follow.'[21] Jaspers' step into the breach, as it were, in order to represent his way of thinking about faith, was only one source of his argument with Bultmann, in which the model of 'loving contest' created the singular difficulty of appearing too vehement and, at the same time, too vague on the interpretation of biblical texts. Bultmann highlighted how biblical texts may be explored to greater advantage in the context of hermeneutics, an approach that may unlock the shape of reality revealed in contexts, not just in the words themselves.[22] Jaspers' comments aired the potential difficulty that he raised in his guest lectures, namely, that his perception of contest was not 'loving' enough to achieve communication:

> We may take as an example of this Biblical religion, Christianity with its claim to absolute truth for all. Our knowledge of the extraordinary accomplishments of Christianity, of the noble figures who have lived in this faith and by this faith cannot prevent us from seeing how this fundamental perversion brought forth historical evils that wore the cloak of sacred and absolute truth.[23]

The context of Jaspers' arguments may be explored as they were further unfolded in his inaugural lecture in Basel, *Philosophy and Science* (1948). One aspect of the lecture was to reflect upon possibilities of communication with respect to ideals about the sources and goals of faith in various nuances and contexts, a problem that had been topical for Jaspers ever since his first visit to Sils Maria in 1902. Then, he had formed certain convictions about methods of conducting research in the natural sciences which, he believed, were not altogether remote from the scope of working in the humanities. He had decided to train in medicine to fulfil his personal ambition of inspecting empirical facts and their potential to disclose alternative insights into his underlying philosophical interest in exploring the wider context of life's problems. Jaspers' chosen subject of philosophy and science reappeared in a fitting context in which his learning and experience could be brought to bear upon his definition of the humanist's task.

In his inaugural lecture, Jaspers outlined how the task of philosophy, in general, is to reconcile the practical with an abstract, or theoretical, approach.[24] To elaborate upon the achievement of this leading idea, Jaspers revitalized his critique of Descartes' mathematical language.[25] He outlined in his lecture that, from the seventeenth century onwards, the pendulum had swung in favour of modern science; and he suggested Descartes as a personification of a figure who represented the success story of mathematics which had come to mean everything in modern science.[26] Echoes of Jaspers' 1937 essay on Descartes' rationalism became couched in a benign, even playful, suggestion that, in pursuit of verifiable facts, mathematics as a discipline had stolen a march on any other form of scientific activity. That is to say the mathematical language of Descartes had become a universal standard that Jaspers treated as having scored an unfair advantage over modern philosophy. Jaspers seemed specifically to refer in this context to the objectivity of research methods in the natural sciences, for these sciences were seen to exclude subjective emotion or feeling, whereas emotive elements enter the fabric of research in the humanities (*Geisteswissenschaften*).[27] That distinction was not yet Jaspers' main concern, for he considered a rationalistic agenda for modern philosophy, as set out by Descartes, as being in perpetual conflict with an aspiration for strict or 'pure' science that presents itself in the service of discovering absolute truth. Whilst that agenda made Descartes the rogue genius of modern philosophy, Jaspers saw Galileo's discovery of the earth's motion around the sun as a scientific discovery *par excellence*.[28] Galileo's telescope seemed nearer to Jaspers' approach for its implicit practicality and use than the perceived abstract beauty of mathematical language that, as Jaspers complained, was not even questioned in Kant's time.[29] Moreover, if mathematical language, or the universal validity of that language, were a step forwards for science, it was a giant leap in the wrong direction for philosophy.

The principal argument of the lecture was that mathematics holds sway over reason, in the sense that Jaspers believed to have identified a static ingredient of Cartesian thought, as having intruded upon the critical, or 'transcendental', boundaries of Kantian thinking. These aspects of his working idea of the relationship between philosophy and science appear to have been the underlying message of a comment that Jaspers mentioned in a letter to Gertrud whilst he was working on the manuscript of *Philosophy* (1932) in the mid-1920s that he thought he had discovered the 'singular meaning of the birth of modern science (in the 17th Century)'.[30] His conception of modern science makes sense in the context of his lecture's emphasis on the urgent task of philosophy: namely, to establish the nature of the interconnection between rationality and feeling, intuition, imagination, or genius – the key elements that Jaspers called the *élan vital* of thinking.[31] The process of that reconnection was only to be accomplished by retaining objectivity; and, hence, it was to be sweet revenge for philosophy as a discipline to be respected as infinitely greater than the universal validity of science, in whatever form that may have taken.

Jaspers established the clear separation of philosophy from a universally compelling scientific approach as a fruitful way forward, but his inaugural lecture in Basel drew to a close with an ardent defence of Plato's doctrine of Ideas that surprisingly usurped the convictions of youth:

> How far removed is the truth, whose revelation Plato interprets in his parable of the cave and touches on in his dialectic, this truth that applies to being and to that which is above all being – how fundamentally different it is from the truth of the sciences, which move only amid the manifestations of being without ever attaining to being itself, and how different from the truth of the dogmatic system which holds itself to be in possession of the whole of being.[32]

In this new episode of his life, Jaspers appeared to have found a curious way of overriding all that he had praised in his youth about practical training. His mature exposition about the interconnection of theory and practice also strengthened his conviction of the clear distinction between philosophy and science as a source of their closer interaction. Jaspers hinted that those thinkers who possess a scientific background seem to have the capacity to clarify channels of communication at their disposal.[33] Here was the crux of one of Jaspers' demands of modern scientific research: namely, he sought freedom as an integral part of the process of discovery. Another possible way to that essentially ethical goal of freedom was to question whether 'truth' holds validity for those who do not share such a view of communication as sponsored by a philosophical approach to its foundations.

In this case, Jaspers' model of communication would appear to require considerable adjustment for the approach of modern science that sets its results within specialist fields of knowledge that seem oblivious to other goals of mankind. If scientific discussion is static, or dependent wholly upon objective analysis, then other, philosophical, goals become a reference point for communication that is pursued in the scope of eternal knowledge. Perhaps, these aspects were inherent in Jaspers' definition of philosophy as 'both less and more than science'.[34] Indeed, his attempt to resolve the ambiguities of the interrelation of philosophy and science was at the heart of the message of his book 'On Truth' (1947), that the competence to measure truth lies only within a field that can scrutinize its activities. Jaspers tried to highlight the essential purpose of maintaining an open mind to theories or doctrines of 'truth'. What counts seems to have been the search for individual freedom from any one creative influence, whether a personality or his teaching, whether in the past or the present.

18   'Rencontres' in Geneva

GERTRUD CALLED THEIR 'life in asylum' in Switzerland a challenging break with their past.[1] Yet she was now able to be reunited with her brother Ernst and his wife, Ella, whom they had not seen for six years when Jaspers spoke at the International *Rencontres* in Geneva, one of the first post-war meetings of Europe's intellectual élite, which ran from 2 until 14 September 1946. His brother-in-law, Ernst, was one of the guests along with an illustrious list of Europe's leading intellectuals, including the young English poet Stephen Spender, Maurice Merleau-Ponty, Raymond Aron and Jean Wahl.[2] The Jaspers' reunion with Ernst and Ella was able to take place because Jaspers donated his fee to underwrite the cost of the Mayers' travel from Holland and their accommodation in Switzerland. This fact weighed unduly on Gertrud's conscience, since for the sake of this meeting, she had coerced Jaspers into attending.[3]

On the penultimate day of the conference, Jaspers delivered his speech on the conference theme, *The European Spirit* (1946). His chief concern was with the status of western philosophy and his speech was mirrored in the structure of his essay for the Rome Congress and his 1947 Basel guest lectures. Stephen Spender reviewed Jaspers' appearance as one of the highlights, the other being the contribution by the philosopher, Georg Lukács.[4] What intrigued Spender was 'the Jaspers–Lukács controversy', a clash of views that became symbolic of what Spender reported as 'simply the exposure of the rift between the East and the West.'[5] In a programmatic analysis, Lukács spoke on 'Aristocratic and Democratic

Weltanschauung', a showcase for Marxist-inspired socialist-realism that was to shape life in the GDR after the establishment of separate constitutions nominally split the GDR from the FRG.[6] The Geneva delegates saw Lukács' speech as foreshadowing that ideological polarization of Europe. Spender's analysis of the rhetoric was embellished by his fine observations of the two protagonists' styles:

> Lukács took the view that the intellectual must regard himself as an up-to-date version of the French revolutionary conception of the *citoyen*. He must see himself as the product of social and modern society which is most progressive, most anti-reactionary, most representative of the interests of the 'masses', most vigilant in opposing Fascism, etc. He attacked Jaspers very sharply on the lines of 'social-realist' criticism, saying that Jaspers was a 'broken man' representing the point of view of a bankrupt individualism. These attacks were made rather curious, and perhaps less pointed, by the fact that it was Lukács, of Budapest, who looked physically more broken than the upright, austere, attentive and cordial Jaspers.[7]

If Spender, a representative of the British effort to reintroduce democracy in Germany, was enamoured of Jaspers and courted his company, his delicate bias towards Jaspers' beliefs was genuine: 'As for Jaspers, his personality outshone that of the other delegates, and it was a privilege to be with him. One afternoon he explained to me movingly that it was with the most wonderful sense of joy and relief that he found himself in Geneva. He was amazed at the atmosphere of free discussions in which he found himself, and he felt that he was breathing again for the first time in fifteen years.'[8] Gertrud sensed Spender's warmth of personality and wrote to her brother Gustav that they found Spender and his wife 'enchanting people'; and she commented on the 'friendly atmosphere' of a private meeting with the Spenders at their hotel after the conference.[9] However, the journey to Geneva a year after war ended, and with the added complication of securing visas, had taken its toll on Jaspers' health to the extent that Gertrud decided that there would be no more such arduous trips.

The exaggerated response to Jaspers' and Lukács' appearances, as though they personified nascent divisions in Europe, had little foundation in the actual reflections of the two men, neither the Hungarian Lukács, a self-appointed representative of the Communist bloc nor Jaspers, a libertarian at ease with the Americanization of West Germany and the Marshall Plan. Gertrud was indifferent to the encounter: 'We only ever spoke to Lukács briefly, during the talks and discussions in which he spoke in a longwinded manner.'[10] Lukács himself provided a similarly disinterested account of what he called his 'small confrontation' with Jaspers in Geneva.[11] Their Geneva exchanges were like a barometer of the tensions shaping world politics, but Lukács' attack on Jaspers was mild by comparison to the bitter irony of his later polemics against Jaspers and Heidegger.[12] Jaspers was not impervious to an emerging East–West division in Europe, only he did not waste much breath on it. In his speech, he first clarified the European idea as part of global developments that were to govern the future:

> Marx saw how impossible the state of affairs was in the economic and social sphere. In the sphere of human existence, Kierkegaard and Nietzsche were prophets of the time who tried – in vain – to rouse people from the slumber of self-deception. Christendom is no more than a semblance, said Kierkegaard. God is dead, nihilism is on the way, said Nietzsche. European unity was a weak product of the culture of the upper classes. What was then called Europe was obviously not able to carry on. If we wish to live on a European basis, then we must allow a deeper origin to take effect.[13]

Jaspers thus probed into intellectual perceptions of Europe, and traced them back to what he called the 'axial age'. In other words, he argued for an idea, as opposed to a reality of Europe as a geographical space. What was at stake during the seminal or 'axial' phase of history was not a polarization of modern Europe into an ideological and, as is now clear, historical map of America and Russia. Instead, Europe spanned three continents across time and space. In Jaspers' conception of that space, the diversity of modern Europe's cultural identity was to be dated from a fertile period, around 800 BC to 200 BC, when European unity was represented in common and diverse sources of scriptures and songs: 'It is the time from Homer to Archimedes, the time of the great Old Testament prophets and of Zarathustra, the time of the Upanishads and of Buddha, the time from the Songs of Shiking to Laotse, Confucius, and Tschuang-tse.'[14] The importance of biblical tradition for that watershed of history was that, according to Jaspers' idea, it speeded up a process of discovery that was already under way. Those sources of humanity dating from the 'axial' period were parallel and completely independent experiences in Europe, China and India. Moreover, if Jaspers promoted democracy in his first Geneva speech, it was not as an ideological position intended to provoke a critique from an opponent with a different viewpoint, but as an intellectual affinity for deeper communication amongst world religions. His hostility towards Christian tradition hinged partly upon his desire to encourage an open attitude towards spirituality. That attitude was inherent in the meaning of what he called biblical religion: 'Freedom is dependent on the possibility of truth's being perfected, but truth is manifold and all its forms are in motion; scientific knowledge comes to grief on insuperable antinomies and is limited by the finite and phenomenal. Every perfection in the world at once produces an imperfection. That which appears in time is bound to fall.'[15]

The European idea, in Jaspers' interpretation, hardly coincided with polarities of Judaism and Christianity, with the division of Old and New Testament, but with biblical tradition seen as a vehicle of dynamic change, as compared with the static possibilities of the 'axial' age. The claim to exclusivity of the Christian revelation was dismissed as Jaspers' saw his notion of 'biblical religion' as more relevant in an increasingly secular modern age: '"European" seems, then, to us to be, first, the depth of human communication between independent individuals, and, second, conscious labour for the freedom of public conditions by means of the forms which shape the will in community. But absolute truth, and with it freedom, is never attained; truth is on the way.'[16]

The idea of 'truth' as relative to a constant process of inner renewal, or as a rebirth that derives from continual and inner self-improvement as opposed to the Christian teaching of the bestowal of grace through the redemption of sin, was a reflection of Gertrud's influence. Although she was, like her brother Gustav, not carrying on their parents' devout Jewish traditions and practices, she retained a strong sense of attachment to the words of the Old Testament. Her spiritual life, as she wrote to Gustav, was rather more in tune with her marriage: '[...] I [call] myself a Zionist, because I want Jews to show what is possible for a Jewish individual. And I stand between philosophy and the religion of the prophets when I am uplifted by the idea of God in the Old Testament. "You should make no picture or graven image."'[17] Gertrud's tolerant feelings towards Zionism were modified by her husband's intellectual approach for she was, like Jaspers, naturally opposed to dogmatic interpretation of faith, especially if matched by a fatal complication of nationalism. Her experience of religion was rather more poetical than Jaspers' sceptical approach, as though she were guided by an inner relationship to biblical words. This was also the message of a deeply affectionate eulogy that Jaspers prepared to be spoken in the event of Gertrud's death. This was no morbid preparation, for Jaspers was in the habit of writing letters and texts in the highly likely event of his premature death, and ever since the prospect of their marriage, he had worried that Gertrud would outlive him by many years. His text focused on Gertrud's rejection of beautiful images for the stern presence of inner striving, as drawn from her faith:

As was the case at our wedding, we must again do without the church.

We have lived and thought and chosen together; and now we want the solemn rite of the funeral even without the church. But not without the Bible.

I would like to speak some words that were dear to her:

The Lord has given it, the Lord has taken it, praised be the name of the Lord. Yahweh plants and Yahweh uproots, and you desire great things for yourself? Desire not.

God was for her a cipher – yet more than a cipher: He was the actuality from which she did not sever herself when she doubted. She wrestled with God. I remember, once when she was still young we spent a whole day at the monastery ruin, Paulinzella, a twelfth-century edifice in which Grecian beauty seemed to combine with biblical piety in a wondrous, stern discipline. In the evening when, taking leave, we looked back once more, she suddenly clenched her fist and said: And yet I do not forgive Him for letting Ida (her sister) go insane. My wife understood Job.

But on such occasions she stood at the outer limit. Her centre and actuality was love, love on the part of the human being who, through this love, becomes more than mere changeable transient existence. [...] We have lived this life philosophizing. If there is any substance in what I have presented to the world as philosophy, then it is her I have to thank for it.[18]

Jaspers spoke in Geneva about the 'fruitful polarity' of Christian, Judaic, or Asian elements of western spiritual tradition.[19] That was another way of referring to the philosophical faith in which he lived with Gertrud. In a letter to his parents from Gertrud's family home several months after his marriage, Jaspers had reported on his conversations and impressions of David and Clara Mayer. He called David Mayer a 'very fine person who proves by his manner of expression and topic of conversation that he is an educated individual'.[20] Jaspers further reported that David Mayer rarely left Prenzlau and had always been in the wholesale wool trade, yet his horizons were broad and he was the 'soul of the business'.[21] Gertrud's mother was described as an attentive housewife, who preferred to remain in the background due to modesty. According to Jaspers, David Mayer was reported to have remarked upon Jaspers' personality to Gertrud: 'He is such a dear, pleasant individual – oh, if only he were Jewish!'[22] In response, Jaspers commented to his parents that he understood the remark in the context of David Mayer's devoutness and he highlighted Gertrud's achievement at having found her own way out of the milieu of her family before he became acquainted with her.

Jaspers' experiences of the richness of faith were not to jeopardize his idea of the inherent interdependence of science, technology and philosophy that he identified as European influences to be transmitted across the globe. His marriage had been, until Hitler and the abrupt cancellation of all creativity, a source of possible communication between German and Jewish culture. Jaspers had also experienced that possibility with Ernst Mayer, for his discussions were a source of flourishing vitality of his Christian and Mayer's Jewish traditions in their studies of western philosophy. After experiencing totalitarianism in Germany, Jaspers' emphasis on the ancient sources of mankind's civilization was an attempt to discover in the dim and nebulous past an ever deeper revival of the original openness that he applauded during the 'axial' period when tolerance seemed to be captured in a kind of Golden Age, with the parallel awakening of the world's religions. To promote, in that quasi-religious environment, an increasing sense of common links between Europe, China and India was no longer an exclusively European task. The task was to incorporate modern technological advancements into a supranational framework of civilized existence.[23]

Jaspers' approach towards humanism involved a radical break with the apolitical aspect of his portrait of modern man, as it appeared in the 'Göschen' book, in which he had written, for example, the following study of 'the sophist':

> The emotionalism of his rhetorical professions of resoluteness enables him to slip away like an eel from any resolve which it might trouble him to fulfil. He affirms or rejects just as the fancy takes him. What he says is futile and has no interconnexion with the new succession of time; communication with him is a plunge into fathomless abysses. Nothing grows out of his words, for they are empty chatter.[24]

Jaspers now modified the appearance of modern man from that of vacant intellectualism into that of being the frontier character of mankind, in the sense that consciousness as such was no longer imprisoned by sophistry, but released by a store of creativity awaiting fulfilment and replenishment: 'The dance of life hastens to fill the gaps, and the dance goes on.'[25] In spite of this turnabout in Geneva, it was still unclear how Jaspers proposed to interpret his flirtation with the 'dance' of modern life. The obscurity in his interpretation was significantly addressed in his 1949 definition of humanism, given in his second Geneva speech, 'On the Conditions and Possibilities of a New Humanism' (1949), insofar as his scheme was moving towards his notion of *Existenz*.

The question is not a picture of humanity but how we can grow conscious of mankind's widest possibilities that still lack an image. Only the frame of this picture leaves all possibilities open to fulfilment. Every picture of man already restricts him. [...] But man can grow conscious of himself apart from all nature, in the source of his own heritage, cutting across history in eternity – and he then becomes assured that he is not to be exhausted as a product of nature and history. Man is more than he can know about himself. For that reason, we distinguish between knowledge of mankind as an object that is to be researched infinitely as he becomes a focus of study; and growing aware of mankind in *The Encompassing* that we are and that we can be on the infinite path of our freedom.[26]

Jaspers' basic reorientation on humanism in the immediate post-war years designated a new way of philosophizing, in the sense that his idea of an 'axial' age did not appear to envisage a sweeping Copernican revolution in the manner of Kant. He rather admired Goethe's model, for his attempt to clarify the purpose of thinking more or less approximated to a reform of creativity Jaspers had relied upon in his youth.[27]

On the one hand, Jaspers appeared in Geneva as a philosopher whose emphasis on openness and tolerant conduct in the intellectual sphere was meant to define freedom as a goal to be brought to life through the activity of thinking. On the other hand, his Geneva schedule reflected, with renewed vigour, a deep determination to focus intently on the humanist foundations of contemporary politics. After all, for what purpose had they arrived in Geneva, other than to revitalize their friendship with Ernst Mayer, who had been parted from them by years of political upheaval in Germany?

Their journey to Geneva reminded Gertrud of these lost years, when now in the company of Ernst, she attended an evening concert of Brahms, Schubert and Schumann. And together with Jeanne Hersch, who acted as Jaspers' conference interpreter and translated his speech for French publication, Gertrud listened to a performance of Beethoven's *Fidelio* and reflected, throughout, upon the fact that so many had perished, whilst she had survived.[28] When the Jaspers headed for Crans, in the Swiss Rhone valley, just as they did the following year, after Jaspers' Basel guest lectures, they enjoyed a view across Lake Geneva.[29] They were in a beautiful place where the backdrop of mountain scenery and clear lakes was as though reflected in the humane character of Jaspers' political thinking.

THE GLOBE ON JASPERS' DESK that had inspired his project for a world history of philosophy, as well as his ideas for his Basel lectures and Geneva speeches, was rather symbolic of his growing influence in the international arena.[1] A flourishing friendship with Hannah Arendt was beneficial to the promotion of his work in America, where Arendt devoted herself to editing the first English translation of *The Great Philosophers* (1957), Jaspers' introductions to western philosophy that remain eminently appealing to an English-speaking readership. The pragmatic conception of sub-divisions on paradigmatic, seminal and original thinkers was, however, unlike Bertrand Russell's *History of Western Philosophy*, based on Jaspers' admiration for Hegel's works. That Jaspers stood in awe of Hegel is implied in a neat summary of his aims, included in the text of his posthumously published 'World History of Philosophy' (1982): 'An image that appears modest is apt here: namely, the thinkers of the past were giants, but I, although only a sparrow, take a seat on the giant's head and see further than he.'[2]

The false modesty of this picture reveals the originality of Jaspers' treatment of the gap between past and future that, dispensing with textual props, culminated in an ambiguous yet succinct explanation of his purpose. His approach in his project of world history was to inspire communication by opening new channels of thought; and to move beyond what he previously called an illumination of *Existenz*, yet to do so without revising his early beginnings in philosophy.[3] A deeper understanding of man's historical achievements could only be obtained from an inward projection of thoughts in a realm that shed a brighter light on the origins of mankind. An intriguing question is whether such origins actually become manifest through Jaspers' perspective that, in his 'World History of Philosophy', was defined as follows:

> It is the revelation of Being in humans themselves by virtue of all modes of *The Encompassing* that man is, and of modes in which he exists, that out of his *Existenz* in relation to Transcendence, he becomes historically real, a process that he grasps as his eternal Being; and it is precisely because of this that his Being and knowledge, as his unique accomplishment, are irrevocably bound and united as one.[4]

The capacity to see beyond one's predecessors' achievements may be equated to cognitive processes that are not exactly intuitions, but emerge in Jaspers' work as an appropriation of scenery that appears as though projected onto historical aspects. Such aspects bear only traces of the past in contrast to the present. The contradictory forces of this inward-looking, forward-thinking project still appear connected to Jaspers' idea of *Existenz* which cuts across past and future.[5]

This rather antagonistic relationship of the individual in his approach to history was underlined by Jaspers' ambiguous distinction between science and philosophy, especially evident in his eulogy for Max Weber when he spoke of Weber as a 'Galilei of the human studies'.[6] A similar conviction about Weber's philosophy was extended, albeit in a modified sense, to Weber's younger brother, Alfred, when Jaspers subjected Weber's ideas to close scrutiny in his monograph, *The Origin and Goal of History* (1949).[7] However, if Jaspers' exposition of the 'axial' period of world history met with disagreement from Alfred Weber, it was given a warm welcome from other friends upon their return to Heidelberg, as Gertrud noticed with some relief.[8] The purpose of their return was for Jaspers to give his guest lectures, *Reason and Anti-Reason in Our Time* (1950), at the invitation of the students' association, from 18 to 20 July in the university's *Alte Aula*. It was in this elegant, old lecture theatre where Jaspers had spoken on the guilt question at the reopening of the philosophy faculty only months after the liberation of Heidelberg. Then, as now, he appeared before a packed auditorium.[9] What the public wanted to hear was, according to the local press, 'clarification' and 'discussion' of the present by an intellectual who supplied these things in abundance.[10]

His lectures began on a characteristic note of personal reminiscence: 'Since the day in 1901 when I first entered the University of Heidelberg and these very rooms as a student I have always regarded Reason as the essence of philosophy.'[11] If Jaspers chose to be remembered as a philosopher of reason, he was seeking to change the impression that his 1937 lectures, *The Philosophy of Existence*, had created. Then, he had described philosophy's timeless claim to interpreting man's capacity for freedom. This capacity was, however, also linked to what he defined as man's *Existenz*. In short, his impressive lectures tended towards an emphatic exposition of that idea, in an effort to highlight the individual's responsibility for freedom.[12] A more conciliatory tone could now be detected.[13] Aggressiveness towards the legacy of Marx and Freud seemed a thing of his youth, even though he continued to bracket Communism with psychoanalysis and used the analogy as an argument for the pseudo-scientific status of their work.[14] That these guest lectures should have rejoined a battle with Freud that Jaspers began in Heidelberg was consistent with his views of his role as a critic which, in turn, conditioned his perception about the avenues of creativity legitimately open to him as a thinker. To embellish the scheme that he had defined in Geneva in 1949 as a new form of humanism, Jaspers referred to a metaphor from *Philosophy* (1932), to clarify the purpose of aspects, such as feeling or intuition, that he saw as a wellspring of creativity, even if he omitted to mention their relevance in terms of art. The metaphor of the gift of selfhood nonetheless indicates some form of intuition at play:

> Man knows that he is as it were a gift to himself, without knowing, learning or being made conscious by any reliable experience that he owes himself to another power. He knows that he is a gift to himself without knowing the giver; this state of being a gift to oneself, of owing oneself to oneself, requires all possible exertion, openness and good will.[15]

Jaspers' metaphor of selfhood seems analogous to his idea of knowledge as evoking an experience or intuition about an individual's situation as though bestowed from above. The contact with 'otherness' is rooted only in a transcendent realm of 'striving for betterness in time'.[16] That particular striving seems reminiscent of the challenge put forward in *Philosophy* (1932) where Jaspers' appeal to *Existenz* is that the historical dimension of experience should be internalized. One issue that arises is that such an appeal can only be considered real if the individual is free from delusion, open, and in constant readiness to face life anew. Such a formulation of the ethical dimension of *Existenz* was only achieved in cooperation with Ernst Mayer, who supplied the finely detailed and elaborate revisions of Jaspers' *Philosophy* (1932) in their correspondence. Jaspers himself openly admitted that the metaphors of selfhood, such as 'I did not create myself' or 'what if I remain apart from myself' were devised in association with Mayer.[17] Mayer's significant contribution was to add the self-reflexive dimension of the original German to evoke the pattern of analogies that remain true to the abstract nature of Jaspers' appeal to a world within and beyond the present, a world that still retains the tangibility of a present experience. Jaspers' shift of emphasis to a philosophy of reason mirrored the alteration of his focus that was evident in the conciliatory tone of his guest lectures in Heidelberg. Gertrud's report of their visit listed small, if telling examples, of a rather unfriendly reception by the academics in the university and, as she noted, especially by former colleagues in the philosophy faculty.[18] As it turned out, Jaspers' guest appearance in Heidelberg was to be a final farewell. He would never return after this short visit.

If Jaspers' hope in returning to Heidelberg was to re-establish credibility after his hasty retreat to Switzerland in the spring of 1948, as might be supposed by the conciliatory tone of his lectures, it seemed that the development either came too late or was too unexpected to be fully appreciated. This was surprising considering the moral support that was usually available for Jaspers in Heidelberg. Only the year before, several of his colleagues had rallied round when a controversy flared up with the professor of Romance studies, Ernst Robert Curtius. In an emotional outburst Curtius had condemned Jaspers for his speech 'Our Future and Goethe', made, almost two years previously after Jaspers had collected the Goethe Prize in 1947.[19] The reason for Curtius's rather delayed and polemical criticisms mystified Jaspers, who adamantly refused to enter into public debate.[20] Curtius's main indictments of Jaspers' personality were as follows:

> After 1945 Jaspers clearly announced his ambition to take up the much coveted position of 'praeceptor Germaniae'. He proved our collective guilt as clearly as we can see the sun, so that we can only carry on our lives with a bad conscience. Jaspers, a Wilhelm von Humboldt for our time, gave the German universities a sense of direction, until he turned his back on them.[21]

The Goethe Prize itself carried considerable prestige and was awarded to Jaspers as a mark of personal distinction, to reflect his moral lead in the Nazi era when his actions stood out as those of an individual 'who amidst the collapse and barbarity, as instigated by the demon of power, awakened a sense of duty for the imperative of humanity, free from all the poisons of the time, to give the Goethean spirit both form and influence'.[22]

That Jaspers had justly been awarded the Goethe Prize gained a vote of public support from Heidelberg colleagues who signed their names to an initiative by Karl Heinrich Bauer that appeared in the local *Rhein–Neckar–Zeitung.* The newspaper was keen to gain its share of the publicity and dramatized the affair as the controversy gained momentum. However, Bauer's declaration was published with the opposite intention of causing a sensation, stating that Curtius's article showed something was amiss in the atmosphere of scholarly debate. The Heidelberg announcement read as follows:

> The signatories below, united in their admiration for Karl Jaspers and in concern for the academic level of intellectual debate, regard it as their duty to provide the following declaration: Whatever approach is taken to Karl Jaspers' interpretation of philosophy and Goethe, the attack on him by E.R. Curtius is deeply regrettable. The attack is not objective and it is insulting; it is not reconcilable with the respect owed to Karl Jaspers personally and not worthy of a scholar of the rank of E. R. Curtius. This has to be said clearly before any objective debate on the substance of the essay by E.R. Curtius. [Signed] Karl Heinrich Bauer. Hans Freih. v. Campenhausen, Karl Geiler, August Grisebach, Gustav Radbruch, Otto Regenbogen, Alfred Weber.[23]

If anything, Jaspers' speech, delivered on the anniversary of Goethe's birthday, 28 August 1947, in Frankfurt am Main – where only the stone threshold of Goethe's house had been saved from the ruins – could be seen as a final reckoning with all things German. The speech had been a symbolic leave-taking of Jaspers' native Germany, a subtle sign of his desire to leave Heidelberg, and a measure of all that he considered positive about humanism inside Germany. After all, Goethe's novels had been a source of companion-ship during Jaspers' bachelor years as a medical student in Göttingen.

Curtius had read Jaspers' speech as questioning the literary merits of Goethe scholarship.[24] Jaspers naturally had different motives from those of Goethe scholarship; and, furthermore, his speech was intimately connected to what, in his essay about the guilt question, he had identified as a 'meta-morphosis' of thinking, a parallel connection of his wife's question about her survival. Jaspers' speech earned positive reactions from Gertrud's youngest brother, Fritz Mayer, in Israel.[25] All the same, it was a daring venture for Jaspers to have grouped the results of his reassessment of Goethe's legacy under the headline, 'Goethe's limitations'.[26] He deliberately distinguished his personal treatment of Goethe from the literary, which was typical of his opposition to authority. Even if the standards of Goethe scholarship necessarily revered Goethe's spirit through the resplendent and refined radiance of editions of his poetical works, correspondence and conversations, it was at least legitimate, as Jaspers contended, to question the authority of the legacy that Goethe scholarship had made accessible. Jaspers attempted to examine the propensity to worship idols and opinions that were held sacrosanct even once they were long since outdated. The need for the leadership of a paradigmatic figure became highly questionable for Jaspers through his reading of Goethe. Goethe's example was indeed a model for Jaspers' appeal for 'metamorphosis' after 1945, something that is not clear from the speech alone but rather from Jaspers' lifelong appropriation of Goethe. Nonetheless, Jaspers was not convinced that Goethe's approach to empirical experiment was appropriate in an age of universal scientific discovery. He argued that to emulate Goethe was singularly unproductive; and to read Goethe was to recognize a deficit of reason even if that deficit were inadequate proof of Goethe's legacy as standing or falling. Ultimately for Jaspers, Goethe's personality inspired the opposite of what Goethe symbolized because, since his time in Göttingen, Jaspers regarded a reform of an intuitive approach as compelling for scientific discovery.

On that score, Jaspers appeared uncharacteristically dogmatic, although he did not reject Goethe's genius out of hand. His essay on Leonardo da Vinci, published in 1953, revealed his deep humility towards those in possession of creative talent. Like Goethe, Leonardo was to be revered as a great mind, whose unique capacity was the ability to transform his observations and so define the essence of mankind's frontier character. In admiration for Leonardo's *Mona Lisa*, or *The Last Supper*, Jaspers went some way in his analysis to undo a potentially dogmatic aspect of his reference to 'Goethe's limitations'. The deficit of reason that he criticized as Goethe's contradictory and intuitive practice of science was now seen as being as miraculous as Leonardo's genius.[27] At the same time, he naturally saw Leonardo and Goethe as men of their time. Neither genius was capable of understanding the shipwreck of modern life, something that now only modern science could achieve. For Jaspers, the deepest insights into mankind's situation were to be gained from the force of reason shedding light upon the innate human capacity to destroy that which in the age of Goethe had seemed indestructible: human spirit that furthers the lot of mankind.[28]

That was a focus of at least one of the many radio broadcasts that Jaspers gave during his years in Basel, when he spoke in 1956 on the consequences of the atom bomb. As a result of his broadcast, he received so many letters from listeners that he decided to turn his lecture into a book. The original text of *The*

Atom Bomb and the Future of Man (1958) seems daunting due to its stylistic similarity to Jaspers' second book, 'Psychology of World Visions' (1919). The structure of each work includes many detailed excursions into problems that highlight the historical context of his arguments and, as such, are offset in small print from the main body of the text.[29] The English text of Jaspers' study of the atom bomb gives pride of place to a central metaphor – the notion of building a 'dam' to stem the tide of man's desire for self-destruction.[30] That notion was carried through the book, from an opening comparison to mankind's situation facing the tide of human history and the need for 'dykes' to protect communities.[31] Jaspers concluded that the preventative mechanisms to avoid the planet's destruction could only be derived from an ability to reflect upon the very prospect of that destruction.

In her dedication for Karl Jaspers in the preface to a collection of essays, Hannah Arendt wrote about the 'Noahs floating around out there on the world's seas trying to bring their arks as close together as they can'.[32] Jaspers liked Arendt's metaphor for it demonstrated that mankind's ability to discover his capacity to save the planet highlighted the danger of the possession of tools to accelerate his demise. He was adamant that totalitarian states – his chosen model, now outdated, was Russia and hence the resultant arms race between America and Russia – remained an uncommon threat to world peace. The potential danger of depriving communities of freedom was only to be balanced by ensuring that the means to patrol the development of weapons of mass destruction is within the grasp of the modern statesman. Jaspers' conception of mankind's survival was based on his vision not just of the participation of rogue states but of the modern scientist, whom he saw compelled to probe into the recesses of his conscience, as well as the philosopher, whose purpose was to inspire an ethic of open exhange amongst those with scientific knowhow and those in the position of the statesman, whose goal is to rescue the future of mankind.[33] That goal is accompanied by the constant possibility of 'shipwreck', if a peace is obtained without openness, transparency, and truth on all sides. In that sense, Jaspers' book on the atom bomb followed on from his closer inspection of philosophy and science, of world history and truth in politics, the central themes of his later philosophy that were concentrated into a single book. In respect of his achievement, he was awarded the Peace Prize of the German Book Trade, a prize that he collected in Frankfurt, flanked by Hannah Arendt who delivered the *laudatio* speech. Jaspers now sought to promote Arendt's work as a different form of ambassadorship for his very own cause, that of harnessing reason in pursuit of peace.

PART VI

'In my end is my beginning'

Dawn points, and another day
Prepares for heat and silence. Out at sea the dawn wind
Wrinkles and slides.

T. S. Eliot, *East Coker*[1]

20 *Butterflies in Sils Maria*

WHEN JASPERS ARRIVED AT THE Hotel Alpenrose, Sils Maria, in August 1902, he came to a decision that exerted manifold changes for the future. The climate itself transformed an otherwise dreary month of convalescence into a late summer of exhilarating walks across fields and meadows, near the shores of Sils' lake, in the Upper Engadine.

In a different valley, almost half a century later, Jaspers visited Bad Ragaz, to deliver a speech for the Swiss Philosophical Society's conference for the centenary of Schelling's death (20 August 1854). Jaspers' talk was developed into his book on Schelling's 'greatness and fatality' in which he explored the idea that Schelling's life lacked an about-turn that, inwardly, could have reformed his approach to thinking. That omission in Schelling's life may have hindered what Jaspers saw as a development of ideas, dormant in the works yet not within the grasp of the actual man.[2] Schelling's downfall was his innate propensity for Romanticism, an intellectual problem to do with the personality, and, as such, integral to the gradual dissipation of Schelling's creative powers. Jaspers disapproved of Schelling's Romanticism because the tolerance of the Romantic spirit for inner introspection without change culminated in so-called 'negative' and 'positive' poles in his philosophy, unlike the inward development of Kant's works.

Jaspers insisted on that polarization of Schelling's works, a distinction made by Schelling himself, in an attempt to enhance the profile of his system in comparison to the influential output of his main rival, Hegel. Schelling's predicament was that his productive capacities were cast adrift; and Jaspers saw such aimless drifting as a telling sign of Schelling's inability, inwardly, to adapt to a later life that fell, indisputably, under Hegel's shadow. The decline of Schelling's creative powers had fascinated Jaspers well before his talk in Bad Ragaz.[3] Gustav Mayer first introduced Jaspers to Schelling, when he gave Jaspers a copy of Schelling's collected works.[4] Mayer's biography of Friedrich Engels contained a fine portrait of Engel's interpretation of the social and historical context in which Schelling berated Hegel's works in the late lectures on the mythology of the revelation that marked Schelling's return to the lecture theatre in Berlin in 1842:

> Schelling claimed here, as is known, that Hegel actually possessed no system at all, but merely measured out his days in the anxious waste of his thoughts: whilst Schelling personally busied himself with positive philosophy, Hegel only indulged in the negative and accepted its completion and production in his name. If Hegel, nonetheless, gained a place amongst the great thinkers, then he earned this merely because he was the only one who acknowledged the basic thought of a philosophy of identity, whilst all others declared it flat and shallow.[5]

That Jaspers should later have used the rift between Schelling and Hegel as a starting point for his attack on Schelling's Romanticism was curious, not least in view of Gertrud's participation in his research. Their evenings in Basel were taken up by her readings from the correspondence of 'the Romantics', (Caroline Schlegel's letters to Schelling and also Schelling's letters to Hegel and Fichte).[6] Gertrud would draw Jaspers' attention to sections of the correspondence; and, perhaps, the unusually intense portrait of Caroline Schlegel, Schelling's first wife, as a source of Schelling's Romanticism in the introduction to the biography owes much to Gertrud's influence: 'Encouraging, appealing (*appellierend*), instructive, Caroline at first appears to have an effect, then she attempts to influence in an interpretative manner, finally she only admires, is sent into raptures, approves everything. In the marriage all criticism is extinguished.'[7]

The harmony of Schelling's marriage to Caroline was seen as a source of a decline in his critical thinking, a factor that could not be said of Jaspers' marriage that was based on a 'communicative' relationship with Gertrud. Her involvement in the development of Jaspers' research was to prepare the way for his conceptual thinking as she did now with the Schelling project. Jaspers' sister, Erna, had a different role and was recruited as a second proof reader and entrusted with the task of preparing a new index for the third edition of *Philosophy* (1932) that Jaspers revised that same year.[8] The 'afterword' to the new edition of *Philosophy* showed traces of the preparations of the book on Schelling since it all but resembled Schelling's *Letter on Dogmatism and Criticism* (1795). Schelling's interpretation of Kant was, however, an attempt to assert the waywardness of pre-Kantian thinking whereas, for Jaspers, it was rather Idealists, like Schelling, who were to be pronounced wayward in their appropriation of Kant. In this regard, Jaspers defined the existentialist approach of French philosophy as the 'dogmatic' element of contemporary debate (Sartre), whereas his appeal for reason was, not unlike Schelling's original discourse, represented as a desire to revitalize and extend the boundaries of critical thinking.

Jaspers' perception of his *Philosophy* as a response to Kant was, to some extent, motivated by his determination to strengthen the critical echo for his work which had been impoverished by the decline of polemical argument to which Idealists, like Schelling, had contributed. Jaspers further underlined Schelling's 'illumination' (*Erhellung*) as a source of the title and method for the second volume of his *Philosophy*.[9] This invoked the influential pattern of Schelling's *Philosophy of Art* (1802), or the notion of art as the 'organon' of philosophy and Schelling's appreciation of the compelling beauty of a spoken word, that is, his idea of the *Logos* as the culmination of Reason in its closest appropriation of vocal speech.[10] The importance of Schelling's influence was implied, too, in Ernst Mayer's contribution to the *Festschrift* for Jaspers' seventieth birthday on 23 February 1953. Jaspers dedicated his Schelling book to Mayer whose essay for the *Festschrift* was one of the last texts he wrote before he died on 10 October 1952. Upon reading Mayer's study, Jaspers informed Ella, Ernst's widow, that the contribution taught him better how to see himself.[11] Notably, Mayer praised the beauty of Jaspers' language, inasmuch as he found an aesthetic quality in Jaspers' *Philosophy* (1932) and 'On Truth' (1947). That quality had been encouraged by Mayer's critique of the finer distinctions of Jaspers' use of words that developed in progression from the earlier to the later period of his philosophizing. This essential disharmony in the different periods of Jaspers' thinking lent his works their perspicuity. In the later period of his work, his task had been one of creating a language of ciphers through intuitivism, whereas his earlier illumination of *Existenz* illustrated what Mayer called a way to explore reality in ever closer approximation of truth.[12]

Jaspers seemed to appreciate Mayer's contribution to his *Festschrift* more than the official reception held in his honour at the University of Basel, where the Jaspers hosted a private luncheon, attended only by close family and friends, amongst them Jaspers' publisher, Klaus Piper and wife, Renato de Rosa, Robert Oboussier, Lotte Waltz, Jaspers' sister, Erna and her son Enno and his wife, Herta. At this reception, Jaspers delivered a speech in which he paid particular tribute to Erna for her 'solidarity'.[13] The private luncheon may, indeed, have overshadowed the rest of the day's ceremony, and Hans-Georg Gadamer, who had travelled to Basel, with the Dean of Heidelberg's philosophy faculty, Hans Schaefer, to present Jaspers with an honorary doctorate from Heidelberg University was apparently upset to be shown a seat in a drafty corridor while only the Dean was allowed an audience with Jaspers.[14]

In *Philosophy* (1932), the strictest of formulations of ideas was to discipline and focus the mind on the ethos of Jaspers' model of 'existential communication' that was defined as follows: 'The first step of proper understanding beyond the firmness of conceptual identity is to comprehend what has been said in the whole of the idea; the second step in existential communication is to accept into the historical present what has been said in the idea.'[15] Jaspers' family relations between father and son, or husband and wife, exemplified an unspoken understanding of the possibility for connections between lives that are apart, when otherwise, they could be brought together. One of the fascinations of Jaspers' definition of communication remains, however, an intimation of striving for harmony between two individuals so that the harmony achieves a timeless, eternal aspect.

Jaspers' study of that striving amongst equals suggests new perspectives or standpoints through openness to the other's dimension, something that was exemplified in an endeavour to emulate what his father's paintings depicted, namely, a landscape that was exposed to different nuances that were to be represented in a way that was as true to life as possible. Upon his father's death, Jaspers requested that he be allowed to keep his father's paintings and sketches that were listed on his sister's inventory of the family heirlooms.[16] This other visual influence on Jaspers' philosophical endeavours could perhaps be identified on the day after he had first arrived in Sils Maria when he had written to his parents that, with the intensity of the sun beating through the icy chill of the wind, he felt that he could almost touch the show of colour on butterflies hovering over flowers in the meadows. He was sorely tempted to capture the butterflies in a net and, rather than study them on the wing, contemplate a new study of their forms: 'The meadows in the valley are full of flowers and butterflies. The latter are so numerous and available in such wonderful colours that I would like to try and collect them. Here, I can only get hold of a butterfly net; and if I happen to go to St Moritz, I could get a fluid to kill the animals.'[17]

Perhaps one of the most enduring facets of the visual dimension of Jaspers' thinking, as evidenced in his activities in Sils Maria, was his intention as a young man to inspect Kant's *Critique of Pure Reason*.[18] Indeed, Kant's influence was to remain the significant one for Jaspers. It therefore comes as no surprise that Kant's sea-faring metaphor, with the mariner in sight of the 'territory of pure understanding' that is to be distinguished from the 'land of truth' was also an inspiration for Jaspers' later description of 'Philosophical Life'.[19] In the following extract from the twelve lectures that were broadcast as *An Introduction to Philosophy* (1950), Jaspers illustrated the situation of a philosopher, who navigates towards the ever-distant point on a far horizon that he never reaches. He spoke as though the memories of his youth were momentarily present, having glimpsed the hazardous problems implicit in his life's work:

Having now oriented himself on secure dry land – through realistic observation, through the special sciences, through logic and methodology – the philosopher, at the limits of this land, explores the world of ideas over tranquil paths. And now like a butterfly he flutters over the ocean shore, darting out over the water; he spies a ship in which he would like to go on a voyage of discovery, to seek out the one thing which as transcendence is present in his existence. He peers after the ship – the method of philosophical thought and philosophical life – the ship that he sees and yet can never fully reach; and he strives to reach it, sometimes strangely staggering and reeling. We are butterflies of this sort, and we are lost, if we relinquish our orientation on dry land. Yet we are not content to remain there. That is why our flutterings are so unsure and perhaps so foolish to those who sit secure and content on dry land, and are intelligible only to those who have been seized by the same unrest.[20]

21 *'Child Hannah'*

Hannah Arendt's post-war reunion with Karl Jaspers took place in Basel, around Christmas 1949, when Jaspers wrote to her husband, Heinrich Blücher: 'My wife and I are very happy. One takes courage oneself from someone like Hannah, in whom not only steadfastness and trust but also the exuberance of creative work is so evident. That kind of reality is the only reality there is today.'[1] The reality that Jaspers referred to was enshrined in a world for which he felt responsible, ever since he accepted Heidegger's reference for Arendt as one of his first doctoral scholars in 1926. Even then, Jaspers recognized Arendt's future lay not merely in the field of academic philosophy, a factor that entered his examiner's report for her doctoral dissertation, 'The Concept of Love in Augustine' (1929).[2] Jaspers' exacting analysis of her contribution (for he did not award her the highest possible grade), showed that he was struck by the creativity of her interpretation:

A philosophical interpretation of Augustine demands the ability to perceive, by reading a text that is largely rhetorical and preacher-like, the relevant thought structures and the pearls that, now and then, leap out in their brilliance to intensify the intellectual content. An arduous reading of this kind confronts the reader, only from time to time, with his actual object. The writer of this dissertation has that gift of reading.[3]

Apart from Jaspers' reservations about certain methodological aspects of Arendt's work, he highlighted her capacity to bring to life concepts in such a way as to illuminate their present reality, what he called Arendt's 'objective philosophizing'.[4] Several decades later, when the roles were reversed and Arendt had the opportunity to file a report on her former teacher's contribution, she returned to Jaspers' observation about objective thinking. In her *Laudatio* speech for Jaspers' German Peace Prize (1958), she spoke of his *Philosophy* (1932) as having set a standard that had caused communicative problems for other contemporaries in his field. Her praise was for what she called Jaspers' 'spatial' thinking:

> In this space perpetually illuminated by a speaking and listening thoughtfulness, Jaspers is at home; this is the home of his mind, because it is a room in the literal sense of the word, just as the *ways* of thinking taught by his philosophy are, in the original sense, paths that open up a space. Jaspers' thought is spatial because it forever remains in reference to the world and the people in it, not because it is bound to any available space. In fact, the opposite is the case, for his deepest aim is to 'create space' in which the *humanitas* of man can appear pure and luminous.[5]

Whilst the Enlightenment tradition of Lessing and Kant was a cornerstone of their world, Jaspers and Arendt's reference points differed, especially with regard to metaphors that characterized their thinking: Kant's 'reversal' (*Umkehr*), Schelling's 'illumination' (*Erhellung*), Hegel's 'light points' (*Lichtpunkte*) – each element was defined by Jaspers on paths that he explored as signs (*signa*) of *Existenz*.[6] To appreciate Jaspers' signs as leading to another dimension of his language highlights how his metaphysics included symbols, or ciphers replete with further meaning leading on from the direction of his thought trails. The pattern of those thought trails may be seen as Jaspers' point of departure to think through what he defined as 'I myself', 'communication', 'historical consciousness' and 'freedom'.[7]

Ernst Mayer described Jaspers' *Philosophy* and its representation of reality as 'independent of time'.[8] That independence is inherent in the special disharmony of Jaspers' language, or in his refusal to appropriate tradition by transforming past influences into his philosophical works. His phrases, like the gift of selfhood, allude to possibilities of a cipher language, whose essential quality emerges as the restless nature of his metaphors through their concentration, something that Ernst Mayer called 'inner action'.[9] This restless activity lends Jaspers' language an aesthetic quality that seems to provide a basis for his association with artistically gifted individuals, such as Heidegger and Arendt, who were somehow drawn closer to Jaspers' world because of their differences. Jaspers' trains of thought were not entirely separate from the pictorial or spatial dimension in which his concepts become intangible, perhaps as fragile as the high-pitched tone of his voice that was distorted in later years by the worsening of the illness.[10] Jaspers counted on those occasions when he could freely entertain his thoughts by discussing Arendt's projects and drawing her ideas, once again, into the room of his thoughts.

If Arendt grew to appreciate Basel as a focal point of her world, it was because Jaspers' conversations followed her home: 'I'm happy to have your letter, and my living and thinking are still completely in the grip of our talks in Basel. It's nice to continue them mentally on walks in a spring such as I have never seen before in Paris. It's like a dream world filled with blossoms.'[11] The perpetual motion of their thinking carried Jaspers into a world that Arendt experienced through travel.[12] Although his lifestyle was almost totally sedentary, except for the daily walk in the nearby Schützenmatt Park, in central Basel, the distance separating Jaspers and Arendt was overcome by their correspondence. Their reality was not esoteric, a life of pure fiction or a dream world divorced from practical demands. There was keen anticipation in the Jaspers household of Arendt's presence, and Gertrud came to regard Arendt as a member of their family. She worried about 'the Hannah child' (*Hannahkind*) and after Arendt's visits, noted an uplifting mood in her household.[13]

Jaspers became an increasingly protective guardian towards Arendt, who accompanied them on holiday to the Villa Nemmet in St Moritz, owned by their Heidelberg friends, Jaspers' doctor, Wilhelm Waltz and his wife, where the Jaspers were accustomed to stay.[14] Jaspers urged Arendt to present her work in an ever bolder fashion, but she had difficulty mentioning her totalitarianism study, for fear of Heidegger's unwillingness to respect her success as an author in her own right.[15] Jaspers' political philosophy, undergoing a revival in his Basel years, was also inspired by his interest in Arendt's major post-war work, *The Origins of Totalitarianism* (1951), to which he had contributed a preface for the first German edition.[16] He planned to explore what he considered the source of Arendt's success in an unpublished book that owed much to his belief in a level of objectivity that he never ceased to admire in the works of Max Weber. Weber was more of an unconscious presence in Jaspers' old age, as was shown by an anecdote he related, prior to the publication of Arendt's book:

I had a remarkable dream last night. We were together at Max Weber's. You, Hannah, arrived late, were warmly welcomed. The stairway led through a ravine. The apartment was Weber's old one. He had just returned from a world trip, had brought back political documents and artworks, particularly from the Far East. He gave us some of them, you the best ones because you understood more of politics than I. I picture you now correcting the proofs for your big book. Shouldn't you perhaps re-read Max Weber on the archetype (and on other things too)?[17]

Weber's insights into the cogs turning the wheels of modern society were, for Jaspers, a reference on the nobility of Germany's past political and social tradition. His recommendation for Arendt to inspect Weber's methodology of 'ideal types' was out of concern that her book, of all her works, was to attain perfect clarity and overcome any hint of involvement in systems of 'total' thought. Arendt, however, was still inclined to be cautious about Weber as she had been in 1932, after an initial inspection of Jaspers' Weber study.

One of Arendt's concerns, that Jaspers was uninterested in politics because of his generation's education in the humanities, turned out not to be the case when Jaspers increasingly became a radical commentator on Germany. He sparked off a controversy when in a television interview with Thilo Koch, filmed on 10 August 1960, the interviewer's questions drew him out of his reserve to voice thoughts that were an example of what he saw as problems in prevailing attitudes of the time: 'For years I have held the view that the demand for reunification is not only unrealistic, but politically and philosophically an unrealistic form of self-reflection.'[18] In the context of Germany's ideological division, Jaspers' comments were inflammatory. Unity had to be achieved; and to that end the goal of German unification was written into the FRG's constitution. Jaspers appeared to have undermined public confidence in the constitutional framework of democracy; and whilst he still spoke for freedom as a principle of unity, he added that unity was only to be guaranteed by the democratic participation of the GDR in the future of Germany as a whole. When his sister-in-law, Ella Mayer, returned home to Holland, after a short holiday in Basel, she noted how Jaspers' interview had transformed Ausstraße 126 into 'a mad house'.[19] Jaspers had received several hundred letters that repudiated his comments and apparent acceptance of the GDR, which was not officially recognized by the FRG until the Brandt era in the late 1960s. The various letters hurled embittered insults at Jaspers, so much so, that Gertrud felt that Joseph Goebbels, the Nazi propaganda minister, was standing in the wings in control of everything.[20]

The outcry over Jaspers' interview motivated him to embellish his arguments in a series of articles published in August and September editions of the German weekly, *Die Zeit*. These articles were the basis of Jaspers' book, 'Freedom and Unity' (1961), in which his longstanding hostility towards Bismarck's nation-state was openly defined alongside his belief that even the slightest shadow of 'collective guilt' was a wholly improper foundation to unify what was then a divided country. Almost a year to the day of Jaspers' interview, the Berlin Wall was built. His compelling analysis of the once hotly disputed Oder-Neiße border, the historical fault line dividing Germany, gained something of a visionary quality.[21] His analysis of a parliamentary debate in the FRG that occupied members of all parties in 1965 when the need arose to renew laws to bring to justice former Nazi war criminals was equally contested. He gave an interview with Rudolf Augstein, for the German news weekly, *Der Spiegel*, which ran the piece under the headline, 'For genocide there is no redemption'. Jaspers' comments were clearly motivated by his recollections of Gertrud's experiences, for he repeatedly clarified Augstein's questions by emphasizing that the Nazi régime had been a 'criminal state'.[22] His anxiety about it being a duty not to forget survivors of Nazi war crimes became an unwritten theme of his book, 'Where is the Federal Republic heading?' (1965). The failure, inwardly, to re-examine outworn attitudes, he saw as a chronic German habit. This had been a constant theme of his ever since his Heidelberg lectures on the guilt question, yet Jaspers now further underlined the supra-historical element of his political commentary in alignment with his principle of protecting the humane purpose of freedom and truth in politics. In his 'Answer. To critics of my study "Where is the Federal Republic Heading?"' (1967) Jaspers highlighted details of one member of his family's political commitment: his uncle, Theodor Tantzen, had participated in Weimar democracy as a liberal member of parliament (DDP) and Minister President of Lower Saxony from 1924.[23] Tanzen had narrowly escaped the fate of those involved in the 20 July plot against Hitler and was reinstated as a member of the liberal FDP after the war by the British.

Meanwhile, a furore arose over Arendt's coverage of the trial of Adolf Eichmann in Israel. Jaspers avidly read the original English text of Arendt's *Eichmann in Jerusalem. A Report on the Banality of Evil* (1961).[24] Immediately, he wrote to Arendt in solidarity: 'I have read your book now from the first to the last line. I consider it marvellous in its subject matter. It bears witness, in its intent, to your uncompromising desire for truth. In its mind-set, I find it profound and full of despair; in the way it is written, it is a further demonstration of your literary powers.'[25] Jaspers planned to develop his thoughts in a defence of Arendt's text. The ideas for his book, that was never published, informed several interviews in which he discussed the method of Arendt's report and Weber's 'objectivity' as being relevant to gaining an understanding of Arendt's achievement.[26] Whilst Jaspers identified Arendt's literary talent as the source of that achievement, he was careful to note, in his correspondence with her, a slight difference of emphasis regarding his interpretation of the subtitle of her report. He himself had perhaps inspired the book's subtitle,[27] yet his lecture on Kant's 'radical evil', given in Zurich in 1936, showed why he sought to emphasize the need to remain objective about Arendt's work.

In the English edition of her book on totalitarianism, Arendt distinguished, in a literary sense, 'absolute' from 'truly radical' evil.[28] Jaspers had emphasized how Kant's 'radical evil' was an inadequate representation of recent history. In *Metaphysics*, he underlined how a traditional approach to the contours of rational thinking required far-reaching revisions so that they reflected what he saw as the compelling reality of modern times. The appearance of that reality had been memorably stated in the final word of Jaspers' *Metaphysics*: 'It is not by enjoying perfection, but only through suffering in the knowledge of the world's unrelenting nature, and, unconditionally, by remaining true to the self in communication that possible *Existenz* can achieve what may not be planned and what becomes nonsensical as a wish: in shipwreck to experience Being.'[29] Jaspers' metaphor of 'shipwreck' signalled his own particular reorientation on the conditions of humanism. Those conditions depended upon the possibility of open communication among free individuals. Arendt understood that Jaspers' belief in the power of communication was one reason why she had failed to broker a reunion between Heidegger and Jaspers, and that Heidegger's complicity in the Nazis' control of the university was not something Jaspers could forgive. In an unguarded moment, however, Jaspers had mentioned to his parents, his appreciation of Heidegger's world: 'Perhaps he will visit when you are here to listen to Furtwängler. Papa would, I believe, enjoy his company. He is totally rooted in his home turf and near to nature. His most prized thing is the "Hütte" that he built for himself high in the mountains. From there, he looks across the whole of the Black Forest onto the chain of the Alps.'[30] However, Jaspers' brief friendship with Wilhelm Furtwängler, in the late 1920s, and his deep sympathy for Heidegger's creativity were now not necessarily foremost in his mind.[31]

A month before submitting the manuscript of *Philosophy* (1932), Jaspers again disagreed with Ernst Mayer, this time about his dedication of the book to Gertrud. This matter was rather delicate. Mayer's devotion to Jaspers' *Philosophy* was second to none. Thanks to Mayer, Jaspers' trains of thought became concentrated in a way that produced metaphors illuminating the 'signs' of *Existenz*. When Mayer objected to Jaspers' dedication because of its personal aspect, Jaspers implied that Gertrud's personality was an ultimate symbol for his model of communication, and acted as an anonymous appeal to the reader to study the thought trails in their connection to his world and his conception of selfhood.[32] The starting point and outcome of *Philosophy*, a work written in devotion to the objectivity of thinking and the individual's life experience, was defined in a letter, composed when Jaspers was in the midst of preparing his original manuscript:

Heidelberg, 2 October 1927

Dear parents!

[…] It is two years ago that I had the fine conversation with Papa in Scheveningen that, from time to time, repeatedly goes through my mind. Papa doubted audaciously and in an honest manner in the idea of immortality and I could only agree with him in the sense that an endless, temporal continuity of life, as we know it here, is something that we know nothing about and for which there is not the slightest point of proof. The pain of things passing away and of departing is unstoppable. Yet all the same, we are only conscious that our being in this temporal process is not exhausted, even if we cannot see beyond the limit of our appearance. Our belonging together is only ephemeral on days when we feel no love; in every moment of love we are certain of an unspeakable presence of eternity. We think of that, bound as we are to our sensual intuition (*Anschauung*), in symbols which, as symbols, are true or, at least, tell us something valid. That was how I felt yesterday, when in thoughts of you I felt myself at one with you from times that are unthinkable; and this is a state of being that is not to be destroyed. That state can be, in the triviality of everyday life and in the forgetfulness of objective activity, temporarily cast in darkness. It is an irreplaceable contentment inwardly to follow, at such moments, Papa on the shore and in the dunes, to have mother's love and cleverness present, to think about childhood, about my grand-parents, about the present-day when I know that you are cheerful and

content, in spite of all the disappointments and the suffering that you
have not gone without. […]
Fond greetings!
Your Kally[33]

Jaspers' symbols, or ciphers of transcendence as he called them in his
retirement lectures in 1961, imply manifold perceptions of reality that fluctuate
according to their relationship to the individual situation. This situation seems
generalized, as it were, into a symbolic picture of life. However, the picture
transcends a possible connection to any singular vision of the world.

Jaspers' family and friends were as precious to his intellectual life as the
many accolades that poured in – the Erasmus Prize (1959), the honorary
doctorate from the Sorbonne (1959) and the Order of Merit (1964), one of the
highest awards from the FRG. Jaspers found faith in his father's capacity to
capture trails of nature in his drawings, trails which resembled glimpses of
immortality, whose pictorial character still fascinated him. Perhaps he believed
he had captured a final glimpse of the proportions of his task when he selected
Cusa's use of metaphors, especially on the purpose of the game in his late study,
Nicholas of Cusa (1964):

> Our erratic search for the way is illustrated by a comparison with a
> game Cusanus invented, 'the ball game' (which is the title of one of his
> works, *De ludo globi*). It is played with a wooden ball with a spherical
> hollow off-centre. When the ball is bowled, it does not, since one side
> is heavier than the other, roll in a straight line, but takes a spiral path.
> The players toss the ball over a surface divided into ten concentric
> circles. At the centre is the king – Christ. The winner is the player
> whose ball has touched the greatest number of circles and comes
> closest to the centre.[34]

In Jaspers' world, the game of life was only as serious as the purpose of the
player whom he saw as integrated into friendships in a way that leads to the
possibility of suspending the impact of time through communication of the
sort that is unique and irreplaceable. That belief in communicating with others
was reaffirmed in Jaspers' father's gift to Gertrud of a writing bureau, built in
1634. This old piece of furniture was considered a family heirloom, having been
handed down from generation to generation, at least since the time of Jaspers'
great grandfather, Johann Friedrich Jaspers, who had purchased the desk when
co-owner of the company, Delius & Co. Jaspers' father gave the desk to

Gertrud on her birthday, and his explanations about the value of the heirloom caused him to fall under the spell of recollection and to recount how, as a four- or five-year-old boy, he was accustomed to creep into the family's farm in Sanderbusch and to sit on the open leaf of the bureau, with the sole aim of playing with the lighter flints, hidden away in one of the bureau's recesses. The flints had belonged to a large, old rifle with a bayonet, a relic of his father's involvement in the not too distant revolutionary year of 1848. Jaspers' father seemed only too pleased for Gertrud to keep his mementoes of the family's connection to Germany's liberal past: 'I am delighted that you appreciate this old piece of furniture, for which I have feelings of piety, and, from my heart, I gladly leave it to you.'[35] Gertrud had been welcomed wholeheartedly into the Jaspers' family.

On 26 February 1969, her ninetieth birthday, Gertrud, the life and soul of Jaspers' intellectual life, sent a telegram to Hannah Arendt to inform her of the news: 'Karl died Central European Time 13.43. Trude.'[36]

Appendix: Karl Jaspers' Family Correspondence

Every care is taken to provide a faithful and accurate rendition of the original German text of Jaspers' handwritten letters, reproduced in this biography according to the current rules of German spelling. All forms of address to individuals appear as in the original, upper case German spelling. Common abbreviations are usually rendered in full, and any unclear terms are inserted in brackets. In those rare cases where a word simply proved illegible, a question mark is placed after the word in brackets. The references to dates have been standardized, according to the pattern adopted in the original letters.

Letters to pages 1 to 45 (Part I)

pages 7 to 10

Karl Jaspers to parents:

Norderney, 10. Juli 1898

Liebe Eltern!

Heute ist nun schon eine Woche unserer Ferien um. Das ist schade, doch freue ich mich auch, dass ich in 3 Wochen wieder nach Hause komme. Ich habe es hier wirklich brillant. Fr. Busch meint, ich sehe schon viel frischer aus. Mein Husten ist allerdings noch nicht ganz weg. Tags huste ich kaum, aber Fr. Busch sagt, ich hustete nachts. Ich bekomme jeden Morgen und Abend Milch, in der Emser Salz aufgelöst ist. Schmeckt abscheulich, nützt, glaube ich, gar nicht. Gestern hatte Fr. Busch Schwester Hedwig Busch, die hier die Küche besorgt, Geburtstag. Soviel Blumen, wie die gekriegt hat, habe ich noch nicht gesehen. Eine ganze Stube war voll gestellt. Gestern Abend war ich mit W. Salfeld und Fridow Schneider am Strand, um die Sonne untergehen zu sehen. Es war wunderschön. Die Sonne tauchte vollständig ins Meer, am Horizont war keine Wolke. Heute will ich wieder baden. Wenn es mir gut bekommt, was es bis jetzt immer getan hat, Morgen wieder. Was mir eigentlich am Strande fehlt, das ist eine Reisedecke um die Beine zu schlagen. Bei solchem Winde, wie jetzt, ist das eigentlich nötig. Ich habe wohl meinen Mantel umgeschlagen, aber dann ist es mir oben zu kalt. W. Salfeld hat eine mitgenommen, ich brauche dieselbe auch mit. W. Salfeld will gerne mit mir Tennis spielen, wenn ihr meint, dass es sich lohnt, schickt mir die Schläger mit 2 Bällen. Wenn aber nicht, schadet es auch nichts. Meine Photographien kann ich hier schlecht entwickeln, das würde zu teuer sein. Wenn es euch recht ist, möchte ich mir wohl so einen Faulenzerstuhl kaufen, der zusammengeklappt werden kann, er kostet 2.25 [Mark]. Herzlich danke ich Dir, liebe Mama, für Deinen lieben Brief. Es ist zu nett von Dir, dass Du mir jeden Tag schreibst, Du machst mir eine große Freude damit. Mit 150 Mark komme ich natürlich für die ganzen 4 Wochen nicht aus. Die Pension kostet allein 180 Mark. Außerdem habe ich bis jetzt circa 32 Mark ausgegeben [...] Ich glaube, dass ihr mir nach acht bis 14 Tagen am besten noch 150 Mark schickt. Ich bringe ja, was ich nicht brauche, wieder mit, und dann kann ich nicht in Verlegenheit kommen. Wir wollen jetzt zum Baden.

    Herzlichen Gruß
    Euer Kally

Karl Jaspers to parents [postcard]:

[Norderney, 9. VII. 98]

[Liebe Eltern],

Heute schreibe ich Euch keinen Brief, da ich nicht mehr so viel weiß zu schreiben. Gestern waren wir in den Dünen, wo ein Unwetter ausbrach. Wir flüchteten rasch nach Hause. Leider ist mir, als wir auf eine hohe Düne stiegen, mein Schirm entzwei gegangen. Er ist vom Wind umgeklappt und es sind 3 Stangen abgebrochen. Da das Gestell sehr kompliziert ist und alles miteinander zusammenhang, muss eventuell das ganze Gestell neu. Ich möchte Euch nun fragen, ob ich mir einen neuen Schirm kaufen soll oder diesen heil machen lassen, was sehr teuer werden würde, oder ob ich eigentlich überhaupt keinen nötig habe. Gestern Abend ist ein Fridow Schneider aus Hameln hier angekommen (15 Jahre alt, ganz nett). Dieser hat ein Zimmer für sich allein, trotzdem er doch später gekommen ist als ich. Es geht mir sehr gut. Alles ist brillant. Willy Salfeld bessert sich nach meinem Wunsche. Ich schlafe jetzt ganz gern mit ihm, man muss sich ja an alles gewöhnen. Herzlichen Dank für Mamas Karte.

Mit herzlichem Gruß
Euer Kally

pages 13 to 19
Karl Jaspers to parents:

Badenweiler, 27. April 1901

Meine liebe Eltern!

[...] Herr Dr Fr[aenkel] hält es für notwendig, dass ich im nächsten Semester nicht studiere und eine gründliche Kur zu meiner Erholung und Kräftigung durchmache. [...] Eine solche Kur wird ja jedenfalls nicht billig, aber ich glaube, dass Papas Mittel es gestatten, wo es sich um meine Gesundheit, also um mein ganzes späteres Leben handelt.

[...] Ich bin kein Meister im deutschen Stil und verstehe es gar nicht und halte es auch für unzweckmäßig, etwas in schönerem Lichte darzustellen, als es ist. Daher schreibe ich Euch ganz offen, kann Euch aber versichern, dass mir nach allem, was Herr Dr Fr. sagt (und er hat mir versprochen, ganz offen zu sein) die Sache nicht zum Aufregen ist, dass ich mich vielmehr freuen muss, dass die Ursache meines häufigen Unwohlseins endlich entdeckt ist und beseitigt werden kann. [...] Wir waren gewohnt, Lungenkrankheit immer als eine Todeskrankheit anzusehen. Das ist offenbar eine ganz irrige Auffassung, wenn keine Tuberkeln, wie bei mir, dabei sind. Ich habe auch erst einen Schreck bekommen, mich aber bald besser belehren lassen.

Ihr schreibt mir nach dem Europäischen Hof wohl einen <u>Eilbrief</u>, damit ich rasch Klarheit bekomme, wohin ich will und, falls Prof. Bäumler mir dasselbe rät, mich in Badenweiler einnisten kann.
Mit herzlichem Gruß Euer Kally

Dr Albert Fraenkel to Karl Jaspers, senior:

B[adenweiler], 27. 4. 01

Sehr verehrter Herr Jaspers,

Mitte der Woche hatten wir zum ersten Mal die Freude, Ihren Karl bei uns zu sehen.

Es fiel mir auf, dass ihn die kleine Fußtour von Müllheim herauf erschöpft hatte und dass er lange kurzatmig blieb. So konnte ich der Versuchung nicht widerstehen, die Ursache dafür zu ergründen.

Die Untersuchung ergab, dass es sich um eine Erkrankung der linken Lunge handelt, die mit Eiterung einhergeht und die Neigung zur Schrumpfung und Heilung an einer Stelle verrät. Die mikroskop[ische] Untersuchung des Auswurfs bestätigt frühere Resultate, dass es sich <u>nicht</u> um eine tuberkulöse Erkrankung handelt. Wahrscheinlich liegt der Beginn des Leidens weit zurück. Die Neigung zu Fieber und „Influenzen“ in früherem und letztem Jahr stehen in Zusammenhang mit der Erkrankung der Lunge. [...] Durch diese Veränderungen erklärt sich zwanglos der schlechte Ernährungszustand und sein zeitweise mangelhaftes Befinden.[...]

Unter den klimatischen Kurorten, die für einen Aufenthalt in Frage kommen, steht Badenweiler mit obenan. [...]

Es tut mir Leid, Ihrem verständigen, lieben Sohn die Enttäuschung des Studienaufschubes bereiten zu müssen und Ihnen diese Berichte zu senden, aber es erscheint mir als ärztliche und Freundschaftspflicht, hier einzugreifen [...].

Ich harre Ihres Bescheids und bin mit herzlichen Grüßen auch an Ihre Frau Gemahlin

Ihr treu ergebener

Fraenkel

Karl Jaspers to Father:

Badenweiler, 21. V. 01

Lieber Papa!

Ich zeichne sehr gern, aber der Lehrer taugt nichts. Gestern zeichnete ich eine alte Eiche nach der Natur. Den Stamm bekam ich ganz nett, aber das Blattwerk konnte ich nicht charakteristisch wiedergeben; darauf bat ich den Lehrer, er möchte es mir zeigen. Er zeichnete nun nebenan auf dem Papier Blatt für Blatt. Der ganze Baum würde schließlich mehrere Quadratmeter einnehmen. Ich sagte ihm das. Da zeichnete er Blatt für Blatt kleiner. Das wurde eine Kritzelei, auch das sagte ich ihm, worauf er nicht im Stande war, mir das richtig vorzumachen. Er brauchte bloß Phrasen, um mir das mündlich zu erklären. Dazu kostet die Stunde 3 Mark. 3 Stunden habe ich gehabt; ich werde sie wohl ganz aufstecken und allein zeichnen. [...]

Herzlichen Gruß allen!

Dein Karl

Father to Karl Jaspers:

Oldenburg, den 14ᵗᵉⁿ Juni 1901

Lieber Kally!

[...] Die Malutensilien habe ich zusammengesucht, Mutter hat sie Dir zugesandt. Außerdem lasse ich Dir von einer Farbenfabrik direkt auf eine Anzahl Tuben – ich meine 15 Stück – zugehen. Ich bitte Dich, nach Empfang derselben mir ein Verzeichnis der Tuben nach Namen der Farben zuzusenden, damit ich die Rechnung kontrollieren und bezahlen kann.

Die Chinesische Tusche liegt im Farbenkasten. Zum Anreiben habe ich eine <u>kleine</u> Porzellanpalette angelegt, welche Du bequem mit ins Freie nehmen kannst. Ich empfehle Dir, angeriebene Tusche in den Blechdeckel des Kastens zu übertragen, aus dem man bequem malen kann. Du kannst aber auch direkt von der Porzellanpalette malen. Die Blechbüchse für Wasser mit abnehmbaren Näpfen an beiden Enden kennst Du wohl.

Das kleine Brett habe ich als Zeichenbrett im Freien benutzt; eine Schachtel Heftnägel habe ich angelegt. Es ist sehr bequem zum Aquarellieren.

Einen Block mit <u>Aquarell</u>-Papier konnte ich hier leider nicht bekommen.

Statt Tusche kannst Du auch Sepia benutzen; mit Tusche kann man aber viel feiner tönen.

In dem Handbuch für Aquarell-Malerei findest Du die Dir zugesandten Farben alle aufgeführt. Die Benennungen sind mitunter nicht gleichlautend; an einer Stelle, welche ich durch Eselsohren bezeichnet habe, findest Du unter den gedruckten Namen teilweise Namen, welche ich daneben geschrieben habe. [...]

Das Handbuch musst Du sorgfältig wiederholt studieren; ich habe einige Blätter angelegt, auf welchen ich Mischungsstudien gemacht habe. Bei schlechtem Wetter empfehle ich Dir ähnliche Studien zu machen, welche sehr instruktiv sind.

Kann ich Dir von hier noch Auskunft geben, so bitte ich zu fragen. [...]

Herzlichen Gruß Dir!

Dein Papa

Karl Jaspers to parents:

Sils, 1. VIII. 02

Liebe Eltern!

[...] Wenn an den hohen kahlen Bergen, an denen keine Spur menschlicher Tätigkeit zu sehen ist, die Wolken hinfegen, glaubt man anwesend zu sein bei der Bildung des Planeten in vormenschlichen Zeiten. Der Eindruck ist vor allem immer ein gewaltig imponierender und schrecklicher. Während beim Anblick des Meeres die Gesetz-mäßigkeit und Regelmäßigkeit befriedigt und beruhigt, geht von dieser Landschaft, wo in den gezackten Formen und klobigen Massen Willkür und Regellosigkeit zu herrschen scheint, eine ganz entgegen-gesetzte Stimmung aus; darin zu schwelgen, ist schon fast dekadent. Manche werden es erhebend finden, die Kleinheit des Menschen zu empfinden vor dem klotzigen Bergriesen; das kann man in edler Weise vor der endlosen Fläche des Meeres, das in regelmäßigem Wellen-schlag ans Land schlägt oder vor dem sternbedeckten Himmel, in dem man die Gesetzmäßigkeit wenigstens ahnt. Hier sträubt man sich den scheinbar willkürlichen Naturgewalten unterzuordnen; man möchte am liebsten die frech in den Himmel ragenden Spitzen herunterreißen. Die Landschaft hat eine ähnliche Schönheit, wie die Darstellung der Riesen in Wagners Ring – die gegen Wind und Wolken stand-haltenden Gipfel scheinen weniger die unentwegte Manneskraft zu zeigen als dessen Trotz und Unverschämtheit – der Drache Böcklins in der Schackgallerie oder der Riese Polyphem bei Homer. Es scheint bezeichnend, dass Nietzsche sich hier fünf Jahre aufgehalten haben soll. Mein Befinden ist <u>vorzüglich</u>.

Herzlichen Gruß

Euer Kally

pages 31 to 37
Karl Jaspers to parents:

Heidelberg, 28. Okt. 1901

Liebe Eltern!

Die höchstfeierliche Immatrikulation am Sonnabend machte sich sehr lächerlich. Alle Studenten saßen in dem allerdings sehr schönen Saal ganz still und andachtsvoll, als der Rektor mit Gefolge hereinkam. Er gibt eine sehr stotterige, alberne Ansprache (natürlich war es ein Theologe) und dann ging jeder einzelne Student hin und schrieb seinen Namen in das Matrikelbuch und erhielt dafür eine Legimitationskarte. Es entstand ein allgemeines Herumlaufen, wozu der Rektor noch immer eine möglichst würdige und feierliche Miene machte. Solch eine dumme Formalität, die einen auch noch wohl imponieren soll, könnte man gut lassen. [...]

Herzlichen Gruß ihm und Euch von Eurem Kally

Father to Karl Jaspers:

Kissingen, den 11ten Mai 1902

Lieber Kally!

[...] Ich habe in diesen Tagen durchgeblättert: „Rangierbahnhof", „Recht der Mütter" und „Halbtier". Ich muss sagen, dass ich die Tendenz nicht für schlüssig halten kann, wenngleich sie sehr heikle Themata behandelt. Mein Geschmack ist sie nicht, sie schreibt mir viel zu langweilig und ihre Auffassungen sind sehr verfehlbar. Aber, wie gesagt, für unsittlich halte ich ihre Schriften nicht, höchstens für ungesund im Empfinden. Alles in allem möchte ich Dich bitten in den Kreisen, welche dort verkehren, recht vorsichtig zu sein und namentlich das, was dort an Auffassungen vorgetragen wird, mit ruhiger und mühloser Kritik aufzunehmen. [...] Ich hatte nie Gelegenheit, in solchen Kreisen zu verkehren, und kann mir denken, dass es ganz interessant sein kann. Aber Vorsicht! Es wäre mir lieb, wenn Du Dich in München noch etwas nach den Leuten erkundigen möchtest. [...]

Mit herzlichem Gruß!
Dein Papa

Karl Jaspers to Father:

München, 13. V. 02

Lieber Papa!

[...] Wie schön ist es dadurch für mich, dass ich das Gefühl haben
kann, mit Dir alles besprechen und eine vorurteilsfreie Meinung
erwarten zu können. Nun inbetreff der Angelegenheit selbst etwas sehr
Kurioses. Die Dame, die ich für H. Böhlau hielt, weil sie mir unter allen
durch ihr anziehendes, geistvolles Gespräch hervorzuragen schien, ist
es gar nicht, sondern eine andere, die mir schon wegen ihrer
Wichtigtuerei mit der Philosophie und ihr Vordrängeln im Gespräch
unangenehm aufgefallen war. Nebenbei habe ich noch nichts von ihr
gelesen. Mein letzter Brief muss sehr unklar gewesen sein, dass Du
[mich] in dem Kreise einer Künstler- oder Schriftstellerclique
vermutest. Es ist nur ein <u>philosophischer</u> Abend und es sind besonders
Studierende der Philosophie dort. Wenn der Kreis irgendwie
dekadent, demoralisierend oder ungesund wäre, würde ich ein
genauso miserables Urteil über so was haben. Man spricht über
philosophische Themata, Idealität von Raum und Zeit, Parallelismus
von Psychischem und Physischem, Willensfreiheit u. a. Darüber
brauche ich mich gerade sowenig zu erkundigen, als über alles, was ich
selbst durch eigene Anschauung beurteilen kann. Du kannst ganz
sicher sein, dass ich da in keine schlechte Gesellschaft gekommen bin;
auch kann ich ohne Anmaßung behaupten, dass ich mich schon
genügend mit Philosophie beschäftigt habe, um nicht beliebigen
neuen Anschauungen ohne Kritik zu verfallen. [...]
   Herzlichen Gruß
   Dein Kally

pages 44 to 45

Karl Jaspers to parents:

Venedig, auf dem Lido
13/IV/02

L[iebe] Eltern!

[...] Die Stadt Venedig ist sehr malerisch und verkommen, man hat
das Gefühl, wenn die Fremden nicht da wären, würde es bald ganz
verlassen sein. Wenn man irgendwohin will, setzt man sich in eine

Gondel; in ganz Venedig gibt es kein Pferd und kein Wagengerassel. Wie angenehm wäre das für Papa; ich habe überhaupt oft in Italien gedacht, wie schön es für mich und Euch wäre, wenn Ihr mit hier wäret. [...] Wegen des großen Andrangs im Lokal durfte ich nicht länger sitzen und bin nach einem Spaziergang am Strande nach Venedig zurückgefahren und dann mit einer Gondel in der Lagune gewesen, um den Sonnenuntergang zu sehen. Es war nicht schöner als in Norderney oder auf dem Feldberg, aber ganz anders und auch bezaubernd in der Farbenpracht. Eine Schilderung wäre von mir doch nichts wert. In Goethes italienischer Reise soll eine schöne Stelle darüber erhalten sein. [...]

Herzlichen Gruß von
Eurem Kally

Letters to pages 47 to 107 (Part II)

pages 57 to 61

Enno Jaspers to parents:

Heidelberg, 27. April 1909

Liebe Eltern!

[...] Fr. Mayer ist körperlich recht herunter. Sie arbeitet wie ein Pferd und ruiniert damit für den Augenblick ihre Nerven. Sie wird sich jedoch nach dem Examen nach Kallys und ihrer Meinung sehr schnell wieder erholen. Sie ist ein prächtiges Menschenkind. Sie zu beschreiben ist zu schwer. Sie ist vollständig anders, als ich mir dachte. Mehr Gemüt als einseitiger Intellekt, echt weiblich, dabei anscheinend sehr klug. Sie hat viel hinter sich. Ihr Verkehr mit Kally ist rein freundschaftlich. Anders fasst sie ihn auch nicht auf. Sie sagte z. B. einmal: „Wenn ich Ihren Bruder geheiratet hätte, was nun ja nicht mehr in Frage kommt, etc. ..." Sie beurteilt Kallys Körper genau wie K. selbst. [...]

Herzlichen Gruß, auch an Erna
Euer
Enno

Walter Calé to Julia Gottschalk [Undated letter]:

Meine liebe Julia,

Wenn Du diese Zeilen bekommst, leb ich nicht mehr.

Der eine Grund ist in vielen Enttäuschungen und in der Überspannung von allem in mir.

Der andre: dass ich eine große Treulosigkeit gegen dich begangen habe, davon wirst Du hören. Mein Leben ist zerbrochen, es ist nichts wert. Vergiss mich!

Zwei Bitten hab ich: Verbrenn alles von mir, wenn Du kannst.

Und komme meinetwegen <u>nicht!</u> nach Berlin. Ich verdien's nicht.

Sei zum letzten Mal gegrüßt, Begleiterin. Wie schwer ist das alles. Ich wünsche Dir ein gutes Leben. Ich habe Dich, als ich Dich liebte, wahrhaft geliebt.

Walter

David Mayer to Karl and Henriette Jaspers:

Prenzlau, 27. Sept. 1910

Hochgeehrter Herr Jaspers
Hochverehrte Frau Jaspers

Durch Ihren liebenswürdigen Brief und durch die freundlichen Zeilen Ihr[er] verehrten Frau Gemahlin haben Sie uns hoch erfreut.

Es hat lange gewährt, ehe unsere Gertrud sich den Eltern offenbarte und eingestanden hat, dass sie ihr Herz vergeben und sich in Liebe mit einem Mann zusammengefunden habe, dem sie nicht nur aufrichtig in Liebe zugetan sei, sondern hochschätze und hochachte. Freilich hat dies Geständnis, wie Sie, hochgeehrter Herr Jaspers, richtig bemerken, mir einen schweren Kampf um meine Zustimmung bereitet. Es war[en] keine Vorurteile, von denen ich mich frei weiß, die ich beseitigen musste, sondern ein Ringen mit Grundsätzen, die auf festgewurzelter Pietät gegen meine Vorfahren beruhen, von denen ich nicht abweichen konnte. Jetzt rechne ich mit Tatsachen und bringe dem jungen Paar meinen väterlichen Segen aus treuem Herzen entgegen. Möge unseren lieben Kindern, die ja unmittelbar vor ihrer ehelichen Verbindung stehen, Glück und Harmonie, Gesundheit und stete Zufriedenheit zuteil werden, zur größten Freude der beiderseitigen Eltern. Das ist wohl unser gemeinschaftlicher Glückwunsch, den wir für unsere Kinder hegen.

Ich habe von meiner Gertrud und von allen Seiten nur Gutes und Liebes von Ihnen und Ihrer gesamten Familie gehört, ich hoffe, es wird die Zeit nicht fern sein, dass wir uns kennen lernen und aussprechen können.

Meine Tochter wird hoffentlich, ich habe das feste Vertrauen zu ihr, sich stets bestreben, in kindlicher Liebe, sich die Zuneigung der Eltern ihres Gatten zu erhalten und zu verdienen.

Mit hochachtungsvollen und wenn Sie es, hochgeehrter Herr Jaspers gestatten, mit freundschaftlichsten Grüßen für Sie, Ihre hochgeschätzte Frau Gemahlin und alle Ihre Angehörigen.

Ihr ergebener
David Mayer

pages 68 to 74
Karl Jaspers to parents:

Heidelberg, 20/10/11

Liebe Eltern!

[...] Ich lege einen Brief bei, den Husserl mir auf meine Arbeit schrieb. Husserl ist einer der ersten, wenn nicht der erste Philosoph, der zur Zeit tätig ist. Er ist vor allem Logiker. Ich habe eine von ihm geübte Methode zum Teil in meiner Arbeit angewandt. Man spricht von „Phänomenologie". Ich hatte ihm bescheiden geschrieben, dass mir seine <u>einzelnen</u> Analysen sehr überzeugend gewesen seien, dass ich aber eigentlich nicht klar wüsste, was Phänomenologie eigentlich sei – das war als Angriff gemeint, denn ich glaube, er weiß es selber nicht. Das schreibe ich damit Ihr die Beziehung zu meinem <u>Briefe</u> in seinem Briefe versteht. Ich habe mich über den Brief sehr gefreut, wenngleich er etwas väterlich ist. Aber dass Husserl, der auf diesem Gebiet der erste und urteilsfähigste ist, meine Arbeit anerkennt, ist mir viel wert. [...]

Herzliche Grüße
Euer Kally

Karl Jaspers to Father:

Heidelberg, 20. 6. 13

Lieber Papa!

[...] Ich werde Euch nicht so bald wieder ein solches Buch schicken – wenn ich es überhaupt noch einmal kann – und es ist doch das Resultat meiner bisherigen wissenschaftlichen Arbeit. Es könnte gewiss viel besser sein, aber <u>relativ</u> bin ich zufrieden; und ich weiß, dass es über das Thema kein Buch gibt, das nur annähernd so gut wäre. Dieser Vergleich mit anderen <u>psychiatrischen</u> Büchern will aber nicht viel sagen. Denn die Psychiater taugen durchweg nichts und die Konkurrenz auf <u>wissenschaftlichem</u> Gebiet ist mit ihnen leicht.

Ich habe das Buch, lieber Papa, Dir gewidmet. Es ist das keine konventionelle Widmung (wie sie bei Dr.-Arbeiten, aber nicht bei solchen Arbeiten üblich ist). Eigentlich möchte ich Dir ein philosophisches Buch so schicken können, in dem ich die Weltanschauung des Vertrauens auf unsere Vernunft, in der ich mich mit Dir so einig fühle, formuliere, ohne dem philiströsen Stumpfsinn des „aufgeklärten" Ungläubigen zu verfallen. Aber ich fürchte, ich werde nicht alt genug, um das fertig zu kriegen. Dass ich Euch und Gertrud habe, das ist ein Glück, das nur wenigen zuteil wird, und das das Unglück gering erscheinen lässt, das meine Krankheit mir das „äußere" Leben und den Erfolg verfuscht.

Dazu kommt als zweites, lieber Papa, dass ich mich in den Grundanschauungen, sobald ich sie mit den Anschauungen auch mir sonst befreundeter Menschen vergleiche, mit Dir innerlichst verwandt fühle; wenn auch die Formulierungen und Gestaltungen, die wir im Leben gewinnen, zwischen uns natürlich verschieden sind – sind wir doch zwei Generationen angehörig. [...] So bitte ich Dich, lieber Papa, die Widmung gerne anzunehmen. Sie bedeutet mir mehr, als alle Freude, die ich Dir mit einem äußeren Erfolge machen könnte.

Herzlichst Dein Kally

Karl Jaspers to Mother:

Heidelberg, 20. 6. 13

Liebe Mutter!

Du hast in Deinem ganzen Leben Dich immer so rührend in zweite Linie gestellt, dass ich weiß: es ist Dir recht, dass ich das Buch Papa zugeeignet habe, obgleich ich es ebenso gut Dir oder Gertrud widmen könnte. [...] In meiner Widmung an Papa liegt allerdings ein Gefühl eingeschlossen, dass ich bei einer Widmung an Euch Frauen nicht haben könnte: ein Gefühl von Männerfreundschaft, das mir im Leben nie beschieden gewesen ist und das ich in dem sonst so spröden Verhältnis zu unserem Papa von Zeit zu Zeit intensiv gefühlt habe. [...]

Gertrud und ich führen ein schönes Leben. Sie ist von einem so unglaublichen Verständnis für mich und einer so innigen Liebe, dass es mir oft ein Rätsel ist. Ein solches Leben muss doch noch weitere Früchte tragen.

Viele innige Grüße
Dein Kally

pages 77 to 86
Karl Jaspers to parents:

Heid[elberg], 27. 2. 10

Liebe Eltern!

[...] Freitag war ich mit Gruhle bei Max Weber. [...] Den Mann kannte ich ja schon vom Ansehen und besonders aus seinen Schriften. Ich mag ihn besonders gern leiden. Er ist ein seltener „Mann" unter den Gelehrten und voll Begeisterung für die Erkenntnis als solche. Seine Begabung ist hervorragend. Jedenfalls ist es der klügste Mann, mit dem ich bis jetzt persönlich gesprochen habe. [...] Ich habe im allgemeinen eine Antipathie gegen geistliche und gelehrte Leute. Die man kennen lernt sind durchweg persönlich nicht vertrauenerweckend, unzuverlässig, eitel, aufgeregt, Affektmenschen. Ihnen fehlt das männliche, solide, zielbewusste. Ganz anders Max Weber. Er flößt auf den ersten Blick dies Vertrauen eines Mannes ein. Nur ein Zug wirkt ein wenig beängstigend. Es geht oft ein erregtes Flattern über sein Gesicht, die Augen werden eigentümlich stechend und man fürchtet, dass er jeden Augenblick möchte geisteskrank werden, wie er schon einmal 2 Jahre es fast war. Es ist, wie wenn ein mächtiger Wille dauernd ein Nervensystem bändige, das sich empören will. Keine Spur von sich gehen lassen. Seine Frau wirkt ihm gegenüber besänftigend auf eine feine Art. Man merkt, dass er ihr viel zu verdanken hat. Diese Ehe scheint etwas sehr Schönes zu sein. [...] Ich wurde, wie jedes Mal, sehr freundlich zum Wiederkommen und einfachen telephonischen Anmelden gebeten. Aber ich zweifle, ob ich dahin passe. Die Leute sind zu klug. Ich glaube, ich kann nichts bieten. [...]

 Herzlichen Gruß
 Euer Kally

Karl Jaspers to parents:

               Heidelberg, 13/6/19

Liebe Eltern!

[...] Oft denke ich bei dem Wesentlichsten, das ich in meinem Buch – indirekt – zum Ausdruck bringen wollte, an Euch beide. Wenn ich Papas Aquarelle ansehe, was ich oft Tag für Tag mit Bewusstsein tue, so empfinde ich in ihnen dasselbe. Man kann mit Begriffen und in der Kunst das letzthin Gleiche sagen. Aber es ist nur verständlich für Menschen gleicher Artung und nur dann, wenn die Aufnahmefähigkeit für das besondere Medium da ist, das an sich gleichgültig ist. Ich möchte gar nicht, dass Ihr etwa mein Buch lesen würdet. Das wäre eine schreckliche Quälerei. Denn eine äußerliche Voraussetzung ist eine gewisse Kenntnis philosophischer Begriffe. Aber ich bin auch gar nicht traurig darüber. Denn das Wesentliche fühle ich uns gemeinsam. Und Papa ist es in manchen Bildern reiner gelungen als mir. Bei Papa ist so vieles unmittelbar und unreflektiert einfach selbstverständlich, dass er viel mehr in seiner Existenz hat, was ich erst suche. [...].

 Herzliche Grüße
 Euer Kally

Karl Jaspers to Father:

Heidelberg, 25/12/19

Lieber Papa!

Dein liebes Geschenk – für das Du Mutter die Verantwortung zuschiebst und das wir ihr mitzudanken haben – war uns eine große und herrliche Überraschung gestern Abend. Ich sehe mir mit großer Liebe und vielen zum Teil auch wehmütigen Gedanken an Euch und Dich diese Bilder an, die mir ohne Ausnahme im Spiegel Deines Wesens die Welt schöner Kindheitserinnerungen zeigen. [...] Die meisten Menschen werden in Deinem Alter leicht [...] kleinlich, zeigen die weniger angenehmen Eigenschaften, die sie immer hatten, nur noch deutlicher, und gehen in den Lapalien des Alltags mit inadäquater Erregtheit auf. Aus Deinen Bildern strahlt mich die andere Seite des menschlichen Alters an, die mir zwar bei Dir nicht neu ist, diese Ruhe und Abgeklärtheit, die in langen inneren Kämpfen erworben ist, die nicht ein Wissen und Vernünfteln ist, sondern die man von alters her Weisheit nennt und nennen darf.

Über den Wert Deiner Bilder willst Du nichts klargemacht haben und nennst sie allzubescheiden Deine „Fabrikate". Ich bin auch in Kunstdingen kein Sachverständiger, sondern freue mich, wo ich Empfindung spüre und in mir widerklingen fühle, und nenne dann das Bild gut. So ist es mit Deinen. Sie sind für mich so echt, zunächst ohne im Äußeren der Sauberkeit und Sorgsamkeit, mit der alles gemacht und hergerichtet ist. Im Einzelnen könnte ich sehr Vieles nennen: die schöne Weite und Tiefe der Bilder, die unfehlbar wohltätigen Proportionen in der Anordnung, den leuchtend weißen Dünensand in dem durchweg dunklen Wetter der Bilder, die Baumformen und Gebüsche, wie sie auf Spiekeroog zum Teil ganz entwickelt, zum Teil zwanghaft und verkrüppelt sind und die entlaubten, toten Äste schaurig in die Luft strecken, das schwarze Meer oder der fern hinter dem Watt blinkende schmale Wasserstreifen, zum Teil das Wogen und Wühlen wilder Natur, dann wieder die friedliche Ruhe (Heering) oder italienische Formenschönheit (besonders in Kiefern). Jedes Bild sagt mir etwas. Ich glaube, dass ein Sach- verständiger, ganz abgesehen von den persönlichen Empfindungen, die mir die Bilder so wertvoll machen, jedenfalls gleichsam die handwerkliche Tüchtigkeit in der Malweise anerkennen würde. Man sieht, dass Du einmal richtig gelernt und geübt hast, dass Du dieses Malen, wie alles, was Du im Leben angefangen hast, gleich gründlich und planmäßig betrieben hast.

Die Neigung zum Stilisieren und charakteristischen Betonen primitiver Formen, die zum Teil wohl auf der Herstellung ohne die Natur nach Skizzen beruht, lässt Afra Geiger die Bilder als „merkwürdig modern" empfinden, sie war auch ganz begeistert. Uns werden sie immer ein köstlicher Besitz sein. [...] Es ist ein schönes Weihnachtsfest! [...]

Dein Kally

Karl Jaspers to parents:

Heidelberg, 16. Juni 1920

Liebe Eltern!

Dass Max Weber tot ist, werdet Ihr in der Zeitung gelesen haben. Er ist an der Grippe gestorben. Was das bedeutet, ermessen im Augenblick nicht viele Menschen. Ich bin wie gelähmt, aber zugleich von enthusiastischer Liebe – ganz unpersönlich – für diesen Geist. Er ist der einzige Philosoph unserer Zeit und ich zweifle nicht, dass er in Zukunft als solcher auch erkannt wird. Die Welt ist für mich wie verändert. Im Geistigen waren wir so geborgen, weil uns Max Webers Existenz die Garantie war, dass auch das Größte gegenwärtig noch möglich ist. Nun fühle ich geistig niemanden mehr über mir und die geistige Welt scheint mir leer.

[...] Nun sind wir Kleinen übrig und müssen uns in der Wissenschaft nach unseren Kräften einrichten. Ich fühle, dass auf uns nun eine andere Verantwortung fällt. Wenn die Flamme erloschen ist, müssen die glimmernden Funken genährt werden.

Mir ist es nun wie ein Vermächtnis, was Max Weber beim Weggang im Dunkeln noch zu mir zuletzt sagte: Er sagte zu meinem letzten Buch in seiner Freundlichkeit: „es hat sich <u>sehr</u> gelohnt", dann zweimal mit Pathos wiederholend: „ich <u>danke</u> Ihnen für das Buch" und dann: „ich wünsche Ihnen weiter gute Produktivität". Zuletzt noch: „an anderer Stelle werde ich mich noch über Ihr Buch äußern". Das kann er nun nicht mehr. Aber ich habe das Gefühl, dass er in mir doch einen solchen glimmernden Funken sah und ich will mit aller Kraft mich bemühen, was ich noch in der Philosophie – um dieses allgemeine, unklare Wort zu brauchen – leisten kann, und darin seine

Idee und seine Werke der Jugend begreiflich zu machen versuchen.

Das sind Impulse, die einen in solchem Moment ergreifen. Zugleich ist der Tod nahe und die Lust, lebend zu wirken, getragen von dem Bewusstsein des Endes, aber auch des unfasslichen Sinnes.

Ich lege Euch den letzten Brief von Gertrud bei, mit der Bitte, ihn gleich zurückzuschicken. Am Abend telefonierte sie mir dann noch das Ende. [...]

Alles Gute!

Herzlichst Euer Kally

pages 94 to 102

Enno to Karl Jaspers:

Bremen, 20. März 1907

Lieber Kally!

[...] Meine Tätigkeit ist die denkbar langweiligste: Sie besteht aus: 1) Geld einzahlen, 2) Geld einkassieren, 3) zur Post und zur Reichsbank laufen und 4) kopieren und registrieren. Bei den ersten drei Beschäftigungsarten kommt es nur auf die Muskeln der Beine an und bei der vierten ist es nötig, dass man von dem vielen Herumlaufen noch nicht ganz einschläft; Verstand ist aber immer höchst überflüssig, zuweilen sogar lästig. Nach einem halben Jahr wird diese Tätigkeit ja für mich zu Ende sein, aber viel interessanter wird es dann auch nicht. Die ganze Beschäftigung eines Bankbeamten besteht schließlich nur aus Abschreiben von einem Blatt Papier auf ein anderes. [...]

Frdl. Gruß

Enno

Enno to Karl Jaspers:

Bremen, 5. Juli 1907

Lieber Kally!

[...] Du bist nun ja in der glücklichen Lage, das Schildern persönlicher Dinge stets durch allgemeine Betrachtungen ersetzen zu können. So kommst Du denn auch dazu, Dich zum Schreiben von persönlichen Dingen nicht zu zwingen und Deinen Neigungen und Anlagen freien Lauf zu lassen. Wenn Du dann schreibst, Du erlebtest nichts Persön-liches, so ist das töricht. Es ist ja ein angenehmes Gefühl, sich selbst als bedauernswert zu schildern und das auch zu glauben, wo es in Wirklichkeit doch verkehrt ist, aber im Allgemeinen soll man sich so etwas doch nicht vorreden. Du bist durch Deinen Körper an vielem verhindert, aber einen Mangel an persönlichen Erlebnissen daraus abzuleiten, scheint mir nicht berechtigt.

Nächstens mehr!

Frdl. Gruß

Enno

Karl to Enno Jaspers:

Oldenburg, 3. 10. 14

Lieber Enno!

[...] Manchmal werden hier auch wichtigtuerische Dinge gemacht: Die Dozenten Deutschland[s] veröffentlichten eine Erklärung, dass „Militarismus" und Geist der Wissenschaft nicht zu trennen wären und dass wir jetzt alle zusammengehören. Indem ich das <u>jetzt</u> innerlich betonte, habe <u>ich</u> auch unterschrieben. Es richtet sich gegen Engländer, die erklärt haben, deutsche Wissenschaft und deutscher Militarismus sei[en] zu trennen. Nur gegen letzteren werde Krieg geführt. Ich bin durchdrungen davon, dass eigentliche Wissenschaft kontinuierlich nur in Deutschland gedeiht. Anderswo sind einzelne Größe und Nachahmung Deutschlands. Nirgends ist ein „Niveau" wirklicher Wissenschaft vorhanden. Ich möchte nicht zu einer fremden wissenschaaftlichen Organisation gehören. Angesichts realer Möglichkeiten wird einem das doch klar. [...]

Viele herzliche Grüße. Lasse es Dir recht gut gehen!

Dein Kally

Gertrud Jaspers to parents:

[Heidelberg], 18. V. 15

Liebe Eltern, [...]

Kally geht es sehr gut, ich bin glücklich darüber. Sein Kolleg ist gut besucht, bisher war folgende Statistik:

Jungens	Mädchen
11	19
17	22
11	24
13	29

Ihr seht, es wächst die weibliche Zuhörerschaft. Leider – sie sehen gar zu dumm aus. Ich bin begierig aufs Bezahlen. Neulich bei der Bismarckfeier hörte ich folgendes Gespräch von 2 Studentinnen. Die Erste: „Ja, er ist furchtbar groß, ich sehe ihn öfters auf der Hauptstraße, da sieht er komisch aus wegen der Größe." Die Zweite: „Jaspers soll bedeutend sein." Die Erste: „Ja, er ist wohl der Bedeutendste, den wir jetzt hier haben."

Ihr könnt Euch denken, dass ich es gern hörte. Kally wäre wohl böse, wenn er wüsste, ich schreibe Euch das. Ich will ihm nachher die Schuld beichten. Euch macht es doch auch Spaß.

Sowie Ihr von Enno hört, erfahren wir es doch auch?

Herzliche Grüße

Eure Gertrud

Karl to Enno Jaspers:

Heidelberg, 24. 3. 16

Lieber Enno!

Eben erhalte ich Deinen lieben Brief. Mir ist das natürlich zuerst ein Schreckensschuss – wir sind so verwöhnt, ohne Sorge an Dich denken zu können; dass ich aber gar kein Recht zu solchen Gefühlen habe, ist mir sofort klar. Deine Art, so schlicht und illusionslos von den Realitäten zu schreiben, tat mir wohl, ich liebe die Männlichkeit in Dir, der ich mich so fern und doch auch nahe fühle. [...] Ich glaube an Deinen guten Stern in Deinem Schicksal: von ganzem Herzen wünsche ich Dir große Leistungen, aber auch, dass Du für Leistungen des Friedens lebendig und aktiv bleibst.

Du bist doch ein Mann, der sich wichtig genug ist, um nicht etwas zu wagen, wenn es keinen Sinn hat. Bei Deiner Freiwilligkeit möchte ich darum jubeln, wenn sie nicht so sorgenschwer wäre. Sie lässt mich ahnen, dass Du eine Steigerung Deines Lebens erfährst in der Zusammenraffung des Lebenssinnes auf Leistung (man sagt auch „Werk") hin, eine Steigerung, die wir in unserem ungefährlicheren Tun nicht kennen.

Verzeih mir, lieber Enno, dass ich auf Deinen schlichten Brief so wortreich antworte: der Handelnde hat es leichter, unpathetisch zu sein.

Herzliche Grüße von Deinem
Kally

Gertrud ist auf der Reise nach Prenzlau, ich schicke ihr Deinen Brief nach.

Letters to pages 111 to 129 (Part III)

Karl Jaspers to parents:

Heidelberg, 12/7/17

Liebe Eltern!

[...] Die große Politik ist auch nicht gerade ermutigend. Es ist klar, dass die Idee des „Aufdiekniezwingen" Englands Unsinn ist. Ein Statusquo-Friede kann allein in Betracht kommen. Sagt unsere Regierung das offen, wie Erzberger es will, so kann das <u>vielleicht</u> für die feindlichen Völker etwas bedeuten. Leider liegt die Sache nur so, dass sie dann andere Gründe finden werden, aus denen sie uns klein schlagen wollen. Aber der Versuch mit der Formel: „ohne Annexionen" muss bald mal gemacht werden, so wenigstens sagen die Instinkte [von] immer mehr Menschen, von denen man nicht behaupten kann, dass sie ihre Nerven verloren haben. Wir müssen doch Frieden bekommen, wie es auch geht. Enno ist jetzt auch dieser Ansicht, wenn er auch hinzufügt, was richtig ist, dass wir keine Meinung haben können, die auf Kenntnis der wirklichen Lage beruht.

Herzliche Grüße
Euer Kally

Karl Jaspers to parents:

Heidelberg, 8. Okt. 1918

Liebe Eltern!

[...] Am Dienstag, 2 Tage vor Ernennung von Prinz Max, hatten wir politischen Abend. Ich stellte die mögliche Alternative: Entweder: Annahme von Wilsons 14 Punkten (damit Verzicht auf Elsass-Lothringen, wenigstens die Möglichkeit es zu verlieren). Bei Annahme retten wir unsere Existenz. Oder: Es wird abgelehnt; dann wären alle Kräfte, die noch in uns sind, gewollt, und ein Kampf <u>kann</u> vielleicht doch noch uns retten, gerade weil wir vorher dies äußerste Friedensangebot gemacht haben. Darauf ging ein Sturm der Entrüstung gegen mich los. Friedensangebot jetzt sei falsch. Die Ablehnung würde die Stimmung völlig ruinieren. So schlecht stünde es gar nicht um uns usw. Als einige Tage nachher alles so geschah, kam es mir merkwürdig vor. Nun bin ich gespannt, was diese Nationalliberalen das nächste Mal sagen. Jetzt werden sie gewiss alles richtig und selbstverständlich finden. [...]

Herzliche Grüße
Euer Kally

Gertrud Jaspers to parents:

[Prenzlau], 9. II. 19

Liebe Eltern,

[...] Nachts um 3 Uhr wachte das Wirtschaftsfräulein auf durch lautes Klopfen an der Haustür. Da sie den Abschlussschlüssel nicht gleich fand, ging sie auf die Veranda und fragte, was los sei. Da schrieen ihr Soldaten zu, machen Sie sofort auf, sonst schlagen wir die Türen ein. Sie ging nun an die Tür von Wendland, fand den samt Burschen völlig angezogen und die schrieen nun auch in barschem Ton mit ihr. Anstatt auf den Schlüssel zu warten, schlugen die Soldaten mit Kolben Haustür und Wohnungstür ein. 20–30 Soldaten mit Handgranaten und Revolvern stürmten in alle Zimmer, zerschlugen alle Glasfenster der Türen etc. Meinen Geschwistern, die notdürftig angezogen, frierend dastanden, hielten sie Revolver vor und schrieen fortwährend, „Radek ist hier versteckt, wir wollen ihn haben, sagen Sie, wo er ist." Den Worten meines Bruders wurde kein Glauben geschenkt. [...] Die Eheleute getrennt, das Haus durchsucht, als belastendes Material fassten sie in der wissenschaftlichen Arbeit einen der Zettel, auf dem „Liebknecht" stand. Natürlich Wilhelm Liebknecht der Vater, was die unwissenden Führer nicht wussten und – mein Bild – das an Kallys Krankenbett gemachte, von dem sie behaupteten, es sei die Rosa Luxemburg. Keine Erklärungen halfen. Selbst die Kinder wurden nicht geschont. Unter ihren Betten mit Revolvern etc. vorgehalten nach Radek gesucht, man sagte ihnen allerdings, sie sollten sich nicht ängstigen. [...] Schließlich fand man den Brief, der an dem Abend an mich geschrieben war, wollte den lesen. Mein Bruder weigerte sich, indem er sagte, dass er dem Richter ihm zeigen würde, aber nicht dieser ihn überfallenden Bande. [...] Nun aber genug.

Mit herzlichen Grüßen
Eure Gertrud

pages 121 to 123
Karl Jaspers, Diary, 1905:

27/28. 1. 05:

Ich las in letzter Zeit Nietzsches Zarathustra. Das Werk setzte mich sehr in Erstaunen; nach allem Schelten über Nietzsche erwartete ich nicht viel und war aufs Höchste überrascht, eine glänzende, bis ins Einzelne bedeutsame Leistung eines großen Dichters zu lesen. Das Dichterische fiel mir vor allem auf; die wundervollen Bilder und Visionen, die auf eine so wunderbar feine Weise dargestellt sind, dass jedes Wort seine große Bedeutung hat, packten mich mächtig. Der rein philosophische Inhalt, der der verstandesmäßigen Beurteilung unterliegt, ist nicht allzu hochstehenden Naturen von großer Bedeutung; alle Urteile sind zwar sicher von großer Einseitigkeit, aber fasst man sie nicht als absolut wahr auf, sondern als Ausdruck bestimmter seelischer Zustände, wird man sie von großer Bedeutung finden. Ein großer Psychologe scheint mir Nietzsche zu sein; reine Schilderung psychologischer Bestände und Vorgänge sind sehr wahr und ergreifend und in den scheinbar verkehrtesten Aussprüchen finde ich Bestätigungen für die Lipp'schen Anschauungen über das Streben der Individualität nach freiem sich Ausleben, nach Vervollkommnung.

[Karl Jaspers, Tagebuch, 1905, *LE.*]

Karl Jaspers to parents [undated postcard]:

Liebe Eltern!

Herzliche Grüße müssen in diesem Augenblick genügen. Wir nutzen jede Stunde dieser kurzen Zeit. In warmer Sonne bei schönem Wind unter Zitronen und Mangen, überall zahllose Eidechsen, klarste Luft, die Sterne bis nahe an den Horizont ganz hell – und darin die großartigen antiken Ruinen dieser Stadt, in der Plato seine Philosophie verwirklichen wollte – es ist so schön, dass man ganz still wird. Morgen nach Taormina, dann Girgenti, dann Palermo. Dort kann uns eine Karte erreichen.

Herzlichste Grüße

Euer K.

Letters to pages 139 to 183 (Part IV):

pages 150 to 153

Karl Jaspers to parents:

Heidelberg, 28. August 1933

Liebe Eltern!

[...] Jetzt ist eine neue Universitätsverfassung herangekommen nach dem Führerprinzip: Der Rektor wird vom Ministerium ernannt, die Dekanen vom Rektor. Gewählt wird nicht mehr. Die Körperschaften, soweit sie noch bestehen bleiben, erhalten einen nur beratenden Charakter, abgestimmt wird nicht mehr. Die frühere Gelehrten-„republik" ist zu Ende. Nach meinen Erfahrungen von ihr ist mir das ganz recht, besonders wenn ich selber Rektor werden könnte oder ein Name, dem ich dasselbe Vertrauen schenke wie mir! Entschuldigt den Übermut! [...] Herzliche Grüße

Euer Kally

Karl Jaspers to parents:

Heidelberg, 25. 12. 38

Liebe Eltern!

[...] Der Zufall wollte, dass ich wohl das letzte Gespräch mit ihm hatte, mittags um 12 Uhr, – abends 7 Uhr starb er. Nach meinem Gespräch soll er kaum mehr zu hellem Bewusstsein erwacht sein. Während unseres Gespräches versank er schon manchmal, kam dann schnell zu sich und sprach sinnvoll, sachlich, wie immer. Er war ein sehr kluger und ein guter Mensch. In der Medizin ist er durch Entdeckung eines Heilmittels, das schon Tausenden Jahre ihres Lebens geschenkt hat, unsterblich, denn dieses Heilmittel ist keine Zufallsentdeckung, sondern es ist durch Jahrzehnte in methodischer Forschung gefunden. Dass er aus aller Welt Zuschriften erhielt über die Anwendung und Einführung, war ihm noch in den letzten Wochen eine große Befriedigung. Dass er es seit dem 1. Okt. selbst nicht mehr verbreiten

durfte, war ihm ein Schmerz, den er kaum verwinden konnte. Das Helfen war sein Lebenselement. Dies war ihm entzogen und der Tod kam fast wie natürlich, als er dieses Lebenselement nicht mehr hatte. Vor einiger Zeit schenkte er seinen Blutdruckmessapparat (der erste, der von diesem Typus ca. 1909 gebaut wurde und den er seitdem besaß, und mit dem er alle seine Patienten untersucht hatte) einem jungen englischen Arzte, der seine Methode gelernt hatte – ähnlich und doch ganz anders, wie Papa einst sein Gewehr verschenkte, da es niemand in der Familie erben konnte. Mir ist es ein wirklicher Schmerz, dass er nicht mehr da ist. Ich habe ihn nicht nur sehr viel persönlich zu verdanken durch seine ärztliche Beratungen, sondern ich sprach von Zeit zu Zeit besonders gern mit ihm. Denn er war ungewöhnlich klug, manchmal fast visionär in seinem Erkennen der Zusammenhänge, dabei so nüchtern, sachlich, wie es ein wissenschaftlicher Mensch ist. Am Dienstag wird er bestattet. Für Euch habe ich einen Kranz bestellt, ich denke einen sehr schönen. Wir schicken einen üppigen Strauß roter Nelken. Er hat Verschwendung verdient. [...]
    Herzlichste Grüße
    Euer Kally

pages 157 to 158
Karl Jaspers to parents:

                         Scheveningen, 22. 8. 35
Liebe Eltern!

Ich sitze auf dem Balkon unseres Zimmers mit dem Blick auf das weite Meer. Den ganzen Tag hört man leise von fern das Geschrei der Badenden, ständig erinnert an die Lebensfreude der Menschen, was wohl tut, wenn man nicht zu nahe dabei ist. Das Meer ist glatt, gar keine Brandung, die Segel spiegeln sich im Wasser, als ob man im Zeichenalbum wäre. Der Strand weithin ist übersät mit Menschen. Der Himmel den ganzen Tag strahlend, der Ostwind (Landwind) kaum spürbar. Liest man draußen Zeitung, rührt sich das Blatt nicht. Es ist das ein unnatürliches Wetter und wird gewiss bald anders. Für den Anfang ist es schön, zumal man, wenn man älter wird, alles schön findet, wie es die Natur gerade zeigen will.
    Trudlein [...] meint, es [das Baden] sei einer der Weisen hohen Lebensglücks. Julia und ich sahen vom Balkon aus zu (sie hielt sich hier

im Zimmer an) und geht aus dem Hotel mit Bademantel an den Strand [...] Wir bekamen ausgezahlt und haben nun genug Geld für den Aufenthalt. Umständlich ist es allerdings mit diesen Reise-Devisen. Man besorgte es vom Hotel aus. [...]

Gegen Abend machen wir auch einen Gang am Wasser. [...]
Herzliche Grüße
Euer Kally

Henriette Jaspers to Karl and Gertrud Jaspers:

[Oldenburg, 27. September 1935]

Meine geliebte Gertrud! Mein lieber, lieber Kally!

Im Herzen voll Dank feiere ich Euren Silberhochzeitstag und wünsche Euch Glück auf Eurem weiteren Lebensweg! So viel Sonne, so viel Liebe hast du, liebes Trudelein, in mein Leben gebracht und ich gehe zurück in die Erinnerung, – wie Kally Dich als seine Freundin in unser Haus brachte, wie Deine Liebe zu meinem lieben Sohn leuchtend in mein Herz schien und wie ich fühlte, dass Du auch seine Mutter lieb gewannst! Und seit all den langen Jahren seh' ich Dich als seine treuste Gefährtin, in Freude und Sorge und Ihr beide wurdet zu einer unlöslichen Einheit! Täglich begleiten meine Gedanken Euer schönes Leben in der Arbeit, im tiefen Ernst und alles Schwere, was gekommen ist, wird durch die Stütze Deines Mannes, liebe Gertrud, Deine liebe Seele stark erhalten! Möchten sich alle Sorgen bald klären. Was uns beide miteinander verbindet, lieber Kally, das kann ich nicht aussprechen. Es ist etwas von Gott Kommendes, diese Liebe, die mein Inneres mit immer gleichem Feuer durchtränkt! Wenn ich in Deiner Philosophie lese, bist Du mir täglich lebendig nahe und ich empfinde Unvergängliches. Möchte Eure Gesundheit Euch beiden erhalten bleiben und Euer Leben und Wirken weiter gesegnet sein!

Ich schreibe bald wieder und grüße Euch beide!
Eure Mutter

pages 165 to 166
Karl Jaspers to parents:

Heidelberg, 28. 6. 37

Liebe Eltern!

Heute bekam ich meine Versetzung in den Ruhestand, nach §6 des Gesetzes vom 7. April 1933, ohne weitere Begründung (in den Paragraphen ist die Rede von „im Interesse des Dienstes" und „zur Vereinfachung der Verwaltung" – der Paragraph verliert am 1. Juli seine Gültigkeit). Über Höhe der Pension und über andere Konsequenzen (ob ich als inaktiver Professor gelte, dann also der Universität noch nominell angehöre, oder nicht) weiß ich noch nichts.

Es schmerzt mich sehr, liebe Eltern, Euch diesen Abschluss meiner öffentlichen Laufbahn mitteilen zu müssen, nachdem ich eigentlich ein langes Leben Euch nur Erfolge mitteilen konnte. Meine Arbeit kann ich für mich fortsetzen. Ob ich noch gedruckt werde, muss ich sehen. Aber <u>dass</u> ich meine Arbeit habe, und darin ganz bestimmte Pläne und sinnvolle Linien, macht aus der Tatsache eine neue Aufgabe: intensiver und schneller zu arbeiten als es während der Zeit, wo ich Vorlesungen halte, möglich ist. Solange wir zu leben haben, kann unser Leben ergiebig bleiben. Dass ich auf die Jugend verzichten muss, ist schwer. Ich erhielt den Brief vor 2 Stunden, 10 Minuten vor der Vorlesung. Die Hörer wissen noch nichts. Sie empfingen mich, wie immer, mit dem Begrüßungsgetrampel. Am Ende der Vorlesung brach ein außerordentlicher Beifall aus, der mich – gegen alle Gewohnheit – weit auf den Korridor begleitete: ich muss also eine eindrucksvolle Vorlesung gehalten haben. Auf diese Freude muss ich verzichten, und auf das Gefühl, in deutscher Jugend Funken zu streuen. Das gedruckte Wort kann nie das lebendige ersetzen. Es ist meine Begabung, reden zu können, die einzige. Man will sie nicht mehr und ich bin es zufrieden. Noch habe ich die Hoffnung auf Arbeit.

Wir freuen uns, im August Euch zu besuchen. […]

Ich werde, denke ich und hoffe ich, weiter munter durch die Welt gehen – oder jedenfalls nicht anders als vorher.

Ihr erzählt es wohl Erna, Eugen und Enno.

Herzlichst Euer Kally

pages 175 to 181
Karl Jaspers to parents:

Heidelberg, 15. 1. 39

Liebe Eltern!

Es <u>kann</u> sein – und Julia hält es für wahrscheinlich – dass ich in einiger Zeit ein Angebot in Oxford bekomme. <u>Absolute</u> Diskretion ist notwendig, da jedes Gerede Universitätssachen stören kann und aus anderen Gründen. Das Angebot wäre überraschend und ein Glücksfall. Aber wir werden um die Frage nicht herum kommen, ob wir es wagen sollen, ein Angebot für zwei Jahren anzunehmen, ohne sicher vorher zu wissen, was daraus wird. Wenn uns eine Verlängerung auf wahrscheinlich in Aussicht gestellt würde, würde ich zufrieden sein. Fast niemand gewinnt im Ausland in unserer Lage eine lebenslänglich gesicherte Stellung. Die Leute in Oxford sollen über meine Krankheit informiert worden sein. Die Pension würde ich wohl verlieren (nach analogen Fällen: man genehmigt nicht die Wohnsitzverlegung ins Ausland, was Streichung der Pension zur Folge hat, wenn man dann doch umzieht.) Es wird aber eine Überlegung sein, die zwischen zwei Risiken abwägt. Das Angebot an sich wäre großartig, ja märchenhaft: ich hätte <u>nur</u> die Aufgabe, meine Bücher zu schreiben. So etwas ist nur in einer aristokratischen, konservativen Gesellschaft möglich. Das Einkommen – die Höhe ist uns noch nicht genannt – würde bescheiden, aber wahrscheinlich zu einem gesunden Leben ausreichend sein. Hoffentlich geht es Euch gut.

Herzlichste Grüße Euch allen
Euer Kally

Karl Jaspers to Erna Dugend:

Heidelberg, 5. 2. 1941

Liebe Erna!

Unsere Gedanken, meine Sehnsucht, unsere Liebe treffen sich täglich. Ich mag heute aber nicht gern schreiben.

Seit Mitte Januar spricht eine Sache, die wir Mutter absichtlich nicht mitteilten, weil wir erst den Abschluss abwarten wollten. Ich bin zu Gastvorlesungen nach Basel für zunächst 2 Jahre mit 10,000 frcs. Jahresgehalt eingeladen. Natürlich streng vertraulich. Mit dem hiesigen Rektor habe ich schon gesprochen. Wir möchten nicht „auswandern", sondern unseren Rückhalt hier bewahren, alle Genehmigungen bewirken, auch für unsere beider Rückkehr nach Heidelberg. Das ist wohl alles sehr unwahrscheinlich. Vermutlich wird am Ende nichts daraus. Nun fährt unsere Freundin Gabriele nach Berlin und ich würde gern wünschen, dass sie mit Stephan spricht, seine Meinung und Rat einholt. Kannst Du mir wohl gleich eben, postwendend, seine Adresse, ich werde Gabriele einen Brief mitgeben zum persönlichen Überreichen, und Titel mitteilen? Die Schweizer sind rührend. Das Angebot ist unter heutigen Umständen phantastisch, Einreise und alle anderen Schwierigkeiten seitens der Schweiz beseitigt.

Herzliche Grüße Euch allen
Dein Kally

Letters to pages 185 to 222 (Part V)

pages 187 to 188
Karl Jaspers, Diary

30. 3. [45]:

[...] Kein Strom, kein Wasser, kein Gas. Wir suchen uns einzurichten. Für kurze Zeit reicht ein Spirituskocher. Wasser wird von der Quelle zum Klingentor geholt. Die Jugend ist bester Laune. Als ob es ein großartiger Spaß wäre, ein Indianerleben einzurichten: aber zugleich besonnen und tätig.

Da kam um 8 Uhr Frau v. J. und berichtet: Heute Morgen kamen Amerikaner auf der Neuenheimerlandstraße, fanden alle Brücken gesprengt, standen mit Panzern davor. Dann entdeckten sie das Bootshaus nahe der neuen Brücke, nahmen die Paddelboote und paddelten über den Fluss, landeten am Gymnasium und quartierten sich dort [ein]. Sie müssen auch oberhalb über den Neckar gekommen sein. Denn sie sind von Schlierbach her in die Stadt gekommen, sind auf dem Rathaus und verfügen dort.

Frau v. J. kam, um uns Glück zu wünschen, dass uns endlich Trudlein frei ist.

Ein Augenblick ohne Worte. Es ist wie ein Wunder, dass wir noch leben. [...]

Um 10 Uhr beginnt wieder das Schießen, im Westen, nicht mehr so ganz nah. Aber ein Zeichen, dass hier noch nicht alles in Ordnung ist.

Leute auf der Straße behaupten, die Amerikaner seien erst auf der Neuenheimer Seite. In der Plöck hat das Dolmetscherinstitut und ein anderes Haus eine weiße Fahne gesetzt.

11 Uhr Artillerie heftig und nah, fast wie gestern. Es ist die Besetzung Heidelbergs offenbar noch nicht abgeschlossen. Jedoch: eben Nachricht, am Werderplatz stünden Amerikaner.

Eben höre ich vom Lazarett gegenüber: Befehl von Amerikanern durchgegeben: alle sollen von der Straße gehen, wer auf der Straße ist, ist in Gefahr, beschossen zu werden.

12½ Uhr: Auf der Anlage hinter dem Garten sehe ich 6 Infanteristen, immer ein Einzelner[,] Deckung hinter Baumstämmen suchend. Geschüsse – Zurück nach Osten. In der Plöck vor unserem Hause 3 Infanteristen von einem Amerikaner entwaffnet und gefangen abgeführt.

Nachmittags: Die Stadt südlich des Neckar ist vom Westen her besetzt von wenigen Soldaten. Ein Brückenkopf mit Paddelbooten an der zerstörten Neuenheimer Brücke. Die weiteste Spitze bis zum Lazarett uns gegenüber an der Plöck. Je zwei amerikanische Soldaten patroullieren durch die Plöck, an der Bibliothek herum nach links. Eine Ordnungspolizei mit blauen Binden fordert auf, ab 6 Uhr die Straßen zu räumen, die Stadt sei noch nicht übergeben, Kämpfe seien noch möglich.

Heidelberg ist südlich des Neckar heute Nacht ohne amerikanisches und ohne deutsches Militär. [...]

1. 4. [45]:

Der Umsturz aller Macht ist vollständig. Es ist wie im Märchen, wenn man zwischen diesen Mauern, in denen wir 12 Jahre so Entsetzliches erlebten, diese Anschläge liest und die amerikanischen Menschen sieht, die zu einem großen Teil einen vorzüglichen Eindruck machen [...].

Letters to pages 223 to 238 (Part VI)

pages 236 to 237
Karl Jaspers to parents:

Heidelberg, 2. Oktober 1927

Liebe Eltern!

[...] Es sind zwei Jahre her, dass ich mit Papa das schöne Gespräch in Scheveningen hatte, das mir von Zeit zu Zeit immer wieder durch den Kopf geht. Papa zweifelte tapfer und wahrhaftig an der Unsterblichkeit und ich konnte ihm nur zustimmen in dem Sinn, dass eine endlose, zeitliche Fortsetzung des Lebens, wie wir es hier kennen, etwas ist, von dem wir nichts wissen und für die [es] nicht den geringsten Anhaltspunkt gibt. Der Schmerz der Vergänglichkeit und des Abschieds ist unaufhaltbar. Aber trotzdem sind wir uns doch bewusst, dass unser Sein mit diesem zeitlichen Ablauf nicht erschöpft ist, wenn auch über die Grenze unserer Erscheinung kein Blick geht. Unser Zusammengehören ist nur an den Tagen, an denen wir keine Liebe fühlen, vergänglich, in jedem Augenblick der Liebe ist uns ein unaussagbar Unvergängliches gewiss. Das stellen wir uns, gebunden an unserer sinnlichen Anschauung, in Symbolen vor, die <u>als</u> Symbole wahr sind oder doch uns etwas Gültiges sagen. So war mir gestern zumute, als ich in Gedanken an Euch mich gleichsam von unvordenklichen Zeiten her mit Euch eins fühlte und dies als einen unzerstörbaren Bestand, der uns nur in der Trivialität des Alltags und in der Vergesslichkeit bei sachlicher Tätigkeit vorübergehend verdunkelt werden kann. Es ist mir eine unersetzliche Befriedigung, in solchen Augenblicken Papa am Strande und in den Dünen innerlich zu folgen, Mutters Liebe und Klugheit gegenwärtig zu haben, an die Kindheit zu denken, an die Großeltern, und an die Gegenwart, in der ich Euch heiter und zufrieden weiß trotz aller Enttäuschungen und Leiden, die nicht ausgeblieben sind. [...]
Herzliche Grüße!
Euer Kally

Source Material and Abbreviations

Archives

All references to Karl Jaspers' unpublished correspondence, unless otherwise indicated, are from the Family Archive [*FA*] that forms an integral part of Karl Jaspers' literary estate [*LE*]:

FA = Karl Jaspers' Family Archive
  Karl Jaspers' unpublished family correspondence, 1878–1968.
  Karl and Gertrud Jaspers, unpublished correspondence, 1907–39; 1939–52.

LE = Karl Jaspers' Literary Estate (Nachlaß)
  Karl Jaspers/Ernst Mayer, unpublished correspondence; and all other references to Jaspers' unpublished correspondence and biographical materials.

BL = Bodleian Library, Oxford
  Papers of the Society for the Protection of Science and Learning (SPSL):
  Karl Jaspers MS, SPLS, 315/2.
  Gustav Mayer MS, SPLS.

IISH = International Institute of Social History, Amsterdam
Gustav Mayer's Literary Estate: unpublished correspondence, Karl Jaspers/Gustav Mayer; unpublished correspondence, Gertrud Jaspers/Gustav Mayer.

UAH = University Archive, Heidelberg
Karl Jaspers' Personal Files: UAH: PA 460, 4369 & 4370.

Works by Karl Jaspers

The alphabetical selection of Karl Jaspers' works (including abbreviations used in the notes) is based on texts used for this biography. There is a comprehensive survey of Jaspers' works, broadcasts and interviews in *Primärbibliographie der Schriften Karl Jaspers*, ed. Christian Rabanus (a fully revised edition of the 1978 bibliography edited by Gisela Gefken and Karl Kunert, commissioned by the Karl Jaspers–Foundation), Tübingen and Basel: Francke 2000.

A	*Die Atombombe und die Zukunft des Menschen*, Munich and Zurich: Piper 1983 (first edition 1958).
AB	*Die Atombombe und die Zukunft des Menschen* (Rundfunkvortrag, Oktober 1956), in Karl Jaspers, *Hoffnung und Sorge, Schriften zur Deutschen Politik 1945–1965*, Munich: Piper 1965, pp. 153–72. Also *Die Atombombe und die Zukunft des Menschen* (Vortrag, 1956). Forum Gesellschaft Verlag + Audiothek (=FGA 001) 1983. Aufnahme: Radio der deutschen und rätoromanischen Schweiz.
Antwort	*Antwort. Zur Kritik meiner Schrift „Wohin treibt die Bundesrepublik?"*, Munich: Piper 1967.
AP	*Allgemeine Psychopathologie. Ein Leitfaden für Studierende, Ärzte und Psychologen*, Berlin: Springer 1913.
AuP	*Karl Jaspers. Aneignung und Polemik. Gesammelte Reden und Aufsätze zur Geschichte der Philosophie*, ed. Hans Saner, Munich: Piper 1968.
AT	'Der Arzt im Technischen Zeitalter', in *Der Arzt im technischen Zeitalter*, Munich and Zurich: Piper 1986, pp. 39–58.

AzP	'Arzt und Patient' (1953), in *Karl Jaspers. Der Arzt im technischen Zeitalter*, Munich and Zurich: Piper 1986, pp. 19–38.
C	*Chiffren der Transzendenz*, ed. Hans Saner, Munich: Piper 1970.
C	*Chiffren der Transzendenz* (Vorlesung Sommer Semester 1961, University of Basel). Tape recordings by Noboru Hosô. Auditorium Netzwerk (= 335/1–335/8). Vier-Türme Verlag, Münsterschwarzach 1997.
Descartes	*Descartes und die Philosophie*, Berlin: de Gruyter 1966 (first edition 1937).
Einsamkeit	'Einsamkeit' (1915–16), in Freiheit, pp. 11–30.
EP	*Einführung in die Philosophie* (Zwölf Radiovorträge), Zurich: Artemis 1950.
EU	'Erneuerung der Universität', in *Die Wandlung*, I/1, 1945–6, Heidelberg, pp. 66–74.
FE	*Karl Jaspers, Rudolf Bultmann. Die Frage der Entmythologisierung*, Munich: Piper 1954.
Freiheit	*Karl Jaspers. Das Wagnis der Freiheit. Gesammelte Aufsätze zur Philosophie*, ed. Hans Saner, Munich and Zurich: Piper 1996.
FW	*Freiheit und Wiedervereinigung*, Munich and Zurich: Piper 1990, with foreword by Willy Brandt and afterword by Hans Saner (first edition 1960).
GP	*Die großen Philosophen*, Munich and Zurich: Piper 1981 (first edition 1957).
GP1	*Die großen Philosophen*, (Nachlaß 1, Darstellungen und Fragmente), ed. Hans Saner, with Raphael Bielander, Munich and Zurich: Piper 1981.
GP2	*Die großen Philosophen* (Nachlaß 2, Fragmente, Anmerkungen, Inventar), ed. Hans Saner, with Raphael Bielander, Munich and Zurich: Piper 1981.
GW	'Geleitwort' in *Die Wandlung*, I/1 1945, Heidelberg, pp. 3–6.
H	'Über Bedingungen und Möglichkeiten eines neuen Humanismus', in *Die Wandlung*, IV/1949, Heidelberg, pp. 710–34.
HDE	'Heidelberger Erinnerungen', in *Heidelberger*

	Jahrbücher V/1961, Berlin, Göttingen and Heidelberg: Springer 1961, pp. 1–10.
HS	'Hochschulreform?' (Das Gutachten des Hamburger Studienausschusses für Hochschulreform), in *Die Wandlung*, IV/4, 1949, Heidelberg, pp. 340–8.
HV	*Heimweh und Verbrechen* (Inaugural Diss. zur Erlangung der Doktorwürde der hohen medizinischen Fakultät der Universität Heidelberg vorgelegt von Karl Jaspers), Leipzig: F.C.W. Vogel 1909.
IA	'Die Idee des Arztes' (1953), in *Der Arzt im technischen Zeitalter*, Munich and Zurich: Piper 1986, pp. 7–18.
Idee (1923)	*Die Idee der Universität*, Berlin and Heidelberg: Springer 1923.
Idee (1946)	*Die Idee der Universität* (Schriften der Universität Heidelberg 1), Berlin: Springer 1946.
Idee (1961)	*Die Idee der Universität. Für die gegenwärtige Situation entworfen von Karl Jaspers und Kurt Rossmann*, Berlin, Göttingen and Heidelberg: Springer 1961.
Ideenlehre	*Kants Ideenlehre* (1913/14), in AuP, pp. 159–82.
KJM	*Karl Jaspers. Was ist der Mensch? Philosophisches Denken für alle*, ed. Hans Saner, Munich and Zurich: Piper 2000.
KP	'Zur Kritik der Psychoanalyse' (1950), in *Der Arzt im technischen Zeitalter*, Munich and Zurich: Piper 1986, pp. 59–67.
KS	*Kleine Schule des philosophischen Denkens*, Vorlesungen, gehalten im 1. Trimester des Studienprogrammes des Bayerischen Fernsehens (autumn 1964). Munich: Piper 1997 (first edition 1965).
L	*Karl Jaspers erzählt sein Leben*, Münsterschwarzach: Vier-Türme Verlag 1997.
Leonardo	'Lionardo als Philosoph' (1953), in AuP, pp. 76–120.
MW	*Max Weber. Deutsches Wesen im politischen Denken, im Forschen und Philosophieren*, Oldenburg: Stalling 1932.
MW–Bemerkungen	'Bemerkungen zu Max Webers politischem Denken' (1962), in *Karl Jaspers, Max Weber* (Mit einer Einführung von Dieter Henrich), Munich and Zurich: Piper 1988, pp. 115–26.
MW–Rede	*Max Weber*. Rede bei der von der Heidelberger

	Studentenschaft am 17. Juli 1920 veranstalteten Trauerfeier gehalten von Karl Jaspers, Tübingen: Mohr 1921.
Nachtlied	'Zu Nietzsches Nachtlied' (1950), in AuP, pp. 402–8.
NC	*Nietzsche und das Christentum*, Rede am 12. Mai 1938, gehalten in Hannover, Hameln: Seifert 1946.
NCus	*Nikolaus Cusanus*, Munich: Piper 1964.
NE	*Nietzsche. Einführung in das Verständnis seines Philosophierens*, Berlin: de Gruyter 1947 (first edition 1936).
NLogik	*Karl Jaspers. Nachlaß zur Philosophischen Logik*, Hans Saner, Marc Hänggi eds, Munich and Zurich: Piper 1991.
Notizen	*Karl Jaspers. Notizen zu Martin Heidegger*, ed. Hans Saner, Munich and Zurich: Piper 1978.
OH	*Offener Horizont. Festschrift für Karl Jaspers*, ed. Klaus Piper, Munich: Piper 1953.
P	*Provokationen. Gespräche und Interviews*, ed. Hans Saner, Munich: Piper 1969.
PA	*Philosophische Aufsätze*, Frankfurt am Main and Hamburg: Fischer Bücherei 1967.
PI-III	*Philosophie* (3 Vols: I: *Philosophische Weltorientierung*, II: *Existenzerhellung*, III: *Metaphysik*), Berlin and Heidelberg: Springer 1932.
PhA	*Philosophische Autobiographie*, in *Karl Jaspers. Werk und Wirkung*, ed. Klaus Piper, Munich: Piper 1963, pp. 19–129 (revised edition, Munich: Piper 1977, including chapter on Heidegger, pp. 92–111).
PG	*Der Philosophische Glaube*. Zurich: Artemis 1948. (Gastvorlesungen, gehalten 1947 auf Einladung der freien akademischen Stiftung und der philosophisch-historischen Fakultät der Universität Basel).
PGO	*Der philosophische Glaube angesichts der Offenbarung*, Munich: Piper 1962.
PsA	Psychiatrische Arbeiten 1909–1913. As: 'Eifersuchtswahn. Ein Beitrag zur Frage: „Entwicklung einer Persönlichkeit" oder „Prozeß"?', in *Zeitschrift für die gesamte Neurologie und Psychiatrie*, I/5 (1910), pp. 567–637.

'Die Methoden der Intelligenzprüfung und der Begriff der Demenz. Kritisches Referat', in *Zeitschrift für die gesamte Neurologie und Psychiatrie*, I/6 (1910), pp. 401–52.

'Die Trugwahrnehmungen. Kritisches Referat', in *Zeitschrift für die gesamte Neurologie und Psychiatrie*, IV/4 (1911), pp. 289–354.

'Zur Analyse der Trugwahrnehmungen. (Leibhaftigkeit und Realitätsurteil)', in *Zeitschrift für die gesamte Neurologie und Psychiatrie*, VI/4 (1911), pp. 460–535.

'Die phänomenologische Forschungsrichtung in der Psychopathologie', in *Zeitschrift für die gesamte Neurologie und Psychiatrie*, IX/3 (1912) pp. 391–408.

'Kausale und „verständliche" Zusammenhänge zwischen Schicksal und Psychose bei der Dementia praecox (Schizophrenie)', in *Zeitschrift für die gesamte Neurologie und Psychiatrie*, XIV/2 (1913), pp. 158–263.

'Über leibhaftige Bewußtheiten (Bewußtheitstäuschungen), ein psychopathologisches Elementarsymptom', in *Zeitschrift für Pathopsychologie*, II/2 (1913), pp. 150–61.

PuW	'Philosophie und Wissenschaft', in *Die Wandlung*, 3/8 1948, Heidelberg, pp. 721–33. (Wortlaut der Antrittsvorlesung an der Universität Basel 1948.)
PW	*Philosophie und Welt. Reden und Aufsätze*. Munich: Piper 1963 (first edition 1958).
PWa	*Psychologie der Weltanschauungen*, Berlin: Springer 1919; and sixth (1971) edition, Munich and Zurich: Piper 1994.
RA	*Rechenschaft und Ausblick*, Munich: Piper 1958 (first edition 1951).
RBK	'Das radikal Böse bei Kant' (1935), in *Rechenschaft und Ausblick*, Munich: Piper 1958, pp. 107–36. (Vortrag, gehalten 1936 im Lesezirkel Hottingen, Zürich.)
Schelling	*Schelling. Größe und Verhängnis*, Munich: Piper 1955.
Selbstporträt	*Karl Jaspers – ein Selbstporträt*. Freely spoken text for a film portrait for German radio, directed by Hannes Reinhardt, 1966/67.
SF	*Die Schuldfrage*, Heidelberg: Lambert Schneider 1946.

Studium1	'Karl Jaspers. Studium 1901–1907. Autobiographische Schriften', (Erst veröffentlicht aus dem Nachlaß, bearbeitet von Hans Saner), in *Jahrbuch der Österreichischen Karl–Jaspers–Gesellschaft*, Vol. 9/1996, Elisabeth Salamun-Hybašek and Kurt Salamun eds, Innsbruck and Vienna: Studienverlag, pp. 9–45.
Studium2	'Karl Jaspers: Studium 1901–1907. Teil 2' (bearbeitet von Hans Saner), in *Jahrbuch der Österreichischen Karl–Jaspers–Gesellschaft*, (10/1997), Elisabeth Salamun-Hybašek and Kurt Salamun (eds), Innsbruck and Vienna: Studienverlag, pp. 7–53.
SW	*Schicksal und Wille. Autobiographische Schriften*, ed. Hans Saner, Munich: Piper 1967.
Thesen	'Thesen über politische Freiheit', in *Die Wandlung*, I/6 1946, Heidelberg, pp. 460–5.
U	'Das Unbedingte des Guten und das Böse', in *Die Wandlung*, Heidelberg, I/8 1946, pp. 672–83.
UMP	'Über meine Philosophie' (1941), in Freiheit, pp. 31–58.
UZ	*Vom Ursprung und Ziel der Geschichte*, Frankfurt am Main and Hamburg: Fischer Bücherei 1955 (first edition 1949).
UZG	'Unsere Zukunft und Goethe', in *Die Wandlung*, II/7 1947, Heidelberg, pp. 559–78.
VBR	'Von der biblischen Religion', in *Die Wandlung*, I/5 1946, pp. 406–13.
VE	*Vernunft und Existenz*. Fünf Vorlesungen gehalten vom 25. bis 29. März 1935, Groningen: Wolters 1935.
VLG	'Vom Lebendigen Geist der Universität und vom Studieren'. Zwei Vorträge von Karl Jaspers und Fritz Ernst (1946). *Schriften der Wandlung 1*, Heidelberg: Lambert Schneider 1946, pp. 7–40.
VW	*Vernunft und Widervernunft in unserer Zeit*. (Drei Gastvorlesungen, gehalten auf Einladung des Asta an der Universität Heidelberg 1950), Munich: Piper 1950.
W	*Von der Wahrheit* ('Philosophische Logik 1'), Munich and Zurich: Piper 1983 (first edition 1947).
WBR	*Wohin treibt die Bundesrepublik? Tatsachen, Gefahren, Chancen*, Munich: Piper 1966.
WF	'Wahrheit, Freiheit und Friede', in *Reden zur*

	Verleihung des Friedenspreises des Deutschen Buch-handels 1958, Munich: Piper 1958, pp. 9–26.
WG	*Karl Jaspers. Weltgeschichte der Philosophie. Einleitung.* Aus dem Nachlaß, ed. Hans Saner, Munich and Zurich: Piper 1982.
WP	*Karl Jaspers. Was ist Philosophie? Ein Lesebuch*, ed. Hans Saner, Munich: Piper 1976.
WW	*Karl Jaspers. Werk und Wirkung*, ed. Klaus Piper, Munich: Piper 1963.

Works translated into English

AB	*The Atom Bomb and the Future of Man*, trans. E.B. Ashton, Chicago and London: University of Chicago Press 1963.
BW	*Karl Jaspers. Basic Philosophical Writings. Selections*, ed., trans. and with introductions by Edith Ehrlich, Leonard H. Ehrlich and George B. Pepper, Athens (Ohio) and London: Ohio University Press 1986.
ES	*The European Spirit*, trans. Ronald Gregor Smith, London: The Stanhope Press 1948.
GP	*General Psychopathology* (2 Vols), trans. J. Hoenig, Marian W. Hamilton, foreword by Paul R. McHugh, Baltimore and London: Johns Hopkins University Press 1997 (1963 reprint of seventh, 1959 German edition).
GP1	*Socrates, Buddha, Confucius, Jesus,* (*The Paradigmatic Individuals*), from *The Great Philosophers* Vol. 1, ed. Hannah Arendt, trans. Ralph Manheim, Harcourt Brace: San Diego, New York and London 1962.
GP1-Plato	*Plato and Augustine* (*The Seminal Philosophers*), from *The Great Philosophers* Vol. 1, ed. Hannah Arendt, trans. Ralph Manheim, Harcourt Brace: San Diego, New York and London 1962.
GP1-Kant	*Kant* (*The Seminal Philosophers*), from *The Great Philosophers* Vol. 1, ed. Hannah Arendt, trans. Ralph Manheim, Harcourt Brace: San Diego, New York and London 1962.
GP2-Spinoza	*Spinoza* (*The Original Thinkers*), from *The Great*

	Philosophers Vol. 2, ed. Hannah Arendt, trans. Ralph Manheim, Harcourt Brace Jovanovich: New York and London 1974.
GP2-Cusa	*Anselm and Nicholas of Cusa (The Original Thinkers)*, from *The Great Philosophers* Vol. 2, ed. Hannah Arendt, trans. Ralph Manheim, Harcourt Brace Jovanovich: New York and London 1974.
GP2-Heraclitus	*Anaximander, Heraclitus, Parmenides, Plotinus, Lao-Tzu, Nagarjuna (The Original Thinkers)*, from *The Great Philosophers* Vol. 2, ed. Hannah Arendt, trans. Ralph Manheim, Harcourt Brace Jovanovich: New York and London 1974.
Guilt	*The Question of German Guilt*, trans. E.B. Ashton, New York: Capricorn 1961.
Man	*Man in the Modern Age*, trans. Eden and Cedar Paul, New York: Anchor 1957.
Memoirs, MSa)	*Memoirs*, 1938 manuscript of the early chapters of Jaspers' memoirs on childhood and student life in SW, Studium1 and Studium2.
Nietzsche	*Nietzsche. An Introduction to the Understanding of his Philosophical Activity*, trans. Charles F. Wallraff and Frederick J. Schmitz, Baltimore and London: Johns Hopkins University Press 1997.
P1–3	*Philosophy* (3 Vols) 1: *Introduction to Philosophy*, 2: *Existential Elucidation*, 3: *Metaphysics*, trans. E.B. Ashton, Chicago: Chicago University Press 1969–71.
PA	'Philosophical Autobiography', in *The Philosophy of Karl Jaspers*, ed. Paul Arthur Schilpp; trans. Paul Arthur Schilpp and Ludwig B. Lefebre, (Library of Living Philosophers), Illinois: Open Court 1981 (first edition 1957), pp. 1–94.
PAP	'The Phenomenological Approach in Psychopathology', in *British Journal of Psychiatry*, 114/1968, pp. 1313–23.
PE	*Philosophy of Existence*, trans. and with an introduction by Richard F. Grabau, Philadelphia: University of Pennsylvania Press 1995.
PSP	*The Perennial Scope of Philosophy*, trans. Ralph Manheim, Connecticut: Archon Books 1968.
RE	*Reason and Existenz* (Five Lectures), trans. with an

	introduction by William Earle, London: Routledge & Kegan Paul 1956.
Reason	*Reason and Anti-Reason in Our Time*, trans. Stanley Godman, London: SCM Press 1952.
Self-Portrait	'Karl Jaspers – Ein Selbstporträt. A Self-Portrait', trans. Edith Ehrlich, in *Karl Jaspers Today. Philosophy at the Threshold of the Future*, ed. Richard Wisser and Leonard H. Ehrlich, Washington D.C. 1988, pp. 1–25.
S&vGogh	*Strindberg and van Gogh. (An Attempt at a Pathographic Analysis with Reference to Parallel Cases of Swedenborg and Hölderlin)*, trans. Oskar Grunow and David Woloshin, Tucson, Arizona: The University of Arizona Press 1977.
Theses (1933)	'How can the Universities be Rejuvenated? Some Theses (1933)', in *Karl Jaspers. Philosopher among Philosophers*, ed. Richard Wisser and Leonard H. Ehrlich, Würzburg: Königshausen & Neumann 1993, pp. 312–31.
Truth	*Truth and Symbol* (from *Von der Wahrheit* (1947)), trans. Jean T. Wilde, William Kluback and William Kimmel, London: Vision 1959.
Wisdom	*Way to Wisdom. (An Introduction to Philosophy)*, trans. Ralph Manheim, New Haven and London: Yale University Press 1954. (Translation of twelve radio broadcasts from 1950.)

Published Correspondence

EB/MH	*Elisabeth Blochmann/Martin Heidegger. Briefwechsel. 1918–1969*, ed. Joachim W. Storck, Marbach am Neckar: Deutsche Schillergesellschaft 1989.
HA/MH	*Hannah Arendt/Martin Heidegger. Briefe 1925 bis 1975. Und Andere Zeugnisse*, ed. Ursula Ludz, Frankfurt am Main: Vittorio Klostermann 1999.
HA/KJ	*Hannah Arendt/Karl Jaspers: Correspondence 1926–1969*, ed. Hans Saner and Lotte Köhler, trans. Robert and Rita Kimber, San Diego, New York and London: Harcourt Brace Jovanovich 1992.
KHB/KJ	*Karl Jaspers, K. H. Bauer. Briefwechsel. 1945–1968*, ed.

Renato de Rosa, Berlin, Heidelberg and New York: Springer 1983.

KJ/HZ   Karl Jaspers/Heinrich Zimmer. Briefe 1929–1939. (Aus den Nachlässen zusammengestellt von Hans Saner und Maya Rauch), in *Jahrbuch der Österreichischen Karl–Jaspers–Gesellschaft*, ed. Elisabeth Salamun-Hybašek and Kurt Salamun, Vienna: Studienverlag, Vol. 6/1993, pp. 7–32.

MH/HR   *Martin Heidegger/Heinrich Rickert. Briefe 1912–1933. (Und andere Dokumente)*, ed. Alfred Denker, Frankfurt am Main: Vittorio Klostermann 2002.

MH/KJ   *Briefwechsel 1920–1963. Martin Heidegger/Karl Jaspers*, ed. Walter Biemel and Hans Saner, Munich and Zurich: Piper/Frankfurt am Main: Klostermann 1990.

Notes

Introduction

1. Jaspers' radio lecture entitled *Die Atombombe und die Zukunft des Menschen* (1956) was delivered in October 1956. A recording of this lecture was made by Swiss radio (for further details see Source Material and Abbreviations (AB) below). A few years before his death, Jaspers published the text of his lecture in a collection of his essays about German political life from 1945 to 1965, entitled *Hoffnung und Sorge* (1965).
2. AB, p. 164.
3. The text of Albert Einstein's letter to the President of the United States of America of 15 August 1939 may be found in: Carl Seelig (ed.), *Helle Zeit – Dunkle Zeit. In Memoriam Albert Einstein*, Braunschweig 1986, pp. 100–4.
4. Hannah Arendt, *Karl Jaspers. A Laudatio*, in *Men in Dark Times*, trans. Clara and Richard Winston, especially pp. 74–6.
5. In his illuminating monograph, Charles Wallraff devoted an entire introductory chapter to an outline of 'Disputed Topics', in an endeavour to highlight Jaspers' contribution to the polarized and enduring split of Anglo-American from 'Continental' philosophy. See *Karl Jaspers. An Introduction to His Philosophy*, pp. 11–37.
6. In his reflections on his encounters with many philosophers in his time, Hans-Georg Gadamer noted Jaspers' 'light, observing eye' and the 'voice of the moralist' that Gadamer respected, as coming from a gifted teacher. Cf. Hans-Georg Gadamer, 'Philosophische Begegnungen', in *Gesammelte Werke*, Vol. X, especially on 'Karl Jaspers', pp. 392–400, here pp. 393, 396 and 399 (author's translation).
7. Jeanne Hersch, 'Karl Jaspers als Lehrer', in OH, pp. 440 and 442 (author's translation).

8. E. B. Ashton, 'Translator's Note', in *P1*, p. xiv.

9. E. B. Ashton first mentioned his intention to translate *Philosophy* (*1932*) in correspondence with Karl Jaspers as early as 1961. Cf. E. B. Ashton to Karl Jaspers, 22 July 1961 [*LE*]. However, the first volume of *Philosophy* in English went to press in late 1968. Cf. E. B. Ashton to Karl Jaspers, 30 October 1968 [*LE*]. It is possible that due to the rapid deterioration of his health at that time and because of the sterling job that E. B. Ashton did on many other translations that Karl Jaspers was content to accept, with Hannah Arendt's involvement in overseeing the transferral of the translation rights, Ashton's 'line for line' (*Zeile für Zeile*) method of translation. Cf. E. B. Ashton to Karl Jaspers, 2 July 1966 [*LE*]).

10. Compare the debate upon the publication of Charles Wallraff's scholarly article, 'Jaspers in English: A failure of Communication' (1977). Adolph Lichtigfeld responded to Wallraff's arguments about the character of translations by highlighting the duty of scholars to work between the two idioms of German and English and thoroughly to inspect their interpretations in his 'Jaspers in English: A Failure not of Communication but rather of Interpretation' (1980).

11. Father to Karl Jaspers, Oldenburg, i. Gr., 21 February 1908 [*FA*]. Jaspers referred to this letter in his memoirs, SW, pp. 46f.

12. SW, p. 53 (author's translation).

13. Father to Karl Jaspers, Oldenburg, i. Gr., 21 February 1908 [*FA*].

14. Karl Jaspers to parents, Heidelberg, 18 November 1909 [*FA*].

Chapter 1   A Classical Education

1. The original verse of the poem, 'Sils Maria', by Friedrich Nietzsche reads as follows:

     Hier sass ich, wartend, wartend – doch auf Nichts,
     Jenseits von Gut und Böse, bald des Lichts
     Geniessend, bald des Schattens, ganz nur Spiel,
     Ganz See, ganz Mittag, ganz Zeit ohne Ziel.
     Da, plötzlich, Freundin! wurde Eins zu Zwei –
     – Und Zarathustra gieng an mir vorbei...

     (Friedrich Nietzsche, 'Lieder des Prinzen Vogelfrei' in *Werke V/2* (Nachgelassene Fragmente Frühjahr 1881–Sommer 1882), ed. Giorgio Colli and Mazzino Montinari, Berlin: de Gruyter 1973, p. 333. In Jaspers' personal edition of Nietzsche's collected works (Verlag Alfred Kröner), the words 'ganz nur Spiel, Ganz See, ganz Mittag, ganz Zeit ohne Ziel' were underlined and the word 'Mittag' doubly underlined.

2. Karl Jaspers was born '23 February 1883 at 1.30 p.m.' ('am 23. Februar 1883 um 2¼ Uhr nachmittags') according to his birth certificate [*LE*].

3. For an examination of Bismarck's skilful establishment of a federal, as opposed to parliamentary system of democracy during his period as Chancellor (1871–90), and the battle between the Catholic Church, the individual and the State, Bismarck's introduction of social policies, the repression of social democracy, and other things, see Thomas Nipperdey, *Deutsche Geschichte 1866–1918*, Vol. II., pp. 85–140 and 359–426.

4. Karl Wilhelm Jaspers (1850–1940), was born in Jever, son of Carl Wilhelm Jaspers

(1817–86) and Antoinette Christine Louise Drost (1823–95). Henriette Tantzen (1862–1941), was born in Heering, daughter of Anna Magdalena Lührs (1835–1919) and Theodor Johann Tantzen (1835–93). See authenticated copy of Henriette Tantzen's birth certificate, 26 January 1863, Abbehausen, 28 May 1933 [*LE*]. (The copy was to demonstrate the Jaspers' family's 'Aryan' genealogy to the Nazi state.)

5. Fritz Jaspers (1847–1917) was director of the Hannoversche Glashütte. Upon his early death after an illness, he left a considerable sum of money to his brother's children. See below, p. 117.

6. SW ('Mein Vater'), p. 106; and Hans Saner, *Karl Jaspers*, pp. 10f.

7. Erna Margarete Jaspers (1885–1974); and Enno Jaspers (1889–1931).

8. Inscribed onto the loose leaves of a notebook, with Jaspers' copy of instructions on his confirmation, is a brief record: '1898, 20 March, I, <u>Karl Theodor Jaspers</u>, b. 23 February 1883, christened 12 April q[uot] a[nnis], was confirmed by Vicar Wilkens in the St Lamberti Church.' ('1898, d. 20. März, bin ich, <u>Karl Theodor Jaspers</u> geb. 1883, 23. Februar, getauft 12. April q. a., von Herrn Pastor Wilkens in der S. Lamberti Kirche konfirmiert worden.') [*LE*].

9. SW, p. 41; Hans Saner, *Karl Jaspers*, p. 11; and Karl to Gertrud Jaspers, Oldenburg, 23 December 1911 [*FA*].

10. SW ('Mein Vater'), p. 106; and Hans Saner, *Karl Jaspers*, pp. 10f.

11. See Golo Mann, 'Reorganization from Above', in his *The History of Germany since 1789*, trans. Marian Jackson, pp. 24–35.

12. SW, p. 56; and Karl Jaspers, senior to Gertrud Jaspers, Oldenburg, 24 February 1912 [*FA*].

13. SW, pp. 48f.

14. SW, p. 81.

15. Jaspers' mother mentioned this information in a speech that she personally delivered in Heidelberg on the occasion of Jaspers' fiftieth birthday: '[...] As a sixth form pupil (*Primaner*), Kally's greatest interest was philosophy, along with art. Our librarian, Mosen, came to see Papa at the bank and asked with concern whether he agreed with his son borrowing philosophical books? Papa replied to that: "My son can borrow any book that he wishes."' See Henriette Jaspers, transcript of speech for Karl Jaspers' fiftieth birthday, 23 February 1933 [*FA*]. '([...] Als Primaner war es schon die Philosophie, die neben der Kunst Kallys großes Interesse war. Unser Bibliothekar Mosen [*sic*] kam auf die Bank zu Papa und fragte besorgt, ob es ihm recht wäre, dass sein Sohn sich philosophische Bücher hole? Worauf Papa [sagte]: „Mein Sohn kann sich jedes Buch leihen, das er wünscht."')

16. The business of Jaspers' favourite Uncle Fritz, who managed the glass-making company in Hanover, took him to Posen in the east, or to the city of Hamburg in the north. Other relatives were scattered variously in Brake (Jaspers' aunt, Anna Heddewig), Berlin (Jaspers' uncle Theodor Tantzen) and Emden (Jaspers' cousin, Martha Jaspers, herself an artist).

17. Mother to Gertrud Jaspers, February 1929 (undated); and Gertrud to mother, telegram [of thanks], 27 February 1929 [*FA*].

18. Jaspers devoted the first part of the centrepiece of his *Philosophy* (1932), that is, the second volume of his magnum opus entitled, *Existential Elucidation*, to an exposition

of his conception of 'existential communication' in which he discussed what he understood by 'loving contest'. *P2*, pp. 47–103 and pp. 59ff. (E. B. Ashton's translation of Jaspers' 'liebender Kampf' is 'loving struggle'. Ralph Manheim's suggestion of 'loving contest' in Karl Jaspers' *Way to Wisdom* is preferred as an alternative translation.)

19. Karl to Henriette Jaspers, Spiekeroog, 28 July 1886 [*FA*]. ('Kalli [*sic*] ist richtig munter, er röchelt aber noch immer, hustet richtig des Abends und schläft sehr wenig. Ich glaube, die Kur hat ihm im Allgemeinen und auch speziell gegen das Röcheln doch gut getan. Wir werden das Baden wohl fortsetzen müssen und müssen dann das Übrige abwarten.')

20. Karl Jaspers to parents, Norderney, 10 July 1898 [*FA*]. For Karl Jaspers' original letter, see the Appendix.

21. Henriette to Karl Jaspers, senior, Norderney, 29 July 1891 [*FA*].

22. SW, pp. 101f.

23. Grandfather (Theodor Johann Tantzen) to Kally, Heering, 31 December 1891 [*FA*].

24. Louis Jaspers (1852–1935) and Diedrich or Dietrich Jaspers (1855–1911).

25. The wealth derived from Jaspers' great-grandfather's commercial success as co-owner of the Bremen trading company, 'Delius & Co', SW, p. 39.

26. SW ('Großeltern'), p. 54.

27. Several months after Jaspers' grandfather's death, Louise Jaspers was forwarding her son lists of expenditure, such as for household goods, and Karl Jaspers, senior arranged his mother's financial affairs. Louise Jaspers to Karl Jaspers, senior, Jever, 2 February 1887 [*FA*].

28. Karl Jaspers to Golo Mann, Heidelberg, 25 January 1947 [*LE*].

29. Karl to Henriette Jaspers, Oldenburg, 12 May 1881 [*FA*]. ('Noch etwas über 3 Monate und wir beginnen beide den glücklichen Teil unseres Lebens.')

30. See below, pp. 106–7.

31. School leaving Certificate (*Zeugnis der Reife*), Großherzogliches Gymnasium zu Oldenburg, 19 February 1901 [*LE*]. ('Die Klassiker las er mit gutem Verständnis und Interesse und zeigte mündlich und schriftlich wohlbefriedigende Gewandtheit im Ausdruck.') (The certificate gives results of good (*gut*) for Latin, Greek, German, French and English, very good (*sehr gut*) for history and geography, good (*gut*) for mathematics and satisfactory (*genügend*) for sport.)

32. Jaspers' former pupil, the political thinker and literary critic, Dolf Sternberger, devoted an essay in the *Festschrift* for Jaspers' seventieth birthday in 1953 called 'Notizen über die Prosa von Karl Jaspers', in OH, pp. 431–9. In his essay, Sternberger highlighted the aesthetic quality of Jaspers' prose, its certain 'light, temperate sounding tone', as being characteristic of a thinker who was devoted to the serious nature of his task, ibid., pp. 433f. (author's translation).

33. Karl Jaspers to parents, Norderney, 9 July 1898 (postcard, date as postmark [*LE*]), 9. For Jaspers' original letter, see the Appendix.

34. SW, p. 66.

35. SW, p. 20 (author's translation).

Chapter 2   Young Scientist

1. Karl Jaspers to parents, Badenweiler, 30 April 1901 [*FA*]. ('Meine jetzige Adresse lautet: Badenweiler (Schwarzwald) Diätetische Kuranstalt (Villa Hedwig).')

2. Karl Jaspers, postcard to parents, Freiburg, 17 April 1901 [*FA*]. Cf. Walter Engel, 'Kindheit, Jugend, Studium, Biographische Skizze. Elternhaus und Schule', in Joachim-Felix Leonhard (ed.), *Karl Jaspers in seiner Heidelberger Zeit*, pp. 13–21, here pp. 16f.

3. On the advice of his father, Jaspers visited Dr Fraenkel a number of times before the diagnosis of his illness. Father to Karl Jaspers, Oldenburg, 18 April 1901 [*FA*]. 'Should [...] you feel unwell at all, then I would travel to Badenweiler to consult Dr Fraenkel, perhaps he can prescribe you some useful measures to feel better.' ('Solltest [...] Du Dich überhaupt angegriffen fühlen, so würde ich nach Badenweiler fahren und Dr Fraenkel konsultieren, vielleicht kann er Dir zweckmäßige Wohltuungsmaßnahmen geben.')

4. Karl Jaspers to parents, Badenweiler, 27 April 1901 [*FA*].

5. Karl Jaspers to parents, Badenweiler, 27 April 1901 [*FA*]. For Jaspers' original letter, see the Appendix.

6. Albert Fraenkel to Karl Jaspers, senior, B[adenweiler], 27 April 1901 [*FA*]. For the original text of this letter, see the Appendix.

7. Dr Albert Fraenkel (1864–1938) had contracted tuberculosis in late 1888 and he continued to research the treatment of lung conditions as one of his special interests when he moved in 1891 to Badenweiler, where he established his clinic, Villa Hedwig and the Villa Paul, later renamed the Villa Waldeck. See Wolfgang Huebner, 'Albert Fraenkel', in Georg Weiss (ed.), *Albert Fraenkel. Arzt und Forscher*, pp. 6–15.

8. Telegram to 'Jaspers, freyburgbr. Europäischer Hof, v. oldenburg gr.' 29 March [1901] [*FA*]. ('erfreut dass ursache missbefindens entdeckt mit allem was du tust gern einverstanden, depeschiere resultat baeumlers untersuchung, hier alles wohl papa'.)

9. Karl Jaspers to mother, Badenweiler, 7 May 1901 [*FA*]. By his own reckoning, Jaspers should have weighed about an extra 10 kilos for his height. Karl Jaspers to father, Badenweiler, 8 May 1901 [*FA*]. During the severe food shortages of the First World War, Jaspers' weight fell to 124 pounds, that is, almost the same weight as in 1901 in Badenweiler.

10. Karl Jaspers to mother, Badenweiler, 7 May 1901 [*FA*].

11. Jaspers had gained a total of six kilos (67.5 kilos or 135 pounds). Karl Jaspers to father, Badenweiler, 21 May 1901 [*FA*]. Several days before his departure from Badenweiler (on 15 July), Jaspers reported that his weight had risen to 144.5 pounds. Karl Jaspers postcard to parents, Badenweiler, 9 July 1901 [*FA*].

12. Karl Jaspers to father, Badenweiler, 14 May 1901 [*FA*].

13. Karl Jaspers to mother, Badenweiler, 1 May 1901 [*FA*].

14. Karl Jaspers to parents, Freiburg, 21 April 1901 [*FA*]. 'In the evening, 6–7 o'clock' ('Abends 6–7 Uhr').

15. Karl Jaspers to father, Badenweiler, 21 May 1901 [*FA*]. For Jaspers' original letter, see the Appendix.

16. Father to Karl Jaspers, Kissingen, 22 May 1901 [*FA*]: 'If I should come to Badenweiler in the near future, it would be very nice if we could take a trip together to Basel, to look at the collection of paintings there. Magnificent paintings by Böcklin must be there.'

('Wenn ich nächstens nach Badenweiler kommen sollte, wäre es sehr schön, wenn wir mal zusammen nach Basel fahren könnten, um dort die Gemäldesammlung anzuschauen. Dort müssen wahrscheinlich hervorragende Böcklins sein.')

17. Karl Jaspers, senior to Henriette Jaspers, Badenweiler, 7 June 1901 [*FA*].

18. Karl Jaspers to parents, Badenweiler, 15 June 1901 [*FA*].

19. Father to Karl Jaspers, Oldenburg, 14 June 1901 [*FA*]. For the text of the original letter, see the Appendix.

20. Karl Jaspers to father, Badenweiler, 16 June 1901 [*FA*]. ('Aus Düsseldorf wurden mir geschickt: 15 Farben und genau Sepia, [...] Kobalt Blau, Französisch Blau, Indigo [...], Lampenschwarz, Neapelgelb, Krapplackrosa, Madderbraun, Indischrot, Lichtrot, Gebrannte Siena, Umber, Gebrannte Umber.') The colours may be compared with Max Doerner's handbook ('Malmaterial und seine Verwendung im Bilde', 1921). I am grateful to Gregor Fitzi for his assistance in identifying the names of the watercolours.

21. Karl Jaspers to parents, Darmstadt, 15 July 1901 and 16 July 1901 [*FA*].

22. Karl Jaspers to parents, Norderney, 28 July 1901 [*FA*].

23. Karl Jaspers to parents, Heidelberg, 23 October 1901 [*FA*]: 'Dear parents, [...] During the day, I recline a lot on the chaise longue, I read the *Frankfurter Zeitung* that I have ordered for myself and Schopenhauer, whose philosophy seems to be made for my condition. [...] Greeting from Your Kally.' ('Liebe Eltern! [...] Über Tag liege ich viel auf der Chaiselongue, lese die *Frankfurter Zeitung*, die ich mir bestellte, und Schopenhauer, dessen Philosophie für meinen Zustand gemacht zu sein scheint. [...] Gruß von Eurem Kally.')

24. See below, p. 43. The third of Nietzsche's *Untimely Meditations* (1874), *Schopenhauer as Educator*, may be read as highlighting Jaspers' qualms with regard to Schopenhauer's philosophy. Jaspers' initially positive reaction to Schopenhauer cannot be seen as a moment of epiphany in the way that it was for Nietzsche. See Werner Ross, *Der ängstliche Adler*, Munich: Deutscher Taschenbuch 1999 pp. 133f. and 156–67.

25. Karl Jaspers to parents, Sils [Maria], 1 August 1902 [*FA*]. For Jaspers' original letter, see the Appendix.

26. Georg Brandes, 'An Essay on Aristocratic Radicalism (1889)', in Georg Brandes, *Friedrich Nietzsche*, pp. 3–56, here p. 3. For a characterization of Brandes' lectures on Nietzsche's thought see Werner Ross, *Der ängstliche Adler*, Munich: Deutscher Taschenbuch 1999, pp. 744ff.

27. Nietzsche had dated the thought of the 'eternal recurrence of the same' to August 1881, as he stated in the relevant section of *Ecce Homo* (1889). Nietzsche referred to his memory of walking from Silvaplana through the woods, past a pyramid-formed rock, near Surlei, where he had noted: 'Anfang August 1881 in Sils-Maria,/ 6000 Fuß über dem Meere und viel höher über allen / menschlichen Dingen!' Friedrich Nietzsche, *Werke V/2* (Nachgelassene Fragmente Frühjahr 1881–Sommer 1882), ed. Giorgio Colli and Mazzino Montinari, Berlin and New York: de Gruyter 1973, 11 (141), p. 392.)

28. See below, pp. 121f. and pp. 159f.

29. All excerpts are taken from this letter, quoted after *Memoirs*, MS a), pp. 173–80. The full text of this letter was first published in Studium1, pp. 32–40.

30. *Memoirs*, MS a), p. 174; and Studium1, p. 33.

31. *Memoirs*, MS a), p. 176; and Studium1, p. 36.

32. *Memoirs*, MS a), p. 177; and Studium1, p. 36. 'Die Beschäftigung mit dem menschlichem Körper ist die Grundlage alles anderen Wissens von der menschlichen Psyche und des Studiums der Krankheiten in ihren Ursachen, in ihren Wirkungen und Heilungsmöglichkeiten. [...] Man erfährt, wie nicht nur das existiert, was wir mit bloßem Auge sehen, sondern wie auch im Kleinsten sich Leben regt.')

33. Karl Jaspers to parents, Berlin, 16 October 1902 [*FA*].

34. Jaspers included a description of his daily routine in his early letters to his parents from Heidelberg, as here, Karl Jaspers to parents, Heidelberg, 19 October 1901 [*FA*].

35. In the aftermath of the First World War, the room was converted into a hen house in order to help with food supplies. Gertrud Jaspers to parents, 9 November 1920 [*FA*].

36. *Memoirs*, MS a), p. 141.

37. Karl Jaspers to parents, Berlin, 24 October 1902 [*FA*].

38. Mother to Karl Jaspers, Oldenburg, 25 October 1902 [*FA*]. ('Mit den Anschaffungen, die Dein Studium erfordern, ist Papa ganz einverstanden, Du möchtest Dir den Atlas neu kaufen und ebenso ein Skelett. Papa sagte, alle Hilfsmittel zum Studium sind gut angewandtes Geld und ich denke es mir auch sehr schön für Dich, wenn Du beim Studium in Deinem Zimmer das Skelett vor Augen hast.')

    The skeleton was duly purchased: 'I am to have one of the best quality for 100 Marks. I can also obtain a cheaper anatomical atlas, as I discovered from another medical student.' Karl Jaspers to mother, Berlin, 4 November 1902 [*FA*]. ('Ich soll eines bester Qualität für 100 Mark haben. Einen billigeren anatomischen Atlas kann ich auch bekommen, wie ich von einem Mediziner erfuhr.')

39. Karl Jaspers to parents, Berlin, 20 November 1902 [*FA*]. ('Das Skelett steht als Naturzeichen auf meiner Stube; ich benutze es sehr viel [...].')

40. Karl Jaspers to parents, Berlin, 27 November 1902 [*FA*]. ('Mein Wunsch wäre also: Ein Mikroskop zu 270 Mark mit den notwendigen Utensilien <u>ca. 300–320 Mark</u> und im Laufe des nächsten oder weitnächsten Jahren eine Ölimmersion zu 100 Mark.')

41. *Memoirs*, MS a), p. 191. 'With a small telescope I studied the moon's undulations, saw Jupiter's moons, the stardust, the phases of Venus. I was introduced to geology by a collection of stones that were purchased.' ('Mit einem kleinen Fernrohr studierte ich die Mondgebirge, sah Jupitermonde, Sternnebel, Venusphase. Eine gekaufte Steinsammlung führte mich in Geologie ein.')

42. Ibid., p. 196.

43. Ibid., p. 197.

44. Karl Jaspers to parents, Göttingen, 23 February 1905 [*FA*].

45. The inscription is in ink on page two of the diary entitled, 'Diary 1904/5: Jaspers, Oldenburg in Grand D[uchy] stud. med.' ('Tagebuch 1904/5: Jaspers, Oldenburg i. Grossh[erzogtum] stud. med.' [*LE*].)

46. Jaspers read several popular authors in his early student days. Dostoevsky was fashionable at the time, as were Theodor Fontane and Gottfried Keller. Goethe's *Elective Affinities* and *Wilhelm Meister's Travels* are frequently mentioned. Cf. *Memoirs*, MS a), p. 183; and Karl Jaspers to parents, 15 January 1903 [*FA*]. 'Can mother perhaps send me *Wilhelm Meister's Travels* by Goethe?' ('Kann Mutter mir vielleicht [...] Wilhelm Meisters Wanderjahre von Goethe zusenden?'); and Karl Jaspers to parents, Göttingen, 30 May 1905 [*FA*].

47. Johann Wolfgang Goethe, *Wahlverwandtschaften*, in *Werke*, Vol. 6, p. 417.
48. Johann Wolfgang Goethe, *Elective Affinities*, trans. R. J. Hollingdale, p. 216.
49. See below, pp. 00–00.
50. SW, pp. 109–41, here p. 109.
51. 'About My Existence 1904' ('Über meine Existenz 1904' [*LE*]).
52. Ibid.

> [Stelle ich mir einmal vor, dass ich als Sohn meiner Eltern geboren wäre, so wäre das Resultat, dass ich längst tot sein müsste. So werde ich nur künstlich als kranke Pflanze gestellt unter gesunden und der Erfolg ist, dass die kranke Pflanze, weil ihre Lebensbedingungen ihr auf diese Weise – nachgerade andere wären ihre Vernichtung – das Vegetieren möglich machen in ihrem schließlichen Aussehen den Gesunden fast gleicht. Dies kann den unkundigen Beobachter zu einer verkehrten Meinung über die kranke Pflanze verleiten.]

53. SW, p. 109. (For the chronological overview of his illness that Jaspers provided, see SW, pp. 112f.)
54. SW, p. 112.
55. Karl Jaspers to parents, Göttingen, 22 March 1906 [*FA*].
56. Karl Jaspers to parents, Heidelberg, 25 March 1907 [*FA*].

Chapter 3   *'German Student'*

1. Karl Jaspers, 'Neue Deutsche Biographie', in Richard Wisser, *Karl Jaspers. Philosophie in der Bewährung*, pp. 293–301, here p. 294.
2. *Memoirs*, MS a), p. 140.
3. Friedrich Hölderlin, 'Heidelberg', in *Friedrich Hölderlin, Poems and Fragments*, trans. Michael Hamburger, Cambridge: Cambridge University Press 1980, pp. 132–5, here p. 133.
4. HDE, p. 4.
5. HDE, p. 6 (author's translation).
6. Karl Jaspers to parents, Heidelberg, 28 October 1901 [*FA*]. For Jaspers' original letter, see the Appendix.
7. Karl Jaspers to parents, Heidelberg, 26 October 1901 [*FA*]. Emil Kraepelin (1856–1926) wrote the *Kompendium der Psychiatrie. Zum Gebrauch für Studierende und Ärzte* (1883), the book which Jaspers' work in the field of psychiatry was, as shall be seen, considered to have revised. See further on Kraepelin's contribution, Matthias Bormuth, *Lebensführung in der Moderne*, pp. 30f and 35–7.
8. *Memoirs*, MS a), p. 143: and Studium1, pp. 14 and 41.
9. *Self-Portrait*, p. 5.
10. Kuno Fischer (1824–1907) was something of a legend. A gifted rhetorician, he was an influential intellectual figure whose presence in Heidelberg (from 1872 to 1907) upheld an eminent tradition dating from Hegel's time. (Georg Wilhelm Friedrich Hegel held the first professorship in philosophy at Heidelberg in 1817.) Despite Jaspers' youthful disdain for Fischer, he declared in his 'Heidelberg Memoirs' (1961) that he had learned a great deal from Kuno Fischer's rhetorical talent of creatively representing the lives of

great philosophers, even though he saw Fischer's approach as belonging to the bygone age of the German 'Bildungswelt', now radically changed, for Jaspers, by the contribution of Kierkegaard and Nietzsche, HDE, p. 2.

11. Karl Jaspers to parents, Heidelberg, 9 November 1901 [*FA*].

12. *Memoirs*, MS a), p. 148 and Studium1, pp. 17 and 42: 'Through him I then learned to see Pinturicchio, Botticelli, Melozzo da Forli and, above all, Leonardo. The lectures became the high point of the day.' ('Durch ihn habe ich damals Pinturicchio, Botticelli, Melozzo da Forli, vor allem Lionardo sehen gelernt. Diese Vorlesungen wurden zum Mittelpunkt des Tages.')

13. See below, pp. 43–5

14. The certificates of study (*Scheine*) confirm that Jaspers began to attend law lectures in Heidelberg during the winter semester of 1901/2 [*LE*]. He held certificates for attending lectures on law given by Hermann Strauch (1838–1904) and Georg Jellinek (1851–1911); and for lectures on the history of Italian art given by Henry Thode (1857–1920), Professor of History of Art in Heidelberg from 1893 to 1911.

15. HDE, pp. 8 and 5.

16. Gustav Radbruch, a member of the Social Democratic Party, was Minister of Justice from 1921 to 1922 and for several months in 1923 under the Chancellorship of Gustav Stresemann. Cf. Gustav Radbruch, *Der innere Weg*, Stuttgart 1951, pp. 142–81.

17. In answer to his critics in Paul Arthur Schilpp's 'Library of Living Philosophers' (1957), Jaspers later underlined that his understanding of 'aristocracy' in his thinking was not in reference to the 'materially privileged', see Karl Jaspers, 'About the Question of Aristocracy', in P. A. Schilpp ed., *The Philosophy of Karl Jaspers*, pp. 756–60, here p. 758. Jaspers outlined his notion of 'aristocracy' as based on an ethos of freedom and an approach to the individual's capacity for 'nobility', 'luminosity of the soul', 'power of love', 'veracity and incorruptibility', ibid. A further discussion of the philosophical implication of Jaspers' comments is in Richard Wisser, 'Ein Philosoph denkt sich frei. Karl Jaspers' Denkungsart gegen Doktrinen', in Richard Wisser, *Verantwortung im Wandel der Zeit*, Mainz 1967, pp. 17–45, here especially on 'Die Unvertretbarkeit des Menschen', pp. 21–4.

18. Hermann Glockner, *Heidelberger Bilderbuch*, p. 59. Glockner dates his conversation to his second invitation to Karl and Gertrud Jaspers' home on 12 January 1920, ibid., pp. 53–60.

19. When Glockner's visits to Friedrich Gundolf became a topic of conversation, according to Glockner, the Jaspers were critical of Gundolf's involvement in the George Circle, even expressing their concern that Gundolf's friendship with Glockner was merely in order to initiate him into the Circle, see Hermann Glockner, *Heidelberger Bilderbuch*, p. 58f. That their relations with Gundolf were friendly can be seen by the fact that Gundolf dedicated several poems to Jaspers, one of them dated 1919 and entitled 'Geschichte der Philosophie' ('History of Philosophy'), in Joachim-Felix Leonhard (ed.), *Karl Jaspers in seiner Heidelberger Zeit*, pp. 109f. The Jaspers developed a close friendship with Gundolf and his wife, Elisabeth née Salamon, as is shown by Gertrud's letter to her parents-in-law, upon Gundolf's early death on 12 July 1931, Gertrud Jaspers to parents, Heidelberg, 20 July 1931 [*FA*]:

Dear parents, [...] Elly Gundolf [...] makes me feel immeasurably sorry for her, [...] His poems were for her and could protect her from criticism. Neither Stefan George, nor a representative of the Circle was at the funeral. They had banished Gundolf because of this marriage. He suffered a great deal because of that, since he was not able to hate, and did not cease honouring Stefan George, although he himself grew out of the All-too-human element of the Master. [...] Heidelberg has suffered an irreplaceable loss that we will only grow accustomed to with difficulty, with very great difficulty. [...] Fond greetings, your Gertrud. (Liebe Eltern, [...] Elly Gundolf [...] tut mir maßlos leid, [...] Seine Gedichte sind an sie und könnten sie schützen, wenn die Menschen sie angreifen. Bei der Beerdingung war weder Stefan George noch ein Vertreter des Kreises. Sie hatten Gundolf wegen dieser Ehe in den Bann getan. Er hat sehr darunter gelitten, da er nicht hassen kann, nicht aufhörte Stefan George zu verehren, aber selbst über alles dieses Allzumenschliche des Meisters herauswuchs. [...] Heidelberg hat einen unersetzlichen Verlust erlitten, an den wir uns schwer, sehr schwer gewöhnen werden. [...] Herzliche Grüße, Eure Gertrud.)

20. See below, pp. 116 and 132–5.
21. *Memoirs*, MS a), pp. 144f.

[Meine Kenntnis Heidelbergs musste sich beschränken auf das, was ich in Straßen, auf Wegen, im Café sah und hörte. Merkwürdig ist, dass trotzdem vom ersten Tage an Heidelberg auf mich wirkte als eine Atmosphäre, die bis in die Landschaft geistig und vornehm war. Die Überlieferungen der Stadt bis in die Zeit der Romantik, die Pfälzer Erinnerungen, das Schloss und die alten Barockhäuser, der Neckar mit der alten Brücke – alles dieses war nicht der zureichender Grund. Ein überragendes Kunstwerk fehlte. Die Universitätsbauten waren alt und bescheiden. Die Landschaft am Ausgang des Neckartals war zwar von unvergleichlicher nobler Schönheit, hatte etwas vom Stile Claude Lorrains. Die sanften Berglinien, die Größe des Horizonts, das Rauschen des aus dem Gebirge in die Ebene drängende Neckars am Hackteufel, die gotisch krumme Linienführung der Straßen, gesehen von dem leise verwahrlosenden alten Schloßpark aus, all das hatte etwas Beunruhigendes, das aus den Tiefen der Zeit und der Ferne erwuchs. Aber nichts ist zureichend, um zu erklären, dass ich mich wie von einem genius loci aufgenommen fühlte, dem ich mich zwar noch gar nicht verschrieb, dessen Gegenwart mir aber unendlich wohl tat. Freiburg hatte mich entzückt; es besitzt viel größere Schönheiten als Heidelberg; das Münster ist einzig, die Schwarzwaldberge sind ernster und bedeutender, das ständig fließende klare Gebirgswasser in allen Straßen übt einen Zauber – und doch war mir Freiburg etwas Lokales, Heidelberg atmete etwas Universales, Deutsches, Europäisches. Ich hatte gar keine Neigung, noch einmal nach Freiburg zu gehen. In Heidelberg, so schien es mir, macht der 'Geist der Stadt' aufgeschlossen, während er dort eingeschlossen wurde in bodenständige Geborgenheit. Es war, als ob die Menschen, die am geistigen Leben teilnahmen, in Heidelberg gleichsam einen Meter über dem Boden schwebten (wie ich mich damals ausdrückte).]

22. *Memoirs*, MS a), p. 150.

23. Karl Jaspers to parents, 10 November 1916 [*FA*].

24. Karl Jaspers to parents, Heidelberg, 19 November 1901 [*FA*]. See Studium1, pp. 21 and 42; and HDE, p. 3.

25. Karl Jaspers to parents, Heidelberg, 6 December 1901 [*FA*]. ('Heute war hier großer Klimbim wegen Enthüllung eines Denkmals Kaiser Wilhelms. Sogar der Großherzog war da. Das Denkmal ist aber so schlecht, dass spottweise gemunkelt wurde, es wäre aus dem Warenhaus Tietz. Die faulen Professoren ordneten natürlich an, dass sogenannter dies sein sollte und die Vorlesungen fielen aus.') According to Jaspers, the monument to Kaiser William II was melted down in the First World War, HDE, p. 3.

26. *Memoirs*, MS a), pp. 142 and 150.

27. Karl Jaspers to parents, Heidelberg, 27 November 1901 [*FA*].

28. *Memoirs*, MS a), p. 164.

29. Cf. Matthias Bormuth, *Lebensführung in der Moderne*, pp. 126f. and 152–4; and, for a general background, Martin Green, *The Richthofen Sisters*.

30. Karl Jaspers to father, Munich, 7 May 1902 [*FA*]. ('eine bildschöne junge Frau, der man auch nicht im geringsten die Schriftstellerei anmerke'.) (Hélène Böhlau (1856–1940) was born in Weimar. Amongst her works are *Rangierbahnhof* (1895), *Das Recht der Mütter* (1896), *Halbtier* (1899), and *Ratsmädelgeschichten* (1888).)

31. Mother to Karl Jaspers, Oldenburg, 11 May 1902 [*FA*].

32. Father to Karl Jaspers, Kissingen, 11 May 1902 [*FA*]. For the original text of the letter, see the Appendix.

33. Karl Jaspers to father, Munich, 13 May 1902 [*FA*]. For Jaspers' original letter, see the Appendix.

34. *Memoirs*, MS a), p. 166.

35. Ibid., p. 167.

36. Karl Jaspers to parents, Heidelberg, 19 October 1901 [*FA*].

> [Jeden Nachmittag bin ich bisher zum Schloss hinaufgefahren und habe 1 bis 2 Stunden beim Scheffeldenkmal gesessen. Es ist dort großartig und wenn man länger die Natur ansieht, bekommt man ordentlich ein glückliches Gefühl. Gestern wurde ich unangenehm gestört durch ein paar Burschenschaftler, die sich mir beim Denkmal vorstellten und mich keilen wollten. Ich wurde sie natürlich schnell los, aber alle Poesie war durch die alten Förmlichkeiten dahin. Ich kann mir übrigens denken, wie ein so armer Fuchs in meiner Lage leicht dazu kommt, aus Mangel an Verkehr aktiv zu werden, wenn er nicht meine glückliche Anlage hat, auch wohl allein sein zu mögen.]

37. The so-called 'Karlsbad decrees' of 1819 were in connection with the murder of the author, Kotzbue, by the student Karl Ludwig Sand. Prince von Metternich viewed the student fraternities as a hot-bed of revolutionary activity, since their creed was to pursue a national agenda that was intimately linked to the liberal ideal of freedom which contravened Metternich's conservative and repressive style of government. See Thomas Nipperdey, *Deutsche Geschichte 1800–1866*, Vol. II, especially pp. 279–85.

38. About three hundred members of Heidelberg's fraternities were involved in protests and speech-making at Hambach, in nearby Rheinland-Palatinate. See Eike Wolgast,

'Das bürgerliche Zeitalter (1803–1918), in Wilhelm Doerr, *et al.* (eds), *Semper Apertus* (Vol. II), pp. 1–31, here p. 10.

39. See also below, pp. 70–1.

40. Einsamkeit, p. 11.

41. Cf. Hans Saner, 'Zur Dialektik von Einsamkeit und Kommunikation bei Karl Jaspers', in Kurt Salamun and Elisabeth Salamun-Hybašek eds, *Jahrbuch der Österreichischen Karl–Jaspers–Gesellschaft*, Vol. 1/1988, pp. 53–67, here p. 54.

42. Quoted after Walter Raaflaub, *Ernst Mayer 1883–1952*, p. 21. (Mayer's letter was dated, 19 December 1918.) In the summer semester of 1907, Jaspers would have been in his tenth semester of study, a year (two semesters) before completing his doctorate. Mayer completed his doctorate a year after Jaspers, on 23 March 1910 (ibid., p. 23). Unlike Jaspers, Mayer immediately began to practise as a doctor. Jaspers later confirmed Mayer's friendly response to their first meeting by reiterating Mayer's phrase of 'there comes the first German student', *PA*, p. 41.

Chapter 4   *Italian Postscript*

1. Karl Jaspers to parents, Heidelberg, 20 January 1902 [*FA*].

2. Karl Jaspers to parents, Heidelberg, 13 February 1902 [*FA*].

3. Telegram to 'Studiosus Jaspers, Anlage 39, Oldenburg gr.' 22 February 1902 [*FA*]. (The telegram refers to Jaspers' letter of 21 January 1902 in which he described to his parents the risk of undertaking this journey.)

4. Karl Jaspers, postcard to parents, Lucerne, 2 March 1902 [*FA*].

5. Father to Karl Jaspers, Oldenburg, 10 February 1902 [*FA*].

     [Einen Kreditbrief, den Du vorzuziehen scheinst, kannst Du gern bekommen. Da Du zunächst ja Geld einbringst, braucht es ja nicht so sehr hoch zu sein; andererseits mag ich ihn von der deutschen Bank – wir selbst haben nicht überall direkte Verbindungen – nicht so sehr klein ausstellen lassen. Ich denke also 2000 Lire = 1600 M. Besondere Kosten sind mit der Höhe nicht verbunden. Gültigkeitsdauer bis 1ten Juli d. J., wenn Du auch viel früher zurückkommst. Wo willst Du akkrediert sein? In Rom natürlich, aber auch noch an anderen Orten?]

6. Karl Jaspers to father, Munich, 7 May 1902 [*FA*].

7. Karl Jaspers to parents, Milan, 3 March 1902 [*FA*].

8. Karl Jaspers to parents, Milan, 3 March 1902 [*FA*].

9. Karl Jaspers to parents, Rome, 8 March 1902 [*FA*].

10. Karl Jaspers to parents, Rome, 8 March 1902 [*FA*].

11. Karl Jaspers to parents, Rome, 8 March 1902 [*FA*].

12. *Memoirs* MS a), p. 168. ('Italien war für mich der Beginn des Gewinnens von Welt – während ich vor Italien fast weltlos abstrakt lebte.')

13. Karl Jaspers to parents, Florence, 4 April 1902 [*FA*].

14. Karl Jaspers to parents, Venice, on the Lido ('auf dem Lido'), 13 April 1902 [*FA*].

15. Karl Jaspers to parents, Venice, on the Lido ('auf dem Lido'), 13 April 1902 [*FA*]. For Jaspers' original letter, see the Appendix.

16. At some time, Jaspers had listed the colours of the rainbow in his personal copy of

Kant's *Critique of Judgement* (the sixth edition of Felix Meiner's Reclam text, edited by Karl Vorländer (Leipzig 1924). Jaspers underlined § 42 ('Analytic of the Sublime') by Kant's mention of the 'white colour of the lily', adjacent to which Jaspers listed the colours of the rainbow: 'rot/orange/gelb/grün/blau/indigo/violett'. The list seems incidental, though it may be compared with the catalogue of colours that Jaspers had earlier forwarded to his father from Badenweiler and, in that sense, highlights the personal character of Jaspers' interest in art.

Chapter 5   Gertrud Mayer

1. Friedrich Schiller, 'On Grace and Dignity', in Friedrich Schiller, *Essays and Letters*, Vol. 8, trans. A. Lodge, *et al.*, London, New York and Chicago: The Anthological Society 1901, pp. 175–211, here p. 210.

2. Julia and Ernst Gottschalk, Gertrud's cousins, were related through Gertrud's aunt, Bertha Gottschalk, the elder sister of her mother, Clara Mayer (1845–1912). Both the Gottschalk sisters married into the Mayer family. (Ella Mayer, 'Trude', unpublished manuscript [*LE*]).

3. Gertrud Mayer to Karl Jaspers, Märkisch Friedland, 13 November 1907 [*FA*]. ('Durch Dein Leben begleite ich Dich wohl sicher als liebende Freundin, vielleicht – und lass es uns hoffen – anders.')

4. Jaspers later concluded that the risk of an operation to alleviate his condition was too great. Karl Jaspers to Gertrud Mayer, Heidelberg, 8 April 1910 [*FA*].

5. Gustav Mayer subsidized his father's family business every year. Gertrud Mayer to Karl Jaspers, Berlin, 6 November 1910 [*FA*].

6. Karl Jaspers to parents, Heidelberg, 18 July 1907 [*FA*]. ('[…] ein gewisses menschliches Interesse für eine 28-jährige Dame, Frl. Mayer.')

7. Karl Jaspers, *Memoirs* MS a), 'Marriage' (*Ehe*), p. 24 [*LE*].

8. *PA*, p. 11.

9. *Self-Portrait*, p. 15.

10. Karl Jaspers, *Memoirs* MS a), 'Marriage' (*Ehe*), p. 8.

> [Wir machten eine Fahrt in schnellstem Tempo, am einen Ufer den Neckar hinauf, am anderen zurück, ließen gelegentlich halten, stiegen aus, sahen uns um, fuhren weiter. Die Stimmung des Übermutes, die schnelle Fahrt, die Lust an der Welt und ihrer Schönheit hatte bei aller Distanz zwischen uns, die jede Berührung ausschloss, doch den erotischen Charakter, den wir duldeten, ohne davon zu reden.
>
> Wir sprachen es aus, dass wir ohne Willen aneinander gebunden seien. In diesem Sinne verlobten wir uns: wir wollten nie voneinander lassen, wenn auch nie eine Ehe möglich würde.]

11. *Self-Portrait*, p. 20.

12. Henriette Jaspers, no addressee, 9 September 1907 [*FA*].

> [Und Kally sagte mir: Alles Leben, das ich mit Gertrud Mayer gemeinsam gehabt hab', darf die Welt sehen und wissen, Mutter, und auch in Zukunft wird es so sein, wie es recht und gut für uns beide ist. Du kannst mein Leben nicht mit dem gewöhnlichen Maße messen und wenn es keine

Lebensverbindung mit Gertrud werden kann, so ist es doch ein großes Glück für mich gewesen, ihre liebe Seele kennen gelernt und geliebt zu haben.]

13. Karl Jaspers to parents, Heidelberg, 21 November 1908 [*FA*].

14. Ibid. ('Mit G. Mayer treibe ich nicht viel, da wir uns nach dem Essen fast immer gleich Adieu sagen müssen.')

15. Ibid. ('Ich höre Montags Nachmittags eine Vorlesung von Dr Lask über „erkenntnis-theoretische Probleme". Es ist mir das immer eine besondere Freude, der Gegensatz zu meiner sonstigen Beschäftigung ist ein angenehmer.')

16. Emil Lask's work on *Die Lehre vom Urteil* (1911) can be closely compared to Rickert's philosophy of values. Rickert initially oversaw Lask's literary estate after Lask's death, at the age of forty, on active service in Galicia in May 1915. In his foreword, Rickert highlighted how Lask promised to produce a doctrine of 'world visions'. Heinrich Rickert, 'Persönliches Geleitwort', in Emil Lask, *Gesammelte Schriften I*, ed. Eugen Herrigel, pp. i–xvi, here p. vi.

17. Gertrud Jaspers to Erna Dugend, Heidelberg, 25 June 1911 [*FA*].

18. The story of Gustav Mayer's career as a journalist with the *Frankfurter Zeitung* and the failure of his *Habilitation* in Berlin is examined by Gottfried Niedhart in his *Mayer versus Meyer*.

19. Gertrud Mayer to Karl Jaspers, Prenzlau, 19 August 1908 [*FA*].

20. Karl Jaspers to parents, Heidelberg, 12 November 1907 [*FA*]. ('Zur Zeit lese ich, soviel Zeit bleibt, Dante in einer schönen neuen Übersetzung mit Frl. Mayer. Wir studieren es mit Hilfe von Anmerkungen und historischen Aufsätzen. Es ist unvergleichlich großartig. Allerdings sind wir noch immer in der Hölle. Man braucht viel Vorarbeit, um zum rechten Verständnis und Genuss zu kommen. Dann ist es aber gar nicht schwierig.')

21. Enno Jaspers to parents, Heidelberg, 15 April 1909 [*FA*]. ('Frl. Maier [*sic*] [...] Ein reizendes junges Mädchen! (Verzeiht dem harmlosen Ausdruck bei einem so ernsten Menschen.) Sie sieht aus wie ein 22-jähriger, etwas jüdischer Typus, sehr hübsche, kluge Augen, sehr gewandt. Das ist der oberflächliche Eindruck, den ich bisher gewann, er wird sich bei näherer Bekanntschaft noch vertiefen.')

22. David Mayer (1834–1929).

23. David Mayer to Gertrud Mayer, 17 July 1910. Quoted after Gottfried Niedhart, *Gustav Mayer*, p. 322 (author's translation).

24. Gustav Mayer, 'Aus der Geschichte der Familie Ascher Mayer'.

25. Karl Jaspers, *Memoirs* MS a), 'Marriage' (*Ehe*), pp. 9f.

26. When Heinrich Mayer spoke of his support for the Zionist cause, Gustav Mayer expressed his family's identity as follows: 'We feel at home on the Uckersee and not at the Dead Sea, our culture is German and not Jewish, the slogan that we compare with "Hie Zion" is "Hie Weimar".' Gustav Mayer to Vally Wygodzinski, née Cohn, 17 June 1898, quoted after Gottfried Niedhart, *Gustav Mayer*, p. 321 (author's translation).

27. Ella Mayer, 'Trude', unpublished manuscript [*LE*].

28. Karl Jaspers to Gertrud Mayer, Heidelberg, 29 March 1910 [*FA*]. ('Ethisch ist mir das Alles indifferent. Die Ehe ist kein Gegenstand, den zu erreichen Selbst- und Endzweck wäre. Wenn Du einmal Deinem Vater sagst, dass Du mich liebst und das offen vor ihm tust, bist Du nirgends im Unrecht.') (Footnote reads: 'Mir gegenüber fühle ich von

Deiner Seite weder Recht noch Unrecht, keine Pflicht, sondern Liebe.')

29. Franz-Peter Burkard's comparison to Plato's *Symposium* (204c), is particularly apt in the Jaspers' case, especially regarding the dimension of love as a portal to an idea of the world. Cf. Franz-Peter Burkard, *Ethische Existenz bei Karl Jaspers*, p. 122.

30. C, p. 56.

31. Enno Jaspers to parents, Heidelberg, 27 April 1909 [*FA*]. For the original text of this letter, see the Appendix.

32. The friendship with Walter Calé (1881–1904) was a bond between the sisters, their cousin and Ernst Mayer. Ella Mayer's manuscript sheds light on Julia's character:

> This little girl was from an early age a remarkable apparition, with thick, curly brown hair, bright, quite secretive eyes, at that time, still a happy and rather quiet child. Between her and our Ernst, Trude and Ida, a special friendship formed that, in the case of the girls, was supported by a romantic friendship with their mother, Betty. (Dies kleine Mädchen war schon von früh an merkwürdig in ihrer Erscheinung mit ganz dichtem, krausen, braunen Haar, hellen, etwas geheimnisvollen Augen, damals noch ein frohes, aber doch schon sehr schweigsames Kind. Zwischen ihr und unserm Ernst und Trude und Ida bildete sich eine besondere Freundschaft im Leben aus, bei den Mädchen noch unterstützt durch eine romantische Freundschaft zu ihrer Mutter Betty (Ella Mayer, 'Trude', unpublished manuscript [*LE*.]).

33. Gertrud Mayer was present when Ida Mayer died (1880–1917) and was charged with the task of packing away Ida's belongings.

34. Walter Calé to Gertrud Mayer, 20 March 1903 [*LE*]. ('ich vergesse Dich, wie man einen Ring, einen sehr lieben Ring, vergisst, den man am Finger trägt – weil er immer bei einem ist.')

35. Walter Calé to Julia Gottschalk, undated letter, copied by Gertrud Mayer [*LE*]. For the original text of the letter, see the Appendix.

36. Gertrud Mayer to Karl Jaspers, Prenzlau, 4 October 1907 [*FA*]; and Gertrud to Karl Jaspers, Prenzlau, 3 January 1912 [*FA*].

37. Karl Jaspers to parents, Heidelberg, 28 November 1910 [*FA*]. ('Ich habe sie von allen Verwandten Gertruds am liebsten. Wirklich ein Mensch, nicht bedeutend, sondern auf unserer Stufe, aber so recht aus tiefster Seele ernst.')

38. Karl Jaspers to parents, Heidelberg, 8 May 1908 [*FA*].

39. Karl Jaspers to father, Heidelberg, 4 October 1909 [*FA*].

40. Ibid.

41. Karl Jaspers to Gustav Mayer, Oldenburg, 17 September 1910 [*FA*].

> [Bei der Kürze der Zeit bis zum 29. Sept. ist meine Sorge, durch ein misszuverstehendes Wort über eine Äußerung meines Vaters eine Verzögerung herbeizuführen, wohl begreiflich. Ich werde, wie Sie, aufatmen, wenn wir dies alles hinter uns haben. Aber es ist, glaube ich, für mich noch schwerer: das Gefühl, immer als Fordernder aufzutreten, wo einem ein romanhaftes Glück <u>geschenkt</u> wird, ist entsetzlich.]

42. Karl Jaspers to parents, Heidelberg, 28 June 1910 [*FA*].

43. Gertrud Mayer to 'Liebe Frau, lieber Herr Jaspers', 6 July 1910 [*FA*]. ('Jetzt ist auch mein Vater eingeweiht, er stellt sich, wie ich es nie erträumt habe.')

44. Gertrud Mayer to Karl Jaspers, Prenzlau, 7 August 1910 [*FA*].
45. Karl Jaspers to parents, Zehlendorf, 12 August 1910 [*FA*].
46. Ibid.
47. Karl Jaspers, draft of letter to Theodor Tantzen, Oldenburg, 23 September 1910 [*FA*].
    Dear Theo! On 29 Sept., Gertrud Mayer and I are to be married at our brothers and sisters in Berlin-Zehlendorf. For outsiders this is all rather sudden. I have written a longer letter to grandma to explain this. You'll forgive my brevity then. Fond greetings. Your Kally (Lieber Theo! Am 29. Sept. werden Gertrud Mayer und ich uns bei unseren Geschwistern in Zehlendorf-Berlin verheiraten. Für die Außenstehenden kommt das etwas plötzlich. An Oma habe ich einen längeren Brief geschrieben, dies zu erklären. Du verzeihst mir dann die Kürze. Herzliche Grüße. Dein Kally).
48. Karl Jaspers, senior to David Mayer, Oldenburg, 23 September 1910 [*FA*]. The affection for Gertrud was reiterated in letters from Henriette Jaspers to Clara Mayer, Oldenburg, 23 September 1910 [*FA*]; and Clara Mayer to Henriette Jaspers, Prenzlau, 27 September 1910 [*FA*].
49. David Mayer to Karl and Henriette Jaspers, Prenzlau, 27 September 1910 [*FA*]. For the original text of this letter, see the Appendix.

Chapter 6   *'In the Clinic'*

1. Karl Jaspers to parents, Heidelberg, 18 January 1908 [*FA*]: 'In the afternoon I was in the Psychiatric Clinic, to register, but I only met Dr Gruhle. I can still start on Monday morning at 8.30 a.m.' ('Am Nachmittag war ich in der psychiatr. Klinik, um mich zu melden, traf aber nur Dr Gruhle. Trotzdem kann ich Montagmorgen um 9½ Uhr anfangen.')
2. Karl Jaspers to parents, Heidelberg, Sonntag *ca.* 25 April, in the evening (abends) [*FA*]. (This letter also includes Henriette Jaspers' note to Enno, '08 April 29', that is, 29 April 1908.)
    [Der größte Fehler hiesiger Klinik ist, dass man keine Therapie lernt. Meist huldigt [man] hier dem therapeutischen Nihilismus. Es ist aber insofern nicht schlimm, als die Therapie, wenn man diagnostisch sicher ist, das einfachere darstellt. Und in der Diagnostik könnte ich keine bessere Ausbildung genießen als hier, wegen der Fülle des Materials und wegen des sehr kritischen, wissenschaftl[ichen] Geistes, der in der Klinik herrscht.]
3. Karl Jaspers to parents, Heidelberg, 21 January 1908 [*FA*].
4. Gertrud Jaspers to mother, Heidelberg, 28 November 1912 [*FA*]. (According to Gertrud, Jaspers presented a case at court in near by Mosbach.)
5. Karl Jaspers to parents, Heidelberg, 17 March 1909 [*FA*].
6. Karl Jaspers to parents, Heidelberg, 29 June 1908 [*FA*]:
    Dear parents, [...] my doctoral thesis is [...] a boring, quite impersonal work that you may not in the least bit be excited to read. I even advise you not to. This week, I have to present a scientific talk on modern intelligence tests that I am working on at the moment. [...] Your Kally. (Liebe Eltern, [...] Meine Dr.-Arbeit ist [...] eine langweilige ganz unpersönliche Arbeit, auf deren

Lektüre Ihr durchaus nicht gespannt sein dürft, von der ich Euch sogar abrate. In dieser Woche muss ich in der Klinik ein Referat halten über moderne Intelligenzprüfungen, womit ich augenblicklich sehr beschäftigt bin. [...] Euer Kally).

7. Father to Karl Jaspers, Oldenburg, 9 December 1908 [*FA*].
8. Karl Jaspers to parents, Heidelberg, 6 February 1909 [*FA*].
9. Karl Jaspers to father, Heidelberg, 23 January 1910 [*FA*]: 'The daily routine in the clinic is pleasant. [...] The material in the clinic is magnificent.' ('In der Klinik ist der Betrieb angenehm. [...] Das Material der Klinik ist hervorragend.')
10. Karl Jaspers to parents, Heidelberg, 10 January 1910 [*FA*].
11. Karl Jaspers to Gertrud Mayer, Heidelberg, 7 March 1910 [*FA*]. (Ich sitze auf Kohlen wegen meiner Intelligenzarbeit. Ich habe noch enorm viel zu tun.')
12. The essays are in *Psychiatrische Arbeiten*, pp. 567–637 and 401–52, respectively as 'Eifersuchtswahn. Ein Beitrag zur Frage: Entwicklung einer „Persönlichkeit" oder „Prozeß"?'; and 'Die Methoden der Intelligenzprüfung und der Begriff der Demenz'.
13. Karl Jaspers to parents, Heidelberg, 8 July 1910 [*FA*].
   [Ich schicke Euch meine Eifers[ucht]-Arbeit. War die Intelligenzgeschichte bloß ein Referat, so ist der Kern dieser Arbeit nach meiner Meinung original. Ich halte sie für einigermaßen wertvoll, jedenfalls für die bei weiterem Beste meiner bisherigen Arbeiten. Die Lebensgeschichten haben mir viele Mühe gemacht. Sie sind aus einem großem, vergeblich durchgearbeiteten Material ausgewählt.]
14. HV, pp. 2 and 45–53.
15. Freud's *Interpretation of Dreams* (1900) underlined an interpretation of motives, not the pathology of the dreamer. Jaspers was perhaps concerned that Freud's analysis went through the motions of interpretation, only to draw inappropriate conclusions, and, as Ludwig Binswanger claimed in his review of *General Psychopathology* (1913), Freud's emphasis on the culture of human instinct ('Triebe') was too one-sided for Jaspers. Ludwig Binswanger, 'Karl Jaspers und die Psychiatrie' (1943), in *Karl Jaspers in der Diskussion*, ed. Hans Saner, Munich 1973, pp. 21–32, here p. 29.
16. Jaspers highlighted his particular esteem for French psychiatry, a discipline that he highly recommended to his parents as 'the only one that comes into consideration alongside the German'. ('die einzige, die neben der deutschen in Betracht kommt'). Karl Jaspers to parents, Heidelberg, 20 September 1911 [*FA*]. Jaspers was able to understand Janet's work by, as he noted in this letter, his curious ability to comprehend French texts fluently, albeit with the aid of a dictionary, yet without being able to speak a single word of the French language. The relevance of Pierre Janet's studies to Jaspers' reception of Weber's 'understanding psychology', alongside his positive reception of Freud's early essay on hysteria, as well as the school of C. G. Jung and Eugen Bleuler is reliably illustrated by Matthias Bormuth, *Lebensführung in der Moderne*, pp. 52–8 and 66–8.
17. See Wolfram Schmitt, 'Karl Jaspers als Psychiater und sein Einfluß auf die Psychiatrie', in Joachim-Felix Leonhard ed., *Karl Jaspers in seiner Heidelberger Zeit*, pp. 23–41 and 24.
18. Karl to Gertrud Jaspers, Heidelberg, 22 July 1912 [*FA*]. ('Kurzreferat über Freud. Ich als bellender Hund.')

19. Karl Jaspers to parents, Heidelberg, 13 February 1910 [*FA*]. ('In der Klinik ist nichts Neues. Ich bin bei einem Gutachten über einen Epileptiker. Unsere psycholog. Abende sind in gutem Gange. Auch morgens finden oft Besprechungen statt.')

20. Karl Jaspers to parents, Heidelberg, 21 February 1912 [*FA*]:

    We disagreed on a quite principal question. I was quite sad, as I am convinced that Gruhle has not at all grasped the point and that I am basically right, even if the formulation of my ideas is not fully developed. For that reason, I at once sat down on Friday to write a programmatic essay about this unusual theme in psychiatry. (Wir waren in einer ganz prinzipiellen Frage uneinig. Ich war ganz traurig. Da ich überzeugt bin, dass Gruhle die Pointe gar nicht erfasst hat und dass ich im Prinzip, wenn auch nicht in der Formulierung Recht habe, so habe ich mich gleich am Freitag hingesetzt, über dieses in der Psychiatrie ungewohnt Thema einen programmatischen Aufsatz zu schreiben.)

    At the end of March 1912, Jaspers mentions the completion of his essay (Karl Jaspers to parents, Heidelberg, 24 March 1912 [*FA*]). Incidentally, Jaspers' essay 'The Phenomenological Approach' was first published on 3 April 1912, a matter of weeks after he first mentioned his ideas to his parents.

21. The first edition of *General Psychopathology* (Berlin: Julius Springer, 1913) was published under the subtitle 'A guide for students, doctors and psychologists' (*Ein Leitfaden für Studierende, Ärzte und Psychologen*).

22. Jaspers was particularly inspired by Max Weber's programmatic essay, *Röscher und Knies und die logischen Probleme der historischen Nationalökonomie*, originally published in *Schmollers Jahrbuch* (1903–6). Weber's essay included an analysis of 'Erlebnis' and 'Verstehen', a subject that Jaspers acknowledged as being of interest for his own book (AP, p. 7), as well as alluding to it in an early exchange of letters with Enno. See below, pp. 95–7.

23. AP, p. 13.

24. Karl Jaspers to parents, Heidelberg, 22 May 1913 [*FA*].

25. Gertrud noted Nissl's comments as a sign of Jaspers' imminent success. Gertrud Jaspers to parents, Heidelberg, 15 May 1913 [*FA*]: 'that leaves the previous authors, even Kraepelin, far behind' ('das lässt die bisherigen, auch Kraepelin, weit hinter sich').

26. Karl Jaspers to parents, Heidelberg, 6 June 1913 [*FA*]: 'My book, unbound, will cost 9 Marks, bound, 9.80 Marks and has 340 pages' ('Mein Buch wird ungebunden 9.–, gebunden 9.80 kosten, hat 340 Seiten').

27. *GP1*, p. 305.

28. Edmund Husserl, 'Philosophie als strenge Wissenschaft', in *Logos, I*, 1910/11.

29. Karl Jaspers to parents, Heidelberg, 20 October 1911 [*FA*]. For Jaspers' original letter, see the Appendix.

30. AP, pp. 322f.

31. See Reiner Wiehl, 'Die Heidelberger Tradition der Philosophie zwischen Kantianismus und Hegelianismus. Kuno Fischer, Wilhelm Windelband, Heinrich Rickert', in *Semper Apertus*, Vol. II, Wilhelm Doerr, *et al.* (eds), pp. 413–35, here p. 418.

32. Wilhelm Dilthey, 'Ideen über eine beschreibende und zergliedernde Pyschologie', in *Gesammelte Schriften*, Vol. V, Leipzig and Berlin: B.G. Teubner 1924, pp. 139–240, here p. 194: 'Die Natur erklären wir, das Seelenleben verstehen wir.'

33. Jaspers described Kant as the 'true point of orientation' (*wahrer Orientierungspunkt*) for specialist empirical research, AP, p. 263.

34. Karl to Gertrud Jaspers, Oldenburg, 7 August 1913 [*FA*].

35. AP, p. 4.

36. Mary Warnock summarized Husserl's concept as follows: 'Intentionality no longer describes the simple relation between our glance and what we glance at; it takes on the more constructive, and much more Kantian role of being that feature of our looking at the world which brings it about that there is a world of objects for us to look at.' Cf. 'Edmund Husserl', in Mary Warnock, *Existentialism*, pp. 23–45, here p. 28.

37. Jaspers' terminology continues to attract debate. Cf. Osborne P. Wiggins and Michael Alan Schwartz, 'Edmund Husserl's influence on Karl Jaspers's Phenomenology', in *Philosophy, Psychiatry, Psychology*, pp. 15–36. Wiggin and Schwartz's objective account placed Jaspers' influences in a contemporary setting that is to be weighed against the polemical study of G. E. Berrios, 'Phenomenology and Psychopathology', in *Comprehensive Psychiatry*, pp. 213–20 and a series of polemical articles by Chris Walker, who took pains to demonstrate the influence of Kant on Jaspers' *General Psycho-pathology*.

38. AP, p. 87.

39. IA, p. 13; AzP, pp. 36ff: 'To desire to entrust to the doctor one's conduct in life is the path taken by many modern individuals from seriousness into cosy comfortability.' (Ibid., p. 38, author's translation); AT, p. 50; KP, p. 63.

40. See *Psychiatrische Arbeiten*, pp. 158–263, here p. 170, in 'Kausale und „verständliche" Zusammenhänge zwischen Schicksal und Psychose bei der Dementia praecox (Schizophrenie)'. Jaspers treats Freud's school as the most successful amongst psychological movements; he calls Nietzsche the greatest of all psychologists and refers specifically (as in his first book), to *Menschliches, Allzumenschliches* (1878), *Morgenröte* (1881), *Die fröhliche Wissenschaft* (1882) and *Zur Genealogie der Moral* (1887) as evidence of Nietzsche's greatness, ibid., p. 138.

41. Sigmund Freud, 'Das Ich und das Es,' in *Gesammelte Schriften*, Vol. XIII, ed. Anna Freud, *et al.*, Frankfurt am Main: Fischer 1967, pp. 235–89.

42. Einsamkeit, p. 13.

43. Einsamkeit, pp. 11f.

44. Einsamkeit, p. 12.

45. Einsamkeit, p. 18.

46. Einsamkeit, p. 16 (author's translation).

47. *Man*, p. 167.

48. Karl Jaspers to father, Heidelberg, 20 June 1913 [*FA*]. For Jaspers' original letter, see the Appendix.

49. Karl Jaspers to mother, Heidelberg, 20 June 1913 [*FA*]. For Jaspers' original letter, see the Appendix.

50. It should be noted that Heidelberg University accepted women scholars from the beginning of the nineteenth century. Karl and Gertrud Jaspers were intimately acquainted with many gifted female students. They maintained a close and warm friendship with Marianne Weber, who devoted the early part of her career to researching the social status of women, marriage, family and career. The ethical

character of her works bore the hallmarks of Jaspers' influence, as in her rather idiosyncratic study, *Erfülltes Leben* (1946), which she wrote during the years 1943–1945 and had published after the war.

51. Father to Karl Jaspers, Spiekeroog, 22 June 1913 [*FA*].
52. Mother to Karl Jaspers, Spiekeroog, 13 June 1913 [*FA*].
53. *GP1*, p. 308.
54. *GP1*, p. 21.
55. Henriette Jaspers to Karl Jaspers, senior, Heidelberg, 13 December 1913 [*FA*]. (The original date is noted as '13. Sonnabend Abend'.)
56. Karl Jaspers to parents, Heidelberg, 12 July 1913 [*FA*].
57. Henriette Jaspers to Karl Jaspers, senior, Heidelberg, 13 December 1913 [*FA*]. ('Nun bin ich Dozent. Alles andere ist ziemlich gleichgültig. Mutter hat ja sehr ausführlich berichtet.')

Chapter 7   Max Weber

1. Gertrud Mayer to Karl Jaspers, Prenzlau, 11 July 1909; and Prenzlau, 13 July 1909 [*FA*].
2. Karl Jaspers to parents, Heidelberg, 27 February 1910 [*FA*]. For the original text of Jaspers' letter, see the Appendix.
3. Jaspers later alluded to Weber's 'manic' depressive state in his old age, when he wrote to Hannah Arendt, HA/KJ, Letter 396, Basel, 29 April, 1966, p. 637. He does not anywhere give the precise date of his first meeting with Weber.
4. *BW*, p. 479.
5. Karl Jaspers to parents, Heidelberg, 13 February 1912 [*FA*].
6. Karl Jaspers to parents, Heidelberg, 13 June 1919 [*FA*], for the original text of this letter, see the Appendix. (Jaspers' report of Weber's conversation with General Ludendorff is contained in the second half of this letter. Jaspers mirrors, almost word for word, Marianne Weber's description in *Max Weber*, pp. 702f. She attributed the account to 'friends'. Jaspers' feeling that her citation ought to have been credited to him was most probably correct. See also Joachim-Felix Leonhard ed., *Karl Jaspers in seiner Heidelberger Zeit*, p. 107.)
7. Karl Jaspers to father, Heidelberg, 25 December 1919 [*FA*]. For Jaspers' original letter, see the Appendix.
8. Ideenlehre. Jaspers referred to this text as the product of a student seminar in his 'Reply to My Critics', in Paul Arthur Schilpp ed., *The Philosophy of Karl Jaspers*, p. 791.
9. Afra Geiger is frequently mentioned in Jaspers' private correspondence, see also below, p. 192. She died in Ravensbrück concentration camp, see *HA/KJ*, p. 692.
10. Many of the pictures are reproduced, with analysis, in the new edition of the catalogue of the Hans Prinzhorn collection, *Bildnerei der Geisteskranken*, with an introduction by the Austrian author Gerhard Roth.
11. See Thomas Nipperdey, *Deutsche Geschichte 1866–1918*, Vol. II, *Die Wende von 1916/17*, pp. 815–23, here p. 823.
12. Karl Jaspers to father, Heidelberg, 6 February 1917 [*FA*]. ('Max Weber ist jetzt grundsätzlich optimistisch. Aber man merkt, dass ihm U-Boot-Krieg und Amerika gegen den Strich geht. Er hofft aber auf Erfolg. Wie wir alle hoffen. Schon nach 3

Monaten werden wir in Deutschland ein Gefühl bekommen, wie die Sache läuft. Und wenn die Sache nicht gelingt, so müssen wir möglichst schnell einen Frieden, und zwar *à tout prix,* machen.')

13. Mother to Karl Jaspers, Oldenburg, 13 March 1911 [*FA*].

14. Mother to Karl Jaspers, Oldenburg, 13 March 1911 [*FA*] ('[…] entzückende Persönlichkeit, so weiblich und man fand sie schön, als sie lebendig sprach und freundlich lachte.')

15. Karl Jaspers to parents, Heidelberg 6 December 1932 [*FA*].

16. Karl Jaspers to parents, Heidelberg, 10 February 1917 [*FA*].

17. PS, p. 254. (Dominic Kaegi, *Editorische Notiz.*)

18. Karl Jaspers to father, Heidelberg, 4 August 1917 [*FA*]. ('Gestern Abend hielt ich in unserem politischen Verein meinen Vortrag über Weltanschauung in der Politik. Man war sehr anerkennend, ich soll einen zweiten halten; aber ich hatte das Gefühl, dass niemand recht verstand, was ich wollte. Wenn ich meine Worte aus fremdem Munde wiederhörte, kam es mir vor, als ob sie eine Sprache redeten, die ihnen nicht geläufig war.')

19. PS, p. 255.

20. PS, p. 232.

21. PS, p. 249.

22. PWa, p. 225 (on the 'limit situations' (*Die Grenzsituationen*), author's translation).

23. PWa, Foreword to fourth edition, 1954 p. x.

24. PWa, Foreword to fourth edition, 1954 p. xii.

25. Karl Jaspers to parents, Heidelberg, 9 November 1914 [*FA*].

26. Gertrud Jaspers to parents, Heidelberg, 22 November 1914 [*FA*].

27. Gertrud to Karl Jaspers, Munich, 14 June 1920 [*FA*]. (Eduard Baumgarten confirmed the presence of Else Jaffé and Marianne Weber in Munich in *Max Weber: Werk und Person*, pp. 677f.)

28. Gertrud to Karl Jaspers, Munich, 14 June 1920 [*FA*]. ('Ich kam in ein Sterbehaus'.)

29. Karl to Gertrud Jaspers, Heidelberg, 17 June 1920 [*FA*].

30. Karl Jaspers to parents, Heidelberg, 16 June 1920 [*FA*]. For Jaspers' original letter, see the Appendix.

31. MW–Rede, p. 9.

32. Marianne Weber also described Rickert's importance to Weber in her *Max Weber*, pp. 235, 260, 296 and 353.

33. MW–Rede, p. 9.

34. Jaspers called Rickert's approach the 'Rickert–Windelband school', *PA*, p. 30. Rickert reportedly responded to Jaspers' speech as follows: 'That you construct a philosophy out of Max Weber may be your rightful privilege, but to call him a philosopher is absurd.' Jaspers dissociated himself: 'If you think that you and your philosophy will be known at all in the future, you may perhaps be right, but only because your name is mentioned in a footnote in one of Max Weber's works as the man to whom Max Weber expresses his gratitude for certain logical insights', *PA*, p. 33.

35. Thorsten Paprotny, *Politik als Pflicht*, pp. 111f.

36. MW–Rede, p. 14 (author's translation).

37. Weber's biographer, Eduard Baumgarten, presented Jaspers with facts about Weber's private affairs that suggested to Jaspers the distinct need to reconsider his duty of guarding Weber's good name and reputation. When he was in his eighties, Jaspers, to his torment, was confronted with confidential letters written by Else Jaffé to Weber, that Eduard Baumgarten forwarded. Cf. Dieter Henrich, 'Denken im Blick auf Max Weber' in Jeanne Hersch, *et al.* (eds), *Karl Jaspers Philosoph, Arzt, politischer Denker*, pp. 207–31, here p. 224.

38. Cf. Martin Green, *The Richthofen Sisters*, especially, 'Jaspers', p. 288: 'According to Jaspers, Rickert went on to describe Weber as being up to his death philosophically just one of his own, Rickert's, pupils. It seems likely that Jaspers's account is exaggerated – he was always a myth-maker – but there *was* a fierce, life-long quarrel between Rickert and him, and Max Weber was the cause and symbol of that quarrel.'

39. Jaspers indirectly ensured that material relating to Weber's mental illness could not be placed in the wrong hands when he advised Marianne Weber to destroy a psychiatric file that he knew existed. Dieter Henrich, 'Denken im Blick auf Max Weber', in Jeanne Hersch, *et al.* eds, *Karl Jaspers Philosoph, Arzt, politischer Denker*, pp. 223f; and Eduard Baumgarten, *Max Weber: Werk und Person*, pp. 641f.

40. Karl Jaspers to Ernst Mayer, Heidelberg, 9 October 1932 [*LE*]. (Jaspers considered a number of alternatives: „Ein deutscher Philosoph als Politiker und Forscher". Oder: „Ein deutscher Politiker, Forscher und Philosoph". Oder: „Ein deutscher Politiker, Forscher, Philosoph"')

41. Mayer was closely involved with reading the proofs of the Göschen edition of *Philosophy* (1932), the Max Weber monograph and Jaspers' *Nietzsche* (1936), over which a significant disagreement erupted. See below, pp. 155f. and 158f.

42. HA/KJ, Letter 22, Berlin, 1 January, 1933, pp. 15f.

    [Dear Professor Jaspers, Thank you very much for the Max Weber, which I am delighted to have. There is good reason, however, why I am writing only now to thank you for it: The title and introduction made it difficult for me from the start to comment on the book. It does not bother me that you portray Max Weber as the great German but, rather, that you find the 'German essence' in him and identify that essence with 'rationality and humanity originating in passion'. I have the same difficulty with that as I do with Max Weber's imposing patriotism itself. You will understand that I as a Jew can say neither yes nor no and that my agreement on this would be as inappropriate as an argument against it.]

43. MW–Deutsches Wesen, p. 9.

44. Ibid., pp. 12f. Weber accepted his nomination as the candidate for Hesse-Nassau in December 1918, yet when his nomination did not lead to his election as the party's candidate, he was hastily put forward in Heidelberg for the state of Baden, a candidacy that he turned down. Wolfgang Mommsen, *Max Weber und die deutsche Politik 1890–1920*, Tübingen: Mohr 1974, pp. 329–31.

45. Cf. Ralf Kadereit, *Karl Jaspers und die Bundesrepublik Deutschland*, p. 114.

46. Max Weber, 'Die Typen der Herrschaft', in *Wirtschaft und Gesellschaft*, § 10 on 'charismatic leadership'.

47. Weber's explanation of this ethereal quality was, however, rather alarming because of his reference to the 'bond of blood'. ('Der geläufigste Fall einer Versachlichung des Charisma ist der Glaube an seine Übertragbarkeit durch das Band des Blutes', in *Wirtschaft und Gesellschaft*, especially on 'Umbildung des Charisma', pp. 758–78, here p. 772.)

48. MW–Bemerkungen, pp. 123f. Jaspers' concession was based on a denial of Weber as a 'Nationalist' and 'Imperialist' and of any hint that Weber's ideas paved the way to Hitler.

49. In his *Politics as a Vocation*, (1919) Weber used the phrase 'diabolic forces'. ('Wer Politik [...] betreiben will [...] läßt sich [...] mit diabolischen Mächten ein, die in jeder Gewaltsamkeit lauern', *MWG*, Vol. 1/17, p. 250).

50. HA/KJ, Letter 23, Karl Jaspers to Hannah Arendt, Heidelberg, 3 January 1933, pp. 17f. Jaspers replied:

> How tricky this business with the German character is! [...] My reason for choosing this somewhat odd formulation has to do with my pedagogical impulse. Our nationalistic youth have so much good will and genuine élan tangled up in their confused and wrong-headed jabbering that I wanted to make them aware of the demands on themselves that are inherent in being German while at the same time acknowledging their need to feel pride in being German. [...] The word 'German' is so much misused that one can hardly use it at all anymore.

51. Karl Jaspers to parents, Heidelberg, 25 June 1932. ('Der Verlag und die neue Serie scheinen mir ausgesprochen rechts, sie machen in Konjunktur „Nation"'.)

52. Gertrud Jaspers to Karl Jaspers, senior, Heidelberg, 30 November 1932 [*FA*]:

> Yesterday he [Karl] visited Marianne. Now I also want to read the Max Weber text with a critical eye, the typescript is finished and already in the hands of the editorial assistant, Ernst. [...] Yours, Gertrud. (Gestern war er [Karl] bei Marianne. Ich will jetzt die Max Weber Schrift, die fertig getippt ist und schon in des Mitarbeiters Ernst Händen, auch kritisch durchlesen. [...] Deine Gertrud.)

53. Karl Jaspers to parents, Heidelberg, 18 October 1932 [*FA*]. ('Liebe Eltern! [...] Aber ich bin nicht Ernsts Meinung; mir gefällt die Schrift, Trudelein auch. So werde ich wohl noch etwas feilen und dann unter Ernsts Protest den Druck riskieren. Natürlich wäre es schlimm, wenn Ernst Recht hätte.')

54. Gertrud Jaspers to parents, Heidelberg, 17 November 1932 [*FA*].

55. Quoted after Dieter Henrich, 'Denken im Blick auf Max Weber,' in Jeanne Hersch, *et al.*, (eds), *Karl Jaspers Philosoph, Arzt, politischer Denker*, p. 226. 'You must see in the work what is effective and speaks through the work. Otherwise, you only understand it superficially.' ('Man muss im Werk sehen, was durch dieses Werk wirkt und spricht, sonst versteht man es nur äußerlich', author's translation.)

56. A consensus of opinion is that Jaspers inherited his *Philosophy* (1932), as it were, with Weber's goals in mind. Cf. Godfrey Robert Carr, *Karl Jaspers as an Intellectual Critic*, p. 48; Ernst Moritz Manasse, 'Jaspers's Relation to Max Weber', in Paul Arthur Schilpp ed., *The Philosophy of Karl Jaspers*, pp. 369–91; and Martin Green, *The Richthofen Sisters*, pp. 291f.

57. Cf. Ernst Moritz Manasse, 'Jaspers's Relation to Max Weber', p. 369; and Karl Jaspers, 'Reply to My Critics', in Paul Arthur Schilpp (ed.), *The Philosophy of Karl Jaspers*, p. 854.

Chapter 8   Enno Jaspers

1. Karl Jaspers, pocket book, 'Monat März, April, Mai 1898' [*LE*].
2. Karl Jaspers, 1903 Tagebuch, 22 June 1903: 'Prinzipien für mein Verhalten gegen Enno' [*LE*].
3. Ibid. '5. Kein Ausdruck irgendwelcher Rache'.
4. Karl Jaspers, supplementary notes to memoirs, *ca.* 1905 [*LE*].

    [Karl mehr Philister, ungewandt, weltfremd (durch seine Krankheit eminent gesteigert). [...] Immerhin ethische Neigungen. [...]

    Enno genussbedürftiger, gewandter, weltlustig, hochgehende Affekte. [...] Bildungsbedürfnis vorhanden, aber gegenüber anderen Neigungen zurücktretend. [...] Bedürfnis nach Abwechslung. Neigung zu blasierten Handlung. Wenig Selbsterziehung, lässt sich viel gehen. Alle diese Züge sind auch bei K[arl] ausgeprägt, doch geringer.

    Erna bildet auch hier ein Zwischenglied zwischen den beiden Extremen, nur ein solches, das an Wert beider überragt. Ihre zarte Organisation [...] ihre Gefühle durchweg weit, tief, zuverlässig.]

5. Enno to Karl Jaspers, Bremen, 20 March 1907 [*FA*]. For the original letter, see the Appendix.
6. Karl to Enno Jaspers, Heidelberg, 21 March 1907 [*FA*].
7. Enno to Karl Jaspers, Bremen, 27 June 1907 [*FA*].
8. Enno to Karl Jaspers, Bremen, 5 July 1907 [*FA*]. For the original letter, see the Appendix.
9. Karl to Enno Jaspers, Heidelberg, 6 July 1907 [*FA*]. ('Du hast mich an einer meiner empfindlichsten Stellen getroffen.')
10. Ibid. ('Ein Mensch hat eben nur dann persönliche Erlebnisse, wenn diese [einer] reinen geistigen und gemütlichen Veranlagung adäquat sind.')
11. Ibid.

    [Sicher wollte ich mich auch in meinem letzten Brief nicht als bedauernswert schildern. Vielmehr ist es der Trieb, dass man gern verstanden sein möchte, der mich so oft und immer wieder von meiner Krankheit reden lässt. Wenn ich dann eine solche Antwort und Auffassung finde, wie in Deinem jetzigen Brief, so geht mir immer ein Stich durchs Herz, so missverstanden zu werden.]

12. Enno to Karl Jaspers, Bremen, 10 January 1908 [*FA*]. 'In the evening'. ('Abends.')
13. Karl to Enno Jaspers, Heidelberg, 12 January 1908 [*FA*].
14. Enno to Karl Jaspers, Brake, 8 June 1908 [*FA*].
15. Enno Jaspers to parents [Bournemouth], 14 August 1909 [*FA*].

    [Liebe Eltern! Heute war ich auf der Isle of Wight und zwar in Cowes. [...] Die Stadt ist nur klein, sie ist nach der Seeseite hin eingefasst von sehr hübschen Villen englischer Lords und reicher Leute und hat ihre Bedeutung nur durch den *Royal Yacht Squadron,* der etwa dem deutschen Kaiserlichen Yachtklub entspricht und der seine sämtlichen Yachten hier liegen hat. In der letzten Woche war anlässlich des Aufenthalts des Zaren vor Cowes eine große Regatta, und so lagen außer den englischen Yachten auch viele französische und holländische da vor Anker. Es war wunderhübsch, sie zu besehen. Die Natur ist hier wundervoll. Direkt vom Meer steigen weiße Kreidefelsen in die Höhe, die bei dem blauen Wasser wunderbar schön aussehen. Die Wälder stoßen mit den Kreidefelsen sofort ans Meer und bietet die Natur so einen Anblick, wie ich ihn noch nicht sah. [...] Herzlichen Gruß Enno]

16. Enno Jaspers to parents, Bournemouth, 14 August 1909 [*FA*]. ('Morgens um 8 Uhr bade ich in der See, um 9 Uhr breakfast, um 1¼ lunch, um 7½ dinner, Nachmittags 4 Uhr afternoon-tea.')

17. The London visit was part of a study tour, although it is unclear whether Jaspers took an official holiday, since the visit occurred at the end of August and was connected to a visit to Scheveningen, Holland, which Jaspers later referred to in his letter of 2 October 1927. See below, pp. 236f. See Rector, Heidelberg University, 18 July 1925:

> Dr Karl Jaspers, professor of philosophy at our university, intends to make a study visit to England. I recommend him in friendly support. [Professor Karl] Hampe. Rector of Heidelberg University.
>
> ('Herr Dr Karl Jaspers, ordentlicher Professor der Philosophie an unserer Universität, beabsichtigt mit seiner Frau eine Studienreise nach England zu machen. Ich empfehle ihn freundlicher Aufnahme. Hampe. Rektor der Universität Heidelberg.') (*UAH*: KJ/PA)

18. Karl to Enno Jaspers, Oldenburg, 4 August 1914 [*FA*]. ('Lieber Enno! Meine Sehnsucht zu Dir ist groß. Ich möchte Dir immer etwas Brüderliches und Liebes sagen. Aber so etwas können wir nicht. Nur ein instinktives Vertrauen zum Schicksal, dass Du uns gesund zurückkehrst, lässt das Leben noch möglich erscheinen. Hätte ich doch die Kraft, mit Dir zu gehen, dass wir uns gegenseitig helfen könnten! Ich bin voll Liebe für Dich. Dein Karl.')

19. Karl to Enno Jaspers, Oldenburg, 5 August 1914 [*FA*]. ('Als Du neulich abgereist warst, holten wir Papa ab. Papa und Mutter gingen einzelnen [?] und weinten beide. Aber sie haben beide Mut und glauben nicht anders, als dass Du uns bestimmt zurückkommst.')

20. Jaspers seems to have referred to the national declaration of 16 October 1914, 'Erklärung der Hochschullehrer des Deutschen Reiches', signed by over three thousand university professors, in protest against the British perception of German science as being indistinguishable from Prussian militarism. Cf. Wolfgang Mommsen, *Bürgerstolz und Weltmachtstreben. Deutschland unter Wilhelm II. 1890 bis 1918*, Berlin: Propyläen 1995, p. 838.

21. Karl to Enno Jaspers, Oldenburg, 3 October 1914 [*FA*]. For Jaspers' original letter, see the Appendix.

22. Karl Jaspers to parents, Heidelberg, 27 July 1914 [*FA*].

23. Karl Jaspers to parents, Heidelberg, 28 July 1914 [*FA*]. ('[…] Es ist schrecklich, krank zu sein, aber in solchen Zeiten jämmerlich und niederdrückend. Mir ist das ganze deutsche Reich egal, ich sehe nirgends den Quell irgend einer echten Begeisterung: aber es ist so ein Trieb, dass man auch mitrechnen möchte als Kraft; und statt dessen muss

ich in Konsequenz meines ganzen Daseins kläglich mich durchlügen, um die Existenz zu bewahren.')

24. Karl to Enno Jaspers, Oldenburg, 5 August 1914 [*FA*]. ('Da ist es für die Menschheit nötig, dass wir siegen.')

25. Enno Jaspers to parents, Aumenaucourt, 9 January 1915, copy by Henriette Jaspers [*FA*].

26. Karl to Enno Jaspers, Heidelberg, 8 May 1915 [*FA*].

27. Karl Jaspers to parents, Heidelberg, 25 September 1915 [*FA*].

28. Karl to Enno Jaspers, Heidelberg, 26 November 1915 [*FA*].

29. Karl to Enno Jaspers, Heidelberg, 21 December 1915 [*FA*]. ('Goethes *Campagne in Frankreich* hat uns als Vergleich mit jetzt – sozusagen Tagesbericht und Berichterstattung von 1792 – sehr interessiert. Vielleicht liest Du es auch in Zwischenstunden mal ganz gern, zumal die Orte der Champagne zum Teil vorkommen, die auch jetzt viel genannt waren. Wie war damals ein Krieg gemütlich!')

30. Karl Jaspers to Eugen and Erna Dugend, Heidelberg, 27 April 1915 [*FA*].

31. Gertrud Jaspers to parents, Heidelberg, 18 May 1915 [*FA*]. For Gertrud's original letter, see the Appendix.

32. Karl to Enno Jaspers, Heidelberg, 24 March 1916 [*FA*]. For Jaspers' original letter, see the Appendix.

33. Mother to Gertrud Jaspers, Oldenburg, 24 May 1916 [*FA*]. (Copy of Enno's letter of 20 May 1916.)

34. Mother to Karl and Gertrud Jaspers, Oldenburg, 27 September 1917 [*FA*].

35. Ibid. ('Wir sind ganz glücklich. Wie leicht hätte der Schuss seinen Kopf treffen können!')

36. Parents to Karl and Gertrud Jaspers, Cologne, 12 October 1917 [*FA*].

37. Karl Jaspers to Erna Dugend, Heidelberg, 2 May 1917 [*FA*]. ('Solange Krieg ist, kann man ihm nicht abschlagen. Angesichts des Tods muss der Mensch wissen, was er richtig findet.')

38. Mother to Karl Jaspers, Oldenburg, 21 June 1926 [*FA*]. In the morning 12 o'clock. ('Morgens 12 Uhr.')

39. Karl Jaspers to mother, Heidelberg, 11 January 1926 [*FA*].

40. Charlotte von Arnim was, according to Jaspers' father, a descendant (great granddaughter) of Harry von Arnim (1824–81), one of Bismarck's opponents; and her mother was the daughter of General von Falkenstein. Father to Karl Jaspers, Oldenburg, 15 April 1926 [*FA*].

41. Mother to Karl and Gertrud Jaspers, Berlin-Dahlem, 10 April 1926 [*FA*].

42. Enno Jaspers to father, Berlin-Dahlem, 12 June 1926 [*FA*].

43. Mother to Karl Jaspers, Oldenburg, 20 June 1926 [*FA*].

44. Mother to Karl Jaspers, Oldenburg, 21 June 1926 [*FA*]. In the morning, 12 o'clock. ('Morgens 12 Uhr'). ('Ich habe ihm alles so deutlich gesagt, wie wichtig das Geld für die Familie ist, so dass Papa meinte, nun sollte ich nicht mehr davon sprechen.')

45. Karl Jaspers to parents, Cassel, 22 September 1926 [*FA*].

46. Karl Jaspers to parents, Cassel, 22 September 1926 [*FA*]. References taken from this letter are as follows:

Enno klagt über zu wenig Geld. Ich: „Aber Papa zahlt doch besondere

Ausgaben, wie Reisen; und für das bloße Leben reicht doch das Geld." Enno: „Dafür mach ich die Reise auch nobel. In Weimar habe ich im besten Hotel gewohnt." Auf mein Erstaunen hin: „Ja, das ist aber nötig. Wenn die Leute merken würden, dass ich gar kein Geld habe, so ist alles aus. Wenn sie etwa nach meinem Hotel fragen, oder mir etwa ins Hotel schicken, so muss es 1. Ranges sein." [...] Doch sind solche Wendungen vertraut, er spricht im Ganzen sachlich, vernünftig – man merkt kaum jene Phantasie, wenn man im Gespräch an Enno hingibt. [...] Ich brauche nichts anderes, als Enno lieb haben. Aber ich habe auch Angst nicht nur um ihn, sondern auch vor ihm. Mit sich selbst kann er nichts anfangen, er ist befallen von einer Gier nach Unterhaltung, Betätigung, Erlebnis, die nur mit Geldmitteln zu befriedigen sind, die erheblich sind. Alle Kindlichkeit, Gutmutigkeit, Formlosigkeit ist, sowie ich Enno sehen muss, durchschossen von einem unablässigen, egozentrischen Bemühen um das Geld zur Konsumption, nicht um Geld als Lebensgrundlage, und Fundierung der Zukunft, eben um das Geld, dass er „Dreck" nennt.'

47. Enno to parents, Göttingen, 17 October 1926, forwarded from Oldenburg, 18 October 1926 [*FA*]. ('Ich fühle mich körperlich und geistig so pfiff und leistungsfähig wie nie mehr in den letzten Jahren. Und dies Stärkegefühl gibt mir immerhin ein Vertrauen, ohne dass ich dieses auf konkrete Dinge stützen könnte.')

48. Mother to Gertrud Jaspers, Oldenburg, 19 December 1926 [*FA*].

49. Enno to Karl Jaspers, Hamburg, 7 February 1931 [*FA*]. ('Das Cocain spielt in meinem Leben gar keine Rolle mehr.')

50. Karl to Enno Jaspers, Heidelberg, 28 January 1931 [*FA*].

51. Karl Jaspers to Erna Dugend, 8 February 1931 [*FA*]. ('Enno wird uns unter allen Umständen sein Lebenlang für daran schuldig erklären, dass seine glänzenden Aussichten durch uns ruiniert seien. Das darf uns nicht anfechten.')

52. Telegram to Karl Jaspers, Oldenburg, 8 March 1931 [*FA*]. ('Unser lieber Enno ist gestern Abend 10 Uhr sanft ohne Kampf nach seinem eigenen Willen entschlafen er war seit Donnerstag Nacht hier Euer Kommen gesundheitshalber unrichtig kalter Ostwind viel Grippe Ich schreibe heute ausführlich Wir sind ganz ruhig Wir kommen im Mai zu Euch = Papa Mutter').

53. Henriette Jaspers to Anna Heddewig, Oldenburg, 9 March 1931 [*FA*]. Jaspers also described the circumstances surrounding his brother's death in a later letter to Hannah Arendt. HA/KJ, Basel, 17 August 1966, pp. 651–3.

54. Transcript (handwritten) by Karl Jaspers of Enno Jaspers' final letter, Oldenburg, 8 March 1931 [*FA*].

[Lieber Kally!

[...] So bin ich denn am Ende. Von dem Pulver, dessen Besitz ich Dir gegenüber einst erwähnte, mache ich momentan Gebrauch. Die „Familie" wird sich später mit ernstem Blick und echter Erschütterung erneut überprüfen, wird konstatieren, dass alle „Schuld" bei mir liegt, dass alle Familienmitglieder das Beste gewollt haben etc. Und am Ende wird der alte auf Gold gerichtete Bauerninstinkt feststellen können: Der Mensch ist tot, die Dukaten sind gerettet.

Lebe wohl Dein Enno.]

55. Eugen Dugend to Karl Jaspers, Hamburg, 23 June 1931 [*FA*]. The debt (13,183 Marks) was mostly borne by the family, with Eugen taking care of approximately one quarter of the sum and another quarter of the reduced debt being carried by the rest of the family.
56. Gertrud to Karl Jaspers, Oldenburg, 14 March 1931 [*FA*]. ('Ich dachte: „Staub bist Du und zu Staub sollst Du zurückkehren." [...] Und irgendwie fühlt er vielleicht <u>bejahend</u>, dass wir ihn verklären.')

Chapter 9   *'Ordinarius' in Heidelberg*

1. Vincent van Gogh, *The Complete Letters 1*, Letter 226, 'Saturday evening [1882]', p. 441.
2. Karl Jaspers to parents, Heidelberg, 2 July 1917 [*FA*].
3. Selbstporträt, p. 26; and L.
4. See Ministry of Culture and Education to Senate, Heidelberg University, Karlsruhe, 4 December 1913 [*UAH*: KJ/PA].
5. Carl Neumann (Dean) University of Heidelberg Faculty of Philosophy to Senate, Heidelberg University, Heidelberg, 13 December 1913; and Ministry of Culture and Education to Senate, Heidelberg University, Karlsruhe, 18 December 1913 [*UAH*: KJ/PA].
6. Ministry of Culture and Education to Senate, Heidelberg University, Karlsruhe, 4 July 1916 [*UAH*: KJ/PA].
7. Ministry of Culture and Education to Senate, Heidelberg University, Karlsruhe, 21 November 1916 [*UAH*: KJ/PA].
8. Karl Löwith's survey of this development placed Jaspers as an 'existentialist' on the basis of his understanding of Kierkegaard, an assessment that corresponded to Jaspers' own view of his idea of 'Psychology of World Visions'. See Karl Löwith, *Von Hegel zu Nietzsche*, p. 416. PWa, preface to fourth edition, 1954, p. x.
9. PWa, preface to fourth edition, 1954, p. x; and *PA*, p. 26.
10. Karl Jaspers to parents, Heidelberg, 12 July 1917 [*FA*]. For Jaspers' original letter, see the Appendix.
11. Karl Jaspers to parents, Heidelberg, 8 October 1918 [*FA*]. For Jaspers' original letter, see the Appendix.
12. Karl Jaspers to parents, Heidelberg, 19 October 1918 [*FA*].
13. Karl Jaspers to parents, Heidelberg, 13 February 1912 [*FA*].
14. Cf. Golo Mann, *The History of Germany since 1789*, trans. Marian Jackson, p. 331.
15. Karl Jaspers to parents, Heidelberg, 19 October 1918 [*FA*].
16. Gertrud Jaspers to parents, [Prenzlau], 9 February 1919 [*FA*], for the original text, see the Appendix. That the timing of this raid was reported with a delay is clear by the historical dating of the murder of Karl Liebknecht and Rosa Luxemburg that took place on 15 January 1919. In his memoirs, Gustav Mayer included an account of the break-in that occurred on 29/30 January 1919. The details of Gertrud's account almost exactly mirror Mayer's descriptions. Cf. Gustav Mayer, *Erinnerungen*, pp. 319–25.
17. Karl Jaspers to parents, Heidelberg, 30 April 1914 [*FA*].
18. Karl Jaspers to parents, Heidelberg, 3 May 1918 [*FA*].
19. Karl Jaspers to parents, Heidelberg, 20 November 1920 [*FA*].

> [In der Vorlesungstechnik habe ich insofern eine große Änderung <u>versucht</u>, als ich mich jeweils am Vormittag mit dem Thema der Stunde eingehend befasse, dann aber ganz frei rede und auch dem Gang der Gedanken weitgehend vom Augenblick abhängig mache, mich unmittelbarer an die Hörer wendend. Dadurch wird der Vortrag viel lebendiger, aber auch verbindender [?] am Wort, meine Hörer scheinen aber viel aufmerksamer als früher. Der Saal hat sich noch in den ersten Wochen zunehmend gefüllt und ich kann mit der Frequenz sehr zufrieden sein. Wie allerdings die Wirkung ist, das weiß ich nicht.]

20. Ibid. ('so als ob ich mein besseres Selbst darin ausspräche, an dem gemessen ich wenig wert bin'.)

21. In his memoirs, Golo Mann conveyed the impression of Jaspers, his doctoral supervisor, as being cloistered in the ivory tower of science, especially from the early 1930s onwards. Cf. Golo Mann, 'Karl Jaspers', in *Erinnerungen und Gedanken*, pp. 293–332, here p. 309.

22. See below, pp. 133–5.

23. Karl Jaspers to parents, Heidelberg, 21 October 1917 [*FA*].

24. Karl Jaspers to parents, Heidelberg, 15 January 1917 [*FA*].

25. Karl Jaspers to father, Heidelberg, 13 February 1918 [*FA*]. (The figure quoted was 296,000 Marks.) The timing of the bequest is unclear. Gertrud Jaspers to Erna Dugend, 25 May 1918.

26. This sum of money was doubled at Enno's request. Karl Jaspers, senior to Gertrud and Karl Jaspers, Oldenburg, 25 July 1917 [*FA*].

27. Karl Jaspers to parents, Heidelberg, 15 January 1917 [*FA*].

28. Paul Gottschalk, 'Memoiren eines Antiquars II', in *Börsenblatt für den Deutschen Buchhandel*, No. 7/1966, pp. 102–6.

29. Ibid., p. 104. Karl Jaspers to father, Heidelberg, 28 July 1917; Karl Jaspers to parents, Heidelberg, 9 September 1917; and Karl Jaspers to parents, Heidelberg, 29 October 1917 [*FA*].

30. Karl Jaspers to parents, Heidelberg, 9 September 1917 [*FA*].

31. Karl Jaspers, telegram to parents, 11 December 1919 [*FA*].

32. Ministry of Culture and Education to Senate, Heidelberg University, Karlsruhe, 17 January 1920 (transcript) [*UAH*: KJ/PA].

33. In a letter to Flora Mayer, Jaspers later explained that Gertrud's pension had expired and the salary replaced the income they lost. Karl Jaspers to Flora Mayer, Basel, 10 March 1952 [*IISH*].

34. Gertrud Jaspers to parents, Heidelberg, 22 January 1920 [*FA*]. ('Ordinarius im weltvergessenen Erlangen.')

35. Ibid.

36. Heinrich Rickert, 'Psychologie der Weltanschauungen und Philosophie der Werte', in *Logos* IX/1920, H1, pp. 1–42.

37. Karl Jaspers to parents, Heidelberg, 21 June 1920 [*FA*].

> [Er fühlte sich in seiner philosophischen Existenz mit Recht indirekt in meinem Buche sehr in Frage gestellt. Und diese Kritik will zeigen, dass ich im Prinzip völlig im Irrtum bin. […] Schüler von Rickert finden es ein Zeichen

höchster Anerkennung, dass Rickert einen ganzen Aufsatz über mich schreibt, das habe er noch nie einem Buche angetan. Nun, die Kritik will vernichtend sein!]

38. Jaspers later acknowledged Rickert's critique by admitting that the methodological significance of his work was not clear at the time of writing. PWa, preface to fourth edition, 1954, p. x.

39. Karl Jaspers to parents, Heidelberg, 19 January 1921 [*FA*]. ('Es wäre „gerecht" – glaube ich – wenn ich einen Ruf bekäme.')

40. Ibid. Three hundred copies remained from a total of 1,500 volumes.

41. Ibid. Jaspers' book remained substantially unchanged in view of his broader ambitions. See below, pp. 131–2.

42. SW, pp. 21f (and L).

43. Gertrud and Karl Jaspers to parents, Greifswald, 22 May 1921 [*FA*].

44. Ibid. ('In Berlin wurde ich mit großer Achtung empfangen. Man will mich offenbar gewinnen, hat von mir eine merkwürdig große Meinung. Die „Intrige" hat anscheinend nichts geschadet. Wenn ich <u>jetzt</u> einen Wink gebe, dass ich nach Kiel will, so bekomme ich den Ruf dahin sofort.')

45. Karl Jaspers to Dean, Heidelberg, 8 June 1921 [*UAH*: KJ/PA].

46. Ministry of Culture and Education to Senate, Heidelberg University, Karlsruhe, 29 June 1921 [*UAH*: KJ/PA].

47. Ministry of Culture and Education to Senate, Heidelberg University, Karlsruhe, 21 October 1921 (transcript.) [*UAH*: KJ/PA]. (The basic salary of 13,200 Marks was supplemented by additional bonuses that compared favourably to the basic salary that Greifswald were prepared to provide (12,600 Marks) because Jaspers' previous ten years in service were to be counted towards his pension rights).

48. Jaspers also reported to his parents that the philosopher, Georg Simmel, had visited him on several occasions in the year before his death. On one occasion, they had discussed 'Platonic eros' and the 'possible character of a modern philosopher'. Karl Jaspers to father, Heidelberg, 10 June 1917 [*FA*].

Chapter 10   *Paris, Sicily and Vincent van Gogh*

1. Gertrud Jaspers to parents, Naples, 26 March 1922 [*FA*]. ('Ein Philosoph der modernen Zeit muss lebendig bleiben und nicht im Clubsessel einer engen Welt erstarren.')

2. Karl Jaspers to parents, Heidelberg 15 March 1922 [*FA*].

3. Karl Jaspers to Dean, Heidelberg, 9 March 1922 [*UAH*: KJ/PA].

4. Gertrud Jaspers to parents, Naples, 26 March 1922 [*FA*].

5. Karl Jaspers to parents, Naples, 26 March 1922 [*FA*]. ('Ich fühle mich hier unglaublich wohl und würde – wenn es so etwas gäbe – einen Ruf nach Neapel sofort annehmen – oder vielleicht doch nicht?')

6. Karl Jaspers, Tagebuch, 1905 [*LE*]. During Jaspers' semester in Munich, that is, before he began his medical studies in 1902, he first attended lectures by Theodor Lipps. He possessed Lipps's work on 'Die ethischen Grundfragen' (1895), with the inscription 'Karl Jaspers, stud. jur. München 1902' that Hans Saner referred to in his first edition of Jaspers' memoirs on his undergraduate years. Studium1, p. 43.

7. The pictorial mode of representation may be another way to describe Jaspers' notion of historicity that, as Edith Ehrlich, Leonard H. Ehrlich and George B. Pepper asserted in their edition of Jaspers' *Basic Philosophical Writings*, is 'the exploration of the phenomenon of historicity' that 'involves the imagery of the "unity" of opposites like "time and eternity", "necessity and freedom", "existence and Existenz"', *BPW*, p. 79.

8. Karl Jaspers to parents, postcard, Siracusa, 'Teatro Greco Massimo' [*FA*]. (Postmark, 3 April 1922.) For Jaspers' original words, see the Appendix.

9. Karl Jaspers to parents, Naples, 26 March 1922 [*FA*]. ('So kann das eigentlich Unmögliche, dass ich als kranker Mensch jetzt so reise, allein möglich werden.')

10. Karl Jaspers to parents, Heidelberg, 28 February 1918 [*FA*]: 'Strindberg is a repulsive fellow, but he is very interesting in psychiatric and psychological terms, because he has a brutal honesty.' ('Strindberg ist ein widerwärtiger Kerl, aber psychiatrisch und psychologisch sehr interessant, da er eine brutale Aufrichtigkeit hat.')

11. Maurice Blanchot, *Der Wahnsinn par excellence*, trans. Henning Schmidgen, in *Karl Jaspers', Strindberg und van Gogh*, Berlin: Merve 1998, p. 11.

12. Karl to Gertrud Jaspers, 26 December 1911; and letter dated, Oldenburg, Donnerstag Abend [*FA*]: 'Van Gogh is a phenomenon, in the face of which I could do no other than to ask, where the basis of the mental affliction begins behind all that beauty?' ('Van Gogh ist ein Phänomen, bei dem ich nicht anders konnte, als fragen, wo fängt hinter all der Schönheit, die wahnsinnige Grundlage an?')

13. Karl Jaspers to parents, Heidelberg, 28 April 1912 [*FA*].

14. Karl Jaspers to parents, Paris, 30 April 1912; and to father, 1 May 1912. Jaspers tried, but failed, to hear a lecture by Pierre Janet. Karl Jaspers to mother, Paris, 4 May 1912 [*FA*].

15. Karl Jaspers to father, Paris, 1 May 1912 [*FA*]. ('Worin das Eindruckvolle besteht, weiß ich nicht. Zarte Farben, Grazie auf der einen Seite, kühle Objektivität auf der anderen genügen nicht.')

16. Karl Jaspers to mother, Paris, 4 May 1912 [*FA*].
    [Nach langem Suchen durch langweilige akademische Malereien fanden wir schließlich den Saal mit Impressionisten: Manet, Monet, Pissarro, Renoir, Sisley. Es steht uns diese geschmackvolle und sehr sachliche Malerei nicht nahe, aber wir hatten doch einen bedeutenden Eindruck und große Bewunderung. Die ganze moderne Malerei in Deutschland – die Sezessionisten, Liebermann u.s.w. leiten sich hiervon ab – wie man sagt.]

17. Karl Jaspers to parents, Paris, 7 May 1912 [*FA*]. ('Wir waren von 2–4 in einer Privatsammlung Durand-Ruel. Dort sind vor allem Impressionisten, die in den öffentlichen Sammlungen wenig vorkommen. [...] In einer höchst spießbürgerlichen Wohnung sind alle Wände eingeschlossen Schlaf- und Toilettenzimmer mit kostbarsten Gemälden geradezu tapeziert.') Walter Fielchenfeldt charted the loan of ten paintings by van Gogh to Durand-Ruel in *Vincent van Gogh & Paul Cassirer, Berlin*, Cahier Vincent 2, Rijksmuseum/Vincent van Gogh, Vincent van Gogh Foundation, Amsterdam, p. 12.

18. Karl Jaspers to Erna Dugend, Paris, 12 MAy 1912 [*FA*]. ('Alles rein ästhetische, geschmackvolle, künstlerisch bewegende, wenn auch eine Idee (ich meine ein tiefes Gefühl, nicht einen Gedanken) <u>darin</u> wirksam ist, geht unserer Natur nicht eigentlich nahe.')

19. Gertrud Jaspers to Eugen Dugend, Bonn, 29 September 1912 [*FA*]: 'In Cologne, we saw an interesting van Gogh exhibition.' ('In Köln sahen wir eine interessante van Gogh-Ausstellung.')

20. 'International Art Exhibition of the Society of Friends of West German Art Lovers and Artists in Cologne 1912' (*Internationale Kunst-Ausstellung des Sonderbundes westdeutscher Kunstfreunde und Künstler zu Köln 1912*), illustrated catalogue, Van Gogh Museum, Amsterdam.

21. Ibid.

22. Walter Feilchenfeldt, *Vincent van Gogh & Paul Cassirer, Berlin*, p. 14.

23. The first Dutch edition of letters was published in spring 1914. See 'Memoir of Johanna van Gogh-Bonger', in Vincent van Gogh, *The Complete Letters 1*, p. xi. The first German translation was made available in the same year through Paul Cassirer, who had enquired about the rights as early as 1907. See Walter Feilchenfeldt, *Vincent van Gogh & Paul Cassirer, Berlin*, p. 26.

24. *S&vGogh*, p. 181. Roughly speaking, Jaspers dated the transition in the painting to accord with his notes on van Gogh's correspondence, and his perception of an enhancement of the artist's creative powers from 1888 until the early 1890s. The first complete catalogue of Vincent van Gogh's paintings by J. B. de la Faille, *L'Œuvre de Vincent van Gogh. Catalogue Raisonné* (Paris and Brussels), was not published until 1928.

25. *S&vGogh*, pp. 192f (author's slight amendment to translation).

26. Ibid., p. 187.

27. Ibid., p. 177.

28. Ibid., p. 176.

29. Ibid., p. 202 (author's slight amendment to translation).

30. Hans-Georg Gadamer's study of Heidegger's speech, 'The Truth of the Work of Art' (1960) in his *Heidegger's Ways* was not as illuminating as Jacques Derrida's analysis of the same subject. Cf. Jacques Derrida, *La Vérité en Peinture*, especially 'Restitutions', pp. 293–436. Derrida lent credence to Meyer Schapiro's suggestion that Heidegger had 'imagined everything', by projecting an imaginary idea of the origin of the artwork, using the example of van Gogh's painting of shoes that Heidegger first saw in Amsterdam in 1930 [F 255]. Heidegger interpreted their 'truth' by suggesting their use as peasant shoes, ibid., pp. 313 and 315. Jaspers, too, had viewed an example of Van Gogh's painting of shoes, although the example that he saw, according to Feilchenfeldt's list [F 461], was not the same one as Heidegger. Cf. Walter Feilchenfeldt, *Vincent van Gogh & Paul Cassirer, Berlin*, p. 149.

31. Martin Heidegger, *The Origin of the Work of Art* (1935), in Martin Heidegger, *Poetry, Language, Thought*, trans. Albert Hofstadter, pp. 15–87, here p. 36.

32. *S&vGogh*, p. 178. In her critical assessment of Jaspers' pathography, Marielene Putscher noted that Hans Prinzhorn's collection of artwork by mentally ill patients – a collection of about five thousand paintings and drawings, housed in the Heidelberg Clinic of Psychiatry, and specifically referred to in *S&vGogh* (p. 195) – was a far-reaching interpretation of artistic creativity that had been in the public domain since 1919 and was therefore more original than Jaspers' study. Cf. Marielene Putscher, 'Jaspers und Van Gogh', in *Janus* (1980), 5, here p. 164. In conversation with Silivo Vietta, Hans-

Georg Gadamer recalled having seen one of the original exhibitions of the collection in 1921 which had had a key influence on the place of art in his thinking. Cf. *Hans-Georg Gadamer und Silvio Vietta im Gespräch*, p. 75.

33. *S&vGogh*, p. 203 (author's slight amendments to translation).

34. Ibid., p. 180.

35. Vincent van Gogh, *The Complete Letters 1*, Letter 150 ('Etten, September '81'), p. 239.

36. Ibid., Letter 221, ('31 July '82'), p. 425.

37. *P2*, p. 178 (author's minor amendments to translation.)

38. Petra Stelzer's pioneering attempt in *Ästhetik aus existentieller Erfahrung* to read Jaspers' philosophy as a particular appreciation of art focused on *Erlebnisästhetik* (ibid., p. 133). She looks at Jaspers' conception of communication as essentially humane and motivated by the paradigmatic influence of Schelling's philosophy. Jaspers' practice of 'seeing' concepts by comparison to the medium of painting becomes plausible when read in the context of the symbolic significance of art for his intellectual life.

Chapter 11   Martin Heidegger in the 1920s

1. Gertrud to Karl Jaspers, 4 September 1922 [*FA*].

2. Karl to Gertrud Jaspers, Heidelberg, 6 September 1922 [*FA*]. ('Heidegger habe ich eingeladen mit 1000 Mk. für Reisegeld.') MH/KJ, Letter 11, Heidelberg, 6 September 1922, p. 33. Heidegger later returned the money, with interest. MH/KJ, Letter 64, Marburg, 2 June 1928 and Letter 66, Heidelberg, 6 June 1928, pp. 98 and 100.

3. Karl to Gertrud Jaspers, Heidelberg, 9 September 1922 [*FA*]. ('Wir sind eben tüchtig im Philosophieren.')

4. *PA*, pp. 75/1f. Cf. Hans Saner, MH/KJ, p. 222. (Husserl's birthday was on 8 April.) Jaspers' first mention of Heidegger in his family correspondence is to his sister, to whom he noted his meeting with Heidegger during a three-day visit to Freiburg with Gertrud. Karl Jaspers to Erna Dugend, 10 April 1921 [*FA*].

5. That clash of intellectual horizons was illuminated in Richard Wisser's identification of the point of vitality that emerges in Jaspers' correspondence, in general, and with Heidegger, in particular. Cf. Richard Wisser, 'Zum Briefwechsel Martin Heidegger – Karl Jaspers. Jaspers' Vision einer „kommunikativen Kritik"', in Reiner Wiehl and Dominic Kaegi (eds), *Karl Jaspers – Philosophie und Politik*, pp. 115–31.

6. MH/KJ, Letter 12, Freiburg i. Br., 19 November 1922, p. 33.

7. Ibid. (author's translations).

8. Ibid., p. 35.

9. Ibid. Jaspers proposed articles on Max Weber, as well as the Jewish politician and foreign minister, Walther Rathenau, whose murder on 24 June 1922 conveyed the dangers for public figures whose policies and backgrounds were a target of hatred in the early Weimar period.

10. MH/KJ, Letter 14, Freiburg, 19 June 1923, p. 37.

11. MH/KJ, Letter 6, Heidelberg, 28 June 1921, p. 22.

12. Notizen, Note 15, p. 41. (Heidegger dedicated his dissertation on Duns Scotus (1916) to Heinrich Rickert, his magnum opus, *Being and Time* (1927), to Edmund Husserl and his Kant interpretation, *Kant und das Problem der Metaphysik* (1929), to Max Scheler.)

13. Gertrud to Karl Jaspers, Prenzlau, 12 March 1925 [*FA*]. ('Heidegger kann seiner Natur nach nicht anders als gelehrt und philologisch mit philos[ophisch]-religiösem Animus zu forschen, aber er kann nichts zusammenfassend darstellen.')

14. Heidegger intended to publish his critique as a scholarly review in *Göttingischen Gelehrten Anzeigen*, MH/KJ, Letter 5, Freiburg, 25 June 1921, pp. 20f. The review was accepted for publication on the proviso that it would need considerable editing. The text vanished until it was retrieved from Jaspers' literary estate and first published by Hans Saner, see Martin Heidegger, 'Anmerkungen zu Karl Jaspers' „Psychologie der Weltanschauungen"' (1919/1921), in Hans Saner ed., *Karl Jaspers in der Diskussion*, Munich 1973, pp. 70–100.

15. Notizen, Note 210, p. 225; *PA*, p. 75/7.

16. Heidegger's terminology lapsed into the 'insight of essences', a development of Husserl's 'phenomenology', Martin Heidegger, 'Anmerkungen zu Karl Jaspers' „Psychologie der Weltanschauungen"' in Hans Saner (ed.), *Karl Jaspers in der Diskussion*, p. 73.

17. MH/HR, Letter 27, Freiburg im B., 27. January 1920., p. 49. ('Dieses Buch muß meines Erachtens, gerade weil es sehr viel bietet, von überall her gelernt hat und einem Zug der Zeit entgegenkommt, auf das schärfste bekämpft werden.')

18. Notizen, Note 210, p. 226; *PA*, p. 75/6.

19. Heidegger retained the upper hand by accusing Jaspers of describing the 'Weltanschauung' against a backdrop of what Heidegger called 'a kind of pre-emptive grasp ("Vorgriff")'. That was Heidegger's way of condemning Jaspers' work as being blind to the gesture of transferring 'its vision to a specific tradition'. Martin Heidegger, 'Anmerkungen zu Karl Jaspers' „Psychologie der Weltanschauungen"', in Hans Saner (ed.), *Karl Jaspers in der Diskussion*, p. 74.

20. To Rickert, Heidegger acknowledged that Jaspers carried on where Wilhelm Dilthey finished, MH/HR, Letter 27, p. 50.

21. Martin Heidegger, 'Anmerkungen zu Karl Jaspers' „Psychologie der Weltanschauungen"', in Hans Saner (ed.), *Karl Jaspers in der Diskussion*, p. 76.

22. Ibid., p. 85 (author's translation).

23. Reiner Wiehl noted that Heidegger's review highlighted the merits of Jaspers' 'limit situations' not being a standpoint in psychology, yet Heidegger's method of critique failed to clarify the dynamics of Jaspers' systematic approach. Wiehl suggested that Jaspers' aim was to present an intrinsically humane 'cosmos of world visions' whose philosophical character was to 'shine more brightly in certain locations'. Cf. Reiner Wiehl, 'Karl Jaspers' Psychologie der Weltanschauungen zwischen Metaphysik und Erfahrung', in Reiner Wiehl, *Subjektivität und System*, p. 289 (author's translation).

24. Quoted after Hans Saner, 'Anmerkungen zu Karl Jaspers' „Psychologie der Weltanschauungen"', in Hans Saner (ed.), *Karl Jaspers in der Diskussion*, p. 100.

25. MH/KJ, Letter 9, Freiburg i. Br., 27 June 1922, p. 26.

26. Jaspers' question was rather that of humanity and truth. Cf. Reiner Wiehl, 'Karl Jaspers' Psychologie der Weltanschauungen zwischen Metaphysik und Erfahrung', in Reiner Wiehl, *Subjektivität und System*, p. 282.

27. MH/KJ, Letter 9, Freiburg i. Br., 27 June 1922, p. 26.

28. Ibid.

29. Ibid., p. 29.

30. MH/KJ, Letter 10, Heidelberg 2 July 1922, pp. 30f. ('*Soll* einmal ein Kampf nötig sein, so soll es ein *Kampf* sein.')

31. Karl to Gertrud Jaspers, Heidelberg, 21 July 1923 [*FA*].

32. The introduction of the 'Rentenmark', from mid-November 1923, held back the hyper-inflationary spiral.

33. Karl Jaspers to parents, Heidelberg, 17 January 1923 [*FA*]. ('Adresse: Plöck 66. In der Tat von angenehmer Kürze!')

34. Karl Jaspers to parents, Heidelberg, 17 January 1923 [*FA*].

35. *PA*, p. 75/5 (author's translation). Notizen, Note 68, pp. 92–3. MH/KJ, Letter 19, Heidelberg, 4 November 1923, p. 45.

36. *PA*, p. 75/5. ('Heidegger declared emphatically that he had said nothing of the kind. I replied: "Then the matter does not exist for me anymore and is closed." Heidegger was surprised by my reaction. "A thing like this has never happened to me before" was his puzzling answer', author's amendment to translation.)

37. Arthur L. Kennedy, 'The University as a constituting agent of culture', in Gregory J. Walters (ed.), *The Tasks of Truth*, pp. 97–115, here p. 98.

38. Hanna Buczynska-Garewicz, 'Jaspers and University Self-Governance', in Gregory J. Walters (ed.), *The Tasks of Truth*, pp. 117–28, here p. 117.

39. Idee (1923) ('Die Welt ist nicht der platonische Philosophenstaat', p. 52); Idee (1946), '2. Erziehung (Bildung)', p. 53; and Idee (1961), 'b) Erziehung', p. 87.

40. Idee (1923), p. 43.

41. In the co-edited version of his essay, with Kurt Rossmann, Jaspers stated: 'Humboldt's Idea of the University is no longer viable' (Idee (1961), p. 21). Rossmann determined that to cast out the Humboldtian idea was to throw out the baby with the bath water. His historical survey of *universitas* concluded – at odds with Jaspers' 'picture' – that the problem of the 'mass university' system was merely that of modernizing Humboldt's blueprint, that is, restoring, or even properly establishing a 'cosmos of all sciences' (Idee (1961), p. 240).

42. Idee (1961), pp. 20f.

43. Idee (1961), pp. 4–6 and 13. Jaspers concluded that students themselves were to assume responsibility for their level of satisfaction with teaching, for only by testing academic freedom would it be possible to achieve the idea in practice. Ibid., p. 25.

44. Idee (1923), p. 7.

45. Ibid., p. 39.

46. Ibid., p. 49.

47. Karl to Gertrud Jaspers, Heidelberg, 31 July 1924 [*FA*].

48. Gumbel was reported to have commented: 'I do not intend to say that those fell on the field of dishonour, but they indeed died in the most horrifying way.' ('Ich will nicht sagen, auf dem Felde der Unehre gefallen sind, aber die doch auf gräßliche Weise ums Leben kamen.') Quoted after Eike Wolgast, 'Das zwanzigste Jahrhundert', in Wilhelm Doerr, *et al.* (eds), *Semper Apertus*, Vol. III, pp. 1–54, here p. 8.

49. Joachim-Felix Leonhard (ed.), *Karl Jaspers in seiner Heidelberger Zeit*, p. 94.

50. In November 1924, the disciplinary proceedings against Gumbel were renewed. When the investigative committee reported the following spring, Jaspers submitted a separate

report, as his two colleagues decided to withdraw their signature from Jaspers' recommendation that the evidence was inconclusive. The motion to suspend Gumbel from his teaching duties was finally unanimously carried by the philosophy faculty: Jaspers was the only member to vote against the motion. Joachim-Felix Leonhard (ed.), *Karl Jaspers in seiner Heidelberger Zeit*, p. 98.

51. EB/MH, Letter 45, Heidelberg, 22 March 1933, p. 59.

52. EB/MH, Letter 46, Freiburg, 30 March 1933, p. 61.

53. Ibid.

54. MH/KJ, Letter 115, Heidelberg, 20 April 1933; and *PA*, p. 75/8.

55. Karl Jaspers to Martin Heidegger, Heidelberg, August 23, 1933, trans. by Edith Ehrlich, in Richard Wisser and Leonard H. Ehrlich (eds), *Karl Jaspers. Philosopher among Philosophers*, pp. 332–7, here p. 332.

56. Hannah Arendt later suggested that Heidegger's action was based on a curious dislocation of thought from deed that she explained as an autobiographical recoil from bravado into 'reversal', a gesture that occurred from 1936 onwards when Heidegger, in Arendt's view, turned towards a new reading of Nietzsche's 'Will to Power' and against political culpability. Hannah Arendt, *The Life of the Mind*, Vol. II: *Willing*, pp. 172–94, here pp. 173 and 177. David Farrell Krell noted lapses in Arendt's argument, especially in her association of 'destructiveness' with Heidegger's interpretation of Nietzsche's conception of Will (ibid., pp. 177f). Hence, Farrell Krell underlined the importance of Heidegger's turn to Nietzsche, rather than an autobiographical reversal. David Farrell Krell, in David Farell Krell (ed.), trans. Joan Stambaugh, David Farrell Krell and Frank A. Capuzzi, 'Analysis', *Nietzsche Vol. III–IV* p. 275.

57. Karl to Gertrud Jaspers, Heidelberg, 25 October 1927 [*FA*]: 'Heidegger sends his warm greetings. [...] We are reading individual texts (Schelling) and discussing them.' ('Heidegger lässt Dich herzlich grüßen. [...] Wir lesen einzelne Texte (Schelling) und sprechen darüber'). MH/KJ, Letter 32, Todtnauberg, 24 April 1926, p. 62.

58. Karl to Gertrud Jaspers, Heidelberg, 27 October 1927 [*FA*].

59. Karl to Gertrud Jaspers, Heidelberg, 19 April 1928 [*FA*]: 'I do not warm up as much as sometimes on earlier occasions.' ('Ich werde nicht so warm wie manchmal früher.')

60. Notizen, Note 219, p. 231. ('Schelling once contrasted the act of speaking about something and speaking from an original source', author's translation.) Jaspers' disbelief at Heidegger's project was related to his emphasis on speech as a form of thinking activity. Notizen, Note 247, p. 260. ('To turn towards language seduces into the unserious thought of an aesthetically pleasing image of a linguistic work of art', author's translation.)

61. Karl to Gertrud Jaspers, Heidelberg, 20 April 1928 [*FA*].

62. Nowhere are the differences between Jaspers and Heidegger more subtly portrayed than in Richard Wisser's description of his television interview with Martin Heidegger, and his efforts to respond to the ambiance of Heidegger's conversation. See Richard Wisser, 'Nachdenkliche Dankbarkeit', in *Martin Heidegger im Gespräch*, pp. 29–77.

63. Jaspers planned to include a note on polemics and Heidegger in the afterword to *Philosophy* (1955), (Notizen, Note 113, pp. 134f). Gertrud apparently persuaded Jaspers not to include a section about Heidegger in the first edition of *Philosophical Autobiography*: 'Trudelein says: impossible – means a final break, open: it would then

be no longer – I am mistaken about what is psychologically possible for a person.' ('Trudelein sagt: unmöglich – bedeutet endgültigen Abbruch, offen: das sei dann nicht mehr, – ich irre mich psychologisch über das einem Menschen Mögliche.') Notizen, Note 120, p. 144.

64. Elzbieta Ettinger's claim that Arendt's and Jaspers' theories failed them oversimplified the importance of creativity that both Jaspers and Arendt respected in Heidegger's thinking, Elzbieta Ettinger, *Hannah Arendt, Martin Heidegger*, p. 51.

Chapter 12   Inside Nazi Germany

1. Spinoza, *Ethics*, VP23S (Scholium to Proposition 23 of Part V).
2. *Guilt*, p. 82 (author's minor amendment to translation). Cf. also SF, p. 73.
3. SW, p. 160 (author's translation).
4. Raul Hilberg gives lucid clarifications of the mind-numbing Nazi definition of 'non-Aryans', including the so-called *Mischling* of first- and second-degree and mixed marriages, according to decrees subsequently attached to the Nuremberg Laws of 15 September 1935. See Raul Hilberg, *The Destruction of the European Jews*, Vol. 1, especially chapter four, 'Definition by Decree', pp. 63–80. See also the chapter 'Mischlinge and Jews in Mixed Marriages', in Vol. 2, pp. 417–30. As Hilberg concludes: 'The Jews in mixed marriage were finally made exempt because, in the last analysis, it was felt that their deportation might jeopardize the whole destruction process. It simply did not pay to sacrifice the secrecy of the whole operation for the sake of deporting 28,000 Jews, some of whom were so old they would probably die naturally before the operation was over', ibid., p. 430.
5. SW, p. 162 (author's translation).
6. Ian Kershaw, *Hitler. 1936–1945: Nemesis*, p. 839.
7. See further Ian Kershaw, 'The Making of the Dictator', in *Hitler. 1889–1936: Hubris*, pp. 431–95.
8. Ibid., p. 436.
9. 'Declaration of Oath of Service' ('Leistung des Diensteides'), Heidelberg, 6 November 1934, signed Karl Jaspers, Wilhelm Groh (Rector) *et al.* [*UAH*: KJ/PA]. ('Ich schwöre: Ich werde dem Führer des Deutschen Reiches und Volkes, Adolf Hitler, treu und gehorsam sein, die Gesetze beachten und meine Amtspflichten gewissenhaft erfüllen. So wahr mir Gott helfe.')
10. See 'Declaration of Civil Service Oath' ('Verhandlung über die Leistung des Beamteneides'), 28 October 1920, witnessed (Rector) Prof. Johannes Hoops [*UAH*: KJ/PA].
11. See further Ian Kershaw, *Hitler. 1889–1936: Hubris*, pp. 456–9.
12. Gertrud Jaspers to parents, Heidelberg, 2 April 1933 [*FA*].
13. 'Non-Aryan' doctors were banned under regulations of 22 April 1933. See Joseph Walk, *Das Sonderrecht für die Juden im NS-Staat*, I/71, p. 16. The decree of 2 June 1933 meant that two thousand non-Aryan doctors were affected by the prohibition of treatment for state insured patients, see Raul Hilberg, *The Destruction of the European Jews*, Vol. 1, p. 90. The rules were tightened further in Berlin at the end of June, where claims against dismissal were declared ineffectual. Joseph Walk, *Das Sonderrecht für die Juden im NS-*

Staat, I/157, p. 33. By early July 1933, Fritz Mayer had received his notice of dismissal, with no opportunity for appeal. Fritz Mayer to Gertrud Jaspers, Berlin, 4 July 1933 [*LE*].

14. Paul Gottschalk, 'Memoiren eines Antiquars III', in *Börsenblatt für den Deutschen Buchhandel*, No. 15/1966, pp. 241f.

15. Arthur Mayer to Gertrud Jaspers, New York, 23 September 1940 (transcript) [*FA*].

16. Paul Gottschalk, 'Memoiren eines Antiquars III', in *Börsenblatt für den Deutschen Buchhandel*, No. 15/1966, pp. 243.

17. Walter Raaflaub, *Ernst Mayer 1883–1952*, pp. 42–9.

18. Gertrud Jaspers to Gustav Mayer, 27 May 1945 [*IISH*].

19. These facts are referred to in Gertrud's letter to Erna Dugend, Heidelberg, 14 May 1944 [*FA*]. In early 1944 Germans from British-controlled areas were exchanged for Jewish deportees held at Bergen-Belsen, see Raul Hilberg, *The Destruction of the European Jews*, Vol. 2, p. 594.

20. Gertrud Jaspers to Erna Dugend, Heidelberg, 14 May 1944 [*FA*]. ('Es ist kein Konzentrationslager, kein Arbeitslager.') It is not clear how Heinrich Mayer and his wife were able to leave Bergen-Belsen. In a letter to her brother Gustav, after the war, Gertrud mentioned that Heinrich and his wife were 'freed at the eleventh hour' ('in letzter Stunde befreit'), see Gertrud Jaspers in an unaddressed letter, Heidelberg, 13 April 1945 [*IISH*].

21. Gertrud Jaspers to parents, Heidelberg, 17 July 1933 [*FA*].

22. Fritz Mayer to Gertrud Jaspers, Berlin, 4 July 1933 [*LE*]. ('Ich schenke Dir ganz klaren Wein ein, aber bitte Dich mit mir den Kopf hoch zu halten: Es ist ein auch seelisch schwerer Schlag, mit Gewalt ausgeschaltet zu werden, jedoch wird er getragen in Erkenntnis des jüdischen Schicksals in Verbundenheit mit allen denen, die ohne Schuld das gleiche Leid erdulden!')

23. Gertrud Jaspers to parents, Heidelberg, 17 July 1933 [*FA*].

24. Gertrud Jaspers to parents, Heidelberg, 11 June 1933 [*FA*].

25. Gertrud Jaspers to parents, Heidelberg, 11 June 1933 [*FA*].

> [[…] Als philosophischer Mensch <u>darf</u> ich diese Probleme <u>so hoch</u> nicht stellen! Aber ich würde niemals mehr wie früher gegen den Zionismus kämpfen. Wir hatten die sehr gut geleitete Zeitung: „Jüdische Rundschau", die mich auch in meinem unbändigen Stolz verführt zum Zionismus. Alle dortige Probleme meinte man ertragen zu können gegenüber dieser Diffamierung und bitteren Enttäuschung. Wenn ich so nahe sehe, wie fürchterlich es aussieht bei den Brüdern, wie die Jugend alle Wege hier und draußen versperrt sieht – werde ich von Neuem rabiat. […] Erst jetzt höre ich wieder Kallys <u>Worte</u>, wenn ich auch all die Zeit auf seine Liebe und sein Fordern, das Leben zu ertragen, gehört habe. Man lässt die Juden nicht Wurzel schlagen u. wirft ihnen dann Wurzellosigkeit vor. Ich bin froh, dass ich stets leidenschaftlich zu dieser Frage gestanden habe und mich nie vor ihr drückte. […]]

The Zionist paper, *Jüdische Rundschau*, was closed down in 1938 when Goebbels banned the Jewish press and the *Jüdisches Nachrichtenblatt* was authorized in its place. Cf. Saul Friedländer, *Nazi Germany and the Jews*, pp. 283f.

26. Gertrud Jaspers to parents, Heidelberg, 4 September 1934 [*FA*].

27. Gertrud Jaspers to parents, Heidelberg, 7 July 1933 [*FA*]. The measures to promote Jewish emigration to Palestine were formalized under the terms of the so-called 'Haavara' transfer agreement, concluded in August 1933 by the German Reich and the Jewish Agency for Palestine. In this way, funds passed through a German exporter and were reconstituted to the Jewish émigré upon arrival in Palestine. See Raul Hilberg, *The Destruction of the European Jews*, Vol. 1, pp. 140f; and Joseph Walk, *Das Sonderrecht für die Juden im NS-Staat*, I/229 (28 August 1933), p. 48. This agreement survived until the outbreak of war and a variety of methods had to be resorted to by Jewish émigrés in order to salvage any material reserves as the basis of a new life overseas, see further Raul Hilberg, *The Destruction of the European Jews*, Vol. 1, pp. 139–44.

28. Gertrud Jaspers to mother, Heidelberg, 4 October 1933 [*FA*]. By 8 November 1933, Gertrud had announced her youngest brother's safe arrival in Haifa. Gertrud Jaspers to parents, Heidelberg, 10 November 1933 [*FA*].

29. Fritz Mayer to Gertrud Jaspers, Palestine, postcard, 28 November 1933 [*LE*].

30. See below, pp. 169–72.

31. Dolf Sternberger, 'Jaspers und der Staat', in Hans Saner (ed.), *Karl Jaspers in der Diskussion*, p. 418.

32. Mother to Gertrud Jaspers, Oldenburg, 27 January 1932 [*FA*]: 'Papa said yesterday to me: Kally's "Göschen" book is exquisitely well written; I read to the end of the book and I want to read it again!' ('Papa sagte gestern zu mir: Kallys Göschenbuch ist vorzüglich nett geschrieben; ich las es zu Ende und will es nun nochmal lesen!')

33. In his memoirs, Golo Mann recorded his impression of the 'treatise-like' manner of positive aspects of Jaspers' 'Göschen' edition and he objected to the fact that a direct reference to National Socialism was absent, although the book appeared only 15 months before the Nazi takeover. Golo Mann, 'Karl Jaspers', *Erinnerungen und Gedenken*, pp. 304–8.

34. Mother to Karl Jaspers, Oldenburg, 21 February 1932 [*FA*]. ('Wir haben hier vielleicht bald Nazi-Regierung.')

35. By March 1932, Jaspers' 'Göschen' volume was about to sell in its fourth edition. Gertrud Jaspers to parents, Heidelberg, 1 March 1932 [*FA*].

36. Karl Jaspers' fiftieth birthday, 23 February 1933 [*FA*]. (Typed transcript of speech by Henriette Jaspers [*FA*].)

37. Programme for 'Morning Concert, 23 February 1933' ('Morgenkonzert am 23. Februar 1933') [*LE*].

38. Karl Jaspers to father, Heidelberg, 4 March 1933 [*FA*].

39. Gottfried Niedhart, *Deutsche Geschichte 1918–1933*, pp. 200f.

40. Gertrud to Karl Jaspers, Kampen, 20 August 1932 [*FA*].

41. Karl Jaspers to parents, Heidelberg, 14 September 1932 [*FA*]. ('In der Frage der Aufrüstung handelt es sich zunächst doch im Grunde darum, dass die Regierung von den anderen Mächten bewilligt bekommt, dass sie in irgendeiner Form der Miliz, die S.A. Truppen in die Reichswehr aufnehmen und dadurch Hitler abspenstig machen kann.')

42. *Selbstporträt*, p. 35.

43. *Man*, 'Mental Creation', the section deals with 'art, science and philosophy', pp. 137–56.

44. *Man*, p. 144.

45. Walter Raaflaub, *Ernst Mayer 1883–1952*, p. 45.

46. Gertrud Jaspers to parents, Heidelberg, 12 April 1932 [*FA*].
   [Dass Kally einer Tristan Aufführung bis zum Schluss folgen mochte, überraschte mich wieder, und ich freue mich, dass die Musik ihm etwas bedeutet. Er war philosophisch gegen Wagner–Schopenhauer. Diese Todessehnsucht in der Liebe ist gegen seine Ideen. Ich hörte noch ein Klemperer-Konzert, in dem Schnabel ganz wunderbar ein Beethoven-Klavierkonzert spielte. In den Museen hatten wir großen Genuss.]

47. *P3*, pp. 168–75.

48. *Man*, especially on 'Leadership', pp. 54–8.

49. *Man*, especially on 'Solidarity', pp. 209–11.

50. Gertrud Jaspers to parents, Heidelberg, 23 March 1933 [*FA*]. ('Kally war die Tage von Heidegger ganz absorbiert.')

51. Gertrud Jaspers to parents, Heidelberg, 29 June 1933 [*FA*]. ('Nun ich muss mir sagen: Du bist eine Orientalin, die haben Gastfreundschaft zu pflegen! Und ich muss einfach liebenswürdig schweigen! Hoffentlich kriege ich es fertig. Es muss ja sein für Kally und seine Freundschaft für Heidegger.')

52. Gertrud Jaspers to parents, Heidelberg, 7 July 1933 [*FA*]: 'Heidegger gave a talk, Kally spoke at length with him about it. He stayed with us.' ('Heidegger hielt einen Vortrag, Kally sprach ausführlich mit ihm darüber. Er wohnte bei uns.')

53. Martin Heidegger, 'Die Universität im Neuen Reich', in *Heidelberger Neueste Nachrichten*, No. 150, 1 July 1933. (Quoted after Guido Schneeberger, *Nachlese zu Heidegger*, pp. 73–5, here p. 75. Several references to local newspaper reports of 4 May 1933, are given on Heidegger's membership of the Nazi Party, ibid., pp. 23–5.)

54. *Theses (1933)*, p. 331. Jaspers referred to his reform proposals in his posthumous notes on Heidegger, Notizen, Note 165, pp. 181f.

55. Hans Saner, 'Jaspers's "Theses" on the Question of University Rejuvenation (1933). A Critical Comparison with Heidegger's "Rectorial Address"', in Richard Wisser and Leonard H. Ehrlich (eds), *Karl Jaspers. Philosopher among Philosophers*, pp. 139–52, here p. 140.

56. Karl Jaspers to parents, Heidelberg, 15 June 1933 [*FA*]. ('Ich habe noch den Instinkt, in Heidelberg für jeden Augenblick anwesend sein zu müssen, auch in den Ferien. Man weiß nicht, was passiert. Man hört vielleicht Wichtiges. Und im Herbst stehen vielleicht sehr tiefgreifende Universitätsumgestaltungen bevor.')

57. The public announcement of the 'co-ordination' of the university in Baden, dated Karlsruhe, 21 August 1933, was made in the Freiburg newspaper, *Der Alemanne*, 22 August 1933. (See Guido Schneeberger, 'Der Führergedanke an den Bad. Hochschulen Verwirklicht', in Guido Schneeberger, *Nachlese zu Heidegger*, pp. 113–15.) The same document is reproduced in Bernd Martin (ed.), *Martin Heidegger und das 'Dritte Reich'*, pp. 173–6, together with a letter from the Rector of the university in Halle (pp. 171f.) suggesting that pre-empting the decision to introduce reforms in Baden was largely thanks to Heidegger's initiative of 24 August 1933 in which Heidegger had announced Nazi reforms in Freiburg (p. 173). As Bernd Martin records, on the day after the announcement of the Nazi reforms, the Pro-Rector of Freiburg University noted in his diary 'finis universitatum!' See Bernd Martin, 'Der schwierige Umgang mit der

Vergangenheit', in ibid., pp. 213–19, here p. 214.

58. Hans Saner, 'Jaspers's "Theses" on the Question of University Rejuvenation (1933)', in Richard Wisser and Leonard H. Ehrlich (eds), *Karl Jaspers. Philosopher among Philosophers*, p. 140. Karl Jaspers to Martin Heidegger, Heidelberg, 23 August 1933, trans. by Edith Ehrlich in Richard Wisser and Leonard H. Ehrlich (eds.), *Karl Jaspers. Philosopher among Philosophers*, pp. 332–7, here p. 336. An accompanying letter with Jaspers' *Theses (1933)* noted that his proposals were intended for the Ministry of Education in Karlsruhe, ibid., p. 335.

59. Hans Saner, 'Jaspers's "Theses"' on the Question of University Rejuvenation (1933)', in Richard Wisser and Leonard H. Ehrlich (eds), *Karl Jaspers. Philosopher among Philosophers*, p. 139.

60. Karl Jaspers to Martin Heidegger, Heidelberg, 23 August 1933, in Richard Wisser and Leonard H. Ehrlich (eds), trans. by Edith Ehrlich *Karl Jaspers. Philosopher among Philosophers*, p. 335.

61. Jean Grondin, *Hans-Georg Gadamer*, p. 304. Grondin speculated that Jaspers, whom he bracketed with Heidegger as a 'philosopher close to Gadamer', had 'partly greeted the Nazi takeover' and pointed to the Röhm Putsch (30 June 1934) as the 'day on which their eyes were opened', ibid., p. 203 (author's translation).

62. Hans Saner, 'Jaspers's "Theses"' on the Question of University Rejuvenation (1933)', in Richard Wisser and Leonard H. Ehrlich (eds), *Karl Jaspers. Philosopher among Philosophers*, p. 142.

63. *Theses (1933)*, pp. 326f. In the winter semester 1932/3, compulsory sports activities were introduced by the Heidelberg Students' Association; and from January 1934, two semesters' compulsory sports training was required of all students. In August 1933, all male students in the first four semesters of study were required to complete 'work service' (*Arbeitsdienst*). See Dorothee Mussgnug, 'Die Universität Heidelberg zu Beginn der nationalsozialistischen Herrschaft', in Wilhelm Doerr, *et al.* (eds), *Semper Apertus*, Vol. III, pp. 464–503, here pp. 491f.

64. *Theses* (1933), pp. 326f.

65. *Theses* (1933), p. 313.

66. *Theses* (1933), p. 316.

67. *Theses* (1933), p. 317.

68. The question of leadership completely disappeared from Jaspers' *Theses (1933)* and only indirect allusions were made to 'intrigues', 'pedantry' and the decline of 'personal responsible decision' (*Theses (1933)*, p. 325).

69. Karl Jaspers to parents, Heidelberg, 28 August 1933 [*FA*]. For Jaspers' original letter, see the Appendix.

70. MH/KJ, Letter 122, Freiburg, 16 May 1936, pp. 160f and Letter 123 (a draft only), Heidelberg, 16 May 1936, pp. 162f. A draft letter in which Jaspers planned to point out to Heidegger his disappointment at not receiving any word upon his retirement in 1937 indicates the vacuity of their relationship, Letter 124, Heidelberg, 12 October 1942, pp. 164–6. Jaspers' first letter to Heidegger was sent after he had been in Switzerland for almost one year, Letter 126, Basel, 6 February 1949, pp. 168–71.

71. *PA*, p. 75/9–10.

72. Dorothee Mussgnug, *Die vertriebenen Heidelberger Dozenten*, p. 29.

73. Ibid., pp. 20f.

74. Gertrud Jaspers to parents, Heidelberg, 7 July 1933 [*FA*].

75. Gertrud Jaspers to parents, Heidelberg, 20 February 1939 [*FA*]. Zimmer first accepted a guest lectureship in Oxford, with the assistance of Raymond Klibansky, at the end of 1938, and emigrated to America, in spring 1939, with the aid of his wife's family. Dorothee Mussgnug, *Die vertriebenen Heidelberger Dozenten*, pp. 168–71.

76. Jaspers was obliged to prove prior payment of their expenses by their Dutch hosts because of the restrictions on currency conversion. Karl Jaspers to 'foreign department' of University Heidelberg ('An die Auslandsabteilung der Universität Heidelberg'), Heidelberg, 7 February 1935 [*UAH*: KJ/PA].

77. Karl Jaspers to Rector, Professor Dr Groh, Heidelberg University, Heidelberg, 16 January 1935 [*UAH*: KJ/PA].

78. From 'Psychology of World Visions' (1919) to *Philosophy* (1932), Jaspers illustrated the importance of Kierkegaard and Nietzsche for the development of his conception of *Existenz*.

79. Karl Jaspers to parents, Heidelberg, 20 March 1935 [*FA*].

80. Several days before Jaspers' lectures took place, Gertrud confirmed their arrival in Groningen. Gertrud Jaspers to parents (postcard), Hotel 'De Doelen', Grootemarkt 35, Lees-en schrifjzaal, 22 March 1935 [*FA*].

81. *RE* ('Truth as Communicability'), p. 77.

82. *RE* ('The Encompassing'), p. 52.

83. HA/KJ, Letter 374, Basel, 17 April 1965, p. 596.

84. 'Albert Fraenkel', in Hermann Maas and Gustav Radbruch (eds), *Den Unvergessenen. Opfer des Wahnes 1933 bis 1945*, p. 56.

85. Karl Jaspers to parents, Heidelberg, 25 December 1938 [*FA*]. For Jaspers' original letter, see the Appendix. Albert Fraenkel discovered a therapy (with the use of digitalis) that saved the lives of heart patients. Cf. Wolfgang Heubner, 'Albert Fraenkel', in Georg Weiss (ed.), *Albert Fraenkel. Arzt und Forscher*, pp. 6–16. The original speech 'Zur Digitalistherapie. Über intravenöse Strophanthintherapie', delivered by Albert Fraenkel in 1906 is also reprinted here.

86. The severity of Jaspers' personal experiences undoubtedly convinced him of the need to fine tune his conceptual repertoire. The change of heart that Reiner Wiehl sought from Jaspers is illuminated by the German distinction of humanity (*Menschlichkeit*) from mankind (*Menschheit*), a formality that can be overlooked in the English. That change of focus was magnified in Jaspers' 'classic' essay on guilt. Cf. Reiner Wiehl, 'Moralische Verantwortung – privat und öffentlich', in Maria-Sibylla Lotter (ed.), *Normenbegründung und Normenentwicklung in Gesellschaft und Recht*, pp. 96–106, here pp. 97 and 100.

87. Karl Jaspers to Minister for Science, Education and *Volksbildung*, Heidelberg, 19 September 1935 [*UAH*: KJ/PA].

88. The Ministry of Education gave permission for Jaspers' lecture to take place, Reichs- and Prussian Minister for Science, Education (*Volksbildung*), Berlin, 11 October 1935, to Rector, Heidelberg University [*UAH*: KJ/PA].

89. HA/KJ, note to Letter 31, pp. 693f.

90. Karl Jaspers to Ernst Mayer, Heidelberg, 1 May 1936 [*LE*]. Albrecht Mayer hoped to

become an architect and was preparing for the entrance exam to Zurich's technical college. Walter Raaflaub, *Ernst Mayer 1883–1952*, p. 39.

91. Gertrud Jaspers to parents, Heidelberg, 19 January 1936 [*FA*].

92. RBK, p. 109 (author's translation).

93. Cf. Immanuel Kant, *Religion innerhalb der Grenzen der Reinen Vernunft* ('Dieses Böse ist radikal, weil es den Grund aller Maximen verdirbt […]', B 36.)

94. RBK, p. 114. ('But what is called "radical evil" can have no contingent being, whether it be thought as intrinsic substance, or whether it be considered as absence of Being (*modus deficiens*)' (author's translation).

Chapter 13   Nietzsche Lectures (1916–36)

1. Ernst Mayer to Karl Jaspers, 19 June 1933 [*LE*]. Mayer's biographer dated a working knowledge of Nietzsche, on Mayer's part, to as early as 1915. Mayer received Nietzsche's collected works for Christmas 1933, as a gift from Jaspers and his sister. Walter Raaflaub, *Ernst Mayer 1883–1952*, pp. 102f.

2. Karl Jaspers to Ernst Mayer, Heidelberg, 25 May 1934 [*LE*].

3. Karl Jaspers to Ernst Mayer, Heidelberg, 25 May 1934 [*LE*]. ('Hier ist das Problem: ich will möglichst exakt zitieren, durch Nietzsche sprechen lassen, aber es muss ein Text sein, der sich im Ganzen in glatter Kontinuität liest, ohne über die Anführungsstriche zu stolpern.')

4. Ibid.

5. Jaspers' reversal of the metaphorical character of *Philosophy* (1932) and return to the style of 'Psychology of World Visions' (1919) was deliberate. In this case, one of the subtleties of Jaspers' *Nietzsche* (1936) was withheld from English readers. The translators, Charles F. Wallraff and Frederick J. Schmitz, not unjustifiably, presumed that the constructed façade of Jaspers' original manuscript was not part of the method and merely an obstacle to an English-speaking audience, *Nietzsche*, p. viii.

6. The first part of Jaspers' book was devoted to Nietzsche's biography, and, in part, to a description of Nietzsche's friendship with Richard Wagner. Jaspers' refusal to participate in the debate on Cosima Wagner's influence on Nietzsche, in particular, her connection to the figure of 'Ariadne' in Nietzsche's Dionysus-Dyathrambics underlined his refusal to be drawn into what Jaspers called the 'biographical discussions', *Nietzsche*, p. 226.

7. Karl Jaspers to Ernst Mayer, Heidelberg, 16 July 1934 [*LE*]. [„Was Du zu Wagner schreibst ist <u>sehr</u> wichtig. Da ich Musik nicht eigentlich verstehe, muss die Darstellung natürlich auf Nietzsche reduziert werden.')

8. Karl Jaspers to Ernst Mayer, Heidelberg, 17 October 1935 [*LE*].

9. Ernst Mayer to Karl Jaspers, 6 May 1936 [*LE*]. Mayer's critique (186 pages), was divided into five chapters that covered the contents of Jaspers' book. Mayer sent his manuscript to Jaspers who littered the text with exclamations of such severity that their friendship, lasting from their time as medical students, almost ended. Mayer's final chapter on the rationale for his critique suggested that he regretted Jaspers' lack of 'will to convince and will to be convinced'. Quoted after Walter Raaflaub, *Ernst Mayer 1883–1952*, p. 109.

10. Quoted after ibid., p. 107.

11. Ernst Mayer to Karl Jaspers, 11 November 1936 [*LE*]. ('Sackgasse der Kommunikation.')
    Walter Raaflaub, *Ernst Mayer 1883–1952*, p. 106.

12. Ibid., pp. 110–12.

13. Gertrud Jaspers to Erna Dugend, [no date] January 1935 [*FA*]. ('Die Frage ist unlöslich
    für die Juden. Ich bin gewillt, mich von der Welt zurückzuziehen, wie sie ist und nur
    mit diesem Wissen und der Realität mit den Wenigen zu leben – vaterlandslos.')

14. Karl Jaspers to parents, Heidelberg, 12 August 1935 [*FA*]. ('Wir sollen Zimmer mit Blick
    auf das Meer haben; das ist wichtig.')

15. Karl Jaspers to parents, Scheveningen, 22 August 1935 [*FA*]. For Jaspers' original letter,
    see the Appendix.

16. Mother to Karl and Gertrud Jaspers, Oldenburg, 27 September 1935 [*FA*]. For the
    original text of this letter, see the Appendix.

17. Karl Jaspers to parents, Heidelberg, 29 September 1935 [*FA*].
    [Ich lese es in Deinen Worten, liebe Mutter, die Du für uns alle sprichst und
    in denen Du unser beider unvergänglichen Verbundenheit, die bis in die
    Anfänge meines Bewusstseins als die nie fragliche Selbstverständlichkeit
    unseres Lebens zurückgeht und immer gegenwärtig ist, andeutest. Die Liebe
    zu Euch war mir auch im Philosophieren ein Antrieb; sie durchdringt das
    Buch (die Philosophie), das Trudlein und ich als unser liebstes ansehen.]

18. Karl Jaspers to parents, Heidelberg, 18 October 1935 [*FA*]. ('Wegen Ernst haben wir
    große Sorgen. Die Praxis droht weitgehend zu erliegen. Alle Mitglieder der
    „Arbeitsfront" sind aufgefordert, nicht zum jüdischen Arzt zu gehen. Es ist schlagartig
    fühlbar.') The situation for Ernst Mayer was already critical from April 1933 onwards,
    when Jewish doctors were forbidden to take patients from state-sponsored health
    insurance schemes.

19. Walter Kaufmann objected to Jaspers' 'hundreds of quotations from Nietzsche' that he
    argued were 'shuffled and juxtaposed at will' in a book that, for Kaufmann, represented
    an 'amazing and assuredly unscientific method which defies the canons of philology
    and history'. Walter Kaufmann, *Existentialism: From Dostoevsky to Sartre*, pp. 31f.

20. Jaspers reacted rather sharply to Kaufmann's criticisms of his study, Walter Kaufmann,
    'Jaspers' Relation to Nietzsche', in P.A. Schilpp (ed.), *The Philosophy of Karl Jaspers*, pp.
    407–36. To Hannah Arendt, Jaspers again complained of Kaufmann as a 'lightweight'
    and not an 'undangerous' critic who needed to be reminded of his station: 'For him, I
    am a German, of course, a non-European, with only one foot in the Enlightenment,
    and therefore a highly suspect figure.' In his reply to Kaufmann, Jaspers confessed to
    Arendt that he was 'almost entirely lacking in humour and in the light, ironic touch',
    HA/KJ, Letter 151, Basel, 27 November 1953, pp. 232f.

21. Karl Jaspers to Ernst Mayer, Heidelberg, 11 February 1933 [*LE*]. ('Wir hörten gestern
    Abend Hitler im Radio, heute wieder. Man weiß Bescheid, wenn man ihn hört.')
    Hitler's first speech as Reichschancellor was broadcast on 10 February 1933, when he
    spoke at Berlin's *Sportpalast* and attacked the failed democracy of the Weimar
    Republic, inflation and the 'November traitors' (i.e. Jews) who had caused Germany's
    military defeat in the First World War. See Max Domarus (ed.), *Hitler Reden und
    Proklomationen 1932–1934*, Vol. 2/1: *Triumph*, pp. 203–7.

22. Karl Jaspers to Ernst Mayer, Heidelberg, 16 July 1934 [*LE*]. ('es ist, als ob man aus

strengsehender Gespenstigkeit zu lichtender Leuchtung käme').

23. Max Horkheimer's review of Jaspers' book regretted the lack of direct opposition to National Socialism, Max Horkheimer, 'Bemerkungen zu Jaspers' Nietzsche', in *Zeitschrift für Sozialforschung*, 6/1937, quoted after Martha Zapata Galindo, *Triumph des Willens zur Macht*, p. 138.

24. HA/KJ, Letter 35, Heidelberg, 12 March 1946, p. 34. With hindsight, in the preface to the second edition of *Nietzsche*, published after the war in 1946, Jaspers claimed as follows:
    I tried to prepare this book in complete independence of the situation at the time and thus to offer an objective and timelessly valid interpretation. But in the years 1934 and 1935, I also intended to marshal against the National Socialists the world of thought of the man whom they had proclaimed as their own philosopher. The book grew out of lectures in the course of which many listeners understood what I meant when I quoted Nietzsche's statement: 'We are emigrants. …' This quotation, together with his sympathetic comments about the Jews, has been omitted from the book itself and will not be added now, since it is not pertinent to my main concerns. I do not intend to alter the documentary material in the book. (*Nietzsche*, Preface to the second edition, p. xiv.)

25. *Nietzsche*, Preface to the first edition, Heidelberg, December 1935, p. xi. The critical edition of Nietzsche's works, begun in 1933, was halted by the onset of war. Jaspers wrote in 1946 that 'since Nietzsche could not really become the philosopher of the National Socialists, they eventually abandoned him without further ado'. Preface to the second edition, *Nietzsche*, p. xiv.

26. *Nietzsche*, Preface to the first edition, Heidelberg, December 1935, p. xi.

27. Curt Paul Jantz, *Friedrich Nietzsche*. Vol. II, pp. 12f.

28. Jaspers' main objection to P.C. Möbius's 1902 study was precisely that he took such an unquestioning view of Nietzsche's illness that his analysis of the work became 'absurd', *Nietzsche*, p. 107. Lou Andreas Salomé's early study, *Friedrich Nietzsche in seinen Werken* (1894), which Karl Löwith did much to promote, argued that the life and works were directly related.

29. Jaspers also advertised 'psychological exercises' on Nietzsche in the summer semester of 1918. Nietzsche lectures continued in the winter semester of 1933/4, exercises (*Übungen*) in the summer semester of 1934, lectures in the summer semester of 1935 and exercises in the summer semester of 1936.

30. Karl Jaspers to father, Heidelberg, 15 February 1916 [*FA*].

31. Karl Jaspers to father, Heidelberg, 15 February 1916 [*FA*].

32. Curt Paul Jantz connected the publication of Nietzsche's *Thus Spoke Zarathustra* with the year of Karl Jaspers' birth, Curt Paul Jantz, *Friedrich Nietzsche*, Vol. 2, p. 238.

33. *Nietzsche*, p. 8.

34. *Nietzsche*, p. 107.

35. Kaufmann's criticism of Jaspers' 'authentic Nietzsche' was based on his accusation that Jaspers' theory was one of subjectivizing, and he complained that Jaspers' book 'throws light on the philosophy of Jaspers, who has always closely related his own work to Nietzsche's'. Walter Kaufmann, 'Jaspers' Relation to Nietzsche', in P.A. Schilpp (ed.), *The Philosophy of Karl Jaspers*, p. 407.

36. *Nietzsche*, pp. 310f. Kaufmann objected that Jaspers refused to take seriously 'superman and recurrence, will to power and sublimation, or any other definite concept'. Walter Kaufmann, 'Jaspers' Relation to Nietzsche', in P.A. Schilpp (ed.), *The Philosophy of Karl Jaspers*, p. 431.

37. Martin Heidegger, *Nietzsche* Vol. I, ed. and trans. David Farrell Krell, p. 23 ('according to Jaspers, there is no conceptual truth or conceptual knowledge in philosophy').

38. *Nietzsche*, p. 359.

39. Martin Heidegger, *Nietzsche* Vol. I, ed. and trans. David Farrell Krell, p. 75.

40. Martin Heiddegger, *Nietzsche: Der Wille zur Macht als Kunst*, ed. Bernd Heimbüchel, p. 26 (author's translation). For Heidegger's edited versions of the original lecture compare with *Martin Heidegger: Nietzsche I* Pfullingen: Neske, 1961) pp. 26f.

41. Martin Heidegger, *Nietzsche* Vol. I, ed. and trans. David Farrell Krell, pp. 165–6. ('If we are to grasp Plato's teaching concerning art as "political", we should understand that word solely in accordance with the concept of the essence of the *polis* that emerges from the dialogue itself. [...] Such inquiry into art is "theoretical" in the highest degree. The distinction between political and theoretical inquiry no longer makes any sense at all.')

42. Ibid., p. xl. (See *Martin Heidegger: Nietzsche I*, p. 10.)

43. Hannah Arendt, *The Life of the Mind*, Vol. II: *Willing*, p. 188.

44. Jaspers' personal copy of *Martin Heidegger: Nietzsche I* contained in the opening section (on p. 13) the comment: 'Macht-spruch!' Jaspers later scrawled (on p. 29) that he was uncertain whether Heidegger saw his Nietzsche interpretation as a result of his 'editing' of his original lecture in 1961 or as a statement of fact about his views in the Nazi era – 'Nazi-Zeit?' Arendt had difficulties in brokering a reunion for Heidegger with Jaspers when she visited Heidegger in February 1950 in Freiburg for the first time after the war. All that she could extract was Heidegger's 'confession' that he felt ashamed to visit Jaspers in Heidelberg after 1933. Jaspers' reticence towards Heidegger was underlined in his desire to draw parallels between the private and the public sphere in the discussion of 'guilt'. See HA/KJ, Letter 107, Basel, 7 January 1951 and Letter 109, 4 March 1951, pp. 161 and 167, respectively.

45. The literal 'exclusion zone' was contained in the chapter 'Boundaries and Sources' where Jaspers proposed to situate 'Eternal Recurrence', 'myth', in amongst other aspects, the context of what he called 'faith', that is, in reference to Aeschylus' *Prometheus*, the Old Testament Book of Job and Leibniz. See *Nietzsche*, p. 333. The wider consequences of his proposal are explored in the second part of the third book, 'How Nietzsche is to Be Understood', *Nietzsche*, pp. 417–58.

46. Ibid., p. 107.

47. Ibid.

48. Martin Heidegger, *Nietzsche* Vol. I, ed. and trans. David Farrell Krell, p. 158. A range of topics that Jaspers represented as sources of critical views, namely, what he summarized as 'grand politics' in reference to Nietzsche's historicism and positivism, or essentially, Chapters Three ('History and the present Age') and Four ('Great Politics') of *Nietzsche*, were addressed by Hans-Martin Gerlach, 'Wege der Nietzsche Kritik – Jaspers, Bloch, Lukács', in *Jahrbuch der Nietzsche-Gesellschaft/8*, pp. 308–13.

49. *Nietzsche*, p. 27.

50. Ibid., p. 86.

51. Friedrich Nietzsche, *Fröhliche Wissenschaft*, in *Werke*, Vol. V/2 (260, Book III: 'Ein Mal eins. Einer hat immer Unrecht: aber mit Zweien beginnt die Wahrheit.')

52. *Nietzsche*, p. 188.

53. Ibid., p. 98.

54. Ibid., p. 107.

55. Ibid. ('It cannot be doubted that his poetic power increases. [...] What at first impresses one as accidental and strange may suddenly appear as the most profound truth or the meaningful strangeness of the exceptional. The spirit imports meaning even to the insanity, and so permeates the insane notes that they become indispensable to the work.')

56. Ibid., p. 185.

57. Ibid., p. 190.

58. Ibid., p. 167. ('It is Nietzsche's faith that creates for itself the idea of the overman.')

59. Ibid., p. 97.

Chapter 14   Keeping Faith

1. Paul Sauer (ed.), *Dokumente über die Verfolgung der jüdischen Bürger in Baden-Württemberg durch das nationalsozialistische Regime 1933–1945*, Vol. 2, pp. 360f.

2. Minister of Culture and Education to Rector, Heidelberg, Karlsruhe, 25 June 1937 [*UAH*: KJ/PA].

3. Bruno Blau, *Das Ausnahmerecht für die Juden in Deutschland 1933–1945*, pp. 13–18, here p. 15 (author's translation).

4. Karl Jaspers to parents, Heidelberg, 28 June 1937 [*FA*]. For Jaspers' original letter, see the Appendix.

5. Karl Jaspers to Reichsminister for Education via Minister of Culture and Education, Karlsruhe, Heidelberg, 14 July 1937 [*UAH*: KJ/PA].

6. Jaspers mentioned §4 of the 'Reichstaggesetzes über die Entpflichtung von Hochschullehrern, 21. I. 1935'.

7. Ernst Krieck to Minister of Culture and Education, Karlsruhe, Heidelberg University, (Rector), Heidelberg, 14 July 1937 [*UAH*: KJ/PA].

8. Minister of Culture and Education to Rector, Heidelberg University, Karlsruhe, 20 September 1937 [*UAH*: KJ/PA].

9. Karl Jaspers to parents, Heidelberg, 3 July 1937 [*FA*].

10. *PE*, Epilogue to the Second Edition, p. 97.

11. Ibid., p. 17.

12. Jaspers was obliged to obtain permission to publish his essay on what he presented to the Minister of Education as 'a question concerning Descartes or Cartesianism' ('eine Frage [...] die Descartes oder den Cartesianismus betrifft), Karl Jaspers to Reichsminister for Science, Culture and Education (*Volksbildung*) (Berlin), Heidelberg, 12 February 1936 [*UAH*: KJ/PA].

13. Jaspers rejected Descartes' contribution to modern science, yet he somehow disagreed not with the specifics but with the general idea of an abstract language, such as mathematics, staking a claim to experimental and hypothetical methods of research – the only methods Jaspers seemed inclined to accept as 'scientific' because of the

inherent sincerity of the hypotheses as a test for the research process itself. As Hannah Arendt pointed out, Jaspers' essay needs to be set in the context of a split between the Renaissance world and modern science. In the seventeenth century, the insistence on novelty, as, for instance, Galileo's discovery of the heliocentric system, became elevated in contradistinction to a scientific or mathematical tradition. See Hannah Arendt, *The Human Condition*, p. 249. Aspects of this issue are addressed in relation to Jaspers' inaugural lecture in Basel, see below, pp. 205–6.

14. Karl Jaspers to parents, Heidelberg, 3 June 1933 [*FA*].

15. *PE*, p. 97.

16. Ibid., p. 65.

17. Ibid., pp. 73f.

18. Ibid., pp. 49f.

19. *P2*, p. 262.

20. Ibid., p. 263.

21. Karl to Enno Jaspers, Heidelberg, 5 August 1926 [*FA*]. (This letter included the transcript of Jaspers' original letter to Enno, 29 April 1926.)

22. Ibid. ('Du weißt – theoretisch aus meiner Weltanschauungspsychologie – dass ich an Liebe als Besitz nicht glaube, sondern nur an Liebe in Kommunikation und im liebenden Kampfe. Ich hoffe innig, dass der Abgrund des Schweigens, der sich zwischen uns aufgetan hat, sich wieder schließt, wenn Du alles vertragen kannst. Es mag Zeit vergehen.')

23. Karl Jaspers to parents, Heidelberg, 10 March 1931 [*FA*].

24. *P2*, pp. 264f. (author's amendments to translation).

25. *P2*, p. 266.

26. A string of letters could be cited to demonstrate Jaspers' sense of loss, but one, in particular, stands out as articulating a feeling of guilt. Jaspers wrote this letter to coincide with the date and time of Enno's funeral that he did not attend. Karl Jaspers to parents, Heidelberg, 11 March 1931, 11.30 a.m. ('½ 12')[*FA*].

27. *P2*, p. 266. In *Metaphysics*, the section, 'Law of the Day', establishes an ethical code and the section, 'Passion for the Night', a realm of despair, *P3*, pp. 90–102.

28. Karl to Gertrud Jaspers, Heidelberg, 10 March 1931 [*FA*]. ('Er sagt es ohne Vorwurf, mit der Irrnis der „Leidenschaft zur Nacht"'.)

29. Karl to Gertrud Jaspers, Heidelberg, 10 March 1931 [*FA*]. ('Was dieses Andere ist, ist es erst im Tod.')

30. Mother to Gertrud and Karl Jaspers, Oldenburg, Gartenstr. 28, 7 November 1933 [*FA*]. [Meine liebe Gertrud! Mein lieber Kally! [...] Ich lese Metaphysik. Ganz langsam. Letztens „das Gesetz des Tages und die Leidenschaft der Nacht." So ergreifend schön für mich Seite 109: Gegen den blinden Daseinswillen steht der lichte Raum des Menschen. [...] Ich begleite Dich alle Tage auf Deinen Wegen. [...] Seid innig gegrüßt von Papa und Eurer Mutter]

31. William Shakespeare, *King Lear*, Act 5, Scene 2, ll. 9–11. (Edgar). *P2*, p. 269.

32. Jaspers remarked on his parents' example as a source of encouragement after his dismissal in 1937. See 'Answer to the question: What strengths enable you to live?', in PhA, pp. 238–47, here pp. 238f.

33. Karl Jaspers to Erna Dugend, Heidelberg, 21 December 1937 [*FA*].

34. Karl Jaspers to parents, Heidelberg, 21 December 1937 [*FA*].
35. Karl Jaspers to Erna Dugend, 21 December 1937 [*FA*].
36. Henriette to Karl Jaspers, Oldenburg, 25 December 1937 [*FA*].
37. Karl Jaspers to Erna Dugend, Heidelberg, 30 April 1938 [*FA*].
38. NC, pp. 51f.
39. Paul Sauer (ed.), *Dokumente über die Verfolgung der jüdischen Bürger in Baden-Württemberg durch das nationalsozialistische Regime 1933–1945*, Vol. 2, especially on 'Verordnung über Sühneleistung der Juden deutscher Staatsangehörigkeit. Vom 12. November 1938', p. 61.
40. Karl Jaspers to Erna Dugend, Heidelberg, 20 October 1938 [*FA*]. ('Ich habe seit einiger Zeit so stark dieses Bedürfnis nach dem menschlich Fernen, wenn es in den Wurzeln und doch verwandt ist – und habe mal immer den Globus vor mir auf dem Schreibtisch.')
41. Karl Jaspers to parents, Heidelberg, 26 March 1937 [*FA*].

Chapter 15   Oxford connections, visitors and loyal friends

1. Gertrud Jaspers to parents, Heidelberg, 12 October 1938 [*FA*]. General Secretary, (SPSL) to Gustav Mayer, 27 May 1935 [*BL*: MS, SPSL GM 5/256, 474].
2. Secretary (SPSL) to Gustav Mayer, Oxford, 6 September 1944 [*BL*: MS, SPSL KJ 315/2, 300].
3. Werner Brock to Secretary (SPSL), Cambridge, 30 January 1939 [*BL*: MS, SPSL KJ 315/2, 297].
4. Brock visited the Jaspers in Heidelberg after his emigration. Gertrud Jaspers to parents, Heidelberg, 30 July 1935 [*FA*].
5. Brock forwarded testimonials by H.J. Paton, J. Laird, L. Lévy-Bruhl, Jean Wahl, and an article on Jaspers by Kurt Schneider, 'General Psychopathology' (1913). Werner Brock to Secretary (SPSL), Cambridge, 11 January 1939 (date as postmark) [*BL*: MS, SPSL KJ 315/2, 286].
6. Gertrud Jaspers to parents, Heidelberg, 31 December 1938 [*FA*].
7. Karl Jaspers to parents, Heidelberg, 15 January 1939 [*FA*]. For Jaspers' original letter, see the Appendix.
8. The daughter of Arthur and Fanny Mayer, Dodo Mayer, relocated to Manchester in 1934 (Gertrud to Erna Dugend, Heidelberg, 5 April 1934 (postcard). Julia Gottschalk eventually found a position in a doctor's practice near the Lake District in Cumbria. Julia Gottschalk to Karl and Gertrud Jaspers, Distington, 20 September 1945 [*FA*].
9. KJ/HZ, Oxford, May 1939, pp. 19–23, here pp. 19f.
10. Ibid., p. 20.
11. General Information (SPLS), Allgemeine Auskunft, 12 January 1939 [*BL*: MS, SPSL KJ 315/2, 274].
12. Compare the scholarly debate between Charles Wallraff and Adolph Lichtigfeld previously referred to above, p. 281.
13. Lucien Lévy-Bruhl and Jean Wahl unanimously recommended Jaspers' philosophy. British referees – H.J. Paton, H.H. Price, John Laird and W.D. Ross – supplied detailed reports but their votes suggested a lack of consensus about the merits of Jaspers' work.

14. H.J. Paton cited Kant as being a major influence for Jaspers. He strongly recommended gaining Jaspers as a prestigious guest for any Oxford college and for the university as a whole. H.J. Paton to the President and Fellows of St John's College, Oxford, 2 January 1939 [*BL*: MS SPSL KJ 315/2, 266].

15. H.H. Price, New College, Oxford, to Secretary (SPSL), 12 December 1938 [*BL*: MS SPSL KJ 315/2, 262]. Price provided pertinent criticism of Jaspers' study of Descartes that he thought omitted a necessary and detailed analysis of Descartes' mathematical language.

16. Gertrud Jaspers to parents, Heidelberg, 6 July 1938 [*FA*].

17. When the efforts of Lucien Lévy-Bruhl to secure a position for Jaspers in Paris also ended in failure, the Jaspers remained in Heidelberg. SW, p. 152. KJ/HZ, Heidelberg, 6 April 1939, pp. 18f.

18. In October 1940, the transport of 6,500 Jews from Baden and Württemberg was not the first measure taken against Jews in this region. Polish Jews had already been deported in October 1938 (Paul Sauer (ed.), *Dokumente über die Verfolgung der jüdischen Bürger in Baden-Württemberg durch das nationalsozialistische Regime 1933–1945*, Vol. 2, pp. 232f).

19. Gertrud agreed to use the poison if Jaspers' illness worsened. Gertrud Jaspers to Gustav Mayer, Heidelberg, 31 March 1945 [*IISH*]. See Richard Wisser, *Karl Jaspers: Philosophie in der Bewährung*, p. 272; and Wilhelmine Drescher, *Erinnerungen an Karl Jaspers in Heidelberg*, p. 40.

20. Jaspers stayed in Wassenaar from 1 to 19 August 1939. His journey to Holland does not seem to have been related to his work, but was purely in order to visit Gertrud's relatives, especially Ernst Mayer, with whom he was now reconciled after their disagreement over the Nietzsche book, Karl to Gertrud Jaspers, Wassenaar, 11 August 1939 [*FA*].

21. Karl Jaspers to Gustav Mayer, Wassenaar, 18 August 1939 [*IISH*].

22. Ibid. ('Alle „Ausnahme" ist mir leider <u>fraglich</u> (nicht erörtert und nicht entschieden) im Falle meines Todes. Da liegt meine große Sorge. Es wäre besser, wenn wir Kinder hätten (dann gilt die Ausnahme auch nach dem Tode des Mannes).')

23. At the beginning of June 1932, Jaspers signed a contract with the Evangelist Parish Council. He was to stop paying rent from 1 July 1932 and was, instead, to pay a lump sum of 15,000 Marks. The contract was valid even in the event of Jaspers' death. See Contract, Evangelist Parish Council and Prof. Jaspers [*FA*]). Several days after the contract was signed, Jaspers' father mentioned the transfer of 5,000 Marks, Karl Jaspers, senior to Karl and Gertrud Jaspers, Oldenburg, 4 June 1932 [*FA*].

24. Gertrud Jaspers to parents, Heidelberg, 15 November 1935 [*FA*]. ('Ich tue es, obwohl nicht ohne Scheu.')

25. Gertrud Jaspers to parents, Heidelberg, 1 May 1934 [*FA*].

26. Karl Jaspers to parents, Badenweiler, 23 April 1934 [*FA*].

27. Gertrud Jaspers to parents, Heidelberg, 8 April 1937 [*FA*].

28. Karl and Gertrud Jaspers to parents, Heidelberg, 7 September 1939 [*FA*].

29. Karl Jaspers to parents, Heidelberg, 16 October 1939 [*FA*].

30. Karl Jaspers to father, Heidelberg, 28 September 1939 [*FA*].
    [Es ist doch seit meiner frühesten Kindheit ein Familientag, zumal es mit dem Wechsel der Jahreszeiten, dem Beginn der Hasenjagd zusammenfällt. Dass

    sein eigentlicher Charakter Deine Abwesenheit auf der Jagd und abendliche Heimkehr mit vielen Hasen ist, das ist nun schon [seit] mehr als 25 Jahren vergangen, aber für meine Stimmung wenigstens gehört die Erinnerung daran zu diesem Tag.]

31. Gertrud Jaspers to parents, Heidelberg, 5 October 1939 [*FA*].

32. Karl Jaspers to mother, Heidelberg, 28 December 1937 [*FA*].

33. Karl Jaspers to father and mother, Heidelberg, 9 December 1939 [*FA*].

34. Mother to 'my dear children!', Oldenburg, 24 February 1940 [*FA*].

35. Karl Jaspers' speech for the funeral of Karl Jaspers, senior, 28 February 1940 [*FA*].

36. Erna Dugend to Karl Jaspers, 1 February 1941 [*FA*].

37. Karl Jaspers to Erna Dugend, Heidelberg, 31 January 1941 [*FA*]. ('Mutter […] war der ständige Spiegel unseres Lebens, für alles und jedes interessiert, was uns anging.')

38. Library of University of Basel to Karl Jaspers, Basel, 14 January 1941 (transcript) [*UAH*: KJ/PA].

39. Karl Jaspers to Erna Dugend, Heidelberg, 5 February 1941 [*FA*]. For Jaspers' original letter, see the Appendix. Gabriele and Stephan are quite probably false names. A close friend of Karl and Gertrud Jaspers in Heidelberg, Lotte Waltz, was later involved in arranging Jaspers' relocation to Basel after the war. Gertrud Jaspers to Gustav Mayer, Heidelberg, 7 July 1947 [*IISH*].

40. Karl Jaspers to Reichsminister for Education, Berlin, Heidelberg, 20 February 1941 [*UAH*: KJ/PA].

41. Karl Jaspers to Paul Schmitthenner, Heidelberg, 23 January 1941 [*UAH*: KJ/PA].

42. A study of Pareyson's book was later made by Luigi Quattrocchi, 'Karl Jaspers und die Italienische Philosophie', in WW, pp. 152–64.

43. Paul Schmitthenner (Rector), to Minister for Science, Education and *Volksbildung* Berlin, Heidelberg, 22 February 1941 [*UAH*: KJ/PA].

44. Karl Jaspers to Paul Schmitthenner, Heidelberg, 13 June 1941 [*UAH*: KJ/PA].

45. Gertrud Jaspers to Erna Dugend, 14 June 1941 [*FA*].

46. President of Reichsschrifttumskammer to Karl Jaspers, Berlin, 27 February 1943 and 11 March 1943 [*LE*].

47. Gertrud Jaspers to Gustav Mayer, Heidelberg, 9 September 1945 [*IISH*].

48. Gertrud Jaspers to Erna Dugend, Heidelberg, 2 June 1941 [*FA*].

49. Renato de Rosa (ed.), *Karl Jaspers. Erneuerung der Universität*, p. 421.

50. Karl Jaspers to Erna Dugend, Heidelberg, 15 July 1940 [*FA*]. ('Ich hatte etwas Hunger nach Stoff, gab für eine Weile die Logik auf, kehre aber wohl bald zu ihr zurück.')

51. UMP, p. 23; and KJ/HZ, Heidelberg, 2 March 1938, pp. 14f.

52. WG, p. 117.

53. It is plausible that what Jaspers called, in his letter to Erna, the 'universal history of philosophy' was the very introduction to the *Weltgeschichte* that Hans Saner dated from around 1951/2 (WG, p. 9).

54. Karl Jaspers to Minister of the Interior and Headquarters of the National Representation of German Jews, Heidelberg, 30 August 1942 [*UAH*: KJ/PA]. In his journal, on 6 September 1942, Jaspers referred to the decision to remove his domestic help as a 'turning point'. On 3 October 1942, he noted that he was exceptionally allowed to keep the domestic help and noted 'Evidently, a rare case', SW, pp. 161f. (author's translation).

55. *Geheime Staatspolizei* (Gestapo), Karlsruhe, 6 November 1942 (transcript) [*UAH*: KJ/PA]. For clarification of the definition of 'non-Aryans' in the Nuremberg Laws (15 September 1935), see Raul Hilberg, *The Destruction of the European Jews*, Vol. 1, p. 80.
56. Head of Security Service (SD) to Paul Schmitthenner (Rector), Berlin, 22 January 1943 [*UAH*: KJ/PA].
57. Head of the Security Service (SD) to Paul Schmitthenner (Rector), Berlin, 22 January 1943 [*UAH*: KJ/PA].
58. Gertrud Jaspers to Gustav Mayer, Heidelberg, 13 April 1945 [*IISH*].
59. Gertrud Jaspers to Gustav Mayer, 31 March 1945 [*IISH*].
60. See Paul Sauer (ed.), *Dokumente über die Verfolgung der jüdischen Bürger in Baden-Württemberg durch das nationalsozialistische Regime 1933–1945*, Vol. 2, p. 382.
61. Paul Schmitthenner (Rector) to Security Service of the Reichführers SS, Berlin, Heidelberg, 2 March 1945 [*UAH*: KJ/PA].
62. Gertrud Jaspers to Gustav Mayer, 31 March 1945 [*IISH*].

Chapter 16   'Liberated by Allied Forces'

1. Karl Jaspers, Diary, 30 March 1945 [*LE*]. For the original text of all entries from this diary, see the Appendix.
2. Wilhelmine Drescher, *Erinnerungen an Karl Jaspers in Heidelberg*, p. 41.
3. Karl Jaspers, Diary, 30 March 1945 [*LE*].
4. Karl Jaspers, Diary, 31 March 1945 [*LE*].
5. KHB/KJ, Letter 10, 17 July 1945, pp. 29–32.
6. Renato de Rosa, 'Politische Akzente im leben eines Philosophen' in Renato de Rosa (ed.), *Karl Jaspers. Erneuerung der Universität*, p. 384.
7. Renato de Rosa, 'Der Neubeginn der Universität 1945', in Wilhelm Doerr *et al.* (eds), *Semper Apertus*, Vol. III, pp. 544f.
8. Ibid., p. 545.
9. Karl Jaspers, Diary, 1 April 1945 [*LE*].
10. Renato de Rosa, 'Der Neubeginn der Universität 1945', in *Semper Apertus* Vol. III, p. 546. Jaspers also supplied a short biographical description in which he emphasized, especially with regard to his monograph on Max Weber, his anti-nationalistic understanding of the word 'German'. As part of their programme of denazification, the Americans requested such descriptions from all university professors. KJ/KHB, pp. 1–7.
11. Gertrud Jaspers to Gustav Mayer, 13 April 1945 [*IISH*].
12. Otto Regenbogen, Gustav Radbruch, Alfred Weber, Jaspers, Alfred Weber's companion, Else Jaffé, and Alexander Mitscherlich were present at the meeting. Karl Jaspers, Diary, 4 April 1945 [*LE*]. See Renato de Rosa, 'Der Neubeginn der Universität' 1945' in Wilhelm Doerr, *et al.* (eds), *Semper Apertus*, Vol. III, p. 546.
13. Karl Jaspers, Diary, 6 April 1945 [*LE*].
14. KJ/KHB, p. 89.
15. Gertrud Jaspers to Gustav and Flora Mayer, Heidelberg, 31 March 1945 [*IISH*]. ('Noch erfassen wir es nicht, wir sind gerettet.')
16. Gertrud Jaspers to Gustav Mayer, Heidelberg, 27 May 1945 [*IISH*].
17. Hannah Arendt, 'Organized Guilt and Universal Responsibility' in Jerome Kohn (ed.),

Essays in Understanding 1930–1945, pp. 121–32, here p. 124. Gertrud recalled the hanging of Theodor Haubach, who was connected with the Kreisau Circle and the failed plot to assassinate Hitler. Gertrud Jaspers to Gustav and Flora Mayer, Heidelberg, 31 March 1945 [*IISH*]. Emil Henk's pamphlet about the 20 July 1944 plot is interesting for its viewpoint on the Social Democratic opposition. The text was dedicated to Theodor Haubach, Carlo Mierendorff, Wilhelm Leuschner, Adolf Reichwein and Ludwig Schwamb, who all perished in the wake of the plot's failure. Emil Henk, *Die Tragödie des 20. Juli 1944*.

18. Hannah Arendt, 'Organized Guilt and Universal Responsibility', p. 125.

19. Gertrud Jaspers to Gustav Mayer, Heidelberg, 31 March 1945 [*IISH*].

> [Mein lieber Bruder, mein liebes Florchen, den 1. April, Ostersonntag. Dass ich Euch schreiben kann, offen schreiben kann! Vorläufig stillt schon dies die Sehnsucht. Die letzte Woche konnte ich mich nicht konzentrieren, davor las ich die beiden Bände Engels mit großer Freude, mit großem Interesse. Karl ist freudig bewegt, gealtert, aber schon spürt er wieder produktive Ideen. Er hat mich gehalten – ohne das war ich wieder und wieder in Selbstmordgedanken. Seine Seele hat täglich standgehalten in unbeschreiblicher Liebeskraft. Ich versagte oft. Möge mir das Leben geschenkt sein, ihm zu leben und mit Euch innigst verbunden zu sein, bis der Tod uns scheidet. Eure Trude]

Gustav Mayer's biography of Friedrich Engels was translated as *Friedrich Engels: A Biography*, London: Chapman & Hall 1936.

20. *PA*, p. 63.

21. Gertrud Jaspers to Gustav Mayer, Heidelberg, 13 December 1945 [*IISH*]. ('Ich bin Deutschland für Dich.')

22. Karl Jaspers, Heidelberg, 9 November 1930 [*FA*]. ('Das Buch ist Deins.') The handwriting of the letter is so distorted that it is only just possible to state for sure that the signature is that of Jaspers and not, for instance, that of Gertrud.

23. Gertrud Jaspers to 'my 6 brothers', 25 February 1945 ('opened and gratefully re-read by me on 25. XII. 45'). ('An meine 6 Brüder. Von mir am 25. XII. 45 dankbar geöffnet und nochmals gelesen') [*IISH*]. (I am grateful to Lars Fischer for alerting me to this letter.)

24. Gertrud Jaspers to Gustav Mayer, Heidelberg, 30 July 1946 [*IISH*]. ('Eines Tages ruft die Partei bei ihm an: „Herr Präsident, wir wundern uns, dass Sie noch nicht nachgesucht haben, in die Partei aufgenommen zu werden." Er: „Ich tat es nicht, weil meine Vergangenheit als Demokrat allgemein bekannt ist." Die Partei: „Nun, dann sind Sie hiermit in die Partei aufgenommen.")

25. Gertrud Jaspers to Gustav Mayer, 30 June 1945 [*IISH*].

26. Gertrud Jaspers to Gustav Mayer, 27 May 1945 [*IISH*].

27. With effect from 1 April 1945, Jaspers claimed the rights of a civil servant for life. President, Regional District Mannheim to Rector, Heidelberg University, Heidelberg, 7 September 1945 [*UAH*: KJ/PA].

28. President, Regional District Mannheim to Rector, Heidelberg University, Heidelberg, 14 September 1945 [*UAH*: KJ/PA].

29. Renato de Rosa, 'Politische Akzente im Leben eines Philosophen', in *Karl Jaspers. Erneuerung der Universität*, pp. 405–7. Throughout the controversy over Bauer's credentials, Jaspers supported him. KJ/KHB, pp. 35–9. Bauer was a source of energy that

Jaspers lacked because of his illness, as Jaspers underlined in his letter of 20 June 1945: 'What […] is vital […] is action, action, action!' KJ/KHB, p. 18. Jaspers' friendship and moral support for Bauer contrasted with his breakdown of trust with Martin Heidegger and his confidential recommendation to French occupying forces in Freiburg that Heidegger be quietly removed from his lecturing duties. Jaspers nonetheless later recommended that Heidegger be allowed to return to the university as professor emeritus. See Hugo Ott, *Martin Heidegger unterwegs zu seiner Biographie*, Frankfurt am Main: Campus 1988, pp. 315–17; and Richard Wolin, trans., 'Karl Jaspers, Letter to Freiburg University Denazification Committee (December 22, 1945)', in *The Heidegger Controversy*, pp. 144–51.

30. The early editions of *Die Wandlung* show an unsteady compromise between Sternberger's literary and journalistic interest, Weber's preference for objective facts, and Jaspers' focus on democracy in a newly liberated country. The journal survived several years of occupation, only to be discontinued after the constitution ('Basic Law'), was inaugurated in 1949 in the FRG. See Monika Waldmüller, *Die Wandlung, Eine Monatschrift*, pp. 10–39.

31. EU, p. 66.

32. Ibid., p. 67 (author's translation). This section of the speech, 15 August 1945, was used by Jaspers in his analysis of 'metaphysical guilt', and was acknowledged in his essay, *The Question of German Guilt* as having originated from 'Rejuvenation of the University', first published in *Die Wandlung* (I/1, 1945, pp. 66–74). The author's translation may be compared with E.B. Ashton's 1947 translation of *The Question of German Guilt* (*Guilt*, pp. 71f) and with BW, pp. 399f.

33. The involvement of medical science in Nazi crimes reemerged in connection with Jaspers' attempt to prevent, largely because of his critical opinion of practices of therapy, the foundation of a Clinic for Psychosomatic Medicine at the University of Heidelberg after 1945. For a detailed study of this problem, as well as Jaspers' relations with Alexander Mitscherlich and Victor von Weizsäcker, see Matthias Bormuth, *Lebensführung in der Moderne*, especially pp. 197–232.

34. Karl Jaspers, Letter to Heidegger, 23 August 1933, op. cit., p. 335. ('Some things cut out for the university address 1945').

35. *Theses (1933)*, p. 316.

36. Renato de Rosa, 'Der Neubeginn der Universität 1945' in Wilhelm Doerr, *et al.* (eds), *Semper Apertus*, Vol. III, p. 557.

37. EU, pp. 71f.

38. See below, pp. 204–7.

39. Renato de Rosa, 'Der Neubeginn der Universität 1945' in Wilhelm Doerr, *et al.* (eds), *Semper Apertus*, Vol. III, p. 564.

40. The reply to Sigrid Undset underlined Jaspers' public lectures on the untenable notion of 'collective guilt' that emerged from a 'disregard against mankind's humanity'.

41. Renato de Rosa, 'Der Neubeginn der Universität 1945' in Wilhelm Doerr, *et al.* (eds), *Semper Apertus*, Vol. III, p. 564.

42. VLG, p. 22 (author's translation).

43. GW, p. 4 (author's translation).

44. GW, p. 5. (author's translation). See also Hans Saner, *Karl Jaspers*, p. 135.

45. Thesen, p. 465 (author's translation).
46. Hannah Arendt, 'Organized Guilt and Universal Responsibility', p. 126.
47. Ibid., p. 131. VLG, p. 39.
48. Gertrud Jaspers to Gustav Mayer, Heidelberg, 30 November 1945 [*IISH*].
49. Jaspers defined crimes committed against humanity during 1933 to 1945 as 'criminal'. That the Nazis engineered concentration camps on such a horrific scale carried the need for accountability that he called 'political'. *Guilt*, pp. 51–63.
50. *Guilt*, p. 71 (the translation includes author's amendments).
51. HA/KJ, Letter 43, 17 August 1946, p. 54 ('it seems to me that what you call metaphysical guilt encompasses not only the "absolute", where indeed no earthly judge can be recognized anymore, but also the solidarity which is the political basis of the republic [...]').
52. Gertrud Jaspers to Gustav Mayer, Heidelberg, 1 November 1945 [*IISH*].
53. Gertrud Jaspers to 'my 6 brothers', 25 February 1945 [*IISH*].
54. *Guilt*, p. 73 (the translation includes author's amendments).
55. FW, p. 109.

Chapter 17   Citizens of Basel

1. The nuances of Jaspers' notion of 'truth' are difficult to convey to an English-speaking readership, especially since only about one-tenth of his book 'On Truth' (1947) exists in translation, consisting of the sections *Truth and Symbol* and *Tragedy is not Enough* from Part Three. The pioneering translations of Part One of 'On Truth', including selections of pieces showing Jaspers' use of *Dasein*, *Bewußtsein überhaupt*, *Geist* and *Existenz* are in the anthology prepared by Leonard H. Ehrlich, Edith Ehrlich and George B. Pepper, see *BW*, pp. 137–208. Compare especially the Selections 17–20 in *BW*, pp. 141–58, where the translations are 'Existence (*Dasein*), consciousness-as-such, spirit (*Geist*), and Existenz', *BW*, p. 140. Variations on an appropriate English translation for Jaspers' concept of *Existenz*, for instance, may be found in J. Hoenig and Marian W. Hamilton's reliable translation of Jaspers' *General Psychopathology* (1913), or Richard F. Grabau's equally accessible translation of Jaspers' 1937 lectures, *Existenzphilosophie*, rendered in English as *Philosophy of Existence*.
2. Alfons Grieder's 'Karl Jaspers and the Quest for Philosophic Truth' seeks an ethical approach, only to note that Jaspers' idea of truth is frustratingly lacking an ethical programme.
3. Erna Möhrle, who was housekeeper to Karl and Gertrud Jaspers in Basel from 1952 to 1974, especially highlighted the quietly disciplined continuity of the Jaspers' routine, as well as their particularly kind and human interest in their many house guests, Erna Möhrle, letter to the author, 26 November 1999.
4. Letter of Citizenship (*Bürgerbrief*), (Regierungsrat, Kanton Basel-Stadt), 29 June 1967 [*LE*].
5. There appeared to be a conspiracy in Heidelberg to persuade him to refuse a professorship at Bonn University in 1928. The increase in salary, by approximately one fifth of his previous income, was a considerable enticement to stay. Alfred Weber had thrown an impromptu party, with the Rector of the university, a representative of the

education ministry, Dr Fraenkel, Friedrich Gundolf, Else Jaffé, Karl Wilmanns, Marianne Weber, and others in attendance at a local hotel. Gertrud Jaspers to parents and Karl Jaspers to parents, both Heidelberg, 16 December 1928 [*FA*].

6. Rector, Heidelberg University ('statement of Senate in the meeting of 21 January 1948'), to Karl Jaspers [*UAH:* KJ/PA].

> [Sie haben in der Zeit der Neubegründung der Universität für uns und für die deutschen Universitäten insgesamt gesprochen und mit uns sehen Viele auf Sie als den Mann, der die höchsten abendländischen Traditionen für Deutschland verkörpert. Darum bitten wir Sie, bei uns zu bleiben und Ihrem Werk bei uns die reichste und tiefste Wirkung zu erhalten.]

7. Karl Jaspers to Rector, Heidelberg University, Heidelberg, 26 January 1948 [*UAH:* KJ/PA]. ('der geistesaristokratischen Welt deutschsprachiger Universitäten.')

8. Ibid. ('Ich bleibe Heidelberger, wo auch immer ich wäre.')

9. 'Eine Erklärung von Karl Jaspers', in *Rhein–Neckar–Zeitung*, 24 March 1948.

10. Jaspers' essay was first published with an open letter to the journal's editors by a former student of Alfred Weber, based on Weber's essay, 'Our experience and Our Task'. 'Eine Diskussion (Offener Brief an Herrn Professor Alfred Weber in Heidelberg)', in *Die Wandlung*, I/5, June 1946, pp. 399–402.

11. Having been invited to the Rome Congress of Philosophy in 1946 and, indeed, encouraged by Renato de Rosa to attend, Jaspers was obliged to decline, since the Congress collided with his prior agreement to speak in Geneva. Although several months separated the two meetings, Jaspers realized that his health would not allow him to speak at both venues. See Gertrud Jaspers to Gustav Mayer, 2 November 1946 [*IISH*]. Jaspers released the German text of his essay 'On Biblical Religion' (1946) for publication in the papers of the Rome Congress. See Renato de Rosa (ed.), *Karl Jaspers. Erneuerung der Universität*, pp. 291f.

12. EU, p. 67 (author's translation).

13. VBR, p. 408.

14. VBR, pp. 411f. (author's translation).

15. Compare Adorno's *Negative Dialektik. Jargon der Eigentlichkeit* (1966) in which Adorno's ironical critique revolved, for example, around an image of Max Weber's influence on Jaspers as a guardian and protective force that deprived Jaspers' language of adventure and release from liberal and 'Protestant' motives, Theodor W. Adorno, *Gesammelte Schriften*, Vol. 6, Rolf Tiedemann ed., pp. 428 and 432.

16. *PSP*, p. 77.

17. A summary of the differences could be developed through Jaspers' inspiration from Moses' word on the forbidden 'graven image' of Yaweh, a focus that Charles Wallraff called the 'background', as opposed to the 'foreground' of aspects of the ineffable in Jaspers' thinking. See Charles Wallraff, *Karl Jaspers*, pp. 29–32. According to Wallraff, Jaspers finds feelings and emotions 'cognitive vehicles' depending on subjective experience or the involvement of love, vehicles for exploiting the 'highest cognitive possibilities of man's affective life', ibid., pp. 31f. See further *BW*, 'Philosophy and Religion', pp. 441–74; and especially Leonard H. Ehrlich, *Philosophy as Faith*, pp. 145–57.

18. FE, pp. 59 and 69. ('Rudolf Bultmann. Zur Frage der Entmythologisierung. Antwort an Karl Jaspers', in FE, pp. 59–73).

19. FE, p. 82.

20. *GP1*, p. 69. ('The freedom of Jesus' actions is an essential part of this ethos of the kingdom, a freedom which is grounded not in law but in love.')

21. FE, p. 79 (author's translation).

22. FE, p. 62.

23. *PSP*, pp. 92f.

24. Jaspers hoped to emulate Nietzsche's harnessing of tensions of mind and Nature, philosophy and the individual (*Philosophie der Einzelne*), method and content, theory and practice, in such a way as to combine these polarities into a whole, Karl to Gertrud Jaspers, Heidelberg 2 January 1915 [*FA*]. It is noteworthy that Jaspers' first Nietzsche lecture took place in the following summer semester of 1916, the year after this letter was written.

25. Descartes, pp. 33–49, especially '*mathesis universalis*', pp. 42–8.

26. *Wisdom*, p. 153. (Jaspers' inaugural lecture in Basel is included in this translation of his radio lectures, *An Introduction to Philosophy* (1950), Appendix I, *Philosophy and Science* (1948), pp. 147–67.)

27. The diversity of method in the sciences was studied by Wallraff as 'matter, life, psyche (soul) and mind or spirit', whose overview of various approaches highlights what Jaspers described rather as a polarization of method within what are commonly distinguished as natural sciences, so-called humanities and philosophy. Charles Wallraff, *Karl Jaspers*, pp. 41–5, and especially 'The Nature of Science', p. 55.

28. *Wisdom*, p. 153. See also Leonardo, p. 77.

29. *Wisdom*, p. 153.

30. Karl to Gertrud Jaspers, Heidelberg, 29 June 1924 [*FA*]. ('Mein liebes Trudelein! [...] In dieser Woche ist mir die einzigartige Bedeutung der Entstehung der modernen Naturwissenschaft (im 17. Jahrhundert), d. h. eigentlich den modernen Begriff der „Wissenschaft" sehr plastisch geworden, ihre Größe und ihr Verhängnis.') In the first volume of *Philosophy* (1932), Jaspers devoted a chapter to a detailed exposition of the systematics of philosophy and science, *P1*, pp. 156–225.

31. *Wisdom*, p. 149.

32. *Wisdom*, pp. 153f. (author's amendments to translation).

33. That was an added advantage that Jaspers underlined during his apprentice years as 'human scientist' (*Geisteswissenschaftler*). Karl to Gertrud Jaspers, Heidelberg, 1 January 1915 [*FA*].

34. *Wisdom*, p. 159.

Chapter 18   'Rencontres' in Geneva

1. Gertrud Jaspers to Erna Dugend, Heidelberg, 30 July 1950 [*FA*]. ('unser Leben im Asyl').

2. Norbert Kapferer, 'Das Philosophische Vorspiel zum Kalten Krieg' in *Jahrbuch der Österreichischen Karl-Jaspers-Gesellschaft*, 6/1993, ed. Elisabeth Salamun-Hybašek and Kurt Salamun, Innsbruck and Vienna, pp. 79–106.

3. Gertrud to Gustav Mayer, Heidelberg, 30 July 1946 [*IISH*].

4. Stephen Spender, 'The Intellectuals and the Future of Europe', in *The Gate/Das Tor* (International Review of Literature and Art in English and in German), 1,

January/March 1947, pp. 2–9, here p. 3.

5. Ibid., p. 4.

6. Norbert Kapferer, 'Das Philosophische Vorspiel zum Kalten Krieg', in *Jahrbuch der Österreichischen Karl-Jaspers-Gesellschaft*, 6/1993, ed. Elisabeth Salamun-Hybašek and Kurt Salamun, Innsbruck and Vienna, pp. 89–94.

7. Stephen Spender, 'The Intellectuals and the Future of Europe', pp. 4ff.

8. Ibid., p. 6. Spender's '*German Diary*' in his journals described his responsibility to compile inventories to ensure the removal of Nazi literature from public circulation.

9. Gertrud to Gustav Mayer, Geneva, 15 September 1946 [*IISH*]. ('menschlich bezaubernd').

10. Ibid. ('Lukács sprachen wir nur immer kurz bei den Vorträgen und Diskussionen, in denen er langatmig sprach.')

11. Norbert Kapferer, 'Das Philosophische Vorspiel zum Kalten Krieg', in *Jahrbuch der Österreichischen Karl–Jaspers–Gesellschaft*, 6/1993, ed. Elisabeth Salamun-Hybašek and Kurt Salamun, Innsbruck and Vienna, p. 81. The cordial relations that Jaspers entertained with Lukács during his early Heidelberg years (when Jaspers acted as psychiatrist to Lukács' first wife, Yelena Grabenko) had all but faded. See Georg Lukács to Karl Jaspers, Budapest, 3 May and 23 June 1916, in Georg Lukács, *Selected Correspondence 1902–1920*, ed. Judith Marcus, pp. 260–2.

12. In his 'Destruction of Reason' (1954), Lukács railed against Jaspers' (and Heidegger's) adoption of Kierkegaard's conception of *Existenz* that he called 'Romantic and individualistic cat's wail'. Jaspers was deemed to have a 'wild hatred of the "masses", a cold fear of them, of democracy and socialism'. Georg Lukács, 'Der Aschermittwoch des parasitären Subjektivismus', in Georg Lukács, *Die Zerstörung der Vernunft*, pp. 389–416, here pp. 390 and 415 (author's translations).

13. *ES*, p. 29 (author's minor amendment to translation.)

14. Ibid., pp. 32f.

15. Ibid., pp. 38f.

16. Ibid., p. 36.

17. Gertrud to Gustav Mayer, Heidelberg, 19 December 1945 [*IISH*].

> [[…] ich [nenne] mich Zionist, weil ich will, dass die Juden zeigen, was ihrer Idee entspricht. Und dabei ist das Vaterland die Grundlage, um herauszustellen, was dem jüdischen Menschen möglich. Und ich stehe zwischen Philosophie und prophetischer Religion, lebe, wenn ich im Aufschwung bin mit dem Gottesgedanken des alten Testaments. „Du sollst Dir kein Bild oder Gleichnis machen."]

18. *BW*, pp. 525f. Gertrud died on 28 May 1974, only five years after Jaspers, and at her funeral on 30 May 1974, Jaspers' eulogy was spoken for a private circle of close friends.

19. *ES*, p. 38.

20. Karl Jaspers to parents, Prenzlau, 15 March 1911 [*FA*]. ('ein sehr feiner Mensch, der in Ausdrucksweise und Gesprächthema den gebildeten Menschen erkennen lässt.')

21. Ibid. ('die Seele des Geschäftes').

22. Ibid. ('Er ist ein so lieber, netter Mensch – ach, wäre er doch Jude!')

23. *ES*, p. 62. Jaspers' post-war analysis of world history and his resulting emphasis on the global status of contemporary affairs was another mark of his insistence on

incorporating a supranational perspective into a communicative framework. That was a crucial distinguishing feature of Jaspers' view of the Neo-Conservative position taken by Ernst Jünger, whose monograph *Der Arbeiter: Herrschaft und Gestalt* (1932) was in Jaspers' library and heavily marked, especially in those sections dealing with the nature of the German mentality. Jünger's emphasis on the global or 'planetary' scale of world history was different again from the metaphor that Martin Heidegger coined in his 1949 Bremen speeches. If Heidegger sought an escape route in the metaphor of the *Ge-stell*, his path of salvation in contemplative thinking was not an option that Jaspers considered fruitful, unless combined with the activity of philosophy acting as the conscience 'call' of modern science.

24. *Man*, especially 'The Sophist', pp. 182–5 (author's slight amendment to translation).
25. *ES*, p. 62.
26. H, pp. 712f (author's translation).
27. See, pp. 24 and 220.
28. Gertrud to Gustav Mayer, Geneva, 15 September 1946 [*IISH*].
29. Gertrud to Gustav Mayer, Crans sur Sierre, Valais Suisse (undated, but written a few days after 14 July 1947) [*IISH*].

Chapter 19   Talking Peace

1. For instance, an article in the local Heidelberg newspaper coincided with the announcement of the first edition of Paul Arthur Schilpp's compendium on Jaspers in the Library of Living Philosophers series. See Karl Jaspers, 'Weltgeschichte der Philosophie', in *Rhein–Neckar–Zeitung*, 22/23 Feburary 1958.
2. WG, p. 51 (author's translation).
3. Jaspers' posthumous text contained an occasional unusual use of terminology: 'If we hear true philosophy, we enter into communication with human *Existenz* of the philosophical personality. Philosophy is, in essence, always personal in form. The thoughts that are released and freely floating only gain blood and energy (*Blut und Kraft*) if an *Existenz* accepts them and, in that way, they again become a motive of an entire philosophy' [WG, p. 119, author's translation]. Whether *Blut* in this characterization was a *faux pas*, that is, a momentary lapse into Hitler's *Blut und Boden* ideology, such as might have been plausible, given the date of Jaspers' project from 1937 onwards, or whether the terms merely indicated a sign of old age (for it is not clear exactly when the text was written), is an open question.
4. WG, p. 87 (author's translation).
5. Jeanne Hersch, 'The Central Gesture in Jaspers' Philosophy', in *Journal of the British Society for Phenomenology*, Vol. 17, No. 1, 1986, pp. 3–8, here p. 5.
6. *BW*, p. 479.
7. Jaspers' argument with sociology, as a discipline that essentially reduces man's humanity to an object of study, was underlined by his criticism of Alfred Weber's investigations about the introduction of horsemanship into ancient culture. Weber's discoveries were potential proof of what Jaspers saw as the watershed of world history, the 'axial' age, when Europe and Asia were drawn together in parallel attainment of maturity. At the same time, Jaspers complained, in keeping with his objections to

sociology, that the events of world history defied sustainable explanation. He protested that causal links cannot convincingly be demonstrated in the absence of understanding the limitations of mankind's consciousness of humanity, UZ, pp. 60 and 265f.

8. Gertrud Jaspers to Erna Dugend, Basel, 30 July 1950 [*FA*].

9. Ibid.

10. Edwin Kuntz, 'Philosophie in unserer Zeit (Karl Jaspers vor Studenten der Universität Heidelberg)', in *Rhein–Neckar–Zeitung*, 29/30 July 1950.

11. *Reason*, pp. 7f.

12. In the Foreword to the 1956 second edition of his lectures, Jaspers endeavoured to correct the popular view that, like Heidegger or Sartre, he, too, was an existentialist thinker, *PE*, pp. 45f. He repeated his critique in an interesting introduction to the third edition of *Philosophy* (1932) that was published in 1956.

13. *Reason*, p. 63.

14. Jaspers' critique dissolved into the meek observation that, whilst he had not disagreed entirely with Freud's work, he still objected to the therapeutic practices of psycho-analysis, *Reason*, pp. 92f. Nevertheless, in correspondence with Hannah Arendt, Jaspers avidly followed her illumination of the backdrop to the McCarthy era in which psychoanalysis was seen to play a role that led Jaspers to renew his attack on Freud, especially in an essay for Hans Gruhle's seventieth birthday. See Matthias Bormuth, *Lebensführung in der Moderne*, pp. 240–57.

15. *Reason*, p. 53.

16. FE, p. 79 (author's translation).

17. *PA*, p. 42 (author's translation).

18. Gertrud wrote to her sister-in-law (Gertrud Jaspers to Erna Dugend, Basel, 30 July 1950 [*FA*]), that an official reception, the weekend after Jaspers' lectures, was heartlessly ('ohne Herz') arranged to coincide with a local meeting of the Academy of Sciences (*Akademie der Wissenschaften*). Jaspers belonged to the Academy, but he was not invited. As a result, many of Jaspers' former colleagues in the philosophy faculty were absent from the reception. ('So fehlten die Kollegen der phil[osophischen] Fakultät fast vollständig.) Gertrud's letter implied that they returned to a frosty reception from Heidelberg's Philosophical Seminar. No names were mentioned, yet Hans-Georg Gadamer had already arrived from Leipzig University, where he had given a pro-active Rectoral address under the new Communist régime. Gadamer's Rectoral address may have been irksome to Jaspers (who later refused Walter Ulbricht's invitation for open dialogue in the context of Jaspers' debate on parliamentary democracy in the FRG and hopes for Germany unity), and, certainly, the episode strikes a chord with Gertrud's impression of Gadamer on Jaspers' seventieth birthday. See below, pp. 228 and 341.

19. Curtius's article was originally published in the Zurich edition of *Die Tat*, 2 April 1949, reported in *Die Zeit*, 28 April 1949 and reissued in the local Heidelberg paper, Ernst Robert Curtius, 'Goethe oder Jaspers?', in *Rhein–Neckar–Zeitung*, 7 May 1949.

20. Ernst Robert Curtius, 'Darf man Jaspers angreifen? (In Sachen Curtius–Jaspers)'; and 'Prof. Karl Jaspers schreibt', in *Rhein–Neckar–Zeitung*, 17 May 1949.

21. Ernst Robert Curtius, 'Goethe oder Jaspers?', in *Rhein–Neckar–Zeitung*, 7 May 1949 (author's translation).

22. 'Goethe Prize' [*LE*]. See 'Goethe-Preis 1947 für Karl Jaspers', in *Rhein–Neckar–Zeitung*,

28 August 1947. ('inmitten des Verfalls und der durch die Dämonie der Macht aufgerichteten Barbarei die Forderung des Humanen frei von allen Giften der Zeit verpflichtend erweckte und goethischem Wesen Gestalt und Wirken verlieh.')

23. '"Goethe oder Jaspers?" Zu dem Aufsatz von E. R. Curtius', in *Rhein–Neckar–Zeitung*, 10 May 1949 (author's translation).

24. Curtius argued that it was questionable for Jaspers to reject Goethe's conduct as a scientist (he restricted the matter to Goethe's polemics against Sir Isaac Newton); that Jaspers' rejection of Goethe's treatment of tragedy was considered inaccurate; and that Jaspers unfairly accused Goethe of a 'fickle nature in love'. Ernst Robert Curtius, 'Goethe oder Jaspers?', in *Rhein–Neckar–Zeitung*, 7 May 1949.

25. Fritz Mayer to Gertrud Jaspers, Tel-Aviv, 25 December 1947 [*LE*].

26. UZG, p. 565.

27. Leonardo, p. 89.

28. The laboratory scene in Goethe's *Faust* Part II, with Homunculus in dialogue with Mephistopheles, reads as a sinister sign of man's capacity to undermine his state of being.

29. E.B. Ashton's English translation deliberately omitted this element of Jaspers' original text, for the translation was commissioned, as Ashton noted 'to give only the essence of the original' (*AB*, p. v). Notwithstanding Ashton's first-rate editorial work and the virtual impossibility of his task, his difficulty was to reduce the original text, yet without simplifying the book. Ashton's commission led to many of Jaspers' careful illustrations being omitted from the English, because, as Ashton noted, Jaspers' excursions in small print were about 'specifically German controversies unknown abroad' (ibid.). Unfortunately, Ashton's omissions contained some fascinating material, such as Albert Einstein's 1955 call for a moratorium on nuclear power, the 1957 declaration of the Göttingen scientists, led by Carl Friedrich von Weizsäcker, and additions that highlighted Jaspers' understanding of scientific reasons as to why mankind possesses the capacity to destroy the planet, *AB*, pp. 268–77. This background information was also part of the scenery of Jaspers' book that mirrored his perception of the 'shipwreck' that modern man must contend with, in order to practise a new way of thinking.

30. *AB*, p. 31.

31. Ibid., p. 7.

32. Hannah Arendt, 'Dedication to Karl Jaspers' (first published in Arendt's *Sechs Essays* (1948)), in Jerome Kohn (ed.), *Hannah Arendt. Essays in Understanding 1930–1945*, pp. 212–16, here p. 216.

33. See Gregory J. Walters, 'The Role of "Conversion" (Umkehr) in the Nuclear Age: Moral-Political Dimensions of the Thought of Karl Jaspers', in *Jahrbuch der Österreichischen Karl–Jaspers–Gesellschaft*, ed. Elisabeth Salamun-Hybašek and Kurt Salamun, Innsbruck and Vienna, 2/1989, pp. 88–106.

Chapter 20   Butterflies in Sils Maria

1. T.S. Eliot 'East Coker', from *Four Quartets*, in T.S. Eliot, *Collected Poems 1909–1962*, London: Faber and Faber 1983, p. 197.

2. Schelling, p. 175.

3. Gertrud Jaspers to Erna Dugend, Basel, 5 September 1954 [*FA*].

4. Gertrud Jaspers (postcard) to parents, 23 June 1918 [*FA*].

5. Gustav Mayer, *Friedrich Engels*, Vol. 1, p. 71 (author's translation).

6. Gertrud Jaspers to Erna Dugend, 10 November 1953 [*FA*].

7. Schelling, p. 42.

8. Karl Jaspers to Erna Dugend, Basel, 29 August 1955; and Karl Jaspers to Erna Dugend, Basel, 23 January 1955 [*FA*].

9. *P1*, p. 9. E.B. Ashton's official translation of the second volume of Jaspers' *Philosophy* (1932) was *Existential Elucidation*. The selections provided by Edith Ehrlich, Leonard H. Ehrlich and George B. Pepper from *Illuminations of Existenz* are, strictly speaking, appropriate, *BW*, pp. 61–120.

10. F. W. Schelling, *Philosophie der Kunst*, §73 on 'voice' and 'sound' as the organ of the inner movements of the soul, in *Werke*, Vol. 3, ed. Manfred Schröter, pp. 375–507.

11. Karl Jaspers to Ella Mayer, Basel, 25 February 1953 [*FA*]. ('Ich glaube, ich weiß über mein Tun ein wenig besser Bescheid als vorher.')

12. Ernst Mayer, 'Philosophie und Philosophische Logik bei Jaspers', in OH, pp. 63–72, here, p. 68.

13. Karl Jaspers, 'Greeting of guests at luncheon on my seventieth birthday' ('Begrüßung der Gäste beim Mittagsmahl an meinem siebzigsten Geburtstag' [*LE*]).

14. Jean Grondin, *Hans-Georg Gadamer*, p. 312; Riccardo Dottori (ed.), *Hans-Georg Gadamer*, p. 129. To prevent the incident from being perceived as a *faux pas* on Jaspers' part, Gertrud had attempted to welcome Gadamer as an old friend, not just as a replacement for Jaspers in Heidelberg. In her detailed description of the ceremony, including the reception of the Heidelberg delegation she explains how she had difficulty persuading the delegation to 'warm up' ('sie tauten nicht auf'). Gertrud Jaspers to Hannah Arendt, undated letter (attached to official thank-you note, Basel, February 1953 [*LE*]).

15. *P2*, 'I Myself in Communication and Historicity', pp. 25–129, here, p. 70. Jaspers appropriated Kant's distinction of intellect (*Verstand*) and reason (*Vernunft*), the antinomy that is translated in the post-war era into the political dimension of Jaspers' thinking. See Reiner Wiehl, 'Jaspers' Bestimmung des Überpolitischen', in *Karl Jaspers – Philosophie und Politik*, ed. Reiner Wiehl and Dominic Kaegi, pp. 81–96, here pp. 81f.

16. Karl Jaspers to Erna Dugend, Heidelberg, 20 April 1941 [*FA*].

17. Karl Jaspers to parents, Sils, 31 July 1902 [*FA*]. ('Auf den Wiesen im Tal sind viele Blumen und Schmetterlinge. Letztere sind in wunderschönen Farben so zahlreich vorhanden, dass ich sie mal sammeln möchte. Hier kann ich nun nichts bekommen als ein Schmetterlingsnetz; wenn ich mal nach St. Moritz fahre, auch wohl eine Flüssigkeit, um die Tiere zu töten.')

18. Karl Jaspers to parents, Sils Maria, 9 August 1902 [*FA*].

19. Immanuel Kant, *Critique of Pure Reason*, B 295. See also Charles Wallraff, *Karl Jaspers*, p. 41.

20. *Wisdom*, p. 130 (author's amendments to translation).

Chapter 21   'Child Hannah'

1. HA/KJ, Letter 95, Basel, 28 December 1949, p. 143.
2. Arendt's doctoral thesis was recently reissued in a highly accessible English translation that Arendt had partially prepared before her death in 1974. This critical edition of Arendt's dissertation provides details of her revisions by comparison with the original German manuscript, see Hannah Arendt, *Love and Saint Augustine*. Elisabeth Young-Bruehl's synopsis of Arendt's dissertation may have added credibility to the prevailing view that Heidegger's philosophy was a key influence for Arendt, by following Arendt's perception of Jaspers' thought as 'spatial', as opposed to the 'temporal' tracing of Heidegger's work. See Elisabeth Young-Bruehl, *Hannah Arendt*, especially 'Arendt's Doctoral Dissertation. A Synopsis', pp. 490–500, here p. 490.
3. HA/KJ, Letter 2 (footnote), p. 689 (author's amendment to translation).
4. Ibid., p. 690.
5. Hannah Arendt, 'Karl Jaspers: A Laudatio' trans. Clara and Richard Winston, in *Men in Dark Times*, p. 79.
6. *P1*, p. 47.
7. *P1*, p. 84.
8. Ernst Mayer, 'Philosophie und Philosophische Logik bei Jaspers', in OH, p. 68.
9. Ibid., p. 63.
10. Dolf Sternberger and Ludwig Curtius each emphasized the surprising quality of Jaspers' high-pitched voice. Dolf Sternberger, 'Karl Jaspers (1883–1969)', in Wilhelm Doerr, *et al.* (eds), *Semper Apertus*, Vol. III, pp. 285–98; and Ludwig Curtius, 'Erinnerungen an den Freund', in *Rhein–Neckar–Zeitung*, 22/23 February 1958.
11. HA/KJ, Letter 123, Paris, 17 April 1952, p. 181.
12. Hans Saner recorded how Jaspers lived in considerable modesty, not daring to apply for assistance to employ more than one research assistant. Hans Saner, *Karl Jaspers*, pp. 57f.
13. Gertrud Jaspers to Hannah Arendt, Basel, 11 November 1955 [*LE*].
14. HA/KJ, Letter 128, Basel, 9 July 1952, p. 185.
15. The question of Arendt's independence from Heidegger was an underlying issue of the first letter that she wrote to Heidegger, after their Freiburg reunion, early February 1950. HA/MH, Letter 48, 9 February 1950, pp. 75–7. Heidegger briefly acknowledged receipt of the English edition of Arendt's book, ibid., Letters 73 and 74, pp. 125–9.
16. Karl Jaspers, *Geleitwort*, in Hannah Arendt, *Elemente und Ursprünge Totaler Herrschaft*, Frankfurt am Main: Europäische Verlagsanstalt 1955.
17. HA/KJ, Letter 100, Basel, 20 April 1950, p. 148.
18. FW, p. 110 (author's translation).
19. Ella Mayer to Erna Dugend, Woerden, 4 September 1960 [*FA*]. ('In Basel war [...] „der Teufel los".')
20. Ella Mayer to Erna Dugend, Woerden, 4 September 1960 [*FA*].
21. Willy Brandt, the brainchild of *Ostpolitik* acknowledged the relevance of Jaspers' thinking in a foreword for the new edition of Jaspers' book that was released after German unification in 1990.
22. WBR, p. 21.
23. Antwort, p. 189. Tantzen had shown Jaspers and Gertrud round the parliament

chamber in the German Reichstag during one of their visits to Gertrud's family in Berlin, Gertrud Jaspers to parents, Berlin, 2 October 1929 [*FA*].

24. Jaspers' personal copy of the first edition of Arendt's report (published in English in 1963), shows detailed annotation in the introductory sections on so-called Jewish *Mischehen*, the January 1942 Wannsee Conference (Chapter Six, 'The Final Solution: Killing', which included material about deportations from Holland) and, perhaps most significantly, the penultimate chapter, 'Evidence and Witnesses'. Indeed, Jaspers commented on the final two sentences of the following excerpt from a German physician on the Russian front: 'The totalitarian state lets its opponents disappear in silent anonymity. It is certain that anyone who had dared to suffer death rather than silently tolerate the crime would have sacrificed his life in vain. This is not to say that such a sacrifice would have been morally meaningless. It would only have been practically useless' (Hannah Arendt, *Eichmann in Jerusalem*, p. 211). Here Jaspers wrote in the margin: 'Welches Urteil liegt darin? Wo ist die Grenze der Anwesenheit? Nirgends auf der Erde!' ('What judgement lies in that assertion? Where is the limit of being present? Nowhere on earth!', author's translation.) A similar section was also underlined in Jaspers' German copy of Arendt's text that appeared one year later. Indeed, the similarities between Jaspers' notes on both editions show not only his intense scrutiny of Arendt's achievement which he planned to develop into a book about her report, but, also, that his lack of confidence about the English language was a thing of the past.

25. HA/KJ, Letter 341, Basel, 16 November 1963, p. 531 (author's minor amendment to translation).

26. Jaspers' interviews were with Francois Bondy (1961) and Peter Wyss (1965), in P, pp. 101–21.

27. HA/KJ, Letter 276, Basel, January 3, 1961, pp. 420f.

28. Hannah Arendt, *The Origins of Totalitarianism*, p. ix.

29. *P3*, p. 208 (author's amendments to translation).

30. Karl Jaspers to parents, Heidelberg, 23 April 1928 [*FA*]. ('Vielleicht kommt er, wenn Ihr hier seid, um Furtwängler zu hören. Papa würde sich, glaube ich, mit ihm verstehen. Er ist ganz in seiner Heimat verwurzelt und naturnah. Sein Schönstes ist die „Hütte", die er sich hoch am Berge gebaut hat. Von da sieht er über den ganzen Schwarzwald auf die Alpenkette.')

31. Jaspers' parents stayed in Heidelberg in 1929 to listen to Furtwängler's concerts.

32. Karl Jaspers to Ernst Mayer, Heidelberg, 27 September 1931 [*LE*].

33. Karl Jaspers to parents, Heidelberg, 2 October 1927 [*FA*]. For Jaspers' original letter, see the Appendix.

34. *GP2Cusa*, p. 120.

35. Karl Jaspers, senior to Gertrud Jaspers, Oldenburg, 24 February 1912 [*FA*]. ('Ich freue mich sehr, dass Du dies alte Möbel, für welches ich Pietäts-Gefühle habe, schätzt, und ich habe es Dir von Herzen gerne überlassen.') See SW, p. 56.

36. Gertrud Jaspers to Hannah Arendt, 26 February 1969 [*LE*]. ('Karl gestorben mez. 13.43. Trude.')

Selected Bibliography

Further Reading about Karl Jaspers

Arendt, Hannah, *Karl Jaspers, Wahrheit, Freiheit und Friede. (Reden zur Verleihung des Friedenpreises des Deutschen Buchhandels 1958)*, Munich: Piper 1958.

——, 'Karl Jaspers: A Laudatio', trans. Clara and Richard Winston, in *Men in Dark Times*, New York, San Diego and London: Harcourt Brace 1995, pp. 71–80.

——, 'What is Existential Philosophy?', in Jerome Kohn (ed.), *Hannah Arendt. Essays in Understanding 1930–1945*, New York, San Diego and London: Harcourt Brace 1993, pp.163–87.

Berrios, G.E., 'Phenomenology and Psychopathology: was there ever a Relationship?', in *Comprehensive Psychiatry*, 34/4, July/August 1993, pp. 213–20.

Bormuth, Matthias, *Lebensführung in der Moderne. Karl Jaspers und die Psychoanalyse*, Stuttgart: Fromann-Holzboog 2002.

Burkard, Franz-Peter, *Ethische Existenz bei Karl Jaspers*, Würzburg: Königshausen & Neumann 1982.

Carr, Godfrey R., *Karl Jaspers as an Intellectual Critic*, Frankfurt am Main, Bern and New York: Peter Lang 1983.

di Cesare, Donatella, *Die Sprache in der Philosophie von Karl Jaspers*, Tübingen and Basel: Francke 1996.

Drescher, Wilhelmine, *Erinnerungen an Karl Jaspers in Heidelberg*, Meisenheim: Anton Hain 1975.

Ehrlich, Leonard H., *Philosophy as Faith*, Amherst: University of Massachusetts Press 1995.

Gens, Jean-Claude, *Karl Jaspers. Biographie*, Paris: Bayard 2003.

Grieder, Alfons, 'Karl Jaspers and the Quest for Philosophic Truth', in *Journal of the British Society for Phenomenology*, 17/1, January 1986, pp. 17–35.

Hersch, Jeanne, *Karl Jaspers. Eine Einführung in sein Werk*, Munich: Piper 1990.

Hersch, Jeanne, Jan Milic Lochman and Reiner Wiehl (eds), *Karl Jaspers. Philosoph, Arzt, politischer Denker*, Munich and Zurich: Piper 1986.

Horn, Hermann (ed.), *Karl Jaspers: Was ist Erziehung?*, Munich: Deutscher Taschenbuch 1981.

Kadereit, Ralf, *Karl Jaspers und die Bundesrepublik Deutschland. Politische Gedanken eines Philosophen*, Paderborn, Munich, Vienna and Zurich: Schöningh 1999.

Kaegi, Dominic, 'Was ist metaphysische Schuld?', in Ludwig Pohlmann (ed.), *Selbstorganisation, Jahrbuch für Komplexität in den Natur-, Sozial- und Geisteswissenschaften*, Vol. 10, 1999, Berlin: Duncker & Humblot 2000, pp. 37–59.

Kapferer, Norbert, 'Das Philosophische Vorspiel zum Kalten Krieg. Die Jaspers–Lukács–Kontroverse in Genf 1946', in Elisabeth Salamun-Hybašek and Kurt Salamun (eds), *Jahrbuch der Österreichischen Karl–Jaspers–Gesellschaft*, 6/1993, Innsbruck and Vienna: Studienverlag, pp. 79–106.

Leonhard, Joachim-Felix (ed.), *Karl Jaspers in seiner Heidelberger Zeit*, Heidelberg: Heidelberger Verlagsanstalt 1983.

Lichtigfeld, Adolph, 'Jaspers in English: A Failure not of Communication but rather of Interpretation', in *Philosophy and Phenomenological Research*, XLI (1980), pp. 126–222.

——, *Aspects of Jaspers' Philosophy*, Pretoria: Communications of University of South Africa 1971.

Mann, Golo, 'Karl Jaspers', in *Erinnerungen und Gedanken*, Frankfurt am Main: Fischer 1991, pp. 293–332.

Mayer, Ernst, 'Philosophie und Philosophische Logik bei Jaspers', in Klaus Piper (ed.), *Offener Horizont. Festschrift für Karl Jaspers*, Munich: Piper 1953, pp. 63–72.

Olson, Alan M., *Transcendence and Hermeneutics: An Interpretation of the Philosophy of Karl Jaspers*, The Hague, Boston and London: Martinus Nijhoff 1979.

Paprotny, Thorsten, *Politik als Pflicht. Zur politischen Philosophie von Max Weber und Karl Jaspers*, Frankfurt am Main, Berlin, Bern, New York, Paris and Vienna: Peter Lang 1996.

Piper, Klaus and Hans Saner eds, *Erinnerungen an Karl Jaspers*, Munich: Piper 1974.

Putscher, Marielene, 'Jaspers und van Gogh: oder über Krankheit und Kunst', in *Janus*, 67/1980, pp. 157–69.

Ricoeur, Paul, *Gabriel Marcel et Karl Jaspers. Philosophie du Mystère et Philosophie du Paradoxe*, Paris: Éditions du Temps de Présent 1947.

Rosa, Renato de, 'Der Neubeginn der Universität 1945. K.H. Bauer und Karl Jaspers', in Wilhelm Doerr, *et al.* (eds), *Semper Apertus* (Sechshundert Jahre Ruprecht-Karls-Universität Heidelberg 1386–1986, Festschrift in sechs Bänden), Vol. III: *Das Zwanzigste Jahrhundert 1918–1985*, Berlin, Heidelberg, New York and Tokyo: Springer 1985, pp. 544–68.

——, 'Politische Akzente im Leben eines Philosophen', in Renato de Rosa (ed.), *Karl Jaspers. Erneuerung der Universität. Reden und Schriften 1945/46*, Heidelberg: Lambert Schneider 1986, pp. 301–423.

Sahm, August, 'Die Persönlichkeit und das Werk von Karl Jaspers', in *Jaspers als Blickpunkt für neue Einsichten*, 1/1952, ed. August Sahm and Richard Wisser, Worms: Erich Norberg 1952, pp. 9–20.

Salamun, Kurt, *Karl Jaspers*, Munich: C.H. Beck 1985.

Salamun, Kurt ed., *Philosophie, Erziehung, Universität. Zu Karl Jaspers Bildungs- und Erziehungsphilosophie*, Frankfurt am Main: Peter Lang 1995.

Saner, Hans, *Karl Jaspers mit Selbstzeugnissen und Bilddokumenten*, Hamburg: Rowohlt 1991 (first edition 1970).

——, 'Zu Karl Jaspers' Nachlaß. Ein vorläufiger Bericht. (1969/71)', in Hans Saner (ed.), *Karl Jaspers in der Diskussion*, Munich and Zurich: Piper 1973, pp. 449–63.

——, 'Zur Dialektik von Einsamkeit und Kommunikation bei Karl Jaspers', in Elisabeth Salamun-Hybašek and Kurt Salamun (eds), *Jahrbuch der Österreichischen Karl–Jaspers–Gesellschaft*, 1/1988, Vienna: Studienverlag, pp. 53–67.

——, *Karl Jaspers. Denkwege. Ein Lesebuch*, Munich and Zurich: Piper 1983.

——, 'Jaspers's "Theses" on the Question of University Rejuvenation (1933). A Critical Comparison with Heidegger's "Rectorial Address"', in Richard Wisser and Leonard H. Ehrlich (eds), *Karl Jaspers. Philosopher among Philosophers (Philosoph unter Philosophen)*, pp. 139–52.

Schilpp, Paul Arthur (ed.), *The Philosophy of Karl Jaspers*, (Library of Living

Philosophers), Illinois: Open Court 1981.

Schüßler, Werner, *Karl Jaspers zur Einführung*, Hamburg: Junius 1995.

Stelzer, Petra, *Ästhetik aus existentieller Erfahrung. Versuch einer anthropologischen Kunsterklärung*, Frankfurt am Main: Peter Lang 1995.

Sternberger, Dolf, 'Was Wir von Jaspers gelernt haben. Zu seinem 70. Geburtstag', in *Die Gegenwart*, 28 February 1953, pp. 138f.

——, 'Karl Jaspers (1883–1969)', in Wilhelm Doerr, *et al.* (eds), *Semper Apertus*, Vol. III: *Das Zwanzigste Jahrhundert 1918–1985*, Berlin, Heidelberg, New York and Tokyo: Springer 1985, pp. 285–98.

Veauthier, Frank Werner (ed.), *Karl Jaspers zu Ehren. Symposium aus Anlaß seines 100. Geburtstags*, Heidelberg: Carl Winter 1986.

Wahl, Jean, *La pensée de l'existence*, Paris : Flammarion 1951.

Wallraff, Charles, 'Jaspers in English: A Failure of Communication', in *Philosophy and Phenomenological Research*, XXXVII (1977), pp. 537–48.

——, *Karl Jaspers. An Introduction to His Philosophy*, Princeton: Princeton University Press 1970.

Walters, Gregory J. (ed.), *The Tasks of Truth. Essays on Karl Jaspers' Idea of the University*, Frankfurt am Main: Peter Lang 1996.

Warnock, Mary, *Existentialism*, Oxford and New York: Oxford University Press 1970.

Wiehl, Reiner, 'Die Heidelberger Tradition der Philosophie zwischen Kantianismus und Hegelianismus. Kuno Fischer, Wilhelm Windelband, Heinrich Rickert', in Wilhelm Doerr *et al.* (eds), *Semper Apertus*, Vol. II: *Das Neunzehnte Jahrhundet 1803–1918*, Berlin, Heidelberg, New York and Tokyo: Springer 1985, pp. 413–35.

——, 'Moralische Verantwortung – privat und öffentlich. Überlegungen im Anschluß an Karl Jaspers' Essay über „Die Schuldfrage"', in Maria-Sibylla Lotter (ed.), *Normenbegründung und Normenentwicklung in Gesellschaft und Recht*, Baden-Baden: Nosmos 1999, pp. 96–106.

——, 'Karl Jaspers' Psychologie der Weltanschauungen zwischen Metaphysik und Erfahrung', in Reiner Wiehl, *Subjektivität und System*, Frankfurt am Main: Suhrkamp 2000, pp. 271–92.

Wiehl, Reiner and Dominic Kaegi (eds), *Karl Jaspers – Philosophie und Politik*, Heidelberg: Universitätsverlag C. Winter 1999.

Wiggins, Osborne P. and Michael Alan Schwartz, 'Edmund Husserl's influence on Karl Jaspers's Phenomenology', in *Philosophy, Psychiatry, Psychology*, 4, No. 1, March 1997, pp. 15–36.

Wisser, Richard, *Karl Jaspers: Philosophie in der Bewährung*, Würzburg: Königshausen & Neumann 1995.

——, 'Karl Jaspers: The Person and His Cause, Not the Person or his Cause', in: *International Philosophical Quarterly*, XXXVI, 4 December 1996, pp. 414–27.

——, 'Karl Jaspers: Die Philosophie soll nicht abdanken – Am wenigsten heute', in *Der blaue Reiter. Journal für Philosophie*, 2/1996, pp. 89–92.

Wisser, Richard and Leonard H. Ehrlich (eds), *Karl Jaspers Today. Philosophy at the Threshold of the Future*, Washington D.C. and London: University Press of America 1988.

——, *Karl Jaspers. Philosopher among Philosophers. (Philosoph unter Philosophen)*, Würzburg: Königshausen & Neumann 1993.

——, *Karl Jaspers. Philosophy on the Way to 'World Philosophy'. (Philosophie auf dem Weg zur „Weltphilosophie")*, Würzburg: Königshausen & Neumann 1998.

——, *Karl Jaspers's Philosophy: Rooted in the Present, Paradigm for the Future. (Karl Jaspers' Philosophie: Gegenwärtigkeit und Zukunft)*, Würzburg: Königshausen & Neumann 2003.

Young-Bruehl, Elisabeth, *Freedom and Karl Jaspers's Philosophy*, New Haven and London: Yale University Press 1981.

Works of Historical Interest

Baum, Marie, *Rückblick auf Mein Leben*, Heidelberg: F. H. Kerle 1950.

Blau, Bruno, *Das Ausnahmerecht für die Juden in Deutschland 1933–1945*, Düsseldorf: Allgemeine Wochenzeitung der Juden in Deutschland 1965.

Buselmaier, Karin, Dietrich Harth and Christian Jansen, *Auch eine Geschichte der Universität Heidelberg*, Mannheim: Quadrat 1985.

Curtius, Ernst Robert, *Deutscher Geist in Gefahr*, Stuttgart: Deutscher Verlagsanstalt 1932.

Domarus, Max (ed.), *Hitler Reden und Proklomationen 1932–1945*, 4 Vols, Munich: Süddeutscher Verlag 1965.

Fischer, Kuno, *Die Schicksale der Universität Heidelberg* (Festrede zur 500. Jahr Feier der Ruperto Carola. Gehalten am 4. August 1886), Heidelberg: Winter 1903.

Friedländer, Saul, *Nazi Germany and the Jews (The Years of Persecution 1933 – 1939)*, New York: HarperCollins 1997.

Glockner, Hermann, *Heidelberger Bilderbuch*, Bonn: Bouvier 1969.

Gottschalk, Paul, 'Memoiren eines Antiquars I–IV', in *Börsenblatt für den Deutschen Buchhandel* (Frankfurt), No. 99/1965, pp. 2660–4, No. 7/1966, pp. 100–10, No. 15/1966, pp. 241–8 and No. 22/1966, pp. 477–85.

Graml, Hermann, *Kristallnacht*, Munich: Deutscher Taschenbuch 1988.

Green, Martin, *The Richthofen Sisters*, London: Collins 1973.

Henk, Emil, *Die Tragödie des 20. Juli 1944. Ein Beitrag zur politischen Vorgeschichte*, Heidelberg: Adolf Rausch 1946.

Hilberg, Raul, *The Destruction of the European Jews*, 3 Vols, New York and London: Holmes & Meier 1985.

Kershaw, Ian, *Hitler*, 2 Vols, (*1889–1936: Hubris; 1936–1945: Nemesis*), London: Penguin 2001.

Klibansky, Raymond (ed.), Michael Buselmeier, *Erlebte Geschichte erzählt 1994–1997*, Heidelberg: Wunderhorn 2000.

Löwith, Karl, *My Life in Germany Before and After 1933: A Report*, trans. Elizabeth King, Illinois: University of Illinois Press 1994.

Luxemburg, Rosa, *Politische Schriften I-III*, ed. Wolfgang Abendroth, Ossip K. Flechthein and Iring Fetscher, Frankfurt am Main: Europäische Verlagsanstalt 1966–68.

Maas, Hermann and Gustav Radbruch (eds), *Den Unvergessenen. Opfer des Wahns 1933–1945*, Heidelberg: Lambert Schneider 1952.

Mann, Golo, *The History of Germany since 1789*, trans. Marian Jackson, London: Pimlico 1996.

Martin, Bernd (ed.), *Martin Heidegger und das 'Dritte Reich'*, Darmstadt: Wissenschaftliche Buchgesellschaft 1989.

Mayer, Gustav, *Friedrich Engels. Eine Biographie*, 2 Vols, Cologne: Kiepenhauer & Witsch 1932 (first edition 1919).

——, 'Aus der Geschichte der Familie Ascher Mayer', in *Beilage zum Uckermärkischen Kurier*, 27 July 1924.

——, *Erinnerungen. Vom Journalisten zum Historiker der deutschen Arbeiterbewegung*, ed. Gottfried Niedhart, Hildesheim and Zurich: Olms 1993.

Mussgnug, Dorothee, *Die vertriebenen Heidelberger Dozenten. Zur Geschichte der Ruprechts-Karls-Universität nach 1933*, Heidelberg: Carl Winter 1988.

Naumann, Friedrich, *Mitteleuropa*, Berlin: Reimer 1915.

Niedhart, Gottfried, 'Gustav Mayer. Identitätskonflikte eines deutschen Juden an der Wende vom 19. zum 20. Jahrhundert: Gustav Mayer zwischen jüdischer Herkunft und ungewisser deutscher Zukunft', in *Tel Aviver Jahrbuch für Deutsche Geschichte 1991*, ed. Institut für Deutsche Geschichte, University of Tel Aviv: Bleicher, pp. 315–26.

——, 'Mayer versus Meyer. Gustav Mayers gescheiterte Habilitation in Berlin 1917/1918', in Armin Kohle and Frank Engehausen (eds), *Zwischen Wissenschaft und Politik. Festschrift für Eike Wolgast zum 65. Geburtstag*, Stuttgart: Franz Steiner 2001, pp. 329–44.

——, *Deutsche Geschichte 1918–1933*, Stuttgart: Kohlhammer 1996.

Nipperdey, Thomas, *Deutsche Geschichte*, 3 Vols, Munich: C.H. Beck 1998.

Prinzhorn, Hans, *Bildnerei der Geisteskranken*, ed. Gerhard Roth, New York and Vienna: Springer 1997 (first edition 1922).

Radbruch, Gustav, *Der innere Weg. Aufriss meines Lebens*, Stuttgart: Koehler 1951.

Raff, Dieter, *Deutsche Geschichte*, Munich: Heyne 2001.

Sauer, Paul (ed.), *Dokumente über die Verfolgung der jüdischen Bürger in Baden-Württemberg durch das nationalsozialistische Regime 1933–1945*, 2 Vols, Stuttgart: Kohlhammer 1966.

Schneeberger, Guido, *Nachlese zu Heidegger. Dokumente zu seinem Leben und Denken*, Bern: Suhr 1962.

Schrader, Bärbel and Jürgen Schebera, *Die „Goldenen" Zwanziger Jahre. Kunst und Kultur der Weimarer Republik*, Leipzig: Edition Leipzig 1987.

Sombart, Nicolaus, *Rendezvous mit dem Weltgeist. Heidelberger Reminiszenzen 1945–1951*, Frankfurt am Main: Fischer 2000.

Waldmüller, Monika, *Die Wandlung, Eine Monatschrift*, Marbach am Neckar: Deutsche Schillergesellschaft 1988.

Walk, Joseph, *Das Sonderrecht für die Juden im NS-Staat*, Heidelberg: C. F. Müller 1996.

Weckbecker, Arno, *Die Judenverfolgung in Heidelberg 1933–1945*, Heidelberg: Müller 1985.

Weisert, Hermann, *Die Rektoren der Ruperto Carola zu Heidelberg und die Dekane ihrer Fakultäten 1386–1968*, Heidelberg: Zeitschrift der Vereinigung der Freunde der Studentenschaft der Universität Heidelberg 1968.

Weiss, Georg (ed.), *Albert Fraenkel. Arzt und Forscher*, Mannheim: Boehringer 1964.

Wolgast, Eike, 'Das bürgerliche Zeitalter 1803–1918', in Wilhelm Doerr *et al.* (eds), *Semper Apertus*, Vol. II: *Das Neunzehnte Jahrhundert 1803–1918*, Berlin, Heidelberg, New York and Tokyo: Springer 1985, pp. 1–31.

Wolgast, Eike and Peter Claassen (eds), *Kleine Geschichte der Universität Heidelberg*, Berlin, Heidelberg and New York: Springer 1983.

Other Related Works

Adorno, Theodor, W., *Negative Dialektik. Jargon der Eigentlichkeit*, in Rolf Tiedemann (ed.), *Gesammelte Schriften*, Vol. 6, Frankfurt am Main: Suhrkamp 1973.

Arendt, Hannah, *The Origins of Totalitarianism*, New York: Harcourt Brace 1951.

——, *The Human Condition*, Chicago and London: Chicago University Press 1958.

——, *The Life of the Mind*, 2 Vols, New York, San Diego and London: Harcourt Brace 1978.

——, *Eichmann in Jerusalem. A Report on the Banality of Evil*, Harmondsworth: Penguin 1994.

——, 'Organized Guilt and Universal Responsibility', in Jerome Kohn (ed.), *Essays in Understanding 1930–1945*, New York, San Diego and London: Harcourt Brace 1993, pp. 121–32.

——, *Love and Saint Augustine*, ed. Joanna Vecchiarelli Scott and Judith Chelius Stark, Chicago and London: University of Chicago Press 1996.

Aristotle, *The Complete Works of Aristotle*, ed. W.D. Ross, Oxford: Clarendon Press 1966–.

Baumgarten, Eduard, *Max Weber: Werk und Person*, Tübingen: Mohr 1964.

Benhabib, Seyla, *The Reluctant Modernism of Hannah Arendt*, London: Sage 1996.

Brandes, Georg, *Friedrich Nietzsche* (reprint of 1914 edition), New York: Haskell House 1972.

Derrida, Jacques, *La Vérité en Peinture*, Paris: Flammarion 1978.

Descartes, *The Philosophical Works*, 2 Vols, trans. Elizabeth S. Haldane and G.R.T. Ross, Cambridge: Cambridge University Press 1978/9.

Dottori, Riccardo (ed.), *Hans-Georg Gadamer. Die Lektion des Jahrhunderts*, Münster: LIT 2002.

Ettinger, Elzbieta, *Hannah Arendt, Martin Heidegger*, New Haven and London: Yale University Press 1995.

Feilchenfeldt, Walter, *Vincent van Gogh & Paul Cassirer, Berlin. The Reception of Van Gogh in Germany from 1901 to 1914*, Cahier Vincent 2, Rijksmuseum/ Vincent van Gogh, Vincent van Gogh Foundation, Amsterdam.

Fischer, Kuno, *Logik und Metaphysik der Wissenschaftslehre*, ed. Hans-Georg Gadamer, Heidelberg: Manutius 1998.

Freud, Sigmund, *Gesammelte Werke*, ed. Anna Freud, *et al.*, Frankfurt am Main: S. Fischer 1969–73.

Gadamer, Hans-Georg, *Gesammelte Werke*, 10 Vols, Tübingen: Mohr 1986.

——, *Heidegger's Ways*, trans. John W. Stanley, New York: New York University Press 1994.

Galindo, Martha Zapata, *Triumph des Willens zur Macht: Zur Nietzsche-Rezeption im NS-Staat*, Hamburg: Argument 1995.

Goethe, Johann Wolfgang von, *Elective Affinities*, trans. R. J. Hollingdale, Harmondsworth: Penguin 1971.

——, *Werke* (Hamburg Edition in 14 Vols), ed. Erich Trunz, Munich: Beck 1981.

Görner, Rüdiger, *Nietzsches Kunst, Annäherung an einen Denkartisten*, Frankfurt am Main: Insel Verlag 2000.

Grondin, Jean, *Hans-Georg Gadamer. Eine Biographie.* Tübingen: Mohr 1999.

Gundolf, Friedrich, *Shakespeare und der deutsche Geist*, Berlin: Georg Bondi 1911.

Habermas, Jürgen, *Philosophish-politische Profile*, Frankfurt am Main: Suhrkamp 1981.

Hegel, Georg Friedrich Wilhelm, *Phenomenology of the Spirit*, trans. A.V. Miller, with analysis by J.N. Findlay, Oxford, New York, Toronto, Melbourne: Oxford University Press 1977.

——, *Gesammelte Werke*, ed. Wolfgang Bonsiepen, *et al.*, Hamburg: Felix Meiner 1978–.

Heidegger, Martin, *Martin Heidegger: Nietzsche I-II*, Pfullingen: Neske 1961.

——, *Being and Time*, trans. John Macquarrie and Edward Robinson, New York: Harper & Row 1962.

——, *The Origin of the Work of Art*, in Martin Heidegger, *Poetry, Language, Thought*, trans. Albert Hofstadter, New York, Hagerstown, San Francisco and London: Harper & Row 1971, pp. 15–87.

——, *Nietzsche: Der Wille zur Macht als Kunst*, Collected Works, Vol. II/43, ed. Bernd Heimbüchel, Frankfurt am Main: Vittorio Klostermann 1985.

——, *Schelling: Vom Wesen der menschlichen Freiheit (1809)*, Collected Works, Vol. II/42, ed. Ingrid Schüßler, Frankfurt am Main: Vittorio Klostermann 1988.

——, *Nietzsches Metaphysik*, Collected Works, Vol. II/50, ed. Petra Jaeger, Frankfurt am Main: Vittorio Klostermann 1990.

——, *Kant und das Problem der Metaphysik*, ed. Friedrich Wilhelm von Herrmann, Collected Works, Vol. I/3, Frankfurt am Main: Vittorio Klostermann 1991.

——, *Nietzsche*, 4 Vols, ed. David Farrell Krell, trans. Joan Stambaugh, David Farrell Krell and Frank A. Capuzzi, San Francisco: HarperCollins 1991.

——, *Bremer und Freiburger Vorträge*, Collected Works, Vol. II/79, ed. Petra Jaeger, Frankfurt am Main: Vittorio Klostermann 1994.

——, *Reden und andere Zeugnisse eines Lebensweges 1910–1976*, Collected Works, Vol. I/16, ed. Hermann Heidegger, Frankfurt am Main: Vittorio Klostermann 2000.

Hersch, Jeanne, *Das Philosophische Staunen*, trans. Frieder Fischer and Cajetan Freund, Munich: Piper 2000.

Hölderlin, Friedrich, *Sämtliche Werke und Briefe*, ed. Michael Knaupp, Darmstadt: Wissenschaftliche Buchgesellschaft 1998.

Humboldt, Wilhelm von, 'Über die innere und äussere Organisation der höheren wissenschaftlichen Anstalten in Berlin' (1810?), in *Gesammelte Schriften X*, ed. Bruno Gebhardt, Berlin: Behr 1903, pp. 250–60.

——, *Werke*, 5 Vols, ed. Andreas Flintner and Klaus Giel, Darmstadt: Wissenschaftliche Buchgesellschaft 1960–81.

Hume, David, *The Philosophical Works*, ed. T.H. Green and T.H. Grose, 4 Vols, Aalen: Scientia 1964.

Husserl, Edmund, *Logische Untersuchungen*, in *Gesammelte Werke XVIII–XIX/1–2*, ed. Elmar Holenstein and Ursula Panzer, The Hague: Martinus Nijhoff 1975/84.

James, William, *Pragmatism*, London and Cambridge, Mass.: Harvard University Press 1975.

Jantz, Curt Paul, *Friedrich Nietzsche. Biographie*, 3 Vols, Munich and Vienna: Carl Hanser 1978/9.

Kant, Immanuel, *Werke*, ed. Wilhelm Weischedel, Frankfurt am Main: Insel 1956–64.

——, *Critique of Pure Reason*, trans. Norman Kemp Smith, London: Macmillan 1982.

Kaufmann, Walter, *Existentialism: From Dostoevsky to Sartre*, London: Meridian 1988.

Kierkegaard, *Gesammelte Werke*, Jena: Diederichs 1911.

Klages, Ludwig, *Graphologie I*, in *Gesammelte Schriften*, Vols 7–8, ed. Ernst Frauchiger, Gerhard Funke, Karl J. Groffmann, Robert Heiss and Hans Eggert Schröder, Bonn: Bouvier 1968.

Lask, Emil, *Gesammelte Schriften I–II*, ed. Eugen Herrigel, Tübingen: Mohr 1923.

Lessing, Gotthold Ephraim, *Werke und Briefe*, ed. Wilfried Barner, Frankfurt am Main: Deutscher Klassiker Verlag 1985–.

Löwith, Karl, *Von Hegel zu Nietzsche*, (*Sämtliche Schriften 4*), Stuttgart: JB Metzler 1988.

Lukács, Georg, *Die Zerstörung der Vernunft*, Berlin: Aufbau 1954.

——, *Selected Correspondence 1902–1920*, ed. and trans. Judith Marcus and Zoltán Tar, Budapest: Corvina 1986.

Mann, Thomas, *Buddenbrooks. Verfall einer Familie*, Frankfurt am Main: Fischer 1951.

——, *Betrachtungen eines Unpolitischen*, Frankfurt am Main: Fischer Taschenbuch 2002.

Nietzsche, Friedrich, *Werke* (Collected Works: Critical Edition), ed. Giorgio Colli and Mazzino Montinari, with Wolfgang Müller-Lauter and Karl Pestalozzi, Berlin: de Gruyter 1967–.

Pfeiffer, Ernst (ed.), *Lou Andreas Salomé. Ein Lebensbild*, Frankfurt am Main: Insel 1974.

——, Lou Andreas Salomé, *Friedrich Nietzsche in seinen Werken*, Frankfurt am Main and Leipzig: Insel 2000.

Plato, *The Dialogues of Plato*, 4 Vols, trans. Benjamin Jowett, Oxford: Clarendon Press 1953.

Pollock, Frederick, *Spinoza. His Life and Philosophy*, London: Duckworth 1899.

Raaflaub, Walter, *Ernst Mayer 1883–1952*, Bern, Stuttgart and Toronto: Hans Huber 1986.

Rickert, Heinrich, *Die Grenzen der naturwissenschaftlichen Begriffsbildung. Eine logische Einleitung in die historischen Wissenschaften*, Tübingen and Leipzig: Mohr 1902.

Russell, Bertrand, *History of Western Philosophy*, Routledge: London 1996.

Saner, Hans, *Macht und Ohnmacht der Symbole*, Basel: Lenos 1999.

Schelling, Friedrich Wilhelm Joseph, *Werke*, ed. Manfred Schröter, Munich: Beck 1965.

——, '*Philosophische Briefe über Dogmatismus und Kritizismus*' (1795), in *Werke*, ed. Hartmut Buchner, Wilhelm G. Jacobs and Annemarie Pieper, Stuttgart: Frommann 1982.

Schiller, Friedrich, *Werke*, ed. Julius Petersen and Norbert Oellers, Weimar: Böhlau 1943–.

Schopenhauer, Arthur, *The World as Will and Representation*, 2 Vols, trans. E.F.J. Payne, New York: Dover 1969.

Shakespeare, William, *The Complete Works*, ed. Stanley Wells and Gary Taylor, Oxford: Clarendon Press 1998.

Spinoza, Benedict de, *A Theologico-Political Treatise*, trans. R.H.M. Elwes, New York: Dover 1951.

——, *Ethics*, trans. Edwin Curley, Harmondsworth: Penguin 1996.

Thode, Henry, *Michelangelo und das Ende der Renaissance*, Vols 1–3, Berlin: Grote'sche Verlagsbuchhandlung 1902.

Van Gogh, Vincent, *The Complete Letters*, 3 Vols, London: Thames & Hudson 1988.

Vietta, Silvio (ed.), *Hans-Georg Gadamer und Silvio Vietta im Gespräch*, Munich: Fink 2002.

Weber, Marianne, *Ehefrau und Mutter in der Rechtsentwicklung*, Tübingen: Mohr 1907.

——, *Frauenfragen und Frauengedanken. Gesammelte Aufsätze*, Tübingen: Mohr 1919.

——, *Erfülltes Leben*, Heidelberg: Lambert Schneider 1946.

——, *Max Weber. Ein Lebensbild*, Heidelberg: Lambert Schneider 1950.

Weber, Max, *Gesammelte Aufsätze zur Religionssoziolgie*, Vol. 1, Tübingen: Mohr 1920.

——, *Gesammelte Politische Schriften*, ed. Marianne Weber, Munich: DreiMasken 1921.

——, *Wirtschaft und Gesellschaft*, Tübingen: Mohr 1922.

——, *Gesammelte Aufsätze zur Wissenschaftslehre*, ed. Johannes Winckelmann, Tübingen: Mohr 1973.

——, '*Wissenschaft als Beruf (1917/19). Politik als Beruf 1919*', in *Max Weber Collected Works (MWG)* Vol. 1/17, ed. Horst Baier, Rainer M. Lepsius, Wolfgang J. Mommsen, Wolfgang Schluchter and Johannes Winckelmann, Tübingen: Mohr 1992, pp. 71–111 and pp. 157–252.

Wiehl, Reiner, *Metaphysik und Erfahrung. Philosophische Essays*, Frankfurt am Main: Suhrkamp 1996.

Wolin, Richard ed., *The Heidegger Controversy. A Critical Reader*, London and Cambridge, Mass.: MIT Press 1993.

Young-Bruehl, Elisabeth, *Hannah Arendt. For Love of the World*, New Haven and London: Yale University Press 1982.

Index

References to illustrations are in italics.

Adorno, Theodor W. 335
Aeschylus 325
Aliotta, Antonio 179
Al Raschid Bey, Omar (alias Friedrich Arndt) 37
Alzheimer, Alois 64, 66–8
'archetype', the
  'idealtype', the 'objectivity', Weber's
  conception of 81, 148, 233, 235
Archimedes 210
Arendt, Hannah xix, 89, 90, 130, 159, 161, 190,
  195–7, 216, 222, 230–5, 238, 280, 281, 299, 307,
  315, 316, 324, 326, 327, 332, 334, 340–4, *Ill. 31*
Aristotle 197
Arnim, Charlotte von 103, 305
Arnim, Harry von 305
Aron, Raymond 208
Ashton, E.B. xx, 281, 283, 333, 340, 341
Augstein, Rudolf 234
Augustine, Saint 230, 342
'axial age', the 210, 211, 213, 214, 216, 338

Bach, Johann Sebastian 146
Baden, Prince Max von 113, 258
Barth, Heinrich 203
Barth, Karl 203
Bauer, Karl Heinrich 190, 192, 219, 332, 333
Baumgarten, Eduard 300, 301
Bäumler, Alfred 162
Bäumler, Prof. 14, 15, 18, 241, 284

Beckmann, Max 81
Beethoven Ludwig van 146, 148, 214, 319
Bethmann-Hollweg, Theobald von 82, 113
Beutler, Ernst 167
Binswanger, Ludwig 296
Bismarck, Prince Otto von 3–5, 89, 101, 234, 257,
  281, 305
Bleuler, Eugen 296
Bloch, Ernst 32, 84, 325
Blochmann, Elisabeth 135
Blücher, Heinrich 230
Böcklin, Arnold 16, 19, 20, 244, 285
Böhlau, Hélène 36, 37, 246, 290
Botticelli, Sandro 288
Boven, Maria van 144
Brahms, Johannes 214
Brandes, Georg 19, 285
Brandt, Willy 233, 342
Brecht, Bertolt 147
Brentano, Lujo 32
Brock, Werner 175, 176, 328
bronchiectasis xiv, xxi, 13, 15, 22, 25, 42, 116
Bultmann, Rudolf 203, 204, 335
Burckhardt, Jacob 35, 100
Busch, Frl. 7, 239, 240
Busch, Hedwig 7, 240

Calé, Walter 58, 59, 197, 248, 294, *Ill. 8*
Campenhausen, Hans Freiherr von 219

Cassirer, Paul 124, 311, 312
Cézanne, Paul 124
Chamberlain, Joseph 35
cipher 30, 212, 202, 227, 231, 237
Confucius 210
Cornelius, Karl Maria 21, *Ill. 6*
Croce, Benedetto 120
Curtius, Ernst Robert 218, 219, 220, 340, 341
Curtius, Ludwig 178, 343
Cusa, Nicholas 237

Dante Alighieri 53, 54, 293
Derrida, Jacques 311, 312
Descartes, René xv, 167, 168, 205, 327, 329, 337
Dibelius, Martin 178, 190
Dilthey, Wilhelm 65, 67, 69, 298, 314
Dix, Otto 81
Dostoevsky, Fjodor 286, 324
Drescher, Wilhelmine 178, 330, 332
Driesch, Hans xv, 117
Drost, Helen Sophie 9
Dugend, Enno 166, 228, *Ill. 16*
Dugend, Erna (née Jaspers) xx, 4, 5, 36, 92, 93, 103, 105, 106, 107, 124, 144, 166, 173, 180, 182, 192, 227, 228, 247, 265, 282, 293, 303, 305, 306, 308, 311, 313, 317, 323, 328–31, 337, 340–43, *Ills 16 and 24*
Dugend, Eugen 107, 166, 192, 264, 305, 307, 308, 311, 313, *Ill. 16*
Dugend, Herta 228
Durand-Ruel, Paul-Marie-Joseph 124, 311

Ehrlich, Edith 310, 315, 320, 335, 342
Ehrlich, Leonard H. xi, 310, 315, 320, 335, 336, 342
Eichendorff, Josef Freiherr von 30
Eichmann, Adolf 234, 344
Einstein, Albert xvii, 280, 341
Eisenhower, Dwight David 189
Eliot, T.S. 223, 341
Emmet, Thomas A. 189
Encompassing, The 152, 167, 168, 173, 182, 199, 200, 214, 216, 321
Engels, Friedrich 191, 226, 333, 342
Enlightenment, the xix, 231, 324
Erasmus, Desiderius xvi, 237
Erzberger, Matthias 112, 113, 258
'Eternal Recurrence of the Same', the 20, 160, 161, 163, 285, 326
ethics, ethical xix, 55, 56, 83, 84, 89, 93, 116, 161, 199, 200, 206, 217, 221, 294, 299, 303, 328, 335
'Existence' (*Existenz*) xviii, xx, 25, 74, 127, 132, 152, 160, 163, 167–9, 171, 199, 200, 202, 213, 215–17, 227, 231, 235, 236, 254, 287, 305, 310, 321, 335, 338, 339
existential 72

existentialist 307, 340
existentialism 324
'existential communication' 6, 228, 283
Expressionism 124, 126

Faille, J.B. de la 311
Falkenstein, General 306
Fano, Giulo 21, *Ill. 6*
Ferdinand, Francis, Archduke of Austria 98
Fichte, Johann Gottlieb 117, 226
Fischer, Kuno 31, 32, 35, 69, 287, 288, 298
Fontane, Theodor 286
Fraenkel, Albert xiv, 13–18, 21–3, 25–7, 39, 41, 42, 74, 75, 118, 151–3, 241, 242, 284, 322, 335
fraternity, student (*Burschenschaft*) 11, 28, 38, 39, 290, 291
freedom xvi, xviii, 5, 40, 62, 65, 70, 83, 123, 127, 128, 132, 154, 168, 169, 195, 200, 202, 204, 206, 207, 211, 214, 217, 218, 221, 231, 233, 234, 310, 315, 336
Freud, Sigmund 37, 65, 66, 69–72, 74, 162, 217, 296, 297, 298, 340
Friedrich III (King Friedrich I of Prussia) 55
Furtwängler, Wilhelm 235, 344

Gadamer, Hans-Georg 130, 178, 228, 280, 311, 312, 320, 340, 342
Galileo, Galilei 205, 216, 327
Gauguin, Paul 124, 125
Geiger, Afra 80, 81, 192, 254, 300
Geiler, Karl 219
George, Stefan 33, 162, 288, 289
Glockner, Hermann 33, 288
Goebbels, Joseph 234, 318
Goethe, Johann Wolfgang von xv, xvi, 5, 24, 44, 45, 53, 59, 100, 112, 134, 159, 167, 178, 198, 200, 214, 218–20, 247, 286, 287, 305, 340, 341
Göring, Hermann 173
Gottschalk, Bertha 292, 294
Gottschalk, Ernst 60, 98, 292
Gottschalk, Julia 49, 52, 53, 58, 59, 85, 98, 120, 143, 147, 156, 157, 175, 176, 197, 248, 262, 264, 292, 294, 329, *Ill. 27*
Gottschalk, Paul 60, 117, 120, 129, 143, 144, 147, 292, 308, 317, *Ill. 26*
Grabenko, Yelena 338
Grisebach, August 219
Groh, Wilhelm 317, 321
Gross, Hans xiv, 63
Gross, Otto 36
Grosz, Georges 81
Gruhle, Hans W. 62, 66, 77, 251, 295, 297, 340
guilt xvii, xxi, 83, 106, 128, 141, 142, 170–2, 190, 191, 193, 195, 201, 216, 219, 234, 306, 321, 325, 331, 332, 333, 334

collective guilt 218, 333
  metaphysical guilt 196, 197, 333, 334
Gumbel, Emil Julius 135, 314, 315
Gundolf, Elisabeth (née Salamon) 288, 289
Gundolf, Friedrich 32, 194, 288, 289, 335

Häberlin, Paul xvi, 201
Hahn, Otto xvii
Hamburger, Michael 287
Hampe, Karl 83, 304
Hartshorne, Edward 189
Haubach, Theodor 183, 332
Heddewig, Anna 106, 282, 306
Hegel, Georg Wilhelm Friedrich 69, 87, 112, 117,
  134, 215, 226, 231, 287, 297, 307, 337, 338
Heidegger, Martin xix, 126, 129–33, 135–7, 148–51,
  160–62, 175, 193, 210, 230, 232, 235, 311–16, 319,
  320, 325, 333, 338, 339, 342, *Ill. 20*
Henk, Emil 183, 189, 190, 332
Henrich, Dieter 301, 302
Hersch, Jeanne xx, 178, 179, 214, 280, 301, 302, 338
Hilberg, Raul 316–18, 331
Hindenburg, Paul von 142
Hirschberg, Henriette 55
Hitler, Adolf xvi, xvii, 89, 91, 135, 142–4, 146–50,
  152, 154, 159, 177, 178, 182, 183, 195, 197, 200, 201,
  213, 234, 302, 316, 318, 323, 332, 338
Hofmannsthal, Hugo von 151
Hölderlin (Johann Christian) Friedrich 29, 53,
  123, 287
Homer 19, 20, 210, 244
Hoops, Johannes 317
humanism 30, 116, 123, 130, 134, 135, 201, 204, 213,
  214, 217, 220, 231, 340
Humboldt, Alexander von x
Humboldt, Wilhelm von 30, 116, 133, 134, 194,
  218, 314
Husserl, Edmund 32, 66–70, 129, 130, 249, 297,
  298, 312, 313

Impressionism 123, 124, 310

Jaffé, Else (née Richthofen) 36, 85, 187, 188, 190,
  266, 300, 301, 331, 335
Janet, Pierre 65, 296, 310
Jaspers, Carl Wilhelm 4, 9, 281
Jaspers, Diedrich 8, 283
Jaspers, Enno xv, xxii, 4, 9, 24, 31, 54, 57, 59, 82,
  83, 90, 92–107, 112, 113, 146, 169–72, 247, 255–8,
  282, 293–4, 297, 303–6, 308, 327, *Ills 14, 15 and 16*
Jaspers, Fritz 3, 8, 9, 69, 117, 282
Jaspers, Gertrud (née Mayer Trude/Trudlein)
  xi, xiv–xvi, xxi, xxii, 6, 27, 33, 39, 49–61, 63,
  66, 69, 73, 74, 77, 81, 82, 84–7, 88, 90, 91, 98,
  100–2, 106, 114, 115, 117, 118, 120, 123, 129, 131,
  133, 135–7, 141, 143–9, 151, 154, 156–8, 166, 168,
  171, 172, 175–9, 181–3, 188–92, 197, 199, 200,
  201, 205, 208–14, 218, 219, 226, 230, 232–4,
  236–8, 247, 248, 250, 251, 255–60, 262, 263, 266,
  269, 270, 282, 283, 286, 288, 289, 292–300, 302,
  303, 305–10, 312, 313–19, 321–3, 328–4, *Ills 7, 9,
  11, 13, 16, 22, 23, 24, 25, 27, 28, 29 and 30*
Jaspers, Henriette (née Tantzen) xv, 3–10, 14, 15,
  17, 23, 36, 52, 61, 73–5, 79, 80, 82, 98, 100, 102–7,
  146, 157, 158, 172, 173, 179, 180, 222, 236, 242,
  248, 253, 263, 282, 283, 285, 292, 293, 294, 295,
  299, 304–7, 318, 328, 330, *Ills 2, 16 and 25*
Jaspers, Johann Friedrich 8, 9, 237
Jaspers, Karl Wilhelm, senior xv, xxi, xxii, 3–6,
  8, 9, 12–17, 21–3, 25, 28–30, 33–8, 41–5, 55–7, 60,
  61, 72–6, 78, 79, 80–82, 88, 98, 103–6, 117, 146,
  153, 160, 169, 172, 173, 179, 180, 182, 222, 228,
  235–8, 242, 243, 245, 246, 247, 248, 250, 251, 253,
  268, 281, 282, 283–5, 294, 295, 299, 302, 304,
  306, 308, 318, 329, 330, 343, *Ills 5, 16 and 25*
Jaspers, Louis 8, 9, 283
Jaspers, Louise (née Drost) 9, 282, 283
Jaspers, Martha 282
Jellinek, Georg 288
Jung, Carl Gustav 296
Jünger, Ernst 338

Kant, Immanuel xv, xxi, xxiii, 5, 20, 53, 56, 69,
  81, 96, 154, 193, 203, 205, 214, 225, 227, 229, 231,
  235, 292, 297, 298, 312, 322, 329, 341
Kaufmann, Walter 159, 323, 324, 325
Keller, Gottfried 286
Kierkegaard, Søren 101, 112, 132, 170, 202, 210,
  288, 307, 321, 337
Klages, Ludwig 33, 35, 37
Kleist, Heinrich von 58
Klemperer, Otto 147, 319
Klibansky, Raymond 176, 321
Knauss, Werner 192
Koch, Thilo 233
Kotzbue, August von 290
Kraepelin, Emil 31, 62, 67, 287, 297
Krieck, Ernst 166, 192, 326

Laird, John 328
Lask, Emil 53, 65, 81, 84, 293
'Law of the Day, The' 172, 327
Leibniz, Gottfried Wilhelm 325
Leonardo da Vinci 220, 288, 336, 340
Lessing, Gotthold Ephraim 159, 231
Leuschner, Wilhelm 332
Lévy-Bruhl, Lucien xv, 177, 328, 329
Liebermann, Max 124, 310

Liebknecht, Karl 114, 307
Liebknecht, Wilhelm 115, 259
'limit situations' 128, 131, 168, 169, 171, 300, 313
Lipps, Theodor 121, 260, 309
Lorraine, Claude 34, 289
loving contest 56, 71, 170, 194 203, 204, 283, 327
Löwith, Karl 307, 324
Loye, Fritz zur 22, 27, 33, 35
Ludendorff, Erich 299
Lukács, Georg 32, 84, 208–10, 325, 337, 338
Luxemburg, Rosa 114, 115, 259, 307

Maier, Heinrich xv, 119
Manet, Eduard 123, 310, 311
Manheim, Ralph 283
Mann, Golo 282, 283, 307, 308, 318, 319
Mann, Thomas 9, 83
Marx, Karl 72, 209, 210, 217
Mayer, Albrecht 154, 321
Mayer, Arthur 143, 317, 328
Mayer, Ascher 55, 293
Mayer, Clara 55, 212, 292, 295
Mayer, David 54–7, 59–61, 212, 248, 249, 293,
    295, *Ill. 9*
Mayer, Dodo 328
Mayer, Ella 208, 227, 233, 292, 293, 294, 341, 342, *Ill. 30*
Mayer, Ernst xxii, 27, 40, 50, 52, 88–90, 119, 143,
    144, 147, 154–6, 158, 159, 161, 191, 192, 208, 213,
    214, 217, 227, 231, 236, 269, 291, 294, 301–3, 319,
    322–4, 330, 342, *Ill. 30*
Mayer, Fanny 328
Mayer, Flora 49, 59, 114, 190, 191, 308, 331, 332
Mayer, Fritz 143–5, 219, 220, 317, 318, 340, *Ill. 11*
Mayer, Gustav xi, 49, 50, 52, 54, 57, 59, 60, 114,
    115, 143, 144, 175, 177, 178, 189–91, 209, 211, 226,
    269, 270, 292–4, 307, 317, 328–33, 324–38
Mayer, Heinrich 144, 145, 293, 317
Mayer, Ida 50, 58, 59, 197, 212, 294
Mayer, Jennie 144
Mayer, Joseph 55
Mayer, Otto 144, 145, *Ill. 11*
McCarthy, Joseph R. 339
Melozzo da Forli 288
Merlau-Ponty, Maurice 208
Metternich, Prince Clemens von 290
Michelangelo Buonarroti 43
Mierendorff, Carlo 332
Mitscherlich, Alexander 331, 333
Möhrle, Erna 334
Monet, Claude 123, 310
Mozart, Wolfgang Amadeus 146

Napoleon, Bonaparte (Napoleon I, Emperor of
    France) 4, 38, 55

Naumann, Friedrich 90, 100
Nazi, National Socialist xv, xxi, 33, 91, 141–3,
    145–51, 153, 154, 159, 161, 162, 165, 167, 173, 183,
    187, 189, 190, 192–4, 196, 200, 201, 218, 234, 235,
    282, 316, 317, 318, 319, 320, 324–6, 333, 334, 337
Neumann, Carl 111, 307
Newton, Isaac 340
Nietzsche, Friedrich Wilhelm xv, 1, 19, 20, 38,
    101, 112, 121, 122, 132, 135, 136, 151, 155, 156,
    158–64, 173, 210, 244, 260, 281, 285, 288, 298,
    307, 315, 321–6, 328, 337
nihilism 62, 163, 210, 295
Nissl, Franz 26, 62, 63, 67, 76, 297
Novalis (Friedrich von Hardenberg) 53
Nuremberg Laws, the 154, 157, 168, 183, 316, 331

Oboussier, Robert 144, 147, 228
Oncken, Hermann 82
'Overman', the 160, 163, 325, 326

Papen, Franz von 142, 147
Pareyson, Luigi 181, 330
Parmenides 176
'Passion for the Night, The' 171, 172, 327
Paton, H. J. 176, 177, 328, 329
Paulsen, Friedrich 16
phenomenology 66–70, 249, 298
Pinturicchio (Bernardino di Betto) 288
Piper, Klaus 228
Pissarro, Camille 123, 310
Plato 122, 176, 185, 206, 260, 294, 325
Plessner, Helmuth 144
Price, Henry Habberley 329
Prinzhorn, Hans 81, 300, 312
psychoanalysis 37, 38, 66, 70, 72, 217, 339

Radbruch,Gustav 32, 98, 151, 178, 219, 288, 321, 331
Radek, Karl 114, 115, 259
Rathenau, Walther 312
Regenbogen, Otto 219, 331
Reichwein, Adolf 332
Renaissance, the 32, 35, 43, 44, 327
Renoir, Auguste 123, 310
Rickert, Heinrich 53, 65, 67, 69, 85, 86, 87, 118,
    130, 131, 293, 297, 300, 301, 308, 309, 312, 313
Röhm, Ernst 320
Roosevelt, Franklin D. xviii
Rosa, Renato de x, 179, 181, 182, 228, 330, 331–4,
    335, 336
Ross, W. David 329
Ross, Werner 285
Rossmann, Kurt 133, 314
Roth, Gerhard 299
Russell, Bertrand 215

SA (*Sturmabteilung*) 91, 147
Salditt, Maria 178
Salfeld, Willy 7, 10, 240, 241
Salin, Edgar 197, 200
Salomé, Lou Andreas 19, 324
Sand, Karl Ludwig 290
Saner Hans ix, xi, xiii, xvi, 173, 282, 291, 296, 309, 312–14, 319, 320, 330, 333, 342
Sartre, Jean-Paul 227, 323, 339
Schaefer, Hans 228
Scheffel, Joseph Viktor von 38, 290
Scheidemann, Philipp 114
Scheler, Max 84, 130, 312
Schelling, Friedrich Wilhelm Joseph xvi, 117, 136, 203, 225–7, 231, 315, 316, 341, 341
Schiller, Friedrich 5, 47, 112, 292
Schilpp, Paul Arthur 288, 299, 302, 303, 323, 324, 325, 338
Schlegel-Schelling, Caroline 226
Schmitthenner, Paul 181, 183, 192, 330, 331
Schnabel, Ernst 147, 319
Schneider, Fridow 7, 10, 240, 241
Schneider, Kurt 329
Schopenhauer, Arthur 18, 31, 35, 43, 147, 285, 319
Schubert, Franz 214
Schumann, Robert 214
Schwamb, Ludwig 332
Schwarber, Karl 180
Secession, the Berlin 124, 310
Shakespeare, William 143, 147, 172, 197, 327
Simmel, Georg 85, 309
Sisley, Alfred 123, 310
Socrates 91
'species of eternity' xxii
Spender, Stephen 208, 209, 336, 337
Spinoza, Benedict de xxi, xxii, 5, 16, 139, 316
Springer, Julius 66, 67, 181
Stalling, Gerhard 90
Steinvorth 10–12, 42, *Ill. 3*
Sternberger, Dolf 145, 192, 283, 318, 333, 334, 342
Strassmann, Fritz xviii
Strauch, Hermann 288
Stresemann, Gustav 103, 288
Strindberg, August xv, 122, 123, 132, 310

Tantzen, Anna Magdalena (née Lührs) xxi, 60, 282, 295
Tantzen, Theodor 8, 60, 105, 234, 282, 295, 342
Tantzen, Theodor Johann 8, 282, 283
Thode, Henry 31, 32, 35, 288
Thoma, Richard 82
Transcendence 171, 202, 216, 229
'truth' xvi, xx, xxii, 81, 91, 126, 135, 136, 150, 152, 160, 161, 162, 163, 168, 169, 173, 180, 195, 199, 200, 203–7, 211, 221, 227, 229, 234, 235, 311, 321, 324, 325, 326, 334
Tschuang-tzu 210

Ulbricht, Walter 339
'understanding psychology' 67, 69, 121, 160
Undset, Sigrid 194, 333

Van Gogh-Bonger, Johanna 311
Van Gogh, Vincent xv, xix, 81, *108*, 109, 120–8, 132, 145, 152, 307, 309, 310–12, *Ills 17, 18 and 19*

Wagner, Cosima 322
Wagner, Richard 19, 20, 31, 35, 147, 156, 244, 319, 322
Wahl, Jean 208, 328
Wallraff, Charles 280, 281, 322, 328, 335, 336, 341
Waltz, Lotte 228, 232, 331
Waltz, Wilhelm 232
Warnock, Mary 298
Weber, Alfred 151, 178, 192, 216, 219, 331, 333, 334–6, 338, 339
Weber, Marianne 77, 82, 87, 88, 91, 115, 146, 178, 298, 299, 300–2, 335
Weber, Max xiii, xv, xxii, 8, 32, 33, 36, 38, 66, 67, 69, 75–9, 81–91, 99, 112, 119, 134, 146, 148, 189, 216, 232, 233, 235, 251, 254, 296, 297, 299, 300–3, 312, 332, 325, *Ill. 12*
Weill, Kurt 147
Weimar period, the 8, 90, 130, 133–5, 143, 150, 233, 312, 323
Weizsäcker, Carl Friedrich von 340
Weizsäcker, Viktor von 333
Wendland 114, 115, 259
Wiehl, Reiner x, 297, 312, 313, 321, 322, 341
Wilhelm I, Kaiser 3
Wilhelm II, Kaiser 35, 114, 290
Wilhelminian 9
Wilkens, Vicar 282
'Will to Power, the' 160, 162, 315, 325
Wilmanns, Karl 64, 151, 335
Wilson, Woodrow 113, 258
Windelband, Wilhelm xv, 53, 69, 75, 85, 297, 300
Winning, Charles D. 189
Wisser, Richard x, 287, 288, 312, 315, 319, 320, 329, 330
Wolff, (Marie?) 59
'world vision' (*Weltanschauung*) 73, 83, 84, 96, 112, 118, 131, 132, 170, 209, 250, 293, 300, 313, 327
Wundt, Wilhelm 96
Wygodzinski, Vally (née Cohn) 293

Zimmer, Christiane 151, 178
Zimmer, Heinrich 151, 173, 176, 178, 182, 317, 321
Zionism 144, 145, 211, 293, 317, 337